WELCOME TO

Essentials of
OPERATIONS MANAGEMENT

Operations Management is important, exciting, challenging, and everywhere you look!

Important, because it's concerned with creating all of the products and services upon which we depend. Exciting, because it's at the centre of so many of the changes affecting the world of business. Challenging, because the solutions that we find need to work globally and responsibly within society and the environment. And everywhere, because every service and product that you use – the cereal you eat at breakfast, the chair you sit on, and the radio station you listen to while you eat – is the result of an operation or process.

Our aim in writing *Essentials of Operations Management* is to give you a **comprehensive understanding** of the key issues and techniques of operations management, and to **help you get a great final result** in your course. Here's how you might make the most of the text:

- Get ahead with the latest developments – from the up-to-the-minute *Operations in practice* features in every chapter to the focus on corporate social responsibility in the third chapter – these **put you at the cutting edge**.

- Use the *Worked examples* and *Learning exercises* to improve your use of key quantitative and qualitative techniques, and work your way to **better grades in your assignments and exams**.

- Follow up on the recommended reading at the end of each chapter. The texts are specially selected to enhance your learning and **give you an edge** in your course work.

And in particular, look out for the references to **MyOMLab** in the text, and log on to **www.myomlab.com*** where you can:

- check and reinforce your understanding of key concepts using self-assessment questions, audio summaries, animations, video clips and more;

- practice your problem-solving with feedback, guided solutions and a limitless supply of questions!

- look up key terms in the online glossary (key terms are highlighted in red in the margins of this book).

We want *Essentials of Operations Management* to give you what you need: a comprehensive view of the key areas of the subject, an ambition to put that into practice, and – of course – success in your studies. So, read on and good luck!

Nigel Slack
Alistair Brandon-Jones
Robert Johnston

* P.S. In order to **log in to MyOMLab**, you'll need to **register with the access code** found within the access card included with this book or available to buy online at **www.myomlab.com**

Further reading in
OPERATIONS MANAGEMENT

Take your study and interest in operations management further with these leading texbooks written by the same team of expert authors.

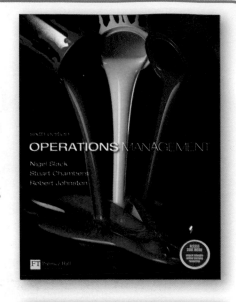

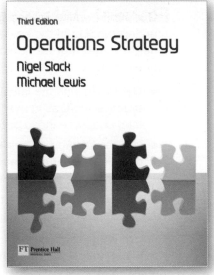

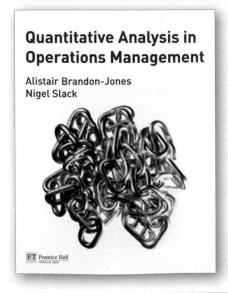

Essentials of
OPERATIONS MANAGEMENT

Nigel Slack

Alistair Brandon-Jones

Robert Johnston

Financial Times
Prentice Hall
is an imprint of

Harlow, England • London • New York • Boston • San Francisco • Toronto • Sydney • Singapore • Hong Kong
Tokyo • Seoul • Taipei • New Delhi • Cape Town • Madrid • Mexico City • Amsterdam • Munich • Paris • Milan

Pearson Education Limited
Edinburgh Gate
Harlow
Essex CM20 2JE
England

and Associated Companies throughout the world

Visit us on the World Wide Web at:
www.pearsoned.co.uk

First published 2011

ISBN: 978-0-273-75242-4

British Library Cataloguing-in-Publication Data
A catalogue record for this book is available from the British Library

Library of Congress Cataloging-in-Publication Data
Slack, Nigel.
   Essentials of operations management / Nigel Slack, Alistair Brandon-Jones,
Robert Johnston.
       p. cm.
   Includes bibliographical references and index.
   ISBN 978-0-273-75242-4 (pbk.)
   1. Production management.   2. Manufacturing processes.   3. Industrial management.
   I. Johnston, Robert, 1953-   II. Brandon-Jones, Alistair.   III. Title.
   TS155.S5617 2011
   658.5--dc22
                                                                    2011000808

10 9 8 7 6 5 4 3 2 1
15 14 13 12 11

Typeset in 10/12pt Minion by 35
Printed and bound by Rotolito Lombarda, Italy

Brief contents

Contents

Guide to 'operations in practice' examples and short cases

Chapter	Location	Company/example	Region	Sector/activity	Company size
Chapter 1 Operations management	p. 2	IKEA	Global	Retail	Large
	p. 7	Acme Whistles	UK	Manufacturing	Small
	p. 8	Oxfam	Global	Charity	Large
	p. 13	Pret A Manger	Europe/USA	Retail	Medium
	p. 18	Formule 1	Europe	Hospitality	Large
	p. 19	Mwagusi Safari Lodge	Tanzania	Hospitality	Small
Chapter 2 Operations strategy	p. 26	Two operations strategies: Flextronics and Ryanair	Global/Europe	Manufacturing service/ transport	Large
	p. 32	Giordano	Asia	Retail	Large
	p. 37	Amazon, what exactly is your core competence?	Global	Retail/business services	Large
	p. 41	Sometimes any plan is better than no plan	Europe	Military	Large
Chapter 3 Social, environmental and economic performance	p. 45	A tale of two terminals	Dubai and UK	Transport	Large
	p. 52	Lower Hurst Farm	UK	Agricultural	Small
	p. 54	Accident recovery	General	Healthcare	Medium
	p. 55	Dabbawalas hit 99.9999% dependability	India	General service	Large
	p. 58	BBC	Global	Media	Large
	p. 59	Aldi	Europe	Retail	Large
Chapter 4 The design of products and services	p. 68	Airbus A380	Europe	Aerospace	Large
	p. 71	Dyson	Global	Design/manufacturing	Large
	p. 74	Square watermelons	Japan	Retail/Agriculture	Various
	p. 76	Daniel Hersheson	UK	Hairdressing	Small
	p. 79	*Art Attack!*	UK	Media	Small
Chapter 5 Process design	p. 91	McDonalds	Global	Quick service	Large
	p. 93	Daimler-Chrysler, Smart car	France	Auto manufacturing	Large
	p. 112	Heathrow	UK	Transport	Large
Chapter 6 Location, layout and flow	p. 119	Tesco	Global	Retail	Large
	p. 121	Tata Nano	India	Manufacturing	Large
	p. 126	Surgery	UK	Healthcare	Medium
	p. 130	Cadbury	UK	Entertainment and manufacturing	Large
Chapter 7 Supply network management	p. 138	Dell	Global	Computer manufacturing	Large
	p. 143	Ford Motor Company	Global	Auto manufacturing	Large
	p. 147	Behind the brand names	Taiwan	Computer manufacturing	Large
	p. 151	Northern Foods	Europe	Food services	Large
	p. 160	TDG	Europe	Logistics services	Large
	p. 161	Seven-Eleven Japan	Japan	Retail	Large

Chapter	Location	Company/example	Region	Sector/activity	Company size
Chapter 8 Capacity management	p. 168	British Airways London Eye	UK	Tourism	Medium
	p. 174	Seasonal products and services	All	Various	Various
	p. 178	Lettuce growing	Europe	Agriculture	Large
	p. 182	Annual Hours Work Plan	UK/Global	Food processing/media	Large
	p. 184	Greetings cards	All	Design	Large
	p. 192	Madame Tussaud's, Amsterdam	Netherlands	Tourism	Medium
Chapter 9 Inventory management	p. 197	UK National Blood Service	UK	Healthcare	Large
	p. 210	The Howard Smith Paper Group	UK	Distribution service	Large
Chapter 10 Planning and control	p. 224	BMW dealership	UK	Service and repair	Medium
	p. 227	Air France	Global	Airline	Large
	p. 233	Accident and Emergency	All	Healthcare	Large
	p. 236	Chicken salad sandwich	All	Food processing	Large
Chapter 11 Lean synchronization	p. 247	Toyota Motor Company	Global	Auto manufacturing	Large
	p. 256	Hospitals	UK	Healthcare	Medium/large
Chapter 12 Quality management	p. 268	Four Seasons Hotel	Global/UK	Hospitality	Large
	p. 270	Tea and Sympathy	USA	Hospitality	Small
	p. 272	Magic Moments	UK	Photography services	Small
	p. 276	Surgical statistics	US	Healthcare	Various
	p. 284	IBM	Canada	IT services	Large
Chapter 13 Operations improvement	p. 290	Taxing quality	Denmark	Public service	Large
	p. 303	Xchanging	Europe	Process outsourcing	Large

Making the most of this book and MyOMLab

Check your understanding

Each chapter opens with a set of **Key questions** to identify major topics. **Summary answers** conclude the chapter. You can check your understanding of each chapter by taking the **Sample tests of self-assessment questions** on MyOMLab at **www.myomlab.com**.

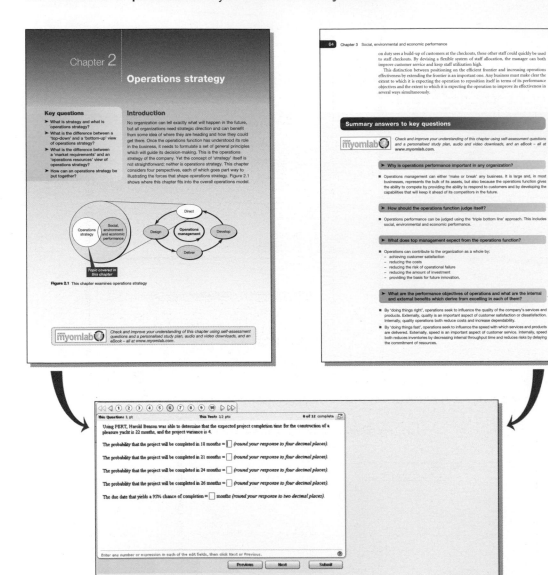

Practice makes perfect

Worked examples show how qualitative and quantitative techniques can be used in operations management. **Learning exercises** at the end of the chapter allow you to apply these techniques, and you can get more practice as well as guided solutions from the **Study plan** on MyOMLab at **www.myomlab.com**.

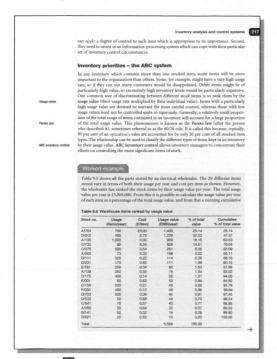

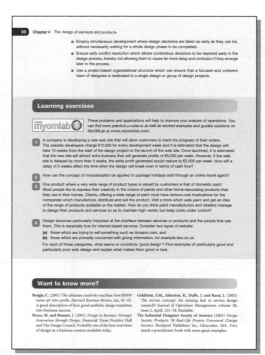

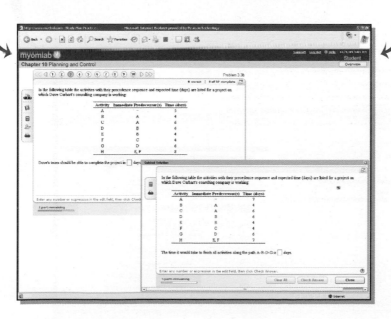

Making the most of this book and MyOMLab (continued)

Analyse operations in action

The **Operations in practice** and **Short case study** features in each chapter illustrate and encourage you to analyse operations management in action. You can see and hear more about how theory is applied in practice in the animations and video clips in the **Multimedia library** in MyOMLab at **www.myomlab.com**.

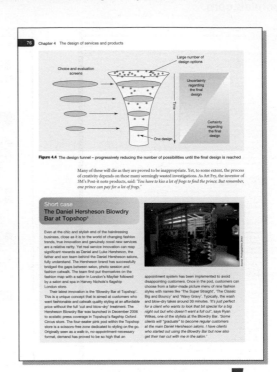

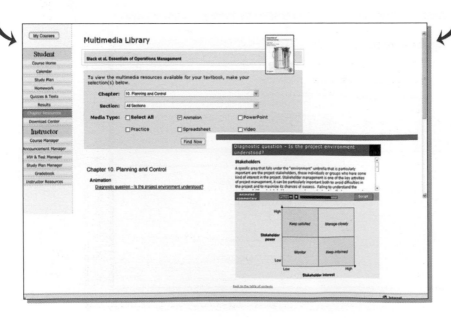

Take a different view

Critical commentaries, together with **Want to know more?** and **Useful websites** at the end of each chapter, show a diversity of viewpoints and encourage you to think critically about operations management. You can find the **Useful websites** in the **Multimedia library** of MyOMLab at **www.myomlab.com**.

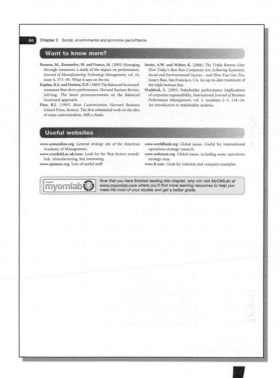

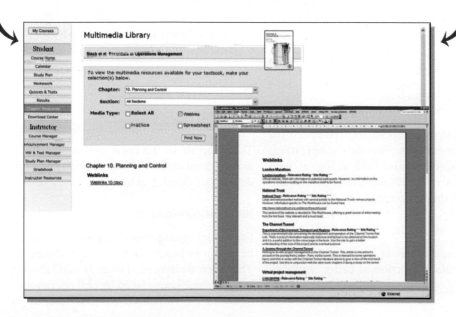

Preface

Introduction

Operations management is *important*. It is concerned with creating the services and products upon which we all depend. And all organizations create and deliver some mixture of services and products, whether that organization is large or small, for profit or not for profit, public or private. Thankfully, most companies have now come to understand the importance of operations. This is because they have realized that effective operations management gives the potential to improve both efficiency and customer service simultaneously. In addition, operations management is *everywhere*, it is not confined to the operations function. All managers, whether they are called Operations or Marketing or Human Resources or Finance, or whatever, manage processes and serve customers (internal or external). This makes at least part of their activities 'operations'.

Operations management is also *exciting*. It is at the centre of so many of the changes affecting the business world – changes in customer preference, changes in supply networks brought about by internet-based technologies, changes in what we want to do at work, how we want to work, where we want to work, and so on. There has rarely been a time when operations management was more topical or more at the heart of business and cultural shifts.

Operations management is also *challenging*. Promoting the creativity which will allow organizations to respond to so many changes is becoming the prime task of operations managers. It is they who must find the solutions to technological and environmental challenges, the pressures to be socially responsible, the increasing globalization of markets and the difficult-to-define areas of knowledge management.

The aim of this book

This book provides a clear, authoritative, well structured and interesting treatment of the essentials of operations management. The text provides both a logical path through the activities of operations management and an understanding of their importance in driving competitive advantage.

More specifically, this text is:

- *Strategic* in its perspective. It is unambiguous in treating the operations function as being central to competitiveness.

- *Conceptual* in the way it explains the reasons why operations managers need to take decisions.
- *Broad* in its coverage of the significant ideas and issues which are relevant to most types of operation.
- *Practical* in exploring the issues and challenges of making operations management decisions. The 'Operations in practice' feature, which starts every chapter, and the short cases that appear throughout, all explore the approaches taken by operations managers in practice.
- *International* in the examples which are used. The descriptions of operations practice come from all over the world.
- *Balanced* in its treatment. This means we accurately reflect the balance of economic activity between service and manufacturing operations.

Who should use this book?

Anyone who is interested in how services and products are created, delivered, and improved.

- *Undergraduates* on business studies, technical or joint degrees should find it sufficiently structured to provide an understandable route through the subject (no prior knowledge of the area is assumed).
- *MBA students* should find that its practical discussions of operations management activities enhance their own experience.
- *Postgraduate students* on other specialist masters degrees should find that it provides them with a well-grounded and critical approach to the subject.

Distinctive features

Clear structure

The structure of the book uses a model of operations management which distinguishes between direct, design, deliver and develop activities.

Illustrations-based

Operations management is a practical subject and cannot be taught satisfactorily in a purely theoretical manner. Therefore, we have used examples and short cases which explain some issues faced by real operations.

Worked examples

Operations management is a subject that blends qualitative and quantitative perspectives; where appropriate, 'worked examples' are used to demonstrate how both types of technique can be used.

Critical commentaries

Not everyone agrees about what is the best approach to the various topics and issues with operations management. This is why we have included 'critical commentaries' that pose alternative views to the one being expressed in the main flow of the text.

Summary answers to key questions

Each chapter is summarized in the form of a list of bullet points. These extract the essential points which answer the key question posed at the beginning of each chapter.

Learning exercises

Every chapter includes a set of problem type exercises. These can be used to check out your understanding of the concepts illustrated in the chapter. These activities can be done individually or in groups.

Want to know more?

Every chapter ends with a short list of further reading which takes the topics covered in the chapter further, or treats some important related issues. The nature of each further reading is also explained.

Useful websites

A short list of web addresses is included in each chapter for those who wish to take their studies further.

To the Instructor...
Teaching and learning resources for *Essentials*

The *Essentials* edition

As an author team, we are always talking with both lecturers and students in an attempt to keep up with the requirements and preferences of our book users. What has become clear is that some of the more introductory courses in operations management do not necessarily need a fully comprehensive text: hence this *Essentials* edition. Based on the approach that has made both *Operations Management* and *Operations and Process Management* market-leading textbooks in the area, *Essentials of Operations Management* provides an effective and authoritative treatment of the subject. Key aspects of the book are:

- Reduced length. Chapter selection has been focused on those topics that extensive research has shown are included in shorter courses. In some cases this has involved incorporating content from more than one chapter of our longer texts.
- Retention of many learning features, including 'operations in practice', 'key questions', 'short cases', 'critical commentaries', 'worked examples', 'summary answers to key questions' and 'learning exercises'.
- Availability of additional cases (both long and short) on the companion website at **www.pearsoned.co.uk/slack**.

We also welcome a new author to our team. Alistair Brandon-Jones from the University of Bath has been behind the scenes for some time and now formally becomes our new writing colleague. Stuart Chambers, who has been part of the team since we started, has now retired from the University of Warwick, and we wish him well in his new mix of activities.

Instructor's resources

A completely new instructor's manual is available to lecturers adopting this textbook, together with Power-Point presentations for each chapter and a Testbank of assessment questions. Visit **www.pearsoned.co.uk/slack** to access these. In addition, the Operations in Practice DVD is available. Please contact your local Pearson Education Sales Consultant (**www.pearsoned.co.uk/replocator**) for further details and to request a copy.

Finally, and most importantly, a new set of online resources to enable students to check their understanding, practice key techniques and improve their problem-solving skills accompanies *Essentials of Operations Management*. Please see below for details of MyOMLab.

The key to greater understanding and better grades in Operations Management!

MyOMLab for instructors

MyOMLab is designed to save you time in preparing and delivering assignments and assessments for your course, and to enable your students to study independently and at their own pace. Using MyOMLab, you can take advantage of:

- A wide range of engaging resources, including movies, PowerPoint slides and animated models with audio commentary.
- Hundreds of self-assessment questions, including algorithmically-generated quantitative values which make for a different problem every time.
- A Homework feature, allowing you to assign work for your students to prepare for your next class or seminar.
- A Gradebook which tracks students' performance on sample tests as well as assessments of your own design.

If you'd like to learn more or find out how MyOMLab could help you, please contact your local Pearson sales consultant at **www.pearsoned.co.uk/replocator** or visit **www.myomlab.com**

To the Student...
Making the most of this book

All academic textbooks in business management are, to some extent, simplifications of the messy reality which is actual organizational life. Any book has to separate topics, in order to study them, which in reality are closely related. The first hint therefore in using this book effectively is to look out for all the links between the individual topics. Similarly with the sequence of topics, although the chapters follow a logical structure, they need not be studied in this order. Every chapter is, more or less, self-contained. Therefore study the chapters in whatever sequence is appropriate to your course or your individual interests. The same applies to revision – study the key chapters and summary answers to key questions.

The book makes full use of the many practical examples and illustrations which can be found in all operations. Many of these were provided by our contacts in companies, but others come from journals, magazines and newspapers. So if you want to understand the importance of operations management in everyday business life look for examples in these sources. There are also examples which you can observe every day. Whenever you use a shop, eat a meal in a restaurant, borrow a book from the library or ride on public transport, consider the operations management issues of all the operations for which you are a customer.

The learning exercises at the end of each chapter are there to provide an opportunity for you to think further about the ideas discussed. Some can be used to test out your understanding of the chapter's key questions. If you cannot answer these you should revisit the relevant parts of the chapter. When you have done this individually try to discuss your analysis with other course members. Most important of all, start off your analysis with the two fundamental questions:

- How is this organization trying to compete (or satisfy its strategic objectives if a not-for-profit organization)?
- What can the operation do to help the organization compete more effectively?

The key to greater understanding and better grades in Operations Management!

MyOMLab for students

MyOMLab has been developed to help students make the most of their studies in operations management. Visit the MyOMLab at **www.myomlab.com** to find valuable teaching and learning material including:

- Self-assessment questions and a personalized Study Plan to diagnose areas of strength and weakness, direct students' learning, and improve results.
- Unlimited practice on quantitative techniques and solving problems.
- Audio downloads, animated models and electronic flashcards to aid exam revision.
- Video clips and short cases to illustrate operations management in action.

Ten steps to getting a better grade in operations management

We could say that the best rule for getting a better grade is to be good! However, there are plenty of us who, while fairly good, don't get as good a grade as we really deserve. So, if you are studying operations management, and you want a really good grade, try following these simple steps:

Step 1 Practice, practice, practice. Use the key questions and the learning exercises to check your understanding. Use the study plan feature in MyOMLab and practice to master the topics which you find difficult.

Step 2 Remember a few **key models**, and apply them wherever you can. Use the diagrams and models to describe some of the examples that are contained within the chapter. You can also use the revision pod casts on MyOMLab.

Step 3 Remember to use both **quantitative and qualitative analysis**. You'll get more credit for appropriately mixing your methods: use a quantitative model to answer a quantitative question and vice versa, but qualify this with a few well chosen sentences. Both the chapters of the book, and the exercises on MyOMLab, incorporate qualitative and quantitative material.

Step 4 There's always a **strategic objective** behind any operational issue. Ask yourself, 'Would a similar operation with a different strategy do things differently?' Look at the operations in practice and short cases in the book.

Step 5 **Research** widely around the topic. Use websites that you trust – we've listed some good websites at the end of each chapter and on MyOMLab. You'll get more credit for using references that come from genuine academic sources.

Step 6 Use **your own experience**. Every day, you're experiencing an opportunity to apply the principles of operations management. Why is the queue at the airport check-in desk so long? What goes on behind the 'hole in the wall' of your bank's ATM machines? Use the videos on MyOMLab to look further at operations in practice.

Step 7 **Always answer the question**. Think 'What is really being asked here? What topic or topics does this question cover?' Find the relevant chapter or chapters, and search the key questions at the beginning of each chapter and the summary at the end of each chapter to get you started.

Step 8 Take account of the three tiers of accumulating marks for your answers.

(a) Firstly, demonstrate your knowledge and understanding. Make full use of the text and MyOMLab to find out where you need to improve.
(b) Secondly, show that you know how to illustrate and apply the topic. The short cases and operations in practice sections, combined with those on MyOMLab, give you hundreds of different examples.
(c) Thirdly, show that you can discuss and analyse the issues critically. Use the critical commentaries within the text to understand some of the alternative viewpoints.

Generally, if you can do (a) you will pass; if you can do (a) and (b) you will pass well, and if you can do all three, you will pass with flying colours!

Step 9 Remember not only **what** the issue is about, but also understand **why**! Read the text and apply your knowledge on MyOMLab until you really understand why the concepts and techniques of operations management are important, and what they contribute to an organisation's success. Your new-found knowledge will stick in your memory, allow you to develop ideas, and enable you to get better grades.

Step 10 Start now! Don't wait until two weeks before an assignment is due. Log on (**www.myomlab.com**), read on, and GOOD LUCK!

Nigel, Alistair, and Bob

About the authors

Nigel Slack is the Professor of Operations Management and Strategy at Warwick University. Previously he has been Professor of Service Engineering at Cambridge University, Professor of Manufacturing Strategy at Brunel University, a University Lecturer in Management Studies at Oxford University and Fellow in Operations Management at Templeton College, Oxford.

He worked initially as an industrial apprentice in the hand-tool industry and then as a production engineer and production manager in light engineering. He holds a Bachelor's degree in Engineering and Master's and Doctor's degrees in Management, and is a chartered engineer. He is the author of many books in the operations management area, including *Operations Management* (with Stuart Chambers and Robert Johnston) sixth edition published by Financial Times Prentice Hall in 2010, *The Manufacturing Advantage*, published by Mercury Business Books, 1991, *Making Management Decisions* (with Steve Cooke), 1991, published by Prentice Hall, *The Blackwell Encyclopedic Dictionary of Operations Management* (with Michael Lewis) published by Blackwell in 2005, *Operations Strategy* together with Michael Lewis, the third edition published by Financial Times Prentice Hall in 2011 and *Perspectives in Operations Management (Volumes I to IV)* also with Michael Lewis, published by Routledge in 2003. He has authored numerous academic papers and chapters in books. He also acts as a consultant to many international companies around the world in many sectors, especially financial services, transport, leisure and manufacturing. His research is in the operations and manufacturing flexibility and operations strategy areas.

Alistair Brandon-Jones is a lecturer in Operations and Supply Management at the University of Bath School of Management, and a visiting lecturer at Warwick Medical School. Previously, he was a Teaching Fellow at Warwick Business School and also worked in a number of logistics and retail roles. He has a Bachelor's degree in Management Science and a Doctorate in Business from the University of Warwick and is widely published in leading operations and supply management journals. *Essentials of Operations Management* is his second text (he co-authored *Quantitative Analysis in Operations Management* with Nigel Slack, published by Financial Times Prentice Hall in 2008).

His main research interest is customer-centric service design. This work focuses on the important role which internal and external customers can have in improving service delivery. His other research focuses on supply strategy and for this work he is the UK lead member for the International Purchasing Survey (www.ipsurvey.org) which explores procurement processes and performance across the globe. Alistair has consulting and executive development experience with organizations around the world, in various sectors including petrochemicals, health, financial services, manufacturing, defence, and government.

Robert Johnston is Professor of Operations Management at Warwick Business School and its Deputy Dean. He is the founding editor of the *International Journal of Service Industry Management* and he also serves on the editorial board of the *Journal of Operations Management* and the *International Journal of Tourism and Hospitality Research*. He is the author of the market leading text, *Service Operations Management* (with Graham Clark), now in its third edition (2008), published by Financial Times Prentice Hall. Before moving to academia Dr Johnston held several line management and senior management posts in a number of service organizations in both the public and private sectors. He continues to maintain close and active links with many large and small organizations through his research, management training and consultancy activities. As a specialist in service operations, his research interests include service design, service recovery, performance measurement and service quality. He is the author or co-author of many books, as well as chapters in other texts, numerous papers and case studies.

Acknowledgements

During the preparation of *Essentials of Operations Management*, the authors relied on colleagues from many universities and colleges around the world. Numerous enthusiasts for promoting operations management were generous in contributing their ideas and experience. Over the years these have included:

Pär Åhlström of the Stockholm School of Economics; Sven Åke Hörte of Lulea University of Technology; Eamonn Ambrose of University College, Dublin; Colin Armistead of Bournemouth University; Alan Betts of ht²; Ran Bhamra of Loughbrough University; Ruth Boaden of Manchester Business School; Emma Brandon-Jones of Bath University; John K Christiansen of Copenhagen Business School; Philippa Collins of Heriot-Watt University; Henrique Correa of Rollins College, Florida; Paul Coughlan, Trinity College Dublin; Stephen Disney of Cardiff University; Doug Davies of University of Technology, Sydney; Tony Dromgoole of the Irish Management Institute; Job de Haan of Tilburg University; Carsten Dittrich, University of Southern Denmark; David Evans of Middlesex University; Paul Forrester of Keele University; Keith Goffin of Cranfield University; Ian Graham of Edinburgh University; Alan Harle of Sunderland University; Norma Harrison of Macquarie University; Catherine Hart of Loughborough Business School; Chris Hillam of Sunderland University; Ian Holden of Bristol Business School; Matthias Holweg of Cambridge University; Mickey Howard of Exeter University; Brian Jefferies of West Herts College; Shirley Johnston; Tom Kegan of Bell College of Technology, Hamilton; Denis Kehoe of Liverpool University; Mike Lewis of Bath University; Peter Long of Sheffield Hallam University; John Maguire of the University of Sunderland; Charles Marais of the University of Pretoria; Roger Maull of Exeter University; Bart McCarthy of Nottingham University; Harvey Maylor of Cranfield University; John Meredith Smith of EAP, Oxford; Michael Milgate of Macquarie University; Keith Moreton of Staffordshire University; Chris Morgan of Cranfield University; Adrian Morris of Sunderland University; Steve New of Oxford University; John Pal of Manchester Metropolitan University; Peter Race of Reading University; Ian Sadler of Victoria University; Andi Smart of Exeter University; Amrik Sohal of Monash University; Alex Skedd of Northumbria Business School; Martin Spring of Lancaster University; Dr Ebrahim Soltani of the University of Kent; Roy Stratton of Nottingham Trent University; Nelson Tang of the University of Leicester; David Twigg of Sussex University; Helen Valentine of the University of the West of England; Roland van Dierdonck of the University of Ghent; Dirk Pieter van Donk of the University of Groningen; and Peter Worthington.

Our academic colleagues at Warwick Business School and Bath School of Management have also helped over the years, both by contributing ideas and by creating a lively work environment. Our thanks go to Nicola Burgess, Nigel Caldwell, Sinéad Carey, Steve Conway, Dan Chicksand, Michaelis Giannakis, Paul Godwin, Andrew Graves, Christine Harland, Adam Joinson, Richard Kamm, Michael Lewis, Sheik Meeran, Niki Panteli, Niall Piercy, Zoe Radnor, Michael Shulver, Rhian Silvestro, Brian Squire, Nick Wake, Helen Walker, Paul Walley, and Baris Yalabik. Mary Walton is the coordinator for the Operations Group at Warwick Business School and her continued efforts at keeping everyone organized are always appreciated.

We were lucky to receive continuing professional and friendly assistance from a great publishing team. Especial thanks to Rufus Curnow, Mary Lince, Angela Hawksbee, Colin Reed, Michelle Morgan, Rob Sykes, Melanie Beard, Philippa Fiszzon, Elizabeth Gain, Sue Gard and Helen MacFadyen.

Finally, to our wives who have supported us through an intense writing period – Angela, Emma and Shirley; our thanks.

Every effort has been made to trace and acknowledge ownership of copyright. The publisher will be glad to hear from any copyright holders who it has not been possible to contact.

Publisher's acknowledgements

We are grateful to the following for permission to reproduce copyright material:

Figures

Figure 7.7 adapted from What is the right supply chain for your product?, *Harvard Business Review*, March–April, pp. 105–16 (Fisher, M.C. 1997); Figure 12.3 adapted from A conceptual model of service quality and implications for future research, *Journal of Marketing*, 49, Fall, pp. 41–50 (Parasuraman, A. et al. 1985).

Tables

Table 11.1 adapted from *Service Management Effectiveness*, Bowen, D.E., Chase, R.B., Cummings, T.G. and Associates (eds). Copyright © 1990 Jossey-Bass. Reproduced with permission of John Wiley & Sons Inc.

Photographs

(Key: b-bottom; c-centre; l-left; r-right; t-top)

ACME: Simon Topman 7; **Alamy Images:** Bildagentur-online 59, British Retail Photography 119, Neil Cannon 2, Bernhard Classen 37, Rob Crandell 32, David Hoffmann Photo Library 52tl, 53tl, 55tl, 57tl, 60tl, Directphoto.org 97t, Les Gibbons 272, Golden Pixels / LLC 6bl, Craig Ingram 45, Michael Jones 112, Medical-on-line 174, Ian Miles / Flashpoint PIctures 233, Stuart Pearce 52, Chris Rout 6c, Alex Segre 13, Adrian Sherratt 71, Van Hilversum 197; **Author's own work:** 18, 19, 97b; © **BMW Group:** 224; **Cadbury World:** 130t; Corbis: Denis Balibous 247, Eleanor Bentall 270, Bernardo Bucci 54, Construction Photography 95, G Flayols / Photocuisine 178, Gianni Giansanti / Sygma 138, Robert Llewellyn 276, Marijan Murat / epa 130b, Claudio Peri / epa 6, Ulrich Perrey / epa 26t, Hcinz von Heyenaber 96t, Thomas White 26b; **Four Seasons Hotels:** Robert Miller 268; **Getty Images:** 74, 93, 115, 74, 93, 115, AFP 55, 91, 121, 161, 227, AFP 55, 91, 121, 161, 227, AFP 55, 91, 121, 161, 227, AFP 55, 91, 121, 161, 227, Burje / Triolo Productions 96c, Getty Images News 143, David Sacks 98, Siri Stafford 6t; **Howard Smith Paper Group:** 210; **Photographers Direct:** Martin Karius 76; **Press Association Images:** Orlin Wagner / AP 184; **Rex Features:** Action Press 6tl, 68, 290, Action Press 6tl, 68, 290, Action Press 6tl, 68, 290, Burger / Phanie 256, Jurgen Hasenkopf 46, Image Source 147, Richard Jones 96b, Charles Knight 303, Per Lindgren 52bl, 53, 55cl, 57bl, 60, Brian Rasic 8; © **The Royal Bank of Scotland Group plc:** 98c; **TDG Logistics:** 160.

In some instances we have been unable to trace the owners of copyright material, and we would appreciate any information that would enable us to do so.

Chapter 1

Operations management

Key questions

➤ What is operations management?

➤ Why is operations management important in all types of organization?

➤ What is the input–transformation–output process?

➤ What is the process hierarchy?

➤ How do operations processes have different characteristics?

➤ What are the activities of operations management?

Introduction

Operations management is about how organizations design, deliver, and improve services and products for their customers. Everything you wear, eat, sit on, use, read or knock about on the sports field comes to you courtesy of the operations managers who organized its creation. Every book you borrow from the library, every treatment you receive at the hospital, every service you expect in the shops and every lecture you attend at university – all have been created. While the people who supervised their creation may not always be called operations managers, that is what they really are. And that is what this book is concerned with – the tasks, issues and decisions of those operations managers who have made the services and products on which we all depend. This is an introductory chapter, so we will examine what we mean by 'operations management', how operations processes can be found everywhere, how they are all similar yet different, and what it is that operations managers do.

 *Check and improve your understanding of this chapter using self-assessment questions and a personalized study plan, audio and video downloads, and an eBook – all at www.myomlab.com.*

Operations in practice IKEA[1]

(All chapters start with an 'Operations in practice' example that illustrates some of the issues that will be covered in the chapter.)

Love it or hate it, IKEA is the most successful furniture retailer ever. With 276 stores in 36 countries, it has managed to develop its own special way of selling furniture. The stores' layout means customers often spend two hours in the store – far longer than in rival furniture retailers. IKEA's philosophy goes back to the original business, started in the 1950s in Sweden by Ingvar Kamprad. He built a showroom on the outskirts of Stockholm where land was cheap and simply displayed suppliers' furniture as it would be in a domestic setting. Increasing sales soon allowed IKEA to start ordering its own self-designed products from local manufacturers. However, it was innovation in its operations that dramatically reduced its selling costs. These included the idea of selling furniture as self-assembly flat packs (which reduced production and transport costs) and its 'showroom–warehouse' concept which required customers to pick the furniture up themselves from the warehouse (which reduced retailing costs). Both of these operating principles are still the basis of IKEA's retail operations process today.

Stores are designed to facilitate the smooth flow of customers, from parking, moving through the store itself, to ordering and picking up products. At the entrance to each store large notice-boards provide advice to shoppers. For young children, there is a supervised children's play area, a small cinema, and a parent and baby room so parents can leave their children in the supervised play area for a time. Parents are recalled via the loudspeaker system if the child has any problems. IKEA 'allow customers to make up their minds in their own time' but 'information points' have staff who can help. All furniture carries a ticket with a code number which indicates its location in the warehouse. (For larger items, customers go to the information desks for assistance.) There is also an area where smaller items are displayed, and can be picked directly. Customers then pass through the warehouse where they pick up the items viewed in the showroom. Finally, customers pay at the checkouts, where a ramped conveyor belt moves purchases up to the checkout staff. The exit area has service points and a loading area that allows customers to bring their cars from the car park and load their purchases.

Behind the public face of IKEA's huge stores is a complex worldwide network of suppliers: 1,300 direct suppliers, about 10,000 sub-suppliers, wholesale and transport operations including 26 Distribution Centres. This supply network is vitally important to IKEA. From

Source: Alamy Images

purchasing raw materials, right through to finished products arriving in its customers' homes, IKEA relies on close partnerships with its suppliers to achieve both ongoing supply efficiency and new product development. However, IKEA closely controls all supply and development activities from IKEA's home town of Älmhult in Sweden.

However, success brings its own problems and some customers became increasingly frustrated with overcrowding and long waiting times. In response IKEA in the UK launched a £150 m programme to 'design out' the bottlenecks. The changes included:

- Clearly marked in-store short cuts allowing customers who just want to visit one area to avoid having to go through all the preceding areas.
- Express checkout tills for customers with a bag only rather than a trolley.
- Extra 'help staff' at key points to help customers.
- Redesign of the car parks, making them easier to navigate.
- Dropping the ban on taking trolleys out to the car parks for loading (originally implemented to stop vehicles being damaged).
- A new warehouse system to stop popular product lines running out during the day.
- More children's play areas.

IKEA spokeswoman Nicki Craddock said: *'We know people love our products but hate our shopping experience. We are being told that by customers every day, so we can't afford not to make changes. We realized a lot of people took offence at being herded like sheep on the long route around stores. Now if you know what you are looking for and just want to get in, grab it and get out, you can.'*

Operations management is a vital part of IKEA's success

IKEA shows how important operations management is for its own success and the success of any type of organization. Of course, IKEA understands its market and its customers. Just as important, it knows that the way it manages the network of operations that design, produce and deliver its products and services must be right for its market. No organization can survive in the long term if it cannot supply its customers effectively. This is essentially what operations management is about – designing, producing and delivering products and services that satisfy market requirements. For any business, it is a vitally important activity. Consider just some of the activities that IKEA's operations managers are involved in.

- Arranging the store's layout to give smooth and effective flow of customers (called process design).
- Designing stylish products that can be flat-packed efficiently (called product design).
- Making sure that all staff can contribute to the company's success (called job design).
- Locating stores of an appropriate size in the most effective place (called supply network design).
- Arranging for the delivery of products to stores (called supply chain management).

- Coping with fluctuations in demand (called capacity management).
- Maintaining cleanliness and safety of storage area (called failure prevention).
- Avoiding running out of products for sale (called inventory management).
- Monitoring and enhancing quality of service to customers (called quality management).
- Continually examining and improving operations practice (called operations improvement).

Importantly, these activities are only a small part of IKEA's total operations management effort. But they do give an indication, first of how operations management should contribute to the businesses success, and second, what would happen if IKEA's operations managers failed to be effective in carrying out any of its activities. Badly designed processes, inappropriate products, poor locations, disaffected staff, empty shelves, or forgetting the importance of continually improving quality, could all turn a previously successful organization into a failing one. Yet, although the relative importance of these activities will vary between different organizations, operations managers in all organizations will be making the same *type* of decision (even if *what* they actually decide is different).

What is operations management?

Operations management
Operations function

Operations management is the activity of managing the resources which create and deliver services and products. The **operations function** is the part of the organization that is responsible for this activity. Every organization has an operations function because every organization produces some type of services and/or products. However, not all types of organization will necessarily call the operations function by this name. (Note that we also use the shorter terms 'the operation' and 'operations' interchangeably with the 'operations function'.) **Operations**

Operations managers

managers are the people who have particular responsibility for managing some, or all, of the resources which comprise the operations function. Again, in some organizations the operations manager could be called by some other name. For example, he or she might be called the 'fleet manager' in a distribution company, the 'administrative manager' in a hospital or the 'store manager' in a supermarket.

Operations in the organization

Three core functions

The operations function is central to the organization because it creates the services and products which are its reason for existing, but it is not the only function. It is, however, one of the **three core functions** of any organization. These are:

- the marketing (including sales) function – which is responsible for *communicating* the organization's services and products (or more generically, offerings) to its markets in order to generate customer requests for service;

- the service/product development function – which is responsible for developing new and modified offerings in order to generate future customer requests for service;
- the operations function – which is responsible for *fulfilling* customer requests for service through the creation and delivery of services and products.

Support functions

In addition, there are the **support functions** which enable the core functions to operate effectively. These include, for example:

- the accounting and finance function – which provides the information to help economic decision-making and manages the financial resources of the organization;
- the human resources function – which recruits and develops the organization's staff as well as looking after their welfare.

Remember that different organizations will call their various functions by different names and will have a different set of support functions. Almost all organizations, however, will have the three core functions, because all organizations have a fundamental need to sell their services, satisfy their customers and create the means to satisfy customers in the future. Table 1.1 shows the activities of the three core functions for a sample of organizations.

Broad definition of operations

In practice, there is not always a clear division between the three core functions or between core and support functions. This leads to some confusion over where the boundaries of the operations function should be drawn. In this book we use a relatively **broad definition of operations**. We treat much of the product/service development, technical and information systems activities and some of the human resource, marketing and accounting and finance activities as coming within the sphere of operations management. We view the operations function as comprising all the activities necessary for the day-to-day fulfilment of customer requests. This includes sourcing services and products from suppliers and transporting them to customers.

Working effectively with the other parts of the organization is one of the most important responsibilities of operations management. It is a fundamental of modern management that functional boundaries should not hinder efficient internal processes. Figure 1.1 illustrates some of the relationships between operations and some other functions in terms of the flow of information between them. Although it is not comprehensive, it gives an idea of the nature of each relationship.

Table 1.1 The activities of core functions in some organizations

Core functional activities	Internet service provider (ISP)	Fast food chain	International aid charity	Furniture manufacturer
Marketing and sales	Promote services to users and get registrations Sell advertising space	Advertise on TV Devise promotional materials	Develop funding contracts Mail out appeals for donations	Advertise in magazines Determine pricing policy Sell to stores
Product/service development	Devise new services and commission new information content	Design hamburgers, pizzas, etc. Design décor for restaurants	Develop new appeals campaigns Design new assistance programmes	Design new furniture Coordinate with fashionable colours
Operations	Maintain hardware, software and content Implement new links and services	Make burgers, pizzas etc. Serve customers Clear away Maintain equipment	Give service to the beneficiaries of the charity	Make components Assemble furniture

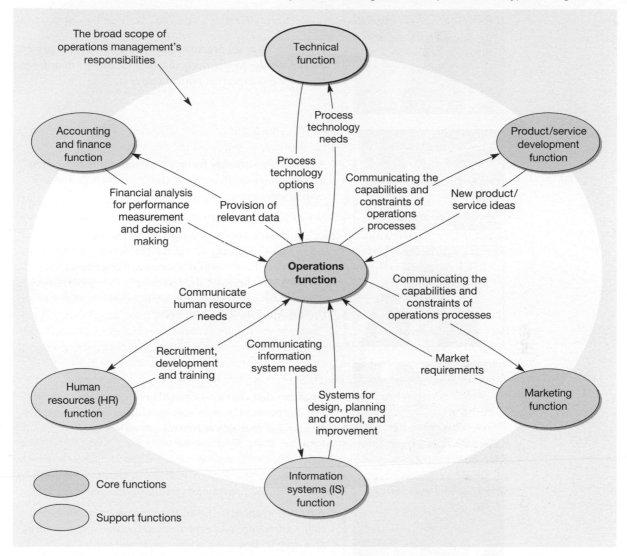

Figure 1.1 The relationship between the operations function and other core and support functions of the organization

Operations management is important in all types of organization

In some types of organization it is relatively easy to visualize the operations function and what it does, even if we have never seen it. For example, most people have seen images of automobile assembly. But what about an advertising agency? We know vaguely what they do – they produce the advertisements that we see in magazines and on television – but what is their operations function? The clue lies in the word 'produce'. Any business that produces something must use resources to do so, and so must have an operations activity. So, the advertising agency and the automobile plant have one important element in common: both have a higher objective – to make a profit from creating and delivering their services or products. Yet not-for-profit organizations also use their resources to produce services, not to make a profit, but to serve society in some way. Look at the following examples of what operations management does in five very different organizations and some common themes emerge.

Physician (general practitioner) – *Operations management uses knowledge to effectively diagnose conditions in order to treat real and perceived patient concerns*

Source: Getty Images

Automobile assembly factory – *Operations management uses machines to efficiently assemble products that satisfy current customer demands*

Source: Rex Features

Management consultant – *Operations management uses people to effectively create the services that will address current and potential client needs*

Source: Alamy Images

Disaster relief charity – *Operations management uses our and our partners' resources to speedily provide the supplies and services that relieve community suffering*

Source: Corbis

Advertising agency – *Operations management uses our staff's knowledge and experience to creatively present ideas that delight clients and address their real needs*

Source: Alamy Images

Whatever terminology is used there is a common theme and a common purpose to how we can visualize the operations activity in any type of organization: small or large, manufacturing or service, public or private, profit or not-for-profit. Operations management uses *resources* to *appropriately create outputs* that *fulfil defined market requirements*. See Figure 1.2. However, although the essential nature and purpose of operations management is the same in every type of organization, there are some special issues to consider, particularly in smaller organizations and those whose purpose is to maximize something other than profit.

Operations management in the smaller organization

Irrespective of their size, all companies need to produce and deliver their products and services efficiently and effectively. However, managing operations in a small or medium-size organization has its own set of problems. Large companies may have the resources to dedicate individuals to specialized tasks, but smaller companies often cannot, so people may have to do different jobs as the need arises. Such an informality may allow a quick response as opportunities present themselves. But decision-making can also become confused as **individuals' roles can overlap in small operations.** However, small operations can also have significant advantages; the short case on Acme Whistles illustrates this.

The role of operations management in smaller organizations often overlaps significantly with other functions

Operations management uses . . .

resources	to	appropriately	create	outputs	that	fulfil	defined	market	requirements
			produce						
experience			change				potential	citizens'	
people		effectively	sell	ideas		match	perceived	client	dreams
machines		efficiently	assemble	products		satisfy	current	customer	demands
knowledge		creatively	move	services		exceed	emerging	society	needs
partners		etc.	cure	etc.		delight	real	etc.	concerns
etc.			shape			etc.	etc.		etc.
			etc.						

Figure 1.2 Operations management uses resources to appropriately create outputs that fulfil defined market requirements

Short case
Acme Whistles[2]

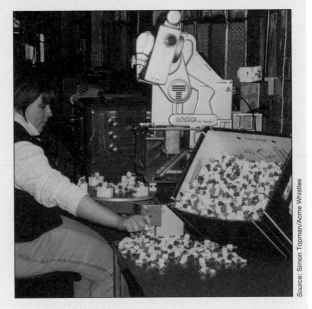

Source: Simon Topman/Acme Whistles

Acme Whistles can trace its history back to 1870 when Joseph Hudson decided he had the answer to the London Metropolitan Police's request for something to replace the wooden rattles that were used to sound the alarm. So the world's first police whistle was born. Soon Acme grew to be the premier supplier of whistles for police forces around the world. *'In many ways'*, says Simon Topman, owner and Managing Director of the company, *'the company is very much the same as it was in Joseph's day. The machinery is more modern, of course, and we have a wider variety of products, but many of our products are similar to their predecessors. For example, football referees seem to prefer the traditional snail-shaped whistle. So, although we have dramatically improved the performance of the product, our customers want it to look the same. We have also maintained the same manufacturing tradition from those early days. The original owner insisted on personally blowing every single whistle before it left the factory. We still do the same, not by personally blowing them, but by using an air line, so the same tradition of quality has endured.'*

The company's range of whistles has expanded to include sports whistles (they provide the whistles for the soccer World Cup), distress whistles, (silent) dog whistles, novelty whistles, instrumental whistles (used by all of the world's top orchestras), and many more types. *'We are always trying to improve our products'*, says Simon, *'it's a business of constant innovation. Sometimes I think that after 130 years surely there is nothing more to do, but we always find some new feature to incorporate. Of course, managing the operations in a small company is very different to working in a large one. Everyone has much broader jobs; we cannot afford the overheads of having specialist people* in specialized roles. But this relative informality has a lot of advantages. It means that we can maintain our philosophy of quality amongst everybody in the company, and it means that we can react very quickly when the market demands it.' Nor is the company's small size any barrier to its ability to innovate. *'On the contrary'*, says Simon, *'there is something about the culture of the company that is extremely important in fostering innovation. Because we are small we all know each other and we all want to contribute something to the company. It is not uncommon for employees to figure out new ideas for different types of whistle. If an idea looks promising, we will put a small and informal team together to look at it further. It is not unusual for people who have been with us only a few months to start wanting to make innovations. It's as though something happens to them when they walk through the door of the factory that encourages their natural inventiveness.'*

Operations management in not-for-profit organizations

Terms such as *competitive advantage*, *markets* and *business*, which are used in this book, are usually associated with companies in the for-profit sector. Yet operations management is also relevant to organizations whose purpose is not primarily to earn profits. Managing the operations in an animal welfare charity, hospital, research organization or government department is essentially the same as in commercial organizations. **Operations have to take the same decisions** – how to create services and products, invest in technology, contract out some of their activities, devise performance measures, and improve their operations performance and so on. However, the strategic objectives of not-for-profit organizations may be more complex and involve a mixture of political, economic, social and environmental objectives. Nevertheless, the vast majority of the topics covered in this book have relevance to all types of organization, including non-profit, even if some terms may have to be adapted.

Operations decisions are the same in commercial and not-for-profit organizations

Short case
Oxfam International[3]

Source: Rex Features

Oxfam International is a confederation of 13 like-minded organizations based around the world that, together with partners and allies, work directly with communities seeking to ensure that poor people can improve their lives and livelihoods and have a say in decisions that affect them. With an annual expenditure that exceeds US$700 million, Oxfam International focuses its efforts in several areas, including development work, long-term programmes to eradicate poverty and combat injustice, emergency relief delivering immediate life-saving assistance to people affected by natural disasters or conflict, helping to build their resilience to future disasters, campaigning and raising public awareness of the causes of poverty, encouraging ordinary people to take action for a fairer world, and advocacy and research that pressures decision-makers to change policies and practices that reinforce poverty and injustice.

All of Oxfam International's activities depend on effective and professional operations management. For example, Oxfam's network of charity shops, run by volunteers, is a key source of income. The shops sell donated items and handcrafts from around the world giving small-scale producers fair prices, training, advice and funding. Supply chain management and development is just as central to the running of these shops as it is to the biggest commercial chain of stores. The operations challenges involved in Oxfam's ongoing 'Clean Water' exercise are different but certainly no less important. Around 80 per cent of diseases and over one-third of deaths in the developing world are caused by contaminated water and Oxfam has a particular expertise in providing clean water and sanitation facilities. The better their coordinated efforts of identifying potential projects, working with local communities, providing help and education and helping to provide civil engineering expertise, the more effective Oxfam is at fulfilling its objectives.

More dramatically, Oxfam International's response to emergency situations, providing humanitarian aid where it is needed, must be fast, appropriate and efficient. Whether the disasters are natural or political, they become emergencies when the people involved can no longer cope. In such situations, Oxfam, through its network of staff in local offices, is able to advise on what and where help is needed. Indeed, local teams are often able to provide warnings of impending disasters, giving more time to assess needs and coordinate a multi-agency response. The organization's headquarters in Oxford in the UK provides advice, materials and staff, often deploying emergency support staff on short-term assignments. Shelters, blankets and clothing can be flown out at short notice from the Emergencies Warehouse. Engineers and sanitation equipment can also be provided, including water tanks, latrines, hygiene kits and containers. When an emergency is over, Oxfam continues to work with the affected communities through their local offices to help people rebuild their lives and livelihoods. In an effort to improve the timeliness, effectiveness and appropriateness of its response to emergencies, Oxfam recently adopted a more systematic approach to evaluating the successes and failures of its humanitarian work. Real-time evaluations, which seek to assess and influence emergency response programmes in their early stages, were implemented during the response to floods in Mozambique and

South Asia, the earthquake in Peru, Hurricane Felix in Nicaragua and the conflicts in Uganda. These exercises provided Oxfam's humanitarian teams with the opportunity to gauge the effectiveness of their response, and make crucial adjustments at an early stage if necessary. The evaluations highlighted several potential improvements. For example, it became evident that there was a need to improve preparation ahead of emergencies, as well as the need to develop more

effective coordination planning tools. It was also decided that adopting a common working approach with shared standards would improve the effectiveness of their response to emergencies. Oxfam also emphasizes the importance of the role played by local partners in emergencies. They are often closer to, and more in tune with, affected communities, but may require additional support and empowerment to scale up their response and comply with the international humanitarian standards.

The new operations agenda

Modern business pressures have changed the operations agenda

The business environment has a significant impact on what is expected from operations management. In recent years there have been new pressures for which the operations function has needed to develop responses. Table 1.2 lists some of these **business pressures** and the operations responses to them. These operations responses form a major part of a *new agenda* for operations. Parts of this agenda are trends which have always existed but have accelerated, such as globalization and increased cost pressures. Part of the agenda involves seeking ways to exploit new technologies, most notably the Internet. Of course, the list in Table 1.2 is not comprehensive, nor is it universal. But very few businesses will be unaffected by at least some of these concerns. When businesses have to cope with a more challenging environment, they look to their operations function to help them respond.

Table 1.2 Changes in the business environment are shaping a new operations agenda

The business environment is changing ...	Prompting operations responses ...
For example,	For example,
• Increased cost-based competition	• Globalization of operations networking
• Higher quality expectations	• Information-based technologies
• Demands for better service	• Internet-based integration of operations activities
• More choice and variety	• Supply chain management
• Rapidly developing technologies	• Customer relationship management
• Frequent new product/service introduction	• Flexible working patterns
• Increased ethical sensitivity	• Mass customization
• Environmental impacts are more transparent	• Fast time-to-market methods
• More legal regulation	• Lean process design
• Greater security awareness	• Environmentally sensitive design
	• Supplier 'partnership' and development
	• Failure analysis
	• Business recovery planning

The input–transformation–output process

Transformation process model

Input resources

Outputs of services and products

All operations create services and products by changing *inputs* into *outputs* using an 'input-transformation-output' process. Figure 1.3 shows this general **transformation process model**. Put simply, operations are processes that take in a set of **input resources** which are used to transform something, or are transformed themselves, into **outputs of services and products**. Although all operations conform to this general input–transformation–output

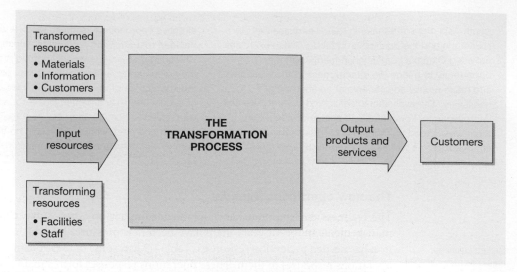

Figure 1.3 All operations are input–transformation–output processes

model, they differ in the nature of their specific inputs and outputs. For example, if you stand far enough away from a hospital or a car plant, they might look very similar, but move closer and clear differences do start to emerge. One is a service operation, creating and delivering services that change the physiological or psychological condition of patients; the other is a manufacturing operation producing products. What is inside each operation will also be different. The motor vehicle plant contains metal-forming machinery and assembly processes, whereas the hospital contains diagnostic, care and therapeutic processes. Perhaps the most important difference between the two operations, however, is the nature of their inputs. The vehicle plant transforms steel, plastic, cloth, tyres and other materials into vehicles. The hospital transforms the customers themselves. The patients form part of the input to, and the output from, the operation. This has important implications for how the operation needs to be managed.

Inputs to the process

Transformed resources

One set of inputs to any operation's processes are **transformed resources**. These are the resources that are treated, transformed or converted in the process. They are usually a mixture of the following:

- **Customers** – operations which process customers might change their *physical properties* in a similar way to materials processors: for example, hairdressers or cosmetic surgeons. Some *store* (or more politely *accommodate*) customers: hotels, for example. Airlines, mass rapid transport systems and bus companies transform the *location* of their customers, while hospitals transform their *physiological state*. Some are concerned with transforming their *psychological state*, for example most entertainment services such as music, theatre, television, radio and theme parks.
- **Materials** – operations which process materials could do so to transform their *physical properties* (shape or composition, for example). Most manufacturing operations are like this. Other operations process materials to change their *location* (parcel delivery companies, for example). Some, like retail operations, do so to change the *possession* of the materials. Finally, some operations *store* materials, such as in warehouses.
- **Information** – operations which process information could do so to transform their *informational properties* (that is the purpose or form of the information); accountants do this. Some change the *possession* of the information, for example market research

Table 1.3 Dominant transformed resource inputs of various operations

Predominantly processing inputs of customers	Predominantly processing inputs of materials	Predominantly processing inputs of information
Hairdressers	All manufacturing operations	Accountants
Hotels	Mining companies	Bank headquarters
Hospitals	Retail operations	Market research company
Mass rapid transport	Warehouses	Financial analysts
Theatres	Postal services	News service
Theme parks	Container shipping line	University research unit
Dentists	Trucking companies	Telecoms company

companies sell information. Some *store* the information, for example archives and libraries. Finally, some operations, such as telecommunication companies, change the *location* of the information.

Often one of these is dominant in an operation. For example, a bank devotes part of its energies to producing printed statements of accounts for its customers. In doing so, it is processing **inputs of material**, but no one would claim that a bank is a printer. The bank is also concerned with processing **inputs of customers**. It gives them advice regarding their financial affairs, cashes their cheques, deposits their cash and has direct contact with them. However, most of the bank's activities are concerned with processing **inputs of information** about its customers' financial affairs. As customers, we may be unhappy with badly printed statements and we may be unhappy if we are not treated appropriately in the bank. However, if the bank makes errors in our financial transactions, we suffer in a far more fundamental way. Table 1.3 gives examples of operations with their dominant transformed resources.

The other set of inputs to any operations process are **transforming resources**. These are the resources which act upon the transformed resources. There are two types which form the 'building blocks' of all operations:

- **facilities** – the buildings, equipment, plant and process technology of the operation;
- **staff** – the people who operate, maintain, plan and manage the operation. (Note that we use the term 'staff' to describe all the people in the operation, at any level.)

The exact nature of both facilities and staff will differ between operations. To a five-star hotel, its facilities consist mainly of 'low-tech' buildings, furniture and fittings. To a nuclear-powered aircraft carrier, its facilities are 'high-tech' nuclear generators and sophisticated electronic equipment. Staff will also differ between operations. Most staff employed in a factory assembling domestic refrigerators may not need a very high level of technical skill. In contrast, most staff employed by an accounting company are, hopefully, highly skilled in their own particular 'technical' skill (accounting). Yet although skills vary, all staff can make a contribution. An assembly worker who consistently misassembles refrigerators will dissatisfy customers and increase costs just as surely as an accountant who cannot add up. The balance between facilities and staff also varies. A computer chip manufacturing company, such as Intel, will have significant investment in physical facilities. A single chip fabrication plant can cost in excess of $4 billion, so operations managers will spend a lot of their time managing their facilities. Conversely, a management consultancy firm depends largely on the quality of its staff. Here operations management is largely concerned with the development and deployment of consultant skills and knowledge.

Marginal notes:
Material inputs
Customer inputs

Information inputs

Transforming resources

Facilities
Staff

Outputs from the process

Some operations create and deliver just services and others just products, but most operations produce a mixture of the two. Figure 1.4 shows a number of operations (including some

'Pure' products
'Pure' service

described as examples in this chapter) positioned in a spectrum from **'pure' product** operations to **'pure' service** operations. Crude oil producers are concerned almost exclusively with
the product which comes from their oil wells. So are aluminium smelters, but they might also
produce some services such as technical advice. Services produced in these circumstances

Facilitating services

are called **facilitating services**. To an even greater extent, machine tool manufacturers produce facilitating services such as technical advice and applications engineering. The services
produced by a restaurant are an essential part of what the customer is paying for. It is both
a manufacturing operation which produces meals and a provider of service in the advice,
ambience and service of the food. An information systems provider may produce software

Facilitating products

'products', but primarily it is providing a service to its customers, with **facilitating products**.
Certainly, a management consultancy, although it produces reports and documents, would
see itself primarily as a service provider. Finally, pure services produce no products, a
psychotherapy clinic, for example.

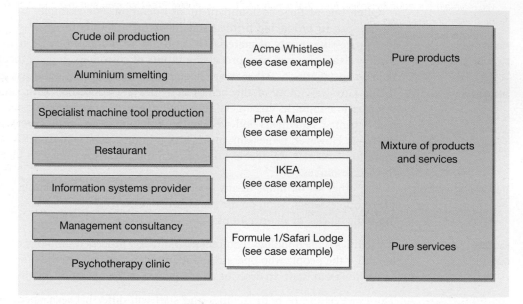

Figure 1.4 The output from most types of operation is a mixture of services and products

Services and products are merging

Increasingly, the distinction between services and products is both difficult to define and
not particularly useful. Internet-based retailers, for example, are increasingly 'transporting'
a larger proportion of their services into customers' homes. Even official statistics have
difficulty in separating services and products. Software sold on a disc is classified as a product.
The same software sold over the Internet is a service. Some authorities see the essential
purpose of all operations processes as being to 'service customers'. Therefore, they argue,

All operations are service
providers

all operations are service providers which may create and deliver products as a part of
serving their customers.

Short case
Pret A Manger[4]

Described by the press as having *'revolutionized the concept of sandwich making and eating'*, Pret A Manger opened their first shop in the mid-1980s, in London. Now they have over 130 shops in UK, New York, Hong Kong and Tokyo. They say that their secret is to focus continually on quality – not just of their food, but in every aspect of their operations practice. They go to extraordinary lengths to avoid the chemicals and preservatives common in most 'fast' food, say the company. *'Many food retailers focus on extending the shelf life of their food, but that's of no interest to us. We maintain our edge by selling food that simply can't be beaten for freshness. At the end of the day, we give whatever we haven't sold to charity to help feed those who would otherwise go hungry. When we were just starting out, a big supplier tried to sell us coleslaw that lasted sixteen days. Can you imagine! Salad that lasts sixteen days? There and then we decided Pret would stick to wholesome fresh food – natural stuff. We have not changed that policy.'*

The first Pret A Manger shop had its own kitchen where fresh ingredients were delivered first thing every morning, and food was prepared throughout the day. Every Pret shop since has followed this model. The team members serving on the tills at lunchtime will have been making sandwiches in the kitchen that morning. The company rejected the idea of a huge centralized sandwich factory even though it could significantly reduce costs. Pret also own and manage all their shops directly so that they can ensure consistently high standards in all their shops. *'We are determined never to forget that our hard-working people make all the difference. They are our heart and soul. When they care, our business is sound. If they cease to care, our business goes down the drain. In a retail sector where high staff turnover is normal, we're pleased to say our people are much more likely to stay around! We work hard at building great teams. We take our reward schemes and career opportunities very seriously. We don't work nights (generally), we wear jeans, we party!'* Customer feedback is regarded as being particularly important at Pret. Examining customers' comments for improvement ideas is a key part of weekly management meetings, and of the daily team briefs in each shop.

The processes hierarchy

So far we have discussed operations management, and the input–transformation–output model, at the level of 'the operation'. For example, we have described 'the whistle factory', 'the sandwich shop', 'the disaster relief operation', and so on. Now look *inside* any of these operations. One will see that all operations consist of a collection of processes (though these processes may be called 'units' or 'departments') interconnecting with each other to form a network. Each process acts as a smaller version of the whole operation of which it forms a part, and transformed resources flow between them. In fact within any operation, the

Processes

mechanisms that actually transform inputs into outputs are these **processes**. A process is 'an arrangement of resources that produce some mixture of products and services'. They are the 'building blocks' of all operations, and they form an 'internal network' within an operation.

Internal supplier
Internal customer

Each process is, at the same time, an **internal supplier** and an **internal customer** for other processes. This 'internal customer' concept provides a model to analyse the internal activities of an operation. It is also a useful reminder that, by treating internal customers with the same degree of care as external customers, the effectiveness of the whole operation can be improved. Table 1.4 illustrates how a wide range of operations can be described in this way.

Table 1.4 Some operations described in terms of their processes

Operation	Some of the operation's inputs	Some of the operation's processes	Some of the operation's outputs
Airline	Aircraft Pilots and air crew Ground crew Passengers and freight	Check passengers in Board passengers Fly passengers and freight around the world Care for passengers	Transported passengers and freight
Department store	Goods for sale Sales staff Information systems Customers	Source and store goods Display goods Give sales advice Sell goods	Customers and goods 'assembled' together
Police	Police officers Computer systems Information systems Public (law-abiding and criminals)	Crime prevention Crime detection Information gathering Detaining suspects	Lawful society, public with a feeling of security
Frozen food manufacturer	Fresh food Operators Processing technology Cold storage facilities	Source raw materials Prepare food Freeze food Pack and freeze food	Frozen food

Within each of these processes is another network of individual units of resource such as individual people and individual items of process technology (machines, computers, storage facilities, etc.). Again, transformed resources flow between each unit of transforming resource. So any business, or operation, is made up of a network of processes and any process is made up of a network of resources. In addition, any business or operation can itself be viewed as part of a greater network of businesses or operations. It will have operations that supply it with the products and services it needs and unless it deals directly with the end-consumer, it will supply customers who themselves may go on to supply their own customers. Moreover, any operation could have several suppliers and several customers and may be in competition with other operations producing similar services to those it produces itself. This network of operations is called the **supply network**. In this way the input–transformation–output model can be used at a number of different 'levels of analysis'. Here we have used the idea to **analyse businesses at three levels**, the process, the operation and the supply network. One could define many different 'levels of analysis': moving upwards from small to larger processes, right up to the huge supply network that describes a whole industry.

This idea is called the **hierarchy of operations** and is illustrated for a business that makes television programmes and DVDs in Figure 1.5. It will have inputs of production, technical and administrative staff, cameras, lighting, sound and recording equipment, and so on. It transforms these into finished programmes, music, videos, etc. At a more macro level, the business itself is part of a whole supply network, acquiring services from creative agencies, casting agencies and studios, liaising with promotion agencies and serving its broadcasting company customers. At a more micro level, within this overall operation there are many individual processes: workshops manufacturing the sets; marketing processes that liaise with potential customers; maintenance and repair processes that care for, modify and design technical equipment; and so on. Each of these individual processes can be represented as a network of yet smaller processes, or even individual units of resource. So, the set manufacturing process could consist of four smaller processes: one that designs the sets, one that constructs them, one that acquires the props, and one that finishes (paints) the set.

Supply network

Operations can be analysed at three levels

Hierarchy of operations

The idea of the internal network of processes is seen by some as being over-simplistic. In reality the relationship between groups and individuals is significantly more complex than that between commercial entities. One cannot treat internal customers and suppliers exactly as we do external customers and suppliers. External customers and suppliers usually operate in a free market. If an organization believes that in the long run it can get a better deal by purchasing goods and services from another supplier, it will do so. Conversely internal customers and suppliers are not in a 'free market'. They cannot usually look outside either to purchase input resources or to sell their output goods and services (although some organizations are moving this way). Rather than take the 'economic' perspective of external commercial relationships, models from organizational behaviour, it is argued, are more appropriate.

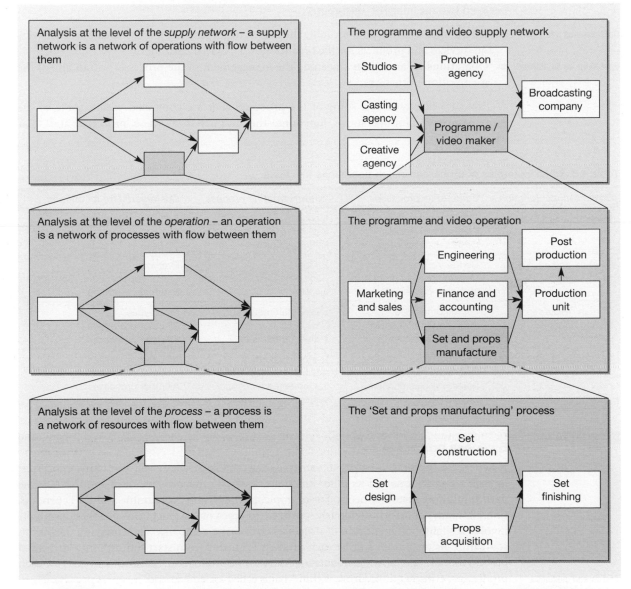

Figure 1.5 Operations and process management requires analysis at three levels: the supply network, the operation, and the process

Operations management is relevant to all parts of the business

All functions manage processes

The example in Figure 1.5 demonstrates that it is not just the operations function that manages processes; **all functions manage processes**. For example, the marketing function will have processes that create forecasts, create advertising campaigns and create marketing plans. These processes also need managing using principles similar to those within the operations function. Each function will have its 'technical' knowledge. In marketing, this is the expertise in designing and shaping marketing plans; in finance, it is the technical knowledge of financial reporting. Yet each will also have a 'process management' role of creating and delivering plans, policies, reports and services. The implications of this are very important.

All managers, not just operations managers, manage processes

As all managers have some responsibility for managing processes, they are, to some extent, operations managers. They all should want to give good service to their (often internal) customers, and they all will want to do this efficiently. So, **operations management is relevant for all functions**, and all managers should have something to learn from the principles, concepts, approaches and techniques of operations management. It also means that we must distinguish between two meanings of 'operations':

Operations as a function

- **'Operations' as a function**, meaning the part of the organization which creates and delivers the services and products for the organization's external customers;

Operations as an activity

- **'Operations' as an activity**, meaning the management of the processes within any of the organization's functions.

Table 1.5 illustrates just some of the processes that are contained within some of the more common non-operations functions, the outputs from these processes and their 'customers'.

Table 1.5 Some examples of processes in non-operations functions

Organizational function	Some of its processes	Outputs from its process	Customer(s) for its outputs
Marketing and sales	Planning process Forecasting process Order taking process	Marketing plans Sales forecasts Confirmed orders	Senior management Sales staff, planners, operations Operations, finance
Finance and accounting	Budgeting process Capital approval processes Invoicing processes	Budgets Capital request evaluations Invoices	Everyone Senior management, requesters External customers
Human resources management	Payroll processes Recruitment processes Training processes	Salary statements New hires Trained employees	Employees All other processes All other processes
Information technology	Systems review process Help desk process System implementation project processes	System evaluation Advice Implemented working systems and aftercare	All other processes All other processes All other processes

Business processes

Whenever a business attempts to satisfy its customers' needs it will use many processes, in both its operations and its other functions. Each of these processes will contribute some part to fulfilling customer needs. For example, the television programme and DVD production company, described previously, creates two types of 'product'. Both of these products involve a slightly different mix of processes within the company. The company decides to reorganize its operations so that each product is created from start to finish by a dedicated process that contains all the elements necessary for its production. So customer needs for each

'End-to-end' business processes

product are entirely fulfilled from within what is called an **'end-to-end' business process**. These often cut across conventional organizational boundaries. Reorganizing (or 're-engineering')

Business process re-engineering

process boundaries and organizational responsibilities around these business processes is the philosophy behind **business process re-engineering** (BPR).

Operations processes have different characteristics

Although all operations processes are similar in that they all transform inputs, they do differ in a number of ways, four of which, known as the four Vs, are particularly important:

Volume
Variety
Variation
Visibility

- The **volume** of their output;
- The **variety** of their output;
- The **variation** in the demand for their output;
- The degree of **visibility** which customers have of the production of their output.

The volume dimension

Repeatability
Systematization

Let us take a familiar example. The epitome of high-volume hamburger production is McDonald's, which serves millions of burgers around the world every day. Volume has important implications for the way McDonald's operations are organized. The first thing you notice is the **repeatability** of the tasks people are doing and the **systematization** of the work where standard procedures are set down specifying how each part of the job should be carried out. Also, because tasks are systematized and repeated, it is worthwhile developing specialized fryers and ovens. All this gives *low unit costs*. Now consider a small local cafeteria serving a few 'short-order' dishes. The range of items on the menu may be similar to the larger operation, but the volume will be far lower, so the repetition will also be far lower and the number of staff will be lower (possibly only one person) and therefore individual staff are likely to perform a wider range of tasks. This may be more rewarding for the staff, but less open to systematization. Also it is less feasible to invest in specialized equipment. So the cost per burger served is likely to be higher (even if the price is comparable).

The variety dimension

Standardized

A taxi company offers a high-variety service. It is prepared to pick you up from almost anywhere and drop you off almost anywhere. To offer this variety it must be relatively *flexible*. Drivers must have a good knowledge of the area, and communication between the base and the taxis must be effective. However, the cost per kilometre travelled will be higher for a taxi than for a less customized form of transport such as a bus service. Although both provide the same basic service (transportation), the taxi service has a high variety of routes and times to offer its customers, while the bus service has a few well-defined routes, with a set schedule. If all goes to schedule, little, if any, flexibility is required from the operation. All is **standardized** and regular, which results in relatively low costs compared with using a taxi for the same journey.

The variation dimension

Consider the demand pattern for a successful summer holiday resort hotel. Not surprisingly, more customers want to stay in summer vacation times than in the middle of winter. At the height of 'the season' the hotel could be full to its capacity. Off-season demand, however, could be a small fraction of its capacity. Such a marked variation in demand means that the operation must change its capacity in some way, for example, by hiring extra staff for the summer. The hotel must try to predict the likely level of demand. If it gets this wrong, it could result in too much or too little capacity. Also, recruitment costs, overtime costs and under-utilization of its rooms all have the effect of increasing the hotel's costs operation compared with a hotel of a similar standard with level demand. A hotel which has relatively level demand can plan its activities well in advance. Staff can be scheduled, food can be bought and rooms can be cleaned in a *routine* and *predictable* manner. This results in a high utilization of resources and unit costs which are likely to be lower than those in hotels with a highly variable demand pattern.

The visibility dimension

Visibility means process exposure

Visibility is a slightly more difficult dimension of operations to envisage. It refers to how much of the operation's activities its customers experience, or how much the operation is **exposed** to its customers. Generally, customer-processing operations are more exposed to their customers than material- or information-processing operations. But even customer-processing operations have some choice as to how visible they wish their operations to be. For example, a retailer could operate as a high-visibility 'bricks and mortar', or a lower-visibility web-based operation. In the 'bricks and mortar', high-visibility operation, customers will directly experience most of its 'value-adding' activities. Customers will have a relatively *short waiting tolerance*, and may walk out if not served in a reasonable time. Customers' perceptions, rather than objective criteria, will also be important. If they perceive that a member of the operation's staff is discourteous to them, they are likely to be dissatisfied (even if the staff member meant no discourtesy), so high-visibility operations require staff with good customer contact skills. Customers could also request goods which clearly would not be sold in such a shop, but because the customers are actually in the operation they can ask what they

High received variety

like! This is called **high received variety**. This makes it difficult for high-visibility operations to achieve high productivity of resources, so they tend to be relatively high-cost operations. Conversely, a web-based retailer, while not a pure low-contact operation, has far lower visibility. Behind its web site it can be more 'factory-like'. The *time lag* between the order being placed and the items ordered by the customer being retrieved and dispatched does not have to be minutes as in the shop, but can be hours or even days. This allows the tasks of finding the items, packing and dispatching them to be *standardized* by staff who need

Customer contact skills

few **customer contact skills**. Also, there can be relatively *high staff utilization*. The web-based organization can also centralize its operation on one (physical) site, whereas the 'bricks and mortar' shop needs many shops close to centres of demand. Therefore, the low-visibility web-based operation will have lower costs than the shop.

Short case
Two very different hotels

Formule 1

Hotels are high-contact operations – they are staff-intensive and have to cope with a range of customers, each with a variety of needs and expectations. So, how can a highly successful chain of affordable hotels avoid the costs of high customer contact? Formule 1, a subsidiary of the French Accor group, manages to offer outstanding value by adopting two principles not always associated with hotel operations – standardization and an innovative use of technology. Formule 1 hotels are usually located close to the roads, junctions and cities which make them visible and accessible to prospective customers. The hotels themselves are made from state-of-the-art volumetric prefabrications. The prefabricated units are arranged in various configurations to suit the characteristics of each individual site. All rooms are nine square metres in area, and are designed to be attractive, functional, comfortable and soundproof. Most importantly, they are designed to be easy to clean and maintain. All have the same fittings, including a double bed, an additional bunk-type bed, a wash basin, a storage area, a working table with seat, a wardrobe and a television set. The reception of a Formule 1 hotel is staffed only from

6.30 am to 10.00 am and from 5.00 pm to 10.00 pm. Outside these times an automatic machine sells rooms to credit card users, provides access to the hotel, dispenses a security code for the room and even prints a receipt. Technology is also evident in the washrooms. Showers and toilets are automatically cleaned after each use by using nozzles and heating elements to spray the room with a disinfectant solution and dry it before it is used again. To keep things even simpler, Formule 1 hotels do not include a restaurant as they are usually located near existing restaurants. However, a continental breakfast is available, usually between 6.30 am and 10.00 am, and of course on a 'self-service' basis!

Mwagusi Safari Lodge

The Mwagusi Safari Lodge lies within Tanzania's Ruaha National Park, a huge undeveloped wilderness, whose beautiful open landscape is especially good for seeing elephant, buffalo and lion. Nestled into a bank of the Mwagusi Sand River, this small exclusive tented camp overlooks a watering hole in the riverbed. Its ten tents are within thatched bandas (accommodation), each furnished comfortably in the traditional style of the camp. Each banda has an en-suite bathroom with flush toilet and a hot shower. Game viewing can be experienced even from the seclusion of the veranda. The sight of thousands of buffalo flooding the riverbed below the tents and dining room banda is not uncommon, and elephants, giraffes, and wild dogs are frequent uninvited guests to the site. There are two staff for each customer, allowing individual needs and preferences to be met quickly at all times. Guest numbers vary throughout the year, occupancy

being low in the rainy season from January to April, and full in the best game viewing period from September to November. There are game drives and walks throughout the area, each selected for customers' individual preferences. Drives are taken in specially adapted open-sided four-wheel-drive vehicles, equipped with reference books, photography equipment, medical kits and all the necessities for a day in the bush. Walking safaris, accompanied by an experienced guide can be customized for every visitor's requirements and abilities. Lunch can be taken communally, so that visitors can discuss their interests with other guides and managers. Dinner is often served under the stars in a secluded corner of the dry riverbed.

Mixed high- and low-visibility processes

Front office

Back office

Some operations have both high- and low-visibility processes within the same operation. In an airport, for example, some activities are totally 'visible' to its customers such as information desks answering people's queries. These staff operate in what is termed a **front-office** environment. Other parts of the airport have little, if any, customer 'visibility', such as the baggage handlers. These rarely-seen staff perform the vital but low-contact tasks, in the **back-office** part of the operation.

The implications of the four Vs of operations processes

'Four Vs' analysis of processes

All four dimensions have implications for the cost of creating services or products. Put simply, high volume, low variety, low variation and low customer contact all help to keep processing costs down. Conversely, low volume, high variety, high variation and high customer contact generally carry some kind of cost penalty for the operation. This is why the volume dimension is drawn with its 'low' end at the left, unlike the other dimensions, to keep all the 'low cost' implications on the right. To some extent the position of an operation in the **four dimensions** is determined by the demand of the market it is serving. However, most operations have some discretion in moving themselves on the dimensions. Figure 1.6 summarizes the implications of such positioning.

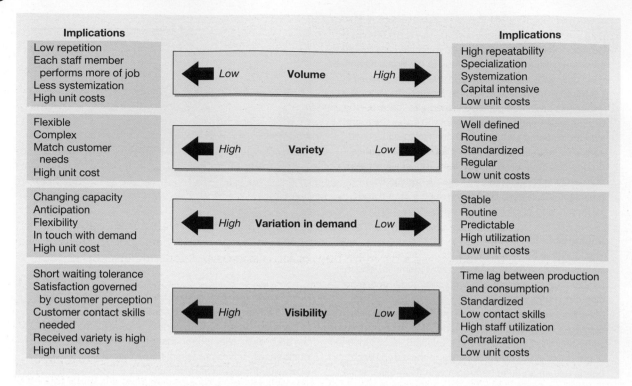

Figure 1.6 A typology of operations

Worked example

Figure 1.7 illustrates the different positions on the dimensions of the Formule 1 hotel chain and the Mwagusi Safari Lodge (*see* the short case on 'Two very different hotels'). Both provide the same basic service as any other hotel. However, one is of a small, intimate nature with relatively few customers. Its variety of services is almost infinite in the sense that customers can make individual requests in terms of food and entertainment. Variation is high and customer contact, and therefore visibility, is also very high (in order to ascertain customers' requirements and provide for them). All of this is very different from Formule 1, where volume is high (although not as high as in a large city-centre hotel), variety of service is strictly limited, and business and holiday customers use the hotel at different times, which limits variation. Most notably, though, customer contact is kept to a minimum. The Mwagusi Safari Lodge hotel has very high levels of service but provides them at a high cost. Conversely, Formule 1 has arranged its operation in such a way as to minimize its costs.

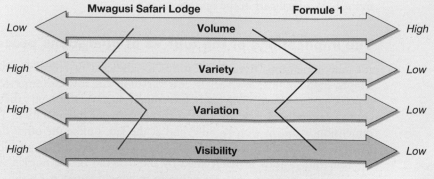

Figure 1.7 Profiles of two operations

The activities of operations management

Operations managers find themselves involved with many different activities within the organization. Many of these are cross-functional, involving managers from other parts of the organization, but other activities are seen as the prime responsibilities of operations managers specifically. These all begin with the letter D.

Directing the overall strategy of the operation. A general understanding of operations and their strategic purpose, together with an appreciation of how operations performance should be assessed is a prerequisite to managing any type of operations. This chapter, together with Chapters 2 and 3, are devoted to this set of activities.

Designing the operation's services, products and processes. Design is the activity of determining the physical form, shape and composition of operations and processes together with the products and services that they produce. Chapters 4–6 deal with these issues.

Delivering to customers. The ongoing creation of services and products must be managed, from choosing and controlling the suppliers of input resources right through to their delivery of products and services to customers. The activities involved in this ongoing delivery are examined in Chapters 7–11.

Developing process performance. Increasingly, it is recognized that for any operation or any process, managers cannot simply routinely deliver services and products in the same way that they always have done. They have a responsibility to develop the capabilities of their processes to improve process performance. These development responsibilities are looked at in Chapters 12 and 13.

The model of operations management

We can now combine two ideas to develop the model of operations management which will be used throughout this book. The first is the input–transformation–output model and the second is the categorization of operations management's activity areas. Figure 1.8 shows how these two ideas go together. The model now shows two interconnected loops of **activities**. The bottom one more or less corresponds to what is usually seen as operations management, and the top one to what is seen as operations strategy. This book concentrates on the former but tries to cover enough of the latter to allow the reader to make strategic sense of the operations manager's job.

Operations activities define operations management and operations strategy

Critical commentary

The central idea in this introductory chapter is that all organizations have operations processes which produce products and services and all these processes are essentially similar. However, some believe that by even trying to characterize processes in this way (perhaps even by calling them 'processes') one loses or distorts their nature, depersonalizes or takes the 'humanity' out of the way in which we think of the organization. This point is often raised in not-for-profit organizations, especially by 'professional' staff. For example the head of one European 'Medical Association' (a doctors' trade union) criticized hospital authorities for expecting a *sausage factory service based on productivity targets*.[5] No matter how similar they appear on paper, it is argued, a hospital can never be viewed in the same way as a factory. Even in commercial businesses, professionals, such as creative staff, often express discomfort at their expertise being described as a 'process'.

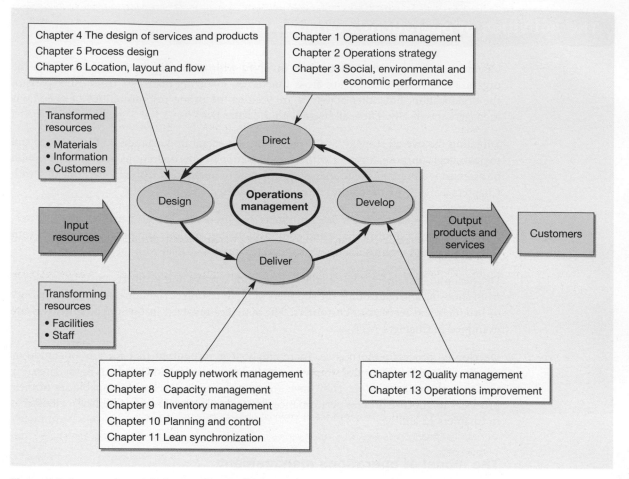

Figure 1.8 A general model of operations management

Summary answers to key questions

Check and improve your understanding of this chapter using self-assessment questions and a personalized study plan, audio and video downloads, and an eBook – all at **www.myomlab.com.**

> ➤ What is operations management?

- Operations management is the activity of managing the resources which are devoted to the creation and delivery of services and products. It is one of the core functions of any business, although it may not be called operations management in some industries.

- Operations management is concerned with managing processes. All processes have internal customers and suppliers. As all management functions also have processes, operations management has relevance for all managers.

> ➤ Why is operations management important in all types of organization?

- Operations management uses the organization's resources to create outputs that fulfil defined market requirements. This is the fundamental activity of any type of enterprise.

- Operations management is increasingly important because today's business environment requires new thinking from operations managers.

➤ What is the input–transformation–output process?

- All operations can be modelled as input–transformation–output processes. They all have inputs of transforming resources, which are usually divided into 'facilities' and 'staff', and transformed resources, which are some mixture of customers, materials and information.
- Few operations create and deliver only services or products. Most produce some mixture of products and services.

➤ What is the process hierarchy?

- All operations are part of a larger supply network which, through the individual contributions of each operation, satisfies end-customer requirements.
- All operations are made up of processes that form a network of internal customer–supplier relationships within the operation.
- End-to-end business processes that satisfy customer needs often cut across functionally based processes.

➤ How do operations processes have different characteristics?

- Operations differ in terms of the volume of their outputs, the variety of outputs, the variation in demand for their outputs, and the degree of visibility they have.
- High volume, low variety, low variation and low customer visibility are usually associated with low cost.

➤ What are the activities of operations management?

- Responsibilities include defining an operations strategy, understanding social, environmental and economic objectives, designing the operation's services, products and processes, delivering to customers, and developing the operation over time.

Learning exercises

These problems and applications will help to improve your analysis of operations. You can find more practice problems as well as worked examples and guided solutions on MyOMLab at www.myomlab.com.

1 Read the short case on Pret A Manger and **(a)** identify the processes in a typical Pret A Manger shop together with their inputs and outputs, **(b)** Pret A Manger also supplies business lunches (of sandwiches and other take-away food). What are the implications for how it manages its processes within the shop? **(c)** What would be the advantages and disadvantages if Pret A Manger introduced 'central kitchens' that made the sandwiches for a number of shops in an area? (As far as we know, they have no plans to do so.)

2 Compare and contrast Acme Whistles and Pret A Manger in terms of the way that they will need to manage their operations.

3 Visit and observe three restaurants, cafés or somewhere that food is served. Compare them in terms of the Volume of demand that they have to cope with, the Variety of menu items they service, the Variation in demand during the day, week and year, and the Visibility you have of the preparation of the food. Think about and discuss the impact of volume, variety, variation and visibility on the day-to-day management of each of the operations and consider how each operation attempts to cope with its volume, variety, variation and visibility.

4 (Advanced) Find a copy of a financial newspaper or magazine (*Financial Times*, *Wall Street Journal*, *Economist*, etc.) and identify one company which is described in the paper that day. Using the list of issues identified in Table 1.1, what do you think would be the *new operations agenda* for that company?

Want to know more?

Chase, R.B., Jacobs, F.R. and Aquilano, N.J. (2004) *Operations Management for Competitive Advantage* (10th edn), McGraw-Hill/Irwin, Boston, MA. There are many good general textbooks on operations management. This was one of the first and is still one of the best, though written very much for an American audience.

Chopra, S., Deshmukh, S., Van Mieghem, J., Zemel, E. and Anupindi, R. (2005) *Managing Business Process Flows: Principles of Operations Management*, Prentice-Hall, Englewood Cliffs, NJ. Takes a 'process' view of operations. Mathematical but rewarding.

Heizer, J. and Render, B. (2006) *Operations Management* (8th edn), Prentice Hall, Englewood Cliffs, NJ. Another good US authored general text on the subject.

Johnston, R. and Clark, G. (2008) *Service Operations Management* (3rd edn), Financial Times-Prentice Hall, Harlow. What can we say! A great treatment of service operations from the same stable as this textbook.

Useful websites

www.opsman.org Useful materials and resources.

www.iomnet.org.uk The Institute of Operations Management site. One of the main professional bodies for the subject.

www.poms.org A US academic society for production and operations management. Academic, but some useful material, including a link to an encyclopaedia of operations management terms.

www.sussex.ac.uk/Users/dt31/TOMI/ One of the longest-established portals for the subject. Useful for academics and students alike.

www.ft.com Useful for researching topics and companies.

www.journaloperationsmanagement.org The home site for the best known operations management journal. A bit academic, but some pages are useful.

Now that you have finished reading this chapter, why not visit MyOMLab at www.myomlab.com where you'll find more learning resources to help you make the most of your studies and get a better grade.

Chapter 2

Operations strategy

Key questions

➤ What is strategy and what is operations strategy?

➤ What is the difference between a 'top-down' and a 'bottom-up' view of operations strategy?

➤ What is the difference between a 'market requirements' and an 'operations resources' view of operations strategy?

➤ How can an operations strategy be put together?

Introduction

No organization can tell exactly what will happen in the future, but all organizations need strategic direction and can benefit from some idea of where they are heading and how they could get there. Once the operations function has understood its role in the business, it needs to formulate a set of general principles which will guide its decision-making. This is the operations strategy of the company. Yet the concept of 'strategy' itself is not straightforward; neither is operations strategy. This chapter considers four perspectives, each of which goes part way to illustrating the forces that shape operations strategy. Figure 2.1 shows where this chapter fits into the overall operations model.

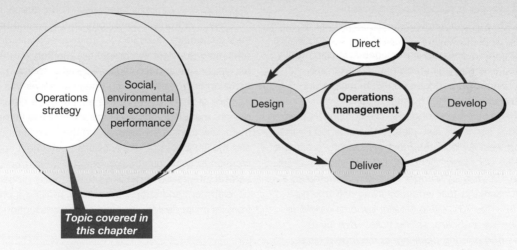

Figure 2.1 This chapter examines operations strategy

Check and improve your understanding of this chapter using self-assessment questions and a personalized study plan, audio and video downloads, and an eBook – all at www.myomlab.com.

Operations in practice Two operations strategies: Flextronics and Ryanair[1]

The two most important attributes of any operations strategy are first that it aligns operations activities with the strategy of the whole organization, and second that it gives clear guidance. Here are two examples of very different businesses and very different strategies which nonetheless meet both criteria.

Ryanair is today Europe's largest low-cost airline (LCAs) and whatever else can be said about its strategy, it does not suffer from any lack of clarity. It has grown by offering low-cost basic services and has devised an operations strategy which is in line with its market position. The efficiency of the airline's operations supports its low-cost market position. Turnaround time at airports is kept to a minimum. This is achieved partly because there are no meals to be loaded onto the aircraft and partly through improved employee productivity. All the aircraft in the fleet are identical, giving savings through standardization of parts, maintenance and servicing. It also means large orders to a single aircraft supplier and therefore the opportunity to negotiate prices down. Also, because the company often uses secondary airports, landing and service fees are much lower. Finally, the cost of selling its services is reduced where possible.

Ryanair has developed its own low-cost Internet booking service. In addition, the day-to-day experiences of the company's operations managers can also modify and refine these strategic decisions. For example, Ryanair changed its baggage handling contractors at Stansted airport in the UK after problems with misdirecting customers' luggage. The company's policy on customer service is also clear. *'We patterned Ryanair after Southwest Airlines, the most consistently profitable airline in the US'*, says Michael O'Leary, Ryanair's Chief Executive. *'Southwest founder Herb Kelleher created a formula for success that works by flying only one type of airplane, – the 737, using smaller airports, providing no-frills service on-board, selling tickets directly to customers and offering passengers the lowest fares in the market. We have adapted his model for our marketplace and are now setting the low-fare standard for Europe. Our customer service'*, says O'Leary, *'is about the most well defined in the world. We guarantee to give you the lowest air fare. You get a safe flight. You get a normally on-time flight. That's the package. We don't, and won't, give you anything more. Are we going to say sorry for our lack of customer service? Absolutely not. If a plane is cancelled, will we put you up in a hotel overnight? Absolutely not. If a plane is delayed, will we give you a voucher for a restaurant? Absolutely not.'*

Source: Corbis

Flextronics is a global company based in Singapore that lies behind such well-known brand names as Nokia and Dell, which are increasingly using electronic manufacturing services (EMS) companies, such as Flextronics, which specialize in providing the outsourced design, engineering, manufacturing and logistics operations for the big brand names. It is amongst the biggest of those EMS suppliers that offer the broadest worldwide capabilities, from design to end-to-end vertically integrated global supply chain services. Flextronics' operations strategy must balance their customers' need for low costs (electronic goods are often sold in a fiercely competitive market) with their need for responsive and flexible service (electronics markets can also be volatile). The company achieves this in a number of ways. Firstly, it has an extensive network of design, manufacturing and logistics facilities in the world's major electronics markets, giving them significant scale and the flexibility to move activities to the most appropriate location to serve customers. Secondly, Flextronics offers vertical integration capabilities that simplify global product development and supply processes, moving a product from its initial design through volume production, test,

Source: Corbis

distribution, and into post-sales service, responsively and efficiently. Finally, Flextronics has developed integrated industrial parks to exploit fully the advantages of their global, large-scale, high-volume capabilities. Positioned in low-cost regions, yet close to all major world markets, Flextronics' industrial parks can significantly reduce the cost of production. Locations include Gdansk in Poland, Hungary, Guadalajara in Mexico, Sorocaba in Brazil, Chennai in India and Shanghai in China. Flextronics' own suppliers are encouraged to locate within these parks, from which products can be produced on-site and shipped directly from the industrial park to customers, greatly reducing freight costs of incoming components and outgoing products. Products not produced on-site can be obtained from Flextronics' network of regional manufacturing facilities located near the industrial parks. Using this strategy, Flextronics says it can provide cost-effective delivery of finished products within 1–2 days of orders.

What is strategy and what is operations strategy?

Strategic decisions

Surprisingly, 'strategy' is not particularly easy to define. Linguistically the word derives from the Greek word '*strategos*' meaning 'leading an army'. Here, by '**strategic decisions**' we mean those decisions which are widespread in their effect on the organization to which the strategy refers, define the position of the organization relative to its environment, and move the organization closer to its long-term goals. But 'strategy' is more than a single decision; it is the *total pattern of the decisions* and actions that influence the long-term direction of the business. Thinking about strategy in this way helps us to discuss an organization's strategy even when it has not been explicitly stated. Observing the total pattern of decisions gives an indication of the *actual* strategic behaviour.

Operations strategy

Operations strategy concerns the pattern of strategic decisions and actions which set the role, objectives and activities of the operation. The term 'operations strategy' sounds at first like a contradiction. How can 'operations', a subject that is generally concerned with the day-to-day creation and delivery of services and products, be strategic? 'Strategy' is usually regarded as the opposite of those day-to-day routine activities. But '*operations*' is not the same as '*operational*'. 'Operations' are the resources that create services and products. 'Operational' is the opposite of strategic, meaning day-to-day and detailed. So, one can examine both the operational *and* the strategic aspects of operations. It is also conventional to distinguish between the '**content**' and the '**process**' of operations strategy. The *content* of operations strategy is the specific decisions and actions which set the operations' role, objectives and activities. The *process* of operations strategy is the method that is used to make the specific 'content' decisions.

'Operations' is not the same as 'operational'

The content and process of operations strategy

Hayes and Wheelwright's four stages of operations contribution

The four-stage model of operations contribution

The ability of any operation to contribute to business strategy can be judged by considering the organizational aims or aspirations of the operations function. Professors Hayes and Wheelwright of Harvard University[2] developed a **four-stage model** which can be used to evaluate the role and contribution of the operations function. The model traces the progression of the operations function from what is the largely negative role of stage 1 operations to its becoming the central element of competitive strategy in excellent stage 4 operations. Figure 2.2 illustrates the four stages.

Stage 1: Internal neutrality. This is the very poorest level of contribution by the operations function. It is inward-looking and reactive, with very little positive to contribute towards competitive success. Paradoxically, its goal is 'to be ignored' (or to become 'internally neutral') by avoiding making mistakes. At least then it isn't holding the company back in any way.

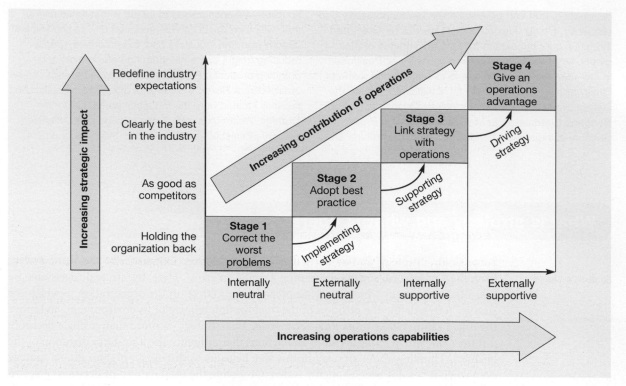

Figure 2.2 The four-stage model of operations contribution

Stage 2: External neutrality. The first step of breaking out of stage 1 is for the operations function to begin comparing itself with similar companies or organizations in the outside market (being 'externally neutral'). This may not immediately take it to the 'first division' of companies in the market, but at least it is measuring itself against its competitors' performance and trying to implement 'best practice'.

Stage 3: Internally supportive. Stage 3 operations are amongst the best in their market. Yet, stage 3 operations still aspire to be clearly and unambiguously the very best in the market. They achieve this by gaining a clear view of the company's competitive or strategic goals and supporting it by developing appropriate operations resources. The operation is trying to be 'internally supportive' by providing a credible operations strategy.

Stage 4: Externally supportive. Yet Hayes and Wheelwright suggest a further stage – stage 4, where the company views the operations function as providing the foundation for its competitive success. Operations looks to the long term. It forecasts likely changes in markets and supply, and it develops the operations-based capabilities which will be required to compete in future market conditions. Stage 4 operations are innovative, creative and proactive and are driving the company's strategy by being 'one step ahead' of competitors – what Hayes and Wheelwright call 'being externally supportive'.

Critical commentary

The idea that operations can have a leading role in determining a company's strategic direction is not universally supported. Both Hayes and Wheelwright's stage 4 of their four-stage model and the concept of operations 'driving' strategy do not only imply that it is possible for operations to take such a leading role, but are explicit in seeing it as a 'good thing'. A more traditional stance taken by some authorities is that the needs of the market will always be pre-eminent in shaping a company's strategy. Therefore, operations should devote all their time to understanding the requirements of the market (as defined by the marketing function within the organization) and devote themselves to their main job of ensuring that operations processes can actually deliver what the market requires. Companies can only be successful, they argue, by positioning themselves in the market (through a combination of price, promotion, product design and managing how products and services are delivered to customers) with operations very much in a 'supporting' role. In effect, they say, Hayes and Wheelwright's four-stage model should stop at stage 3. The issue of an 'operations resource' perspective on operations strategy is discussed later in the chapter.

Perspectives on operations strategy

Different authors have slightly different views and definitions of operations strategy. Between them, four 'perspectives' emerge:[3]

Top-down
Bottom-up

Market requirements

Operations resource
capabilities

- Operation strategy is a **top-down** reflection of what the whole group or business wants to do.
- Operations strategy is a **bottom-up** activity where operations improvements cumulatively build strategy.
- Operations strategy involves translating **market requirements** into operations decisions.
- Operations strategy involves exploiting the **capabilities of operations resources** in chosen markets.

None of these four perspectives alone gives the full picture of what operations strategy is. But together they provide some idea of the pressures which go to form the content of operations strategy. We will treat each in turn (see Figure 2.3).

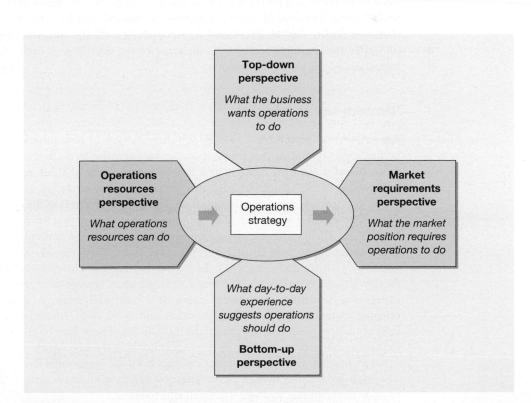

Figure 2.3 The four perspectives on operations strategy

The 'top-down' and 'bottom-up' perspectives

Top-down strategies

Corporate strategy

Business strategy

Functional strategy

A large corporation will need a strategy to position itself in its global, economic, political and social environment. This will consist of decisions about what types of business the group wants to be in, what parts of the world it wants to operate in, how to allocate its cash between its various businesses, and so on. Decisions such as these form the **corporate strategy** of the corporation. Each business unit within the corporate group will also need to put together its own business strategy which sets out its individual mission and objectives. This **business strategy** guides the business in relation to its customers, markets and competitors, and also the strategy of the corporate group of which it is a part. Similarly, within the business, **functional strategies** need to consider what part each function should play in contributing to the strategic objectives of the business. The operations, marketing, product/service development and other functions will all need to consider how best they should organize themselves to support the business's objectives.

So, one perspective on operations strategy is that it should take its place in this hierarchy of strategies. Its main influence, therefore, will be whatever the business sees as its strategic direction. For example, a printing services group has a company which prints packaging for consumer products. The group's management figures that, in the long term, only companies with significant market share will achieve substantial profitability. Its corporate objectives therefore stress market dominance. The consumer packaging company decides to achieve volume growth, even above short-term profitability or return on investment. The implication for operations strategy is that it needs to expand rapidly, investing in extra capacity (factories, equipment and labour) even if it means some excess capacity in some areas. It also needs to establish new factories in all parts of its market to offer relatively fast delivery. The important point here is that different business objectives would probably result in a very different operations strategy. The role of operations is therefore largely one of implementing or 'operationalizing' business strategy. Figure 2.4 illustrates this strategic hierarchy, with some of the decisions at each level and the main influences on the strategic decisions.

'Bottom-up' strategies

The 'top-down' perspective provides an orthodox view of how functional strategies *should* be put together. But in fact the relationship between the levels in the strategy hierarchy is more complex than this. Although it is a convenient way of thinking about strategy, this hierarchical model is not intended to represent the way strategies are always formulated. When any group is reviewing its corporate strategy, it will also take into account the circumstances, experiences and capabilities of the various businesses that form the group. Similarly, businesses, when reviewing their strategies, will consult the individual functions within the business about their constraints and capabilities. They may also incorporate the ideas which come from each function's day-to-day experience. Therefore an alternative view to the top-down perspective is that many strategic ideas emerge over time from operational experience. Sometimes companies move in a particular strategic direction because the ongoing experience of providing products and services to customers at an operational level convinces them that it is the right thing to do. There may be no high-level decisions examining alternative strategic options and choosing the one which provides the best way forward. Instead, a general consensus emerges from the operational level of the organization. The 'high-level' strategic decision-making, if it occurs at all, may confirm the consensus and provide the resources to make it happen effectively.

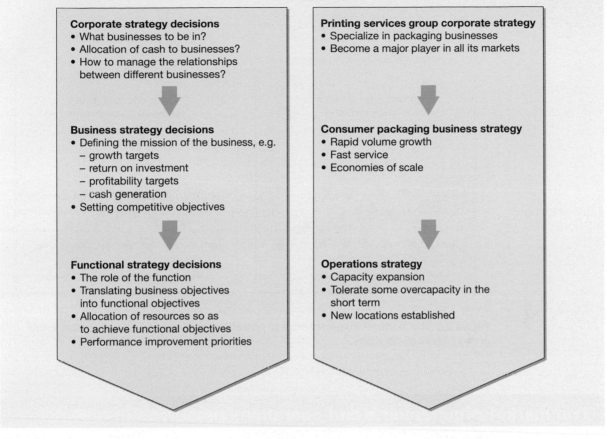

Figure 2.4 The top-down perspective of operations strategy and its application to the printing services group

Suppose the printing services company described previously succeeds in its expansion plans. However, in doing so it finds that having surplus capacity and a distributed network of factories allows it to offer an exceptionally fast service to customers. It also finds that some customers are willing to pay considerably higher prices for such a responsive service. Its experiences lead the company to set up a separate division dedicated to providing fast, high-margin printing services to those customers willing to pay. The strategic objectives of this new division are not concerned with high-volume growth but with high profitability.

This idea of strategy being shaped by operational level experience over time is sometimes called the concept of **emergent strategies.**[4] Strategy is gradually shaped over time and based on real-life experience rather than theoretical positioning. Indeed, strategies are often formed in a relatively unstructured and fragmented manner to reflect the fact that the future is at least partially unknown and unpredictable (see Figure 2.5). This view of operations strategy is perhaps more descriptive of how things really happen, but at first glance it seems less useful in providing a guide for specific decision-making. Yet while emergent strategies are less easy to categorize, the principle governing a bottom-up perspective is clear: shape the operation's objectives and action, at least partly, by the knowledge it gains from its day-to-day activities. The key virtues required for shaping strategy from the bottom up are an ability to learn from experience and a philosophy of continual and incremental improvement.

Emergent strategies

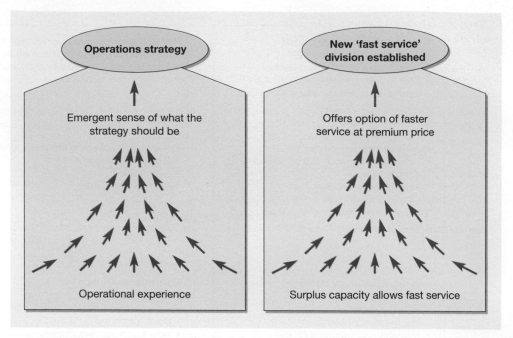

Figure 2.5 The 'bottom-up' perspective of operations strategy and its application to the printing services company

The market requirements and operations resources perspectives

Market-requirements-based strategies

One of the obvious objectives for any organization is to satisfy the requirements of its markets. No operation that continually fails to serve its markets adequately is likely to survive in the long term. Although understanding markets is usually thought of as the domain of the marketing function, it is also of importance to operations management. Without an understanding of what markets require, it is impossible to ensure that operations is achieving the right balance between its performance objectives (quality, speed, dependability, flexibility and cost). For example, the short case Giordano describes a company that designed its operations to fit what it saw as a market that was starting to prioritize quality of service.

Short case
Giordano

With a vision that explicitly states its ambition to be *'the best and the biggest world brand in apparel retailing'*, Giordano is setting its sights high. Yet it is the company that changed the rules of clothes retailing in the fast-growing markets around Hong Kong, China, Malaysia and Singapore, so industry experts take its ambitions seriously. Before Giordano, up-market shops sold high-quality products and gave good service. Cheaper clothes were piled high and sold by sales assistants more concerned with taking the cash than smiling at customers. Jimmy Lai, founder and Chief Executive of Giordano Holdings, changed all that. He saw that unpredictable quality and low levels of service offered an opportunity in the casual clothes market. Why could not value and service, together with low prices, generate better profits? His methods were radical. Overnight he raised the wages of his salespeople by between 30 and 40 per cent, all employees were told they would receive at least 60 hours of training a year and new staff would be allocated a 'big brother' or 'big sister' from among experienced staff to help them develop their service quality skills. Even more startling by the standards of his competitors, Mr Lai brought in a 'no-questions-asked' exchange policy irrespective

of how long ago the garment had been purchased. Staff were trained to talk to customers and seek their opinion on products and the type of service they would like. This information would be immediately fed back to the company's designers for incorporation into their new products. How Giordano achieved the highest sales per square metre of almost any retailer in the region and its founding operations principles are summarized in its 'QKISS' list.

- Quality – do things right.
- Knowledge – update experience and share knowledge.
- Innovation – think 'outside the box'.
- Simplicity – less is more.
- Service – exceed customers' expectations.

The market influence on performance objectives

Operations seek to satisfy customers through developing their five performance objectives. For example, if customers particularly value low-priced products or services, the operation will place emphasis on its cost performance. Alternatively, a customer emphasis on fast delivery will make speed important to the operation, and so on. These factors which define the customers' requirements are called **competitive factors**.[5] Figure 2.6 shows the relationship between some of the more common competitive factors and the operations' performance objectives. This list is not exhaustive; whatever competitive factors are important to customers should influence the priority of each performance objective. Some organizations put considerable effort into bringing an idea of their customers' needs into the operation.

Competitive factors

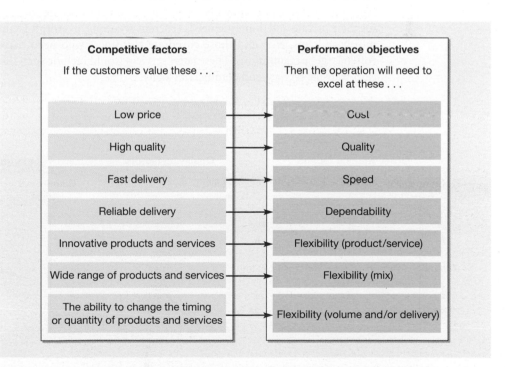

Figure 2.6 Different competitive factors imply different performance objectives

Order-winning and qualifying objectives

Order-winning factors

Qualifying factors

Less important factors

A particularly useful way of determining the relative importance of competitive factors is to distinguish between 'order-winning' and 'qualifying' factors.[6] **Order-winning factors** are those things which directly and significantly contribute to winning business. They are regarded by customers as key reasons for purchasing the service or product. Raising performance in an order-winning factor will either result in more business or improve the chances of gaining more business. **Qualifying factors** may not be the major competitive determinants of success, but are important in another way. They are those aspects of competitiveness where the operation's performance has to be above a particular level just to be considered by the customer. Performance below this 'qualifying' level of performance will possibly disqualify the company from being considered by many customers. However, any further improvement above the qualifying level is unlikely to gain the company much competitive benefit. To order-winning and qualifying factors can be added **less important factors** which are neither order-winning nor qualifying. They do not influence customers in any significant way. They are worth mentioning here only because they may be of importance in other parts of the operation's activities.

Figure 2.7 shows the difference between order-winning, qualifying and less important factors in terms of their utility or worth to the competitiveness of the organization. The curves illustrate the relative amount of competitiveness (or attractiveness to customers) as the operation's performance at the factor varies. Order-winning factors show a steady and significant increase in their contribution to competitiveness as the operation gets better at providing them. Qualifying factors are 'givens'; they are expected by customers and can severely disadvantage the competitive position of the operation if it cannot raise its performance above the qualifying level. Less important objectives have little impact on customers no matter how well the operation performs in them.

Different customer needs imply different objectives

If, as is likely, an operation produces goods or services for more than one customer group, it will need to determine the order-winning, qualifying and less important competitive factors for each group. For example, Table 2.1 shows two types of offerings in the banking industry. Here the distinction is drawn between the customers who are looking for banking services for their private and domestic needs (current accounts, overdraft facilities, savings accounts, mortgage loans, etc.) and those corporate customers who need banking services for their (often large) organizations. These latter services would include such things as letters of credit, cash transfer services and commercial loans.

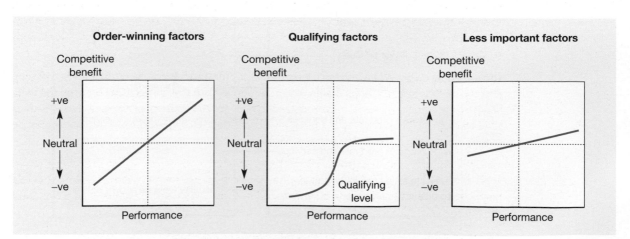

Figure 2.7 Order-winning, qualifying and less important competitive factors

Table 2.1 Different banking services require different performance objectives

	Retail banking	Corporate banking
Products	Personal financial services such as loans and credit cards	Special services for corporate customers
Customers	Individuals	Businesses
Product range	Medium but standardized, little need for special terms	Very wide range, many need to be customized
Design changes	Occasional	Continual
Delivery	Fast decisions	Dependable service
Quality	Means error-free transactions	Means close relationships
Volume per service type	Most services are high-volume	Most services are low-volume
Profit margins	Most are low to medium, some high	Medium to high

Competitive factors		
Order winners	Price Accessibility Speed	Customization Quality of service Reliability
Qualifiers	Quality Range	Speed Price
Less important		Accessibility

Internal performance objectives	Cost Speed Quality	Flexibility Quality Dependability

The service/product life cycle influence on performance objectives

One way of generalizing the behaviour of both customers and competitors is to link it to the life cycle of the services or products that the operation is creating. The exact form of **service/product life cycles** will vary, but generally they are shown as the sales volume passing through four stages – introduction, growth, maturity and decline. The important implication of this for operations management is that services and products will require operations strategies in each stage of their life cycle (see Figure 2.8).

Introduction stage. When a service or product is first introduced, it is likely to be offering something new in terms of its design or performance, with few competitors offering the same service or product. The needs of customers are unlikely to be well understood, so the operations management needs to develop the flexibility to cope with any changes and be able to give the quality to maintain product/service performance.

Growth stage. As volume grows, competitors may enter the growing market. Keeping up with demand could prove to be the main operations preoccupation. Rapid and dependable response to demand will help to keep demand buoyant, while quality levels must ensure that the company keeps its share of the market as competition starts to increase.

Maturity stage. Demand starts to level off. Some early competitors may have left the market and the industry will probably be dominated by a few larger companies. So operations will

Service/product life cycles

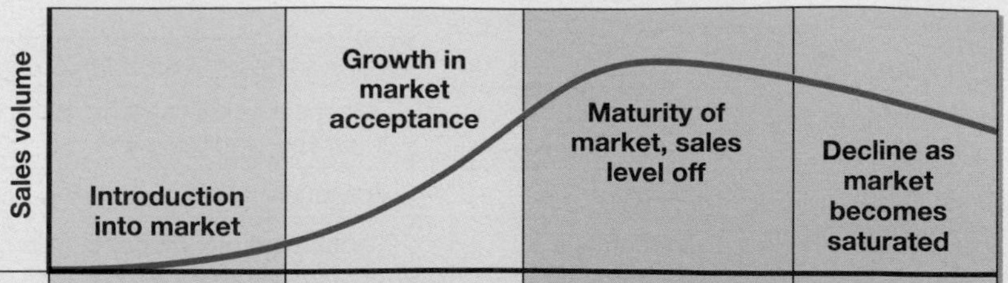

Sales volume	Introduction into market	Growth in market acceptance	Maturity of market, sales level off	Decline as market becomes saturated
Customers	Innovators	Early adopters	Bulk of market	Laggards
Competitors	Few/none	Increasing numbers	Stable number	Declining number
Likely order winners	Product/service specification	Availability	Low price Dependable supply	Low price
Likely qualifiers	Quality Range	Price Range	Range Quality	Dependable supply
Dominant operations performance objectives	Flexibility Quality	Speed Dependability Quality	Cost Dependability	Cost

Figure 2.8 The effects of the life cycle on operations performance objectives

be expected to get the costs down in order to maintain profits or to allow price cutting, or both. This means that cost and productivity issues, together with dependable supply, are likely to be the operation's main concerns.

Decline stage. After time, sales will decline with more competitors dropping out of the market. There might be a residual market, but unless a shortage of capacity develops the market will continue to be dominated by price competition. Operations objectives continue to be dominated by cost.

The operations resources perspective

Resource-based view

The fourth and final perspective we shall take on operations strategy is based on a particularly influential theory of business strategy – the **resource-based view** (RBV) of the firm.[7] Put simply, the RBV holds that firms with an 'above-average' strategic performance are likely to have gained their sustainable competitive advantage because of the core competencies (or capabilities) of their resources. This means that the way an organization inherits, or acquires, or develops its operations resources will, over the long term, have a significant impact on its strategic success. Furthermore, the impact of its 'operations resource' capabilities will be at least as great as, if not greater than, that which it gets from its market position. So understanding and developing the capabilities of operations resources, although often neglected, is a particularly important perspective on operations strategy.

Resource constraints and capabilities

No organization can merely choose which part of the market it wants to be in without considering its ability to produce products and services in a way that will satisfy that market. In other words, the constraints imposed by its operations must be taken into account. For example, a small translation company offers general translation services to a wide range of customers who wish documents such as sales brochures to be translated into another language. A small company, it operates an informal network of part-time translators who enable the company to offer translation into or from most of the major languages in the world. Some of the company's largest customers want to purchase their sales brochures on a 'one-stop shop' basis and have asked the translation company whether it is willing to offer a full service, organizing the design and production, as well as the translation, of export brochures. This is a very profitable market opportunity; however, the company does not have the resources, financial or physical, to take it up. From a market perspective, it is good business; but from an operations resource perspective, it is not feasible.

However, the operations resource perspective is not always so negative. This perspective may identify *constraints* to satisfying some markets but it can also identify *capabilities* which can be exploited in other markets. For example, the same translation company has recently employed two new translators who are particularly skilled at web site development. To exploit this, the company decides to offer a new service whereby customers can transfer documents to the company electronically, which can then be translated quickly. This new service is a 'fast response' service which has been designed specifically to exploit the capabilities within the operations resources. Here the company has chosen to be driven by its resource capabilities rather than the obvious market opportunities.

Intangible resources

An operations resource perspective must start with an understanding of the resource capabilities and constraints within the operation. It must answer the simple questions, what do we have, and what can we do? An obvious starting point here is to examine the transforming and transformed resource inputs to the operation. These, after all, are the 'building

Short case
Amazon, what exactly is your core competence?[8]

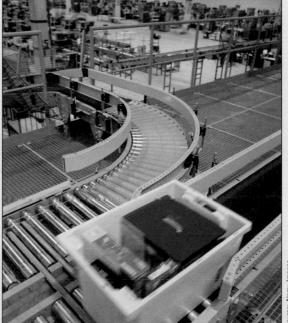

Source: Alamy Images

The founder and boss of Amazon, Jeff Bezos, was at a conference speaking about the company's plans. Although Amazon was generally seen as an Internet book retailer and then a more general Internet retailer, Jeff Bezos was actually pushing three of Amazon's 'utility computing' services. These were: a company that provides cheap access to online computer storage, a company that allows program developers to rent computing capacity on Amazon systems, and a service that connects firms with other firms that perform specialist tasks that are difficult to automate. The problem with online retailing, said Bezos, is its seasonality. At peak times, such as Christmas, Amazon has far more computing capacity than it needs for the rest of the year. At low points it may be using as little as 10 per cent of its total capacity. Hiring out that spare capacity is an obvious way to bring in extra revenue. In addition, Amazon had developed a search engine, a video download business, a service (Fulfilment By Amazon) that allowed other companies to use Amazon's logistics capability including the handling of returned items, and a service that provided access to Amazon's 'back-end' technology.

Amazon's apparent redefinition of its strategy was immediately criticized by some observers. 'Why not', they said, 'stick to what you know, focus on your core competence of Internet retailing?' Bezos's response was clear. 'We *are* sticking to our core competence; this is what we've been doing for the last 11 years. The only thing that's changed is that we are exposing it for [the benefit of] others.' At least for Jeff Bezos, Amazon is not so much an Internet retailer as a provider of Internet-based technology and logistics services.

blocks' of the operation. However, merely listing the type of *resources* an operation has does not give a complete picture of what it can do. Trying to understand an operation by listing its resources alone is like trying to understand an automobile by listing its component parts. To describe it more fully, we need to describe how the component parts form the internal mechanisms of the motor car. Within the operation, the equivalent of these mechanisms is its *processes*. Yet, even for an automobile, a technical explanation of its mechanisms still does not convey everything about its style or 'personality'. Something more is needed to describe these. In the same way, an operation is not just the sum of its processes. In addition,

Intangible resources

the operation has some **intangible resources**. An operation's intangible resources include such things as its relationship with suppliers, the reputation it has with its customers, its knowledge of its process technologies and the way its staff can work together in new product and service development. These intangible resources may not always be obvious within the operation, but they are important and have real value. It is these intangible resources, as well as its tangible resources, that an operation needs to deploy in order to satisfy its markets. The central issue for operations management, therefore, is to ensure that its pattern of strategic decisions really does develop appropriate capabilities within its resources and processes.

Structural and infrastructural decisions

Structure
Infrastructure

A distinction is often drawn between the strategic decisions which determine an operation's **structure** and those which determine its **infrastructure**. An operation's structural decisions are those which we have classed as primarily influencing design activities, while infrastructural decisions are those which influence the workforce organization and the delivery (planning and control) and development (improvement) activities. This distinction in operations strategy has been compared to that between 'hardware' and 'software' in computer systems. The hardware of a computer sets limits to what it can do. In a similar way, investing in advanced technology and building more or better facilities can raise the potential of any type of operation. Within the limits which are imposed by the hardware of a computer, the software governs how effective the computer actually is in practice. The most powerful computer can only work to its full potential if its software is capable of exploiting its potential. The same principle applies with operations. The best and most costly facilities and technology will only be effective if the operation also has an appropriate infrastructure which governs the way it will work on a day-to-day basis. Table 2.2 illustrates both structural and infrastructural decision areas. The table also shows some typical questions which each strategic decision area should be addressing.

Table 2.2 Structural and infrastructural strategic decision areas

Structural strategic decisions	Typical questions which the strategy should help to answer
New service/product design	How should the operation decide which services or products to develop and how to manage the development process?
Supply network design	Should the operation expand by acquiring its suppliers or its customers? If so, what customers and suppliers should it acquire? How should it develop the capabilities of its customers and suppliers? What capacity should each operation in the network have? What number of geographically separate sites should the operation have and where should they be located? What activities and capacity should be allocated to each plant?
Process technology	What types of process technology should the operation be using? Should it be at the leading edge of technology or wait until the technology is established?

Table 2.2 *continued*

Infrastructural strategic decisions	Typical questions which the strategy should help to answer
Job design and organization	What role should the people who staff the operation play in its management? How should responsibility for the activities of the operations function be allocated between different groups in the operation? What skills should be developed in the staff of the operation?
Planning and control	How should the operation forecast and monitor the demand for its offerings? How should the operation adjust its activity levels in response to demand fluctuations? What systems should the operation use to plan and control its activities? How should the operation decide the resources to be allocated to its various activities?
Inventory	How should the operation decide how much inventory to have and where it is to be located? How should the operation control the size and composition of its inventories?
Supplier development	How should the operation choose its suppliers? How should it develop its relationship with its suppliers? How should it monitor its suppliers' performance?
Improvement	How should the operation's performance be measured? How should the operation decide whether its performance is satisfactory? How should the operation ensure that its performance is reflected in its improvement priorities? Who should be involved in the improvement process? How fast should the operation expect improvement in performance to be? How should the improvement process be managed?
Failure prevention, risk and recovery	How should the operation maintain its resources so as to prevent failure? How should the operation plan to cope with a failure if one occurs?

The process of operations strategy

The process of strategy formulation is concerned with 'how' operations strategies are put together. It is important because, although strategies will vary from organization to organization, they are usually trying to achieve some kind of alignment, or 'fit', between what the market wants, and what the operation can deliver, and how that 'alignment' can be sustained over time. So the process of operations strategy should both satisfy market requirements through appropriate operations resources, *and also* develop those resources in the long term so that they can provide competitive capabilities in the longer term that are sufficiently powerful to achieve sustainable competitive advantage.

There are many 'formulation processes' which are, or can be, used to formulate operations strategies. Most consultancy companies have developed their own frameworks, as have several academics. Typically, these formulation processes include the following elements:

- A process which formally links the total organization strategic objectives (usually a business strategy) to resource-level objectives.
- The use of competitive factors (called various things such as order winners, critical success factors, etc.) as the translation device between business strategy and operations strategy.
- A step which involves judging the relative importance of the various competitive factors in terms of customers' preferences.
- A step which includes assessing current achieved performance, usually as compared against competitor performance levels.
- An emphasis on operations strategy formulation as an iterative process.

- The concept of an 'ideal' or 'greenfield' operation against which to compare current operations. Very often the question asked is: 'If you were starting from scratch on a green-field site, how, ideally, would you design your operation to meet the needs of the market?' This can then be used to identify the differences between current operations and this ideal state.
- A 'gap-based' approach. This is a well-tried approach in all strategy formulation which involves comparing what is required of the operation by the marketplace against the levels of performance the operation is currently achieving.

What should the formulation process be trying to achieve?

So what should any operations strategy be trying to achieve? Clearly, it should provide a set of actions that, with hindsight, have provided the 'best' outcome for the organization. However, that really does not help us. What do we mean by 'the best', and what good is a judgement that can only be applied in hindsight? Yet, even if we cannot assess the 'goodness' of a strategy for certain in advance, we can check it out for some attributes that could stop it being a success. Firstly, is the operations strategy comprehensive? Secondly, is there internal coherence between the various actions it is proposing? Thirdly, do the actions being proposed as part of the operations strategy correspond to the appropriate priority for each performance objective? Fourthly, does the strategy prioritize the most critical activities or decisions?

Comprehensive

The notion of 'comprehensiveness' is a critical first step in seeking to achieve an effective operations strategy. Business history is littered with world-class companies that simply failed to notice the potential impact of, for instance, new process technology or emerging changes in their supply network. Also, many strategies have failed because operations have paid undue attention to only one key decision area.

Coherence

As a comprehensive strategy evolves over time, different tensions will emerge that threaten to pull the overall strategy in different directions. This can result in a loss of coherence. Coherence is when the choices made in each decision area do not pull the operation in different directions. For example, if new flexible technology is introduced which allows services or products to be customized to individual clients' needs, it would be 'incoherent' to devise an organizational structure which did not enable the relevant staff to exploit the technology because it would limit the effective flexibility of the operation. For the investment in flexible technology to be effective, it must be accompanied by an organizational structure which deploys the organization's skills appropriately, a performance measurement system which acknowledges that flexibility must be promoted, a new development policy which stresses appropriate types of customization, a supply network strategy which develops suppliers and customers to understand the needs of high-variety customization, a capacity strategy which deploys capacity where the customization is needed, and so on. In other words, all the decision areas complement and reinforce each other in the promotion of that particular performance objective.

Correspondence

Equally, an operation has to achieve a correspondence between the choices made against each of the decision areas and the relative priority attached to each of the performance objectives. In other words, the strategies pursued in each decision area should reflect the true priority of each performance objective. So, for example, if cost reduction is the main organizational objective for an operation, then its process technology investment decisions might err towards the purchase of 'off-the-shelf' equipment from a third-party supplier. This would reduce the capital cost of the technology and may also imply lower maintenance and running costs. Remember, however, that making such a decision will also have an impact on other performance objectives. An off-the-shelf piece of equipment may not, for example, have the flexibility that more 'made-to-order' equipment has. Also, the other decision areas must correspond with the same prioritization of objectives. If low cost is really important then one would expect to see capacity strategies which exploit natural economies of scale, supply network strategies which reduce purchasing costs, performance measurement systems which stress efficiency and productivity, continuous improvement strategies which emphasize continual cost reduction, and so on.

Criticality

In addition to the difficulties of ensuring coherence between decision areas, there is also a need to include financial and competitive priorities. Although all decisions are important and a comprehensive perspective should be maintained, in practical terms some resource or requirement intersections will be more critical than others. The judgement over exactly which intersections are particularly critical is very much a pragmatic one which must be based on the particular circumstances of an individual firm's operations strategy. It is therefore difficult to generalize as to the likelihood of any particular intersections being critical. However, in practice, one can ask revealing questions such as, 'If flexibility is important, of all the decisions we make in terms of our capacity, supply networks, process technology, or development and organization, which will have the most impact on flexibility?' This can be done for all performance objectives, with more emphasis being placed on those having the highest priority.

Short case
Sometimes any plan is better than no plan[9]

There is a famous story that illustrates the importance of having some kind of plan, even if hindsight proves it to be the wrong plan. During manoeuvres in the Alps, a detachment of Hungarian soldiers got lost. The weather was severe and the snow was deep. In these freezing conditions, after two days of wandering, the soldiers gave up hope and became reconciled to a frozen death on the mountains. Then, to their delight, one of the soldiers discovered a map in his pocket. Much cheered by this discovery, the soldiers were able to escape from the mountains. When they were safe back at their headquarters, they discovered that the map was not of the Alps at all, but of the Pyrenees. The moral of the story? A plan (or a map) may not be perfect but it gives a sense of purpose and a sense of direction. If the soldiers had waited for the right map they would have frozen to death. Yet their renewed confidence motivated them to get up and create opportunities.

Summary answers to key questions

Check and improve your understanding of this chapter using self-assessment questions and a personalized study plan, audio and video downloads, and an eBook – all at **www.myomlab.com**.

➤ What is strategy and what is operations strategy?

- Strategy is the total pattern of decisions and actions that position the organization in its environment and that are intended to achieve its long-term goals.

- Operations strategy concerns the pattern of strategic decisions and actions which set the role, objectives and activities of the operation.

- The contribution of operations to overall business strategy can range from stage 1 (holding the business back) to stage 4 (driving business strategy).

> ➤ **What is the difference between a 'top-down' and a 'bottom-up' view of operations strategy?**

- The 'top-down' perspective views strategic decisions at a number of levels. Corporate strategy sets the objectives for the different businesses which make up a group of businesses. Business strategy sets the objectives for each individual business and how it positions itself in its marketplace. Functional strategies set the objectives for each function's contribution to its business strategy.

- The 'bottom-up' view of operations strategy sees overall strategy as emerging from day-to-day operational experience.

> ➤ **What is the difference between a 'market requirements' and an 'operations resources' view of operations strategy?**

- A 'market requirements' perspective of operations strategy sees the main role of operations as satisfying markets. Operations performance objectives and operations decisions should be primarily influenced by a combination of customers' needs and competitors' actions. Both of these may be summarized in terms of the product/service life cycle.

- The 'operations resources' perspective of operations strategy is based on the resource-based view (RBV) of the firm and sees the operation's core competencies (or capabilities) as being the main influence on operations strategy. Operations capabilities are developed partly through the strategic decisions taken by the operation. Strategic decision areas in operations are usually divided into structural and infrastructural decisions. Structural decisions are those which define an operation's shape and form. Infrastructural decisions are those which influence the systems and procedures that determine how the operation will work in practice.

> ➤ **How can an operations strategy be put together?**

- There are many different procedures which are used by companies, consultancies and academics to formulate operations strategies. Although differing in the stages that they recommend, many of these models have similarities.

- Any operations strategy process should result in strategies that are comprehensive and coherent, provide correspondence, and prioritize the most critical activities or decisions.

Learning exercises

These problems and applications will help to improve your analysis of operations. You can find more practice problems as well as worked examples and guided solutions on MyOMLab at www.myomlab.com.

1 Explain how the four perspectives of operations strategy would apply to Ryanair and Flextronics.

2 Compare the operations strategies of Ryanair and a full-service airline such as British Airways or KLM.

3 What do you think are the qualifying or order-winning factors for IKEA described in Chapter 1?

4 Search the Internet site of Intel, the best-known microchip manufacturer, and identify what appear to be its main structural and infrastructural decisions in its operations strategy.

5 **(Advanced)** McDonald's has come to epitomize the 'fast-food' industry. Originally, McDonald's competed on low price, fast service and a totally standardized service offering. They also offered a very narrow range of items on their menu. Visit a McDonald's restaurant and deduce what you believe to be its most important performance objectives. Then try and identify two other chains which appear to compete in a slightly different way. How do these differences in the relative importance of competitive objectives influence the structural and infrastructural decisions of each chain's operations strategy?

Want to know more?

Boyer, K.K., Swink, M. and Rosenzweig, E.D. (2006) Operations strategy research in the POMS Journal, *Production and Operations Management*, vol. 14, issue 4. A survey of recent research in the area.

Hayes, R.H., Pisano, G.P., Upton, D.M. and Wheelwright, S.C. (2005) *Operations, Strategy, and Technology: Pursuing the Competitive Edge*, Wiley, Hoboken, NJ. The gospel according to the Harvard school of operations strategy. Articulate, interesting and informative.

Slack, N. and Lewis, M. (2011) *Operations Strategy*, 3rd edn, Financial Times Prentice Hall, Harlow. What can we say – just brilliant!

Useful websites

www.cranfield.ac.uk/som Look for the 'Best factory awards' link. Manufacturing, but interesting.

www.opsman.org Lots of useful stuff.

www.worldbank.org Global issues. Useful for international operations strategy research.

www.weforum.org Global issues, including some operations strategy ones.

www.ft.com Great for industry and company examples.

Now that you have finished reading this chapter, why not visit MyOMLab at www.myomlab.com where you'll find more learning resources to help you make the most of your studies and get a better grade.

Chapter 3 | Social, environmental and economic performance

Key questions

➤ Why is operations performance important in any organization?

➤ How should the operations function judge itself?

➤ What does top management expect from the operations function?

➤ What are the performance objectives of operations and what are the internal and external benefits which derive from excelling in each of them?

➤ How do operations performance objectives trade off against each other?

Introduction

Operations are judged by the way they perform. There are many individuals and groups doing the judging and there are many different aspects of performance on which the assessment is being made. Here, we take what is called a 'triple bottom line' approach to understand an operation's total performance. If we want to understand the strategic contribution of the operations function, it is important to understand how we can measure its performance. This chapter examines social, environmental, and economic performance before focusing on how operations can impact on the success of the whole organization. Finally, we examine how performance objectives trade off against each other. Figure 3.1 shows where this chapter fits into the overall operations model.

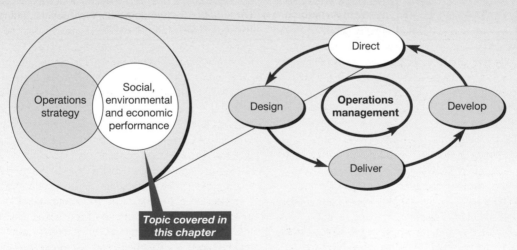

Figure 3.1 This chapter examines social, environmental and economic performance

Check and improve your understanding of this chapter using self-assessment questions and a personalized study plan, audio and video downloads, and an eBook – all at www.myomlab.com.

Operations in practice   A tale of two terminals[1]

On 15 April 2008 British Airways (BA) announced that two of its most senior executives, its director of operations and its director of customer services, would leave the company. They were paying the price for the disastrous opening of British Airways' new Terminal 5 at London's Heathrow airport. The opening of the £4.3bn terminal, said BA's boss, Willie Walsh, with magnificent understatement, 'was not the company's finest hour'. The chaos at the terminal on its opening days made news around the world and was seen by many as one of the most public failures of basic operations management in the modern history of aviation. 'It's a terrible, terrible PR nightmare to have hanging over you', said David Learmount, an aviation expert. 'Somebody who may have been a faithful customer and still not have their luggage after three weeks is not good for their [BA's] image. The one thing that's worse than having a stack of 15,000 bags is adding 5,000 a day to that heap.' According to a BA spokeswoman it needed an extra 400 volunteer staff and courier companies to wade through the backlog of late baggage. So the new terminal that had opened on 27 March could not even cope with BA's full short-haul service until 8 April (two hundred flights in and out of T5 were cancelled in its first three days). This delayed moving its long-haul operations to the new building from Terminal 4 as scheduled on 30 April, which, in turn, disrupted the operations of other airlines, many of which were scheduled to move into Terminal 4 once BA had moved its long-haul flights from there. Sharing the blame with BA was the British Airports Authority (BAA) which was already suffering criticism from passenger groups, airlines and businesses for allegedly poor performance. BAA's non-executive chairman, Sir Nigel Rudd, said he was 'bitterly disappointed' about the opening of the terminal. 'It was clearly a huge embarrassment to the company, me personally, and the board. Nothing can take away that failure. We had all believed genuinely that it would be a great opening, which clearly it wasn't.'

Yet it all should have been so different. T5 took more than six years and around 60,000 workers to build, and it's an impressive building. It is Europe's largest free-standing structure. It was also keenly anticipated by travellers and BA alike. Willie Walsh has said that the terminal 'will completely change his passengers' experience'. He was right, but not in the way he imagined! So what went wrong? As is often the case with major operations failures, it was not one thing, but several interrelated problems (all of which could have been avoided). Press reports initially blamed glitches with the state-of-the-art baggage handling system that consisted

Source: Alamy Images

of 18 km of conveyor belts and was (theoretically) capable of transporting 12,000 bags per hour. Almost inevitably, the baggage handling system experienced problems which had not been exposed in testing. However, BAA, the airport operator, doubted that the main problem was the baggage system itself. The system had worked until it became clogged with bags that were overwhelming BA's handlers loading them onto the aircraft. Partly this may have been because staff were not sufficiently familiar with the new system and its operating processes, but handling staff had also suffered delays getting to their new (and unfamiliar) work areas, negotiating (new) security checks and finding (again, new) car parking spaces. Also, once staff were 'airside' they had problems logging in. The cumulative effect of these problems meant that the airline was unable to get ground handling staff to the correct locations for loading and unloading bags from the aircraft, so baggage could not be loaded onto aircraft fast enough, so baggage backed up, clogging the baggage handling system, which in turn meant closing baggage check-in and baggage drops, leading eventually to baggage check-in being halted.

However, not every airline underestimates the operational complexity of airport processes. During the same year that Terminal 5 at Heathrow was suffering queues, lost bags and bad publicity, Dubai International Airport's Terminal 3 opened quietly with little publicity and fewer problems. Like T5, it is also huge and designed to impress. Its new shimmering facilities are solely dedicated to Emirates Airline. Largely built underground (20 metres beneath the taxiway area) the multi-level environment reduces passenger walking by using 157 elevators, 97 escalators and 82 moving walkways. Its underground baggage handling system is the deepest and the largest of its kind in the world with 90 km of baggage belts handling around 15,000 items

Source: Rex Features

per hour. Also like T5 it handles about 30 million passengers a year.

A key difference between the two terminals was that Dubai's T3 could observe and learn lessons from the botched opening of Heathrow's Terminal 5. Paul Griffiths, the former head of London's Gatwick Airport, who is now Dubai Airport's chief executive, insisted that his own new terminal should not be publicly shamed in the same way. 'There was a lot of arrogance and hubris around the opening of T5, with all the . . . publicity that BA generated', Mr Griffiths says. 'The first rule of

customer service is under-promise and over-deliver because that way you get their loyalty. BA was telling people that they were getting a glimpse of the future with T5, which created expectation and increased the chances of disappointment. Having watched the development of T5, it was clear that we had to make sure that everyone was on-message. We just had to bang heads together so that people realized what was at stake. We knew the world would be watching and waiting after T5 to see whether T3 was the next big terminal fiasco. We worked very hard to make sure that didn't happen.'

Paul Griffiths was also convinced that Terminal 3 should undergo a phased programme with flights added progressively, rather than a 'big bang' approach where the terminal opened for business on one day. 'We exhaustively tested the terminal systems throughout the summer . . . We continue to make sure we're putting large loads on it, week by week, improving reliability. We put a few flights in bit by bit, in waves rather than a big bang.' Prior to the opening he also said that Dubai Airports would never reveal a single opening date for its new Terminal 3 until all pre-opening test programmes had been completed. 'T3 opened so quietly', said one journalist, 'that passengers would have known that the terminal was new only if they had touched the still-drying paint.'

Operations performance is vital for any organization

Operations management is a 'make or break' activity

It is no exaggeration to view operations management as being able to either '**make or break**' any business. This is not just because the operations function is large and, in most businesses, represents the bulk of its assets and the majority of its people, but because the operations function gives the ability to compete by providing customer responsiveness and by developing the capabilities that will keep it ahead of its competitors in the future. For example, operations management principles and the performance of its operations function proved hugely important in the Heathrow T5 and Dubai T3 launches. It was a basic failure to understand the importance of operations processes that (temporarily) damaged British Airways' reputation. It was Dubai's attention to detail and thorough operational preparation that avoided similar problems.

Operations managers face many new challenges as the economic, social, political and technological environment changes. Many of these decisions and challenges seem largely economic in nature. What will be the impact on our costs of adding a new product or service feature? Can we generate an acceptable return if we invest in new technology? Other decisions have more of a 'social' aspect. How do we make sure that all our suppliers treat their staff fairly? Finally, some have an environmental impact. Are we doing enough to reduce our carbon footprint? Furthermore, the 'economic' decisions also have an environmental aspect to them. Will a new product feature make end-of-life recycling more difficult? Will the new technology increase pollution? Similarly the 'social' decisions must be made in the context of their economic consequences. Sure, we want suppliers to treat staff well, but we also need to make a profit. And this is the great dilemma. How do operations managers try to be, simultaneously, economically viable whilst being socially and environmentally responsible?

The triple bottom line

Triple bottom line

One common term that tries to capture the idea of a broader approach to assessing an organization's performance is the '**triple bottom line**' (TBL, or 3BL), also known as 'people, planet and profit'. Essentially, it is a straightforward idea, simply that organizations should measure themselves not just on the traditional economic profit that they generate for their owners, but also on the impact their operations have on society (broadly, in the sense of communities, and individually, for example in terms of their employees) and the ecological impact on the environment. The influential initiative that has come out of this triple bottom line approach is that of 'sustainability'. A sustainable business is one that creates an acceptable profit for its owners, but minimizes the damage to the environment and enhances the existence of the people with whom it has contact. In other words, it balances economic, environmental and societal interests. This gives the organization its 'license to operate' in society. The assumption underlying the triple bottom line (which is not universally accepted) is that a sustainable business is more likely to remain successful in the long-term than one which focuses on economic goals alone. Only a company that produces a balanced TBL is really accounting for the total cost of running its operations. Figure 3.2 illustrates some of the issues involved in achieving the triple bottom line.

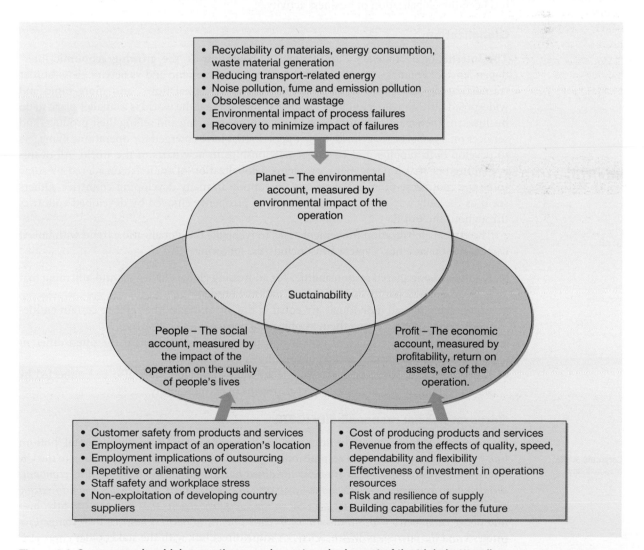

- Recyclability of materials, energy consumption, waste material generation
- Reducing transport-related energy
- Noise pollution, fume and emission pollution
- Obsolescence and wastage
- Environmental impact of process failures
- Recovery to minimize impact of failures

Planet – The environmental account, measured by environmental impact of the operation

Sustainability

People – The social account, measured by the impact of the operation on the quality of people's lives

Profit – The economic account, measured by profitability, return on assets, etc of the operation.

- Customer safety from products and services
- Employment impact of an operation's location
- Employment implications of outsourcing
- Repetitive or alienating work
- Staff safety and workplace stress
- Non-exploitation of developing country suppliers

- Cost of producing products and services
- Revenue from the effects of quality, speed, dependability and flexibility
- Effectiveness of investment in operations resources
- Risk and resilience of supply
- Building capabilities for the future

Figure 3.2 Some ways in which operations can impact each element of the triple bottom line

The social bottom line

The fundamental idea behind the social bottom line is not simply that there is a connection between businesses and the society in which they operate (defined broadly) – that is self-evident. Rather it is that businesses should accept that they bear some responsibility for the impact they have on society and balance the external 'societal' consequences of their actions with the more direct internal consequences, such as profit.

Society is made up of organizations, groups and individuals. Each is more than a simple unit of economic exchange. Organizations have responsibility for the general well-being of society beyond short-term economic self-interest. At the level of the individual, this means devising jobs and work patterns which allow individuals to contribute their talents without undue stress. At a group level, it means recognizing and dealing honestly with employee representatives. This principle also extends beyond the boundaries of the organization. Any business has a responsibility to ensure that it does not knowingly disadvantage individuals in its suppliers or trading partners. Businesses are also a part of the larger community, often integrated into the economic and social fabric of an area. Increasingly, organizations are recognizing their responsibility to local communities by helping to promote their economic and social well-being. Of the many issues that affect society at large, arguably the one that has had the most profound effect on the way business has developed over the last few decades has been the globalization of business activity.

Globalization

The International Monetary Fund defines globalization as 'the growing economic inter-dependence of countries worldwide through increasing volume and variety of cross-border transactions in goods and services, free international capital flows, and more rapid and widespread diffusion of technology'. It reflects the idea that the world is a smaller place to do business in. Even many medium-sized companies are sourcing and selling their products and services on a global basis. Considerable opportunities have emerged for operations managers to develop both supplier and customer relationships in new parts of the world. All of this is exciting but it also poses many problems. **Globalization** of trade is considered by some to be the root cause of exploitation and corruption in many developing countries. Others see it as the only way of spreading the levels of prosperity enjoyed by developed countries throughout the world.

Globalization

The ethical globalization movement seeks to reconcile the globalization trend with how it can impact on societies. Typical aims include the following:

- Acknowledging shared responsibilities for addressing global challenges and affirming that our common humanity doesn't stop at national borders.
- Recognizing that all individuals are equal in dignity and have the right to certain entitlements, rather than viewing them as objects of benevolence or charity.
- Embracing the importance of gender and the need for attention to the often different impacts of economic and social policies on women and men.
- Affirming that a world connected by technology and trade must also be connected by shared values, norms of behaviour and systems of accountability.

Corporate social responsibility (CSR)

Corporate social responsibility

Strongly related to the social 'bottom line' (and to some extent the environmental 'bottom line') is that of **corporate social responsibility** (generally known as CSR). According to the UK government's definition, '*CSR is essentially about how business takes account of its economic, social and environmental impacts in the way it operates – maximizing the benefits and minimizing the downsides. . . . Specifically, we see CSR as the voluntary actions that business can take, over and above compliance with minimum legal requirements, to address both its own competitive interests and the interests of wider society.*' A more direct link with the stakeholder concept is to be found in the definition used by Marks and Spencer, the UK-based retailer. *'Corporate Social Responsibility . . . is listening and responding to the needs of a company's stakeholders. This includes the requirements of sustainable development. We believe that building good relationships with employees, suppliers and wider society is the best guarantee of long-term success. This is the backbone of our approach to CSR.'* The issue of how broader social performance objectives can be included in operations management's activities is of increasing importance, from both an ethical and a commercial point of view.

The environmental bottom line

Environmental sustainability (according to the World Bank) means 'ensuring that the overall productivity of accumulated human and physical capital resulting from development actions more than compensates for the direct or indirect loss or degradation of the environment', or (according to the Brundtland Report from the United Nations) it is 'meeting the needs of the present without compromising the ability of future generations to meet their own needs'. Put more directly, it is generally taken to mean the extent to which business activity negatively impacts on the natural environment. It is clearly an important issue, not only because of the obvious impact on the immediate environment of hazardous waste, air and even noise pollution, but also because of the less obvious, but potentially far more damaging issues around global warming.

From the perspective of individual organizations, the challenging issues of dealing with sustainability are connected with the scale of the problem and the general perception of 'green' issues. Firstly, the scale issue is that cause and effect in the environmental sustainability area are judged at different levels. The effects of, and arguments for, environmentally sustainable activities are felt at a global level, while those activities themselves are essentially local. It has been argued that it is difficult to use the concept at a corporate or even at the regional level. Secondly, there is a paradox with sustainability-based decisions. It is that the more the public becomes sensitized to the benefits of firms acting in an environmentally sensitive way, the more those firms are tempted to exaggerate their environmental credentials, the so-called 'greenwashing' effect.

Environmental protection   Operations managers cannot avoid responsibility for **environmental protection** generally, or their organization's environmental performance more specifically. It is often operational failures which are at the root of pollution disasters and operations decisions (such as product design) which impact on longer-term environmental issues. The pollution-causing disasters which make the headlines seem to be the result of a whole variety of causes – oil tankers run aground, nuclear waste is misclassified, chemicals leak into a river, or gas clouds drift over industrial towns. But in fact they all have something in common. They were all the result of an operational failure. Somehow operations procedures were inadequate. Less dramatic in the short term, but perhaps more important in the long term, is the environmental impact of products which cannot be recycled and processes which consume large amounts of energy – again, both issues which are part of the operations management's broader responsibilities.

Again, it is important to understand that broad issues such as environmental responsibility are intimately connected with the day-to-day decisions of operations managers. Many of these are concerned with waste. Operations management decisions in product and service design significantly affect the utilization of materials both in the short term and in long-term recyclability. Process design influences the proportion of energy and labour that is wasted as well as materials wastage. Planning and control may affect material wastage (packaging being wasted by mistakes in purchasing, for example), but also affects energy and labour wastage. Improvement, of course, is dedicated largely to reducing wastage. Here environmental responsibility and the conventional concerns of operations management coincide. Reducing waste, in all it forms, may be environmentally sound but it also saves cost for the organization. At other times, decisions can be more difficult. Process technologies may be efficient from the operations point of view but may cause pollution, the economic and social consequences of which are borne by society at large. Such conflicts are usually resolved through regulation and legislation. Not that such mechanisms are always effective – there is evidence that just-in-time principles applied in Japan may have produced significant economic gains for the companies which adopted them, but at the price of an overcrowded and polluted road system.

The economic bottom line

An organization's top management represent the interests of the owners (or trustees, or electorate, etc.) and therefore are the direct custodians of the organization's basic purpose. They also have responsibility for translating the broad objectives of the organization into a more tangible form. Broadly they should expect all their operations managers to contribute to the economic success of the organization by **using its resources effectively**. To do this it must be creative, innovative and energetic in improving its processes, products and services. In more detail, effective operations management can give five types of advantage to the business (see Figure 3.3):

Operations can have a significant impact on economic success

- It can reduce the **costs** of producing services and products.
- It can achieve customer satisfaction through good quality and service (and therefore **revenue** in a for-profit organization).
- It can reduce the **risk** of operational failure, because well designed and well-run operations should be less likely to fail, and if they do they should be able to recover faster and with less disruption (this is called *resilience*).
- It can reduce the amount of **investment** (sometimes called *capital employed*) that is necessary to produce the required type and quantity of products and services by increasing the effective capacity of the operation and by being innovative in how it uses its physical resources.
- It can provide the basis for *future* **innovation** by learning from its experience of operating its processes, so building a solid base of operations skills, knowledge and capability within the business.

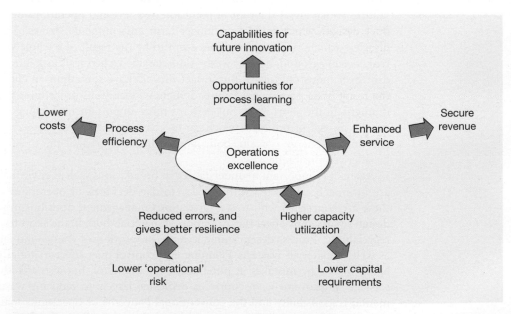

Figure 3.3 Operations can contribute to competitiveness through low costs, high levels of service (securing revenue), lower operational risk, lower capital requirements, and providing the capabilities that determine future innovation

The five operations performance objectives

Five basic 'performance objectives'

Broad stakeholder objectives form the backdrop to operations decision-making, and top management's objectives provide a strategic framework, but running operations at an operational day-to-day level requires a more tightly defined set of objectives. These are the **five basic 'performance objectives'** and they apply to all types of operation. Imagine that you are an operations manager in any kind of business – a hospital administrator, for example, or a production manager at a car plant. What kind of things are you likely to want to do in order to satisfy customers and contribute to competitiveness?

Quality

- You would want to do things right; that is, you would not want to make mistakes, and would want to satisfy your customers by providing error-free services and products which are 'fit for their purpose'. This is giving a **quality** advantage.

Speed

- You would want to do things fast, minimizing the time between a customer asking for services or products and the customer receiving them in full, thus increasing the availability of your services and products and giving a **speed** advantage.

Dependability

- You would want to do things on time, so as to keep the delivery promises you have made. If the operation can do this, it is giving a **dependability** advantage.

Flexibility

- You would want to be able to change what you do; that is, being able to vary or adapt the operation's activities to cope with unexpected circumstances or to give customers individual treatment. Being able to change far enough and fast enough to meet customer requirements gives a **flexibility** advantage.

Cost

- You would want to do things cheaply; that is, create and deliver services and products at a cost which enables them to be priced appropriately for the market while still allowing for a return to the organization; or, in a not-for-profit organization, give good value to the taxpayers or whoever is funding the operation. When the organization is managing to do this, it is giving a **cost** advantage.

The next part of this chapter examines these five performance objectives in more detail by looking at what they mean for four different operations: a general hospital, an automobile factory, a city bus company and a supermarket chain.

The quality objective

Quality is consistent conformance to customers' expectations, in other words, 'doing things right', but the things which the operation needs to do right will vary according to the kind of operation. All operations regard quality as a particularly important objective. In some ways quality is the most visible part of what an operation does. Furthermore, it is something that a customer finds relatively easy to judge about the operation. Is the service or product as it is supposed to be? Is it right or is it wrong? There is something fundamental about quality. Because of this, it is clearly **a major influence on customer satisfaction or dissatisfaction**. A customer perception of high-quality products and services means customer satisfaction and therefore the likelihood that the customer will return. Figure 3.4 illustrates how quality could be judged in four operations.

Quality is a major influence on customer satisfaction or dissatisfaction

Quality inside the operation

When quality means consistently creating and delivering services and products to specification, it not only leads to external customer satisfaction, but makes life easier inside the operation as well.

Quality reduces costs. The fewer mistakes made by each process in the operation, the less time will be needed to correct the mistakes and the less confusion and irritation will be spread. For example, if a supermarket's regional warehouse sends the wrong goods to the supermarket, it will mean staff time, and therefore cost, being used to sort out the problem.

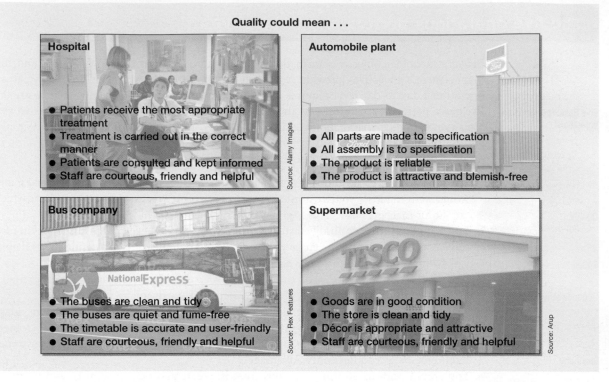

Quality could mean . . .

Hospital
- Patients receive the most appropriate treatment
- Treatment is carried out in the correct manner
- Patients are consulted and kept informed
- Staff are courteous, friendly and helpful

Source: Alamy Images

Automobile plant
- All parts are made to specification
- All assembly is to specification
- The product is reliable
- The product is attractive and blemish-free

Bus company
- The buses are clean and tidy
- The buses are quiet and fume-free
- The timetable is accurate and user-friendly
- Staff are courteous, friendly and helpful

Source: Rex Features

Supermarket
- Goods are in good condition
- The store is clean and tidy
- Décor is appropriate and attractive
- Staff are courteous, friendly and helpful

Source: Arup

Figure 3.4 Quality means different things in different operations

Quality increases dependability. Increased costs are not the only consequence of poor quality. At the supermarket, poor quality could also mean that products run out on the shelves, resulting in lost revenue to the operation. Sorting the problem out could also distract the supermarket management from giving attention to the other parts of the supermarket operation. This in turn could result in further mistakes being made. So, quality (like the other performance objectives, as we shall see) has both an external impact which influences customer satisfaction and an internal impact which leads to stable and efficient processes.

Short case
Organically good quality[2]

'*Organic farming means taking care and getting all the details right. It is about quality from start to finish. Not only the quality of the meat that we produce but also quality of life and quality of care for the countryside.*' Nick Fuge is the farm manager at Lower Hurst Farm located within the Peak District National Park of the UK. He has day-to-day responsibility for the well-being of all the livestock and the operation of the farm on strict organic principles. The 85-hectare farm has been producing high-quality beef for almost 20 years but changed to fully organic production in 1998. Organic farming is a tough regime. No artificial fertilizers, genetically modified feedstuff or growth-promoting agents are used. All beef sold from the farm is home-bred and can be traced back to the animal from which it came.

Source: Alamy Images

'*The quality of the herd is most important*', says Nick, '*as is animal care. Our customers trust us to ensure that the cattle are organically and humanely reared, and slaughtered in a manner that minimizes any distress. If you want to* understand the difference between conventional and organic farming, look at the way we use veterinary help. Most conventional farmers use veterinarians like an emergency service to put things right when there is a problem with an animal. The amount we pay for veterinary assistance is lower because we try to avoid problems with the animals from the start. We use veterinarians as consultants to help us in preventing problems in the first place.'

Catherine Pyne runs the butchery and the mail-order meat business. 'After butchering, the cuts of meat are individually vacuum-packed, weighed and then blast-frozen. We worked extensively with the Department of Food and Nutrition at Oxford Brooks University to devise the best way to encapsulate the nutritional, textural and flavoursome characteristics of the meat in its prime state.

So, when you defrost and cook any of our products you will have the same tasty and succulent eating qualities associated with the best fresh meat.' After freezing, the products are packed in boxes, designed and labelled for storage in a home freezer. Customers order by phone or through the Internet for next-day delivery in a special 'mini-deep-freeze' reusable container which maintains the meat in its frozen state. 'It isn't just the quality of our product which has made us a success', says Catherine. 'We give a personal and inclusive level of service to our customers that makes them feel close to us and maintains trust in how we produce and prepare the meat. The team of people we have here is also an important aspect of our business. We are proud of our product and feel that it is vitally important to be personally identified with it.'

The speed objective

Speed means the elapsed time between customers requesting services or products and receiving them. Figure 3.5 illustrates what speed means for the four operations. The main benefit to the operation's (external) customers of speedy delivery of services or products is that the faster they can have the service or product, the more likely they are to buy it, or the more they will pay for it, or the greater the **benefit they receive** (see the short case 'When speed means life or death').

Speed increases value for some customers

Speed inside the operation

Inside the operation, speed is also important. Fast response to external customers is greatly helped by speedy decision-making and speedy movement of materials and information inside the operation. Speed brings other benefits too.

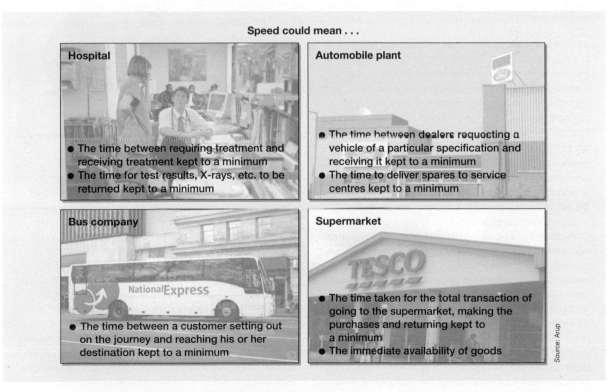

Speed could mean . . .

Hospital
- The time between requiring treatment and receiving treatment kept to a minimum
- The time for test results, X-rays, etc. to be returned kept to a minimum

Automobile plant
- The time between dealers requesting a vehicle of a particular specification and receiving it kept to a minimum
- The time to deliver spares to service centres kept to a minimum

Bus company
- The time between a customer setting out on the journey and reaching his or her destination kept to a minimum

Supermarket
- The time taken for the total transaction of going to the supermarket, making the purchases and returning kept to a minimum
- The immediate availability of goods

Source: Arup

Figure 3.5 Speed means different things in different operations

Speed reduces inventories. Take, for example, the automobile plant. Steel for the vehicle's door panels is delivered to the press shop, pressed into shape, transported to the painting area, coated for colour and protection, and moved to the assembly line where it is fitted to the automobile. This is a simple three-stage process, but in practice material does not flow smoothly from one stage to the next. Firstly, the steel is delivered as part of a far larger batch containing enough steel to make possibly several hundred products. Eventually it is taken to the press area, pressed into shape, and again waits to be transported to the paint area. It then waits to be painted, only to wait once more until it is transported to the assembly line. Yet again, it waits until it is eventually fitted to the automobile. The material's journey time is far longer than the time needed to make and fit the product. It actually spends most of its time waiting as stocks (inventories) of parts and products. The longer items take to move through a process, the more time they will be waiting and the higher inventory will be.

Speed reduces risks. Forecasting tomorrow's events is far less of a risk than forecasting next year's. The further ahead companies forecast, the more likely they are to get it wrong. The faster the throughput time of a process the later forecasting can be left. Consider the automobile plant again. If the total throughput time for the door panel is six weeks, door panels are being processed through their first operation six weeks before they reach their final destination. The quantity of door panels being processed will be determined by the forecasts for demand six weeks ahead. If instead of six weeks, they take only one week to move through the plant, the door panels being processed through their first stage are intended to meet demand only one week ahead. Under these circumstances it is far more likely that the number and type of door panels being processed are the number and type which eventually will be needed.

Short case
When speed means life or death[3]

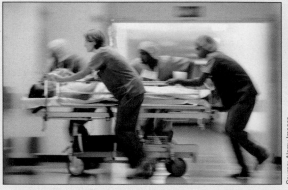

Source: Alamy Images

Of all the operations which have to respond quickly to customer demand, few have more need of speed than the emergency services. In responding to road accidents especially, every second is critical. The treatment you receive during the first hour after your accident (what is called the 'golden hour') can determine whether you survive and fully recover or not. Making full use of the golden hour means speeding up three elements of the total time to treatment – the time it takes for the emergency services to find out about the accident, the time it takes them to travel to the scene of the accident, and the time it takes to get the casualty to appropriate treatment.

Alerting the emergency services immediately is the idea behind Mercedes-Benz's TeleAid system. As soon as the vehicle's airbag is triggered, an on-board computer reports through the mobile phone network to a control centre (drivers can also trigger the system manually if not too badly hurt), satellite tracking allows the vehicle to be precisely located and the owner identified (if special medication is needed). Getting to the accident quickly is the next hurdle. Often the fastest method is by helicopter. When most rescues are only a couple of minutes' flying time back to the hospital speed can really saves lives.

However, it is not always possible to land a helicopter safely at night (because of possible overhead wires and other hazards) so conventional ambulances will always be needed, both to get paramedics quickly to accident victims and to speed them to hospital. One increasingly common method of ensuring that ambulances arrive quickly at the accident site is to position them, not at hospitals, but close to where accidents are likely to occur. Computer analysis of previous accident data helps to select the ambulance's waiting position, and global positioning systems help controllers to mobilize the nearest unit. At all times a key requirement for fast service is effective communication between all who are involved in each stage of the emergency. Modern communications technology can play an important role in this.

The dependability objective

Dependability means doing things in time for customers to receive their services or products exactly when they are needed, or at least when they were promised. Figure 3.6 illustrates what dependability means in the four operations. Customers might only judge the dependability of an operation after the service or product has been delivered. Initially this may not affect the likelihood that customers will select the service – they have already 'consumed' it. **Over time,** however, dependability can override all other criteria. No matter how cheap or fast a bus service is, if the service is always late (or unpredictably early) or the buses are always full, then potential passengers will be better off calling a taxi.

Dependability is judged over time

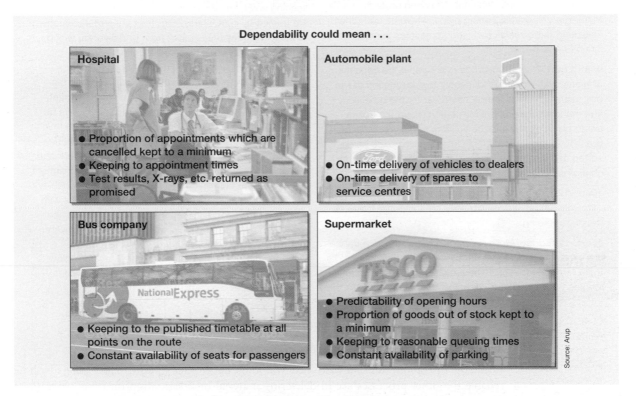

Dependability could mean . . .

Hospital
- Proportion of appointments which are cancelled kept to a minimum
- Keeping to appointment times
- Test results, X-rays, etc. returned as promised

Automobile plant
- On-time delivery of vehicles to dealers
- On-time delivery of spares to service centres

Bus company
- Keeping to the published timetable at all points on the route
- Constant availability of seats for passengers

Supermarket
- Predictability of opening hours
- Proportion of goods out of stock kept to a minimum
- Keeping to reasonable queuing times
- Constant availability of parking

Source: Arup

Figure 3.6 Dependability means different things in different operations

Short case
Dabbawalas hit 99.9999% dependability[4]

Mumbai is India's most densely populated city, and every working day its millions of commuters crowd onto packed trains for an often lengthy commute to their workplaces. Going home for lunch is not possible, so many office workers have a cooked meal sent either from their home, or from a caterer. It is Mumbai's 5,000-strong dabbawala collective that provides this service, usually for a monthly fee. The meal is cooked in the morning (by family or

Source: Getty Images

→

caterer), placed in regulation dabbas or tiffin (lunch) boxes and delivered to each individual worker's office at lunch time. After lunch the boxes are collected and returned so that they can be re-sent the next day. 'Dabbawala' means 'one who carries a box', or more colloquially, 'lunch box delivery man'. This is how the service works:

7am–9am The dabbas (boxes) are collected by dabbawalas on bicycles from nearly 200,000 suburban homes or from the dabba makers and taken to railway stations. The dabbas have distinguishing marks on them, using colours and symbols (necessary because many dabbawalas are barely literate). The dabbawala then takes them to a designated sorting place, where he and other collecting dabbawalas sort (and sometimes bundle) the lunch boxes into groups.

9am–11am The grouped boxes are put in the coaches of trains, with markings to identify the destination of the box (usually there is a designated car for the boxes). The markings include the rail station where the boxes are to be unloaded and the building address where the box has to be delivered. This may involve boxes being sorted at intermediary stations, with each single dabba changing hands up to four times.

10am–12midday Dabbas taken into Mumbai using the otherwise under-utilized capacity on commuter trains in the mid-morning.

11am–12midday Arrive downtown Mumbai where dabbas are handed over to **local dabbawalas**, who distribute them to more locations where there is more sorting and loading on to handcarts, bicycles and dabbawalas.

12midday–1pm Dabbas are delivered to appropriate office locations.

2pm Process moves into reverse, after lunch, when the empty boxes are collected from office locations and returned to suburban stations.

6pm Empty dabbas sent back to the respective houses.

The service has a remarkable record of almost flawlessly reliable delivery, even on the days of severe weather such as Mumbai's characteristic monsoons. Dabbawalas all receive the same pay and at both the receiving and the sending ends, are known to the customers personally, so are trusted by customers. Also, they are well accustomed to the local areas they collect from or deliver to, which reduces the chances of errors. Raghunath Medge, the president of the Bombay Tiffin Box Supply Charity Trust, which oversees the dabbawallas, highlights the importance of their hands-on operations management. *'Proper time management is our key to success. We do everything to keep the customer happy and they help in our marketing.'* There is no system of documentation. The success of the operation depends on teamwork and human ingenuity. Such is the dedication and commitment of the barefoot delivery men (there are only a few delivery women) that the complex logistics operation works with only three layers of management. Although the service remains essentially low-tech, with the barefoot delivery men as the prime movers, the dabbawalas now use some modern technology, for example they now allow booking for delivery through SMS and their web site, (www.mydabbawala.com).

Dependability inside the operation

Inside the operation, internal customers will judge each other's performance partly by how reliable the other processes are in delivering material or information on time. Operations where internal dependability is high are more effective than those which are not, for a number of reasons.

Dependability saves time. Take, for example, the maintenance and repair centre for the city bus company. If the centre runs out of some crucial spare parts, the manager of the centre will need to spend time trying to arrange a special delivery of the required parts and the resources allocated to service the buses will not be used as productively as they would have been without this disruption. More seriously, the fleet will be short of buses until they can be repaired and the fleet operations manager will have to spend time rescheduling services. So, entirely due to the one failure of dependability of supply, a significant part of the operation's time has been wasted coping with the disruption.

Dependability saves money. Ineffective use of time will translate into extra cost. The spare parts might cost more to be delivered at short notice and maintenance staff will expect to be paid even when there is not a bus to work on. Nor will the fixed costs of the operation, such as heating and rent, be reduced because the two buses are not being serviced. The rescheduling of buses will probably mean that some routes have inappropriately sized buses and some services could have to be cancelled. This will result in empty bus seats (if too large a bus has to be used) or a loss of revenue (if potential passengers are not transported).

Dependability gives stability. The disruption caused to operations by a lack of dependability goes beyond time and cost. It affects the 'quality' of the operation's time. If everything in an operation is always perfectly dependable, a level of trust will have built up between the different parts of the operation. There will be no 'surprises' and everything will be predictable. Under such circumstances, each part of the operation can concentrate on improving its own area of responsibility without having its attention continually diverted by a lack of dependable service from the other parts.

The flexibility objective

Flexibility means being able to change in some way

Flexibility means being able to **change** the operation in some way. This may mean changing what the operation does, how it is doing it, or when it is doing it. Specifically, customers will need the operation to change so that it can provide four types of requirement:

Service/product flexibility

- **Service/product flexibility** – the operation's ability to introduce new or modified services and products;

Mix flexibility

- **mix flexibility** – the operation's ability to create a wide range or mix of services and products;

Volume flexibility

- **volume flexibility** – the operation's ability to change its level of output or activity to produce different quantities or volumes of services and products over time;

Delivery flexibility

- **delivery flexibility** – the operation's ability to change the timing of the delivery of its services or products.

Figure 3.7 gives examples of what these different types of flexibility mean to the four different operations.

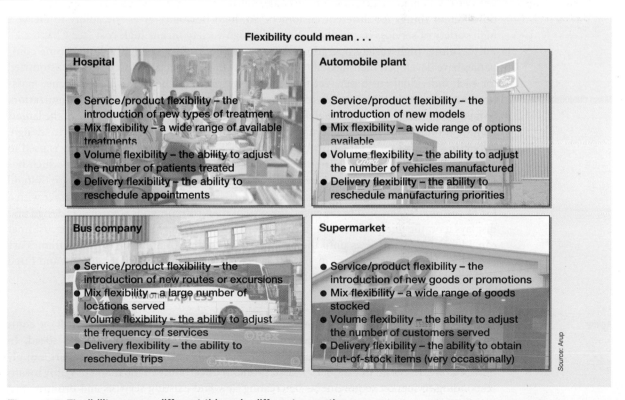

Flexibility could mean . . .

Hospital
- Service/product flexibility – the introduction of new types of treatment
- Mix flexibility – a wide range of available treatments
- Volume flexibility – the ability to adjust the number of patients treated
- Delivery flexibility – the ability to reschedule appointments

Automobile plant
- Service/product flexibility – the introduction of new models
- Mix flexibility – a wide range of options available
- Volume flexibility – the ability to adjust the number of vehicles manufactured
- Delivery flexibility – the ability to reschedule manufacturing priorities

Bus company
- Service/product flexibility – the introduction of new routes or excursions
- Mix flexibility – a large number of locations served
- Volume flexibility – the ability to adjust the frequency of services
- Delivery flexibility – the ability to reschedule trips

Supermarket
- Service/product flexibility – the introduction of new goods or promotions
- Mix flexibility – a wide range of goods stocked
- Volume flexibility – the ability to adjust the number of customers served
- Delivery flexibility – the ability to obtain out-of-stock items (very occasionally)

Source: Arup

Figure 3.7 Flexibility means different things in different operations

Short case
Flexibility and dependability in the newsroom[5]

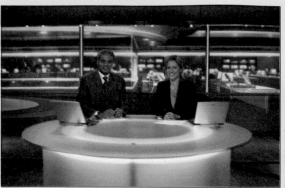

Source: BBC/Jeff Overs

Television news is big business. Satellite and cable, as well as developments in terrestrial transmission, have all helped to boost the popularity of 24-hour news services. However, news perishes fast. A daily newspaper delivered one day late is practically worthless. This is why broadcasting organizations like the BBC have to ensure that up-to-date news is delivered on time, every time. The BBC's ability to achieve high levels of dependability is made possible by the technology employed in news gathering and editing. At one time news editors would have to schedule a video-taped report to start its countdown five seconds prior to its broadcasting time. With new technology the video can be started from a freeze-frame and will broadcast the instant the command to play is given. The team have faith in the dependability of the process. In addition, technology allows them the flexibility to achieve dependability, even when news stories break just before transmission. In the hours before scheduled transmission, journalists and editors prepare an 'inventory' of news items stored electronically. The presenter will prepare his or her commentary on the autocue and each item will be timed to the second. If the team needs to make a short-term adjustment to the planned schedule, the news studio's technology allows the editors to take broadcasts live from journalists at their locations, on satellite 'takes', directly into the programme. Editors can even type news reports directly onto the autocue for the presenter to read as they are typed – nerve-racking, but it keeps the programme on time.

Mass customization

Mass customization

One of the beneficial external effects of flexibility is the increased ability of operations to do different things for different customers. So, high flexibility gives the ability to create a high variety of services or products. Normally high variety means high cost (see Chapter 1). Furthermore, high-variety operations do not usually produce in high volume. Some companies have developed their flexibility in such a way that products and services are customized for each individual customer. Yet they manage to produce them in a high-volume, mass-production manner which keeps costs down. This approach is called **mass customization**. Sometimes this is achieved through flexibility in design. For example, Dell is one of the largest volume producers of personal computers in the world, yet allows each customer to 'design' (albeit in a limited sense) their own configuration. Sometimes flexible technology is used to achieve the same effect. For example, Paris Miki, an up-market eyewear retailer which has the largest number of eyewear stores in the world, uses its own 'Mikissimes Design System' to capture a digital image of the customer and analyse facial characteristics. Together with a list of customers' personal preferences, the system then recommends a particular design and displays it on the image of the customer's face. In consultation with the optician the customer can adjust shapes and sizes until the final design is chosen. Within the store the frames are assembled from a range of pre-manufactured components and the lenses ground and fitted to the frames. The whole process takes around an hour.

Agility

Agility

Judging operations in terms of their **agility** has become popular. Agility is really a combination of all the five performance objectives, but particularly flexibility and speed. In addition, agility implies that an operation and the supply chain of which it is a part (supply networks are described in Chapter 7) can respond to uncertainty in the market. Agility means responding to market requirements by creating new and existing services and products fast and flexibly.

Flexibility inside the operation

Developing a flexible operation can also have advantages to the internal customers within the operation.

Flexibility speeds up response. Fast service often depends on the operation being flexible. For example, if the hospital has to cope with a sudden influx of patients from a road accident, it clearly needs to deal with injuries quickly. Under such circumstances a flexible hospital which can speedily transfer extra skilled staff and equipment to the Accident and Emergency department will provide the fast service which the patients need.

Flexibility saves time. In many parts of the hospital, staff have to treat a wide variety of complaints. Fractures, cuts or drug overdoses do not come in batches. Each patient is an individual with individual needs. The hospital staff cannot take time to 'get into the routine' of treating a particular complaint; they must have the flexibility to adapt quickly. They must also have sufficiently flexible facilities and equipment so that time is not wasted waiting for equipment to be brought to the patient. The time of the hospital's resources is being saved because they are flexible in 'changing over' from one task to the next.

Flexibility maintains dependability. Internal flexibility can also help to keep the operation on schedule when unexpected events disrupt the operation's plans. For example, if the sudden influx of patients to the hospital requires emergency surgical procedures, routine operations will be disrupted. This is likely to cause distress and considerable inconvenience. A flexible hospital might be able to minimize the disruption by possibly having reserved operating theatres for such an emergency, and being able to bring in medical staff quickly that are 'on call'.

The cost objective

To the companies which compete directly on price, cost will clearly be their major operations objective. The lower the cost of creating and delivering their services and products, the lower can be the price to their customers. Even those companies which do not compete on price will be interested in keeping costs low. Every euro or dollar removed from an operation's

Short case
Everyday low prices at Aldi[6]

Source: Alamy Images

Aldi is an international 'limited assortment' supermarket specializing in 'private label', mainly food products. It has carefully focused its service concept and delivery system to attract customers in a highly competitive market. The company believes that its unique approach to operations management make it 'virtually impossible for competitors to match our combination of price and quality'.

Aldi operations challenge the norms of retailing. They are deliberately simple, using basic facilities to keep down overheads. Most stores stock only a limited range of goods (typically around 700 compared with 25,000 to 30,000 stocked by conventional supermarket chains). The private label approach means that the products have been produced according to Aldi quality specifications and are only sold in Aldi stores. Without the high costs of brand marketing and advertising and with Aldi's formidable purchasing power, prices can be 30 per cent below their branded equivalents. Other cost-saving practices include open carton displays which eliminate the need for special shelving, no grocery bags to encourage reuse as well as saving costs, and using a 'cart rental' system which requires customers to return the cart to the store to get their coin deposit back.

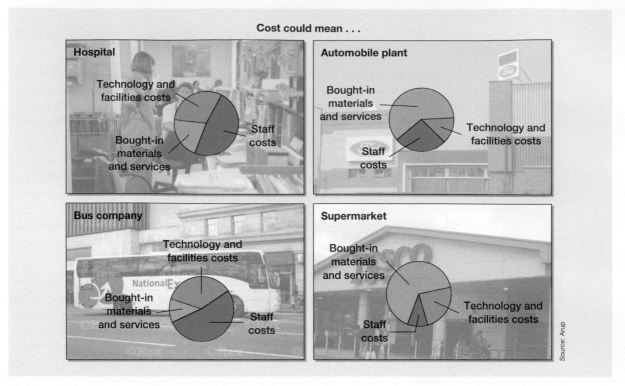

Figure 3.8 Cost means different things in different operations

Source: Arup

Low cost is a universally attractive objective

cost base is a further euro or dollar added to its profits. Not surprisingly, **low cost is a universally attractive objective**. The short-case 'Everyday low prices at Aldi' describes how one retailer keeps its costs down. The ways in which operations management can influence cost will depend largely on where the operation costs are incurred. The operation will spend its money on staff (the money spent on employing people), facilities, technology and equipment (the money spent on buying, caring for, operating and replacing the operation's 'hardware') and materials (the money spent on the 'bought-in' materials consumed or transformed in the operation). Figure 3.8 shows typical cost breakdowns for the hospital, car plant, supermarket and bus company.

Cost reduction through internal effectiveness

Our previous discussion distinguished between the benefits of each performance objective to externally and internally. Each of the various performance objectives has several internal effects, but **all of them affect cost**. So, one important way to improve cost performance is to improve the performance of the other operations objectives (see Figure 3.9).

All performance objectives affect cost

- High-quality operations do not waste time or effort having to re-do things, nor are their internal customers inconvenienced by flawed service.
- Fast operations reduce the level of in-process inventory between and within processes, as well as reducing administrative overheads.
- Dependable operations do not spring any unwelcome surprises on their internal customers. They can be relied on to deliver exactly as planned. This eliminates wasteful disruption and allows the other micro-operations to operate efficiently.
- Flexible operations adapt to changing circumstances quickly and without disrupting the rest of the operation. Flexible micro-operations can also change over between tasks quickly and without wasting time and capacity.

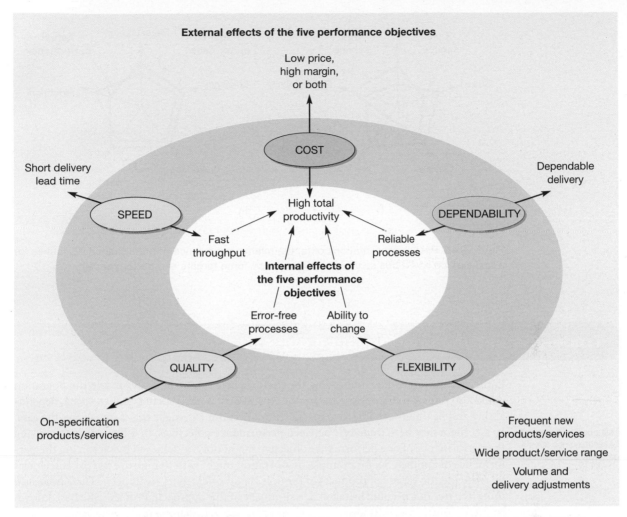

Figure 3.9 Performance objectives have both external and internal effects. Internally, cost is influenced by the other performance objectives

The polar representation of performance objectives

Polar representation

A useful way of representing the relative importance of performance objectives for a product or service is shown in Figure 3.10(a). This is called the **polar representation** because the scales which represent the importance of each performance objective have the same origin. A line describes the relative importance of each performance objective. The closer the line is to the centre, the less important is the performance objective to the operation. Two services are shown, a taxi and a bus service. Each essentially provides the same basic service, but with different objectives. The differences between the two services are clearly shown by the diagram. Of course, the polar diagram can be adapted to accommodate any number of different performance objectives. For example, Figure 3.10(b) shows a proposal for using a polar diagram to assess the relative performance of different police forces in the UK.[7] Note that this proposal uses three measures of quality (reassurance, crime reduction and crime detection), one measure of cost (economic efficiency), and one measure of how the police force develops its relationship with 'internal' customers (the criminal justice agencies). Note also that actual performance as well as required performance is marked on the diagram.

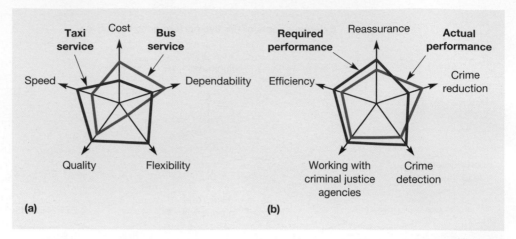

Figure 3.10 Polar representations of (a) the relative importance of performance objectives for a taxi service and a bus service, and (b) a police force targets and performance

Trade-offs between performance objectives

Earlier we examined how improving the performance of one objective inside the operation could also improve other performance objectives. Most notably, better quality, speed, dependability and flexibility can improve cost performance. But externally this is not always the case. In fact there may be a '*trade-off*' between **performance objectives**. In other words improving the performance of one performance objective might only be achieved by sacrificing the performance of another. So, for example, an operation might wish to improve its cost efficiencies by reducing the variety of products or services that it offers to its customers. '*There is no such thing as a free lunch*' could be taken as a summary of this approach. Probably the best-known summary of the trade-off idea comes from Professor Wickham Skinner, who said:

> '*most managers will readily admit that there are compromises or trade-offs to be made in designing an airplane or truck. In the case of an airplane, trade-offs would involve matters such as cruising speed, take-off and landing distances, initial cost, maintenance, fuel consumption, passenger comfort and cargo or passenger capacity. For instance, no one today can design a 500-passenger plane that can land on an aircraft carrier and also break the sound barrier. Much the same thing is true in [operations]*'.[8]

But there are two views of trade-offs. The first emphasizes 'repositioning' performance objectives by trading off improvements in some objectives for a reduction in performance in others. The other emphasizes increasing the 'effectiveness' of the operation by overcoming trade-offs so that improvements in one or more aspects of performance can be achieved without any reduction in the performance of others. Most businesses at some time or other will adopt both approaches. This is best illustrated through the concept of the '**efficient frontier**' of operations performance.

Trade-offs and the efficient frontier

Figure 3.11(a) shows the relative performance of several companies in the same industry in terms of their cost efficiency and the variety of products or services that they offer to their customers. Presumably all the operations would ideally like to be able to offer very high variety while still having very high levels of cost efficiency. However, the increased complexity that a high variety of product or service offerings brings will generally reduce the operation's ability to operate efficiently. Conversely, one way of improving cost efficiency is to severely

There can be a trade-off between an operation's performance objectives

The efficient frontier

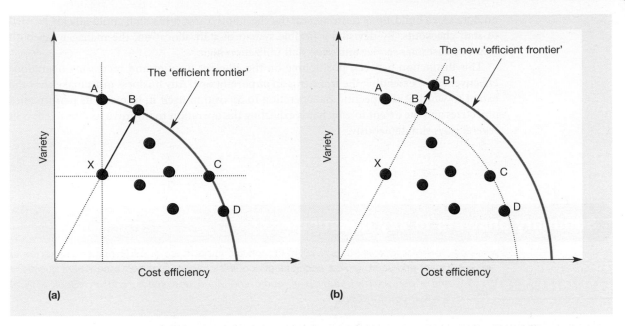

(a) **(b)**

Figure 3.11 The efficient frontier identifies operations with performances that dominate other operations' performance

limit the variety on offer to customers. The spread of results in Figure 3.11(a) is typical of an exercise such as this. Operations A, B, C, D have all chosen a different balance between variety and cost efficiency. However, none is dominated by any other operation in the sense that another operation necessarily has 'superior' performance. Operation X, however, has an inferior performance because operation A is able to offer higher variety at the same level of cost efficiency and operation C offers the same variety but with better cost efficiency. The convex line on which operations A, B, C and D lie is known as the 'efficient frontier'. They may choose to position themselves differently (presumably because of different market strategies) but they cannot be criticized for being ineffective. Of course, any of these operations that lie on the efficient frontier may come to believe that the balance they have chosen between variety and cost efficiency is inappropriate. In these circumstances they may choose to reposition themselves at some other point along the efficient frontier. By contrast, operation X has also chosen to balance variety and cost efficiency in a particular way but is not doing so effectively. Operation B has the same ratio between the two performance objectives but is achieving them more effectively.

However, a strategy that emphasizes increasing effectiveness is not confined to those operations that are dominated, such as operation X. Those with a position on the efficient frontier will generally also want to improve their operations effectiveness by overcoming the trade-off that is implicit in the efficient frontier curve. For example, suppose operation B in Figure 3.11(b) wants to improve both its variety and its cost efficiency simultaneously and move to position B1. It may be able to do this, but only if it adopts operations improvements that extend the efficient frontier. For example, one of the decisions that any supermarket manager has to make is how many checkout positions to open at any time. If too many checkouts are opened then there will be times when the checkout staff do not have any customers to serve and will be idle. The customers, however, will have excellent service in terms of little or no waiting time. Conversely, if too few checkouts are opened, the staff will be working all the time but customers will have to wait in long queues. There seems to be a direct trade-off between staff utilization (and therefore cost) and customer waiting time (speed of service). Yet even the supermarket manager might, for example, allocate a number of 'core' staff to operate the checkouts but also arrange for those other staff who are performing other jobs in the supermarket to be trained and 'on call' should demand suddenly increase. If the manager on duty sees a build-up of customers at the checkouts, these other staff could quickly be used to staff checkouts. By devising a flexible system of staff allocation, the manager can both improve customer service and keep staff utilization high.

This distinction between positioning on the efficient frontier and increasing operations effectiveness by extending the frontier is an important one. Any business must make clear the extent to which it is expecting the operation to reposition itself in terms of its performance objectives and the extent to which it is expecting the operation to improve its effectiveness in several ways simultaneously.

Summary answers to key questions

Check and improve your understanding of this chapter using self-assessment questions and a personalized study plan, audio and video downloads, and an eBook – all at **www.myomlab.com**.

➤ Why is operations performance important in any organization?

■ Operations management can either 'make or break' any business. It is large and, in most businesses, represents the bulk of its assets, but also because the operations function gives the ability to compete by providing the ability to respond to customers and by developing the capabilities that will keep it ahead of its competitors in the future.

➤ How should the operations function judge itself?

■ Operations performance can be judged using the 'triple bottom line' approach. This includes social, environmental and economic performance.

➤ What does top management expect from the operations function?

■ Operations can contribute to the organization as a whole by:
  - achieving customer satisfaction
  - reducing the costs
  - reducing the risk of operational failure
  - reducing the amount of investment
  - providing the basis for future innovation.

➤ What are the performance objectives of operations and what are the internal and external benefits which derive from excelling in each of them?

■ By 'doing things right', operations seek to influence the quality of the company's services and products. Externally, quality is an important aspect of customer satisfaction or dissatisfaction. Internally, quality operations both reduce costs and increase dependability.

■ By 'doing things fast', operations seek to influence the speed with which services and products are delivered. Externally, speed is an important aspect of customer service. Internally, speed both reduces inventories by decreasing internal throughput time and reduces risks by delaying the commitment of resources.

- By 'doing things on time', operations seek to influence the dependability of the delivery of services and products. Externally, dependability is an important aspect of customer service. Internally, dependability within operations increases operational reliability, thus saving the time and money that would otherwise be taken up in solving reliability problems and also giving stability to the operation.

- By 'changing what they do', operations seek to influence the flexibility with which the company creates its offerings. Externally, flexibility can:
  - create new offerings (service/product flexibility);
  - create a wide range or mix of offerings (mix flexibility);
  - create different quantities or volumes of offerings (volume flexibility);
  - create offerings at different times (delivery flexibility).

  Internally, flexibility can help speed up response times, save time wasted in changeovers, and maintain dependability.

- By 'doing things cheaply', operations seek to influence the cost of the company's offerings. Externally, low costs allow organizations to reduce their price in order to gain higher volumes or, alternatively, increase their profitability on existing volume levels. Internally, cost performance is helped by good performance in the other performance objectives.

> ➤ How do operations performance objectives trade off against each other?

- Trade-offs are the extent to which improvements in one performance objective can be achieved by sacrificing performance in others. The 'efficient frontier' concept is a useful approach to articulating trade-offs and distinguishes between repositioning performance on the efficient frontier and improving performance by overcoming trade-offs.

Learning exercises

These problems and applications will help to improve your analysis of operations. You can find more practice problems as well as worked examples and guided solutions on MyOMLab at **www.myomlab.com**.

1 The 'forensic science' service of a European country has traditionally been organized to provide separate forensic science laboratories for each police force around the country. In order to save costs, the government has decided to centralize this service in one large central facility close to the country's capital. What do you think are the external advantages and disadvantages of this to the stakeholders of the operation? What do you think are the internal implications to the new centralized operation that will provide this service?

2 *Step 1.* Look again at the figures in the chapter which illustrate the meaning of each performance objective for the four operations. Consider the bus company and the supermarket, and in particular consider their external customers.

Step 2. Draw the relative required performance for both operations on a polar diagram.

Step 3. Consider the internal effects of each performance objective. For both operations, identify how quality, speed, dependability and flexibility can help to reduce the cost of producing their services.

3 Visit the websites of two or three large oil companies such as Exxon, Shell, Elf, etc. Examine how they describe their policies towards their customers, suppliers, shareholders, employees and society at large. Identify areas of the company's operations where there may be conflicts between the needs of these different stakeholder groups. Discuss or reflect on how (if at all) such companies try and reconcile these conflicts.

Want to know more?

Bourne, M., Kennerley, M. and Franco, M. (2005) Managing through measures: a study of the impact on performance, *Journal of Manufacturing Technology Management*, vol. 16, issue 4, 373–95. What it says on the tin.

Kaplan, R.S. and Norton, D.P. (2005) The Balanced Scorecard: measures that drive performance, *Harvard Business Review*, Jul/Aug. The latest pronouncements on the Balanced Scorecard approach.

Pine, B.J. (1993) *Mass Customization*, Harvard Business School Press, Boston. The first substantial work on the idea of mass customization. Still a classic.

Savitz, A.W. and Weber, K. (2006) *The Triple Bottom Line: How Today's Best-Run Companies Are Achieving Economic, Social and Environmental Success – and How You Can Too*, Jossey-Bass, San Francisco, CA. An up-to-date treatment of the triple bottom line.

Waddock, S. (2003) Stakeholder performance implications of corporate responsibility, *International Journal of Business Performance Management*, vol. 5, numbers 2–3, 114–24. An introduction to stakeholder analysis.

Useful websites

www.aomonline.org General strategy site of the American Academy of Management.

www.cranfield.ac.uk/som Look for the 'Best factory awards' link. Manufacturing, but interesting.

www.opsman.org Lots of useful stuff.

www.worldbank.org Global issues. Useful for international operations strategy research.

www.weforum.org Global issues, including some operations strategy ones.

www.ft.com Great for industry and company examples.

Now that you have finished reading this chapter, why not visit MyOMLab at *www.myomlab.com* where you'll find more learning resources to help you make the most of your studies and get a better grade.

Chapter 4

The design of services and products

Key questions

➤ Why is good service and product design important?

➤ What are the stages in service and product design?

➤ Why and how should service and product design be considered interactively with process design?

Introduction

Services and products are often the first thing that customers see of a company, so they should have an impact. Whilst operations managers may not have direct responsibility for service and product design, they always have an indirect responsibility to provide the information and advice upon which successful development depends. However, operations managers are increasingly expected to take a more active part in design. Unless a service, however well conceived, can be implemented and unless a product, however well designed, can be produced to a high standard, the design can never bring its full benefits. Figure 4.1 shows where this chapter fits into the overall operations model.

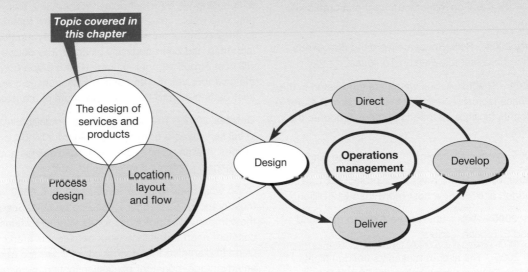

Topic covered in this chapter

Figure 4.1 This chapter examines service and product design

Operations in practice The troubled history of the Airbus A380[1]

It is perhaps inevitable that a major new and complex product like a passenger aircraft will experience a few problems during its development. The history of the Airbus A380 was a long and incident-packed journey from drawing board to reality that illustrates the dangers when the design activity goes wrong. This is the story in brief.

1991 – Airbus consults with international airlines about their requirements for a super-large passenger aircraft.

January 1993 – Airbus rival Boeing says it has begun studies into 'very large' commercial aircraft.

June 1993 – Boeing decides not to go for a super-large passenger aircraft, but instead to focus on designing smaller 'jumbos'. Airbus and its partners set up the A3XX team to start the 'super-jumbo' project.

1996 – Airbus forms its 'Large Aircraft' Division. Because of the size of the aircraft, it is decided to develop specially designed engines rather than adapt existing models.

2000 – The commercial launch of the A3XX (later to be named the A380).

2002 – Work starts on manufacturing the aircraft's key components.

February 2004 – Rolls-Royce delivers the first Airbus engines to the assembly plant in Toulouse.

April 2004 – The first Airbus wings are completed in the North Wales factory. London's Heathrow airport starts to redevelop its facilities so that it can accommodate the new aircraft.

May 2004 – Assembly begins in the Toulouse plant.

December 2004 – EADS reveals the project is €1.45 billion over budget, and will now cost more than €12 billion.

January 2005 – Airbus unveils the A380 to the world's press and European leaders.

27 April 2005 – The aircraft makes its maiden flight, taking off in Toulouse and circling the Bay of Biscay for four hours before returning to Toulouse. A year of flight-testing and certification work begins.

June 2005 – Airbus announces that the plane's delivery schedule will slip by six months.

March 2006 – The plane passes important safety tests involving 850 passengers and 20 crew safely leaving the aircraft in less than 80 seconds with half the exits blocked.

July 2006 – The A380 suffers another production delay. Airbus now predicts a delay of a further six to seven

Source: Rex Features

months. This causes turmoil in the boardrooms of both Airbus and its parent company EADS. The company's directors are accused of suppressing the news for months before revealing it to shareholders. It leads to the resignations of Airbus' chief executive, co-chief executive, and the A380 programme manager.

October 2006 – Airbus infuriates customers by announcing yet a further delay for the A380, this time of a whole year. The first plane is now forecast to enter commercial service around twenty months later than had been originally planned. The delays will cost Airbus another estimated €4.8 billion over the next four years. The company announces a drastic cost-cutting plan to try to recoup some of the losses.

October 2007 – The super-jumbo eventually takes off in full service as a commercial airliner for Singapore Airlines. It wins rave reviews from both airlines and passengers – even if it is two years late!

So what caused the delays? Firstly, the A380 was the most complex passenger jet ever to be built. Secondly, the company was notorious for its internal rivalries, its constant need to balance work between its French and German plants so that neither country had too obvious an advantage, constant political infighting, particularly by the French and German governments, and frequent changes of management. According to one insider, 'the underlying reason for the mess we were in was the hopeless lack of integration [between the French and German sides] within the company'. Eventually it was this lack of integration between design and manufacturing processes that was the main reason for the delays to the aircraft's launch. During the early design stages the firm's French and German factories had used incompatible software to design the 500 km of wiring that each plane needs. Eventually, to resolve the cabling problems, the company had to transfer two thousand German staff from Hamburg to Toulouse. Processes that should have been streamlined had to be replaced by temporary and less efficient ones, described by one French union official as a *'do-it-yourself system'*. Feelings ran high on the shopfloor, with tension and arguments between French and German staff. *'The German staff will first have to succeed at doing the work they should have done in Germany'*, said the same official. Electricians had to resolve the complex wiring problems, with the engineers having to adjust the computer blueprints as they modified them so they could be used on future aircraft. *'Normal installation time is two to three weeks'*, said Sabine Klauke, a team leader. *'This way it is taking us four months.'* Mario Heinen, who ran the cabin and fuselage cross-border division, admitted the pressure to keep up with intense production schedules and the overcrowded conditions made things difficult. *'We have been working on these initial aircraft in a handmade way. It is not a perfectly organized industrial process.'* He claimed, there was no choice. *'We have delivered five high-quality aircraft this way. If we had left the work in Hamburg, to wait for a new wiring design, we would not have delivered one by now.'* The toll taken by these delays was high. The improvised wiring processes were far more expensive than the planned 'streamlined' processes and the delay in launching the aircraft meant two years without the revenue that the company had expected.

However, Airbus was not alone. Its great rival, Boeing, was also having problems. Engineers' strikes, supply chain problems and mistakes by its own design engineers had further delayed its '787 Dreamliner' aircraft. Specifically, fasteners used to attach the titanium floor grid to the composite 'barrel' of the fuselage had been wrongly located, resulting in 8,000 fasteners having to be replaced. By 2011 it looked as if the Boeing aircraft was also going to be two years late.

Why is good design so important?

Good design satisfies customers, communicates the purpose of the service or product to its market, and brings financial rewards to the business. The objective of good design, whether of services or products, is to satisfy customers by meeting their actual or anticipated needs and expectations. This, in turn, enhances the competitiveness of the organization. Service and product design, therefore, can be seen as starting and ending with the customer. Service designers try to put together a service which meets, or even exceeds, customer expectations. Yet at the same time the service must be within the capabilities of the operation and be delivered at reasonable cost. Product designers try to achieve aesthetically pleasing designs which meet or exceed customers' expectations. They also try to design a product which performs well and is reliable during its lifetime. Further, they should design the product so that it can be manufactured easily and quickly. In fact, the business case for putting effort into good service and product design is overwhelming according to the UK Design Council.[2] Using design throughout the business ultimately boosts the bottom line by helping create better products and services that compete on value rather than price. **Design** helps businesses connect strongly with their customers by anticipating their real needs. That in turn gives them the ability to set themselves apart in increasingly tough markets.

Good design enhances profitability

Critical commentary

Remember that not all new services and products are created in response to a clear and articulated customer need. While this is usually the case, especially for offerings that are similar to (but presumably better than) their predecessors, more radical innovations are often brought about by the innovation itself creating demand. Customers don't usually know that they need something radical. For example, in the late 1970s people were not asking for microprocessors, they did not even know what they were. They were improvised by an engineer in the USA for a Japanese customer who made calculators. Only later did they become the enabling technology for the PC and after that the innumerable devices that now dominate our lives.

What is designed in a service or product?

All services and products can be considered as having three aspects:

Concept

Package

Process

- a **concept**, which is the understanding of the nature, use and value of the service or product;
- a **package** of 'component' services and products that provide those benefits defined in the concept;
- the **process** defines the way in which the component services and products will be created and delivered.

The concept

Designers often talk about a 'new concept'. This might be a concept car specially created for an international show or a restaurant concept providing a different style of dining. The concept is a clear articulation of the outline specification including the nature, use and value of the product or service against which the stages of the design (see later) and the resultant product and/or service can be assessed. For example, a concept for a restaurant might be a bold and brash dining experience aimed at the early 20s market, with contemporary décor and music, providing a range of freshly made pizza and pasta dishes. Although the detailed design is important, customers are buying the particular concept. Patients consuming a pharmaceutical company's products are not particularly concerned about the ingredients contained in the drugs they are using nor about the way in which they were made, they are concerned about the notion behind them, how they will use them and the benefits they will provide for them. Thus the articulation, development and testing of the concept is a crucial stage in the design of products and services.

The package of services and products

Normally, the word 'service' implies a more intangible experience, such as an evening at a restaurant or a nightclub, and the word 'product' implies a tangible physical object, such as a car, washing machine or watch. In fact, as we discussed in Chapter 1, most, if not all, operations produce a combination of services *and* products. The purchase of a car includes the car itself and the services such as 'warranties', 'after-sales services' and 'the services of the person selling the car'. The restaurant meal includes products such as 'food' and 'drink' as well as services such as 'the delivery of the food to the table and the attentions of the waiting staff'. It is this collection of services and products that is usually referred to as the 'package' that customers buy. Some of the services or products in the package are **core**, that is they are fundamental to the purchase and could not be removed without destroying the nature of the package. Other parts will serve to enhance the core. These are **supporting services and products**. In the case of the car, the guarantees and leather trim are supporting services and products. The core good is the car itself. At the restaurant, the meal itself is the core. Its provision and preparation are important but not absolutely necessary (in some restaurants you might serve and even cook the meal yourself). By changing the core, or adding or subtracting supporting services and products, organizations can provide different packages and in so doing create quite different concepts. For instance, engineers may wish to add traction control and four-wheel drive to make the two-seater sports car more stable, but this might conflict with the concept of an 'economical' car with 'sensitive handling'.

Core services and products

Supporting services and products

The process

The package of components which make up a service and products, are the 'ingredients' of the design; however, designers need to design the way in which they will be created and delivered to the customer – this is process design. For the new car the assembly line has to be designed and built which will assemble the various components as the car moves down the line. The service processes of the delivery of cars to the showrooms and the sales processes have to be designed to support the concept. Likewise in the restaurant, the manufacturing processes of

Short case
Spangler, Hoover and Dyson[3]

James Dyson

In 1907 a janitor called Murray Spangler put together a pillowcase, a fan, an old biscuit tin and a broom handle. It was the world's first vacuum cleaner. One year later he sold his patented idea to William Hoover whose company went on to dominate the vacuum cleaner market for decades, especially in its United States homeland. Yet between 2002 and 2005, Hoover's market share dropped from 36 per cent to 13.5 per cent. Why? Because a futuristic-looking and comparatively expensive rival product, the Dyson vacuum cleaner, had jumped from nothing to over 20 per cent of the market. In fact, the Dyson product dates back to 1978 when James Dyson noticed how the air filter in the spray-finishing room of a company where he had been working was constantly clogging with powder particles (just like a vacuum cleaner bag clogs with dust). So he designed and built an industrial cyclone tower, which removed the powder particles by exerting centrifugal forces. The question intriguing him was, *'Could the same principle work in a domestic vacuum cleaner?'* Five years and five *thousand* prototypes later he had a working design, since praised for its 'uniqueness and functionality'. However, existing vacuum cleaner manufacturers were not as impressed – two rejected the design outright. So Dyson started making his new design himself. Within a few years Dyson cleaners were, in the UK, outselling the rivals that had once rejected them. The aesthetics and functionality of the design help to keep sales growing in spite of a higher retail price. To Dyson, good *'is about looking at everyday things with new eyes and working*

out how they can be made better. It's about challenging existing technology'.

Dyson engineers have taken this technology one stage further and developed core separator technology to capture even more microscopic dirt. Dirt now goes through three stages of separation. Firstly, dirt is drawn into a powerful outer cyclone. Centrifugal forces fling larger debris, such as pet hair and dust particles, into the clear bin at 500 Gs (the maximum G-force the human body can take is 8 Gs). Secondly, a further cyclonic stage, the core separator, removes dust particles as small as 0.5 microns from the airflow – particles so small you could fit 200 of them on this full stop. Finally, a cluster of smaller, even faster cyclones generate centrifugal forces of up to 150,000 G – extracting particles as small as mould and bacteria.

food purchase, preparation and cooking need to be designed, just like the way in which the customers will be processed from reception to the bar or waiting area and to the table and the way in which the series of activities at the table will be performed in such a way as to deliver the agreed concept.

The design activity is itself a process

The design activity is one of the most important operations processes

Producing designs for services and products is itself a process which conforms to the input–transformation–output model described in Chapter 1. It therefore has to be designed and managed like any other **process**. Figure 4.2 illustrates the design activity as an input–transformation–output diagram. The transformed resource inputs will consist mainly of information in the form of market forecasts, market preferences, technical data, and so on. Transforming resource inputs includes operations managers and specialist technical staff, design equipment and software such as computer-aided design (CAD) systems and simulation packages. One can describe the objectives of the design activity in the same way as we do any transformation process. All operations satisfy customers by producing their services and goods according to customers' desires for quality, speed, dependability, flexibility and cost. In the same way, the design activity attempts to produce designs to the same objectives.

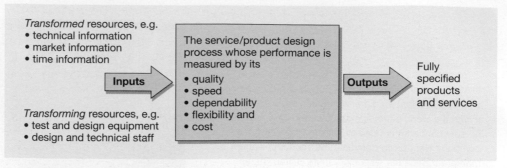

Figure 4.2 The design activity is itself a process

The stages of design – from concept to specification

Fully specified designs rarely spring, fully formed, from a designer's imagination. To get to a final design of a service or product, the design activity must pass through several key stages. These form an approximate sequence, although in practice designers will often recycle or backtrack through the stages. We will describe them in the order in which they usually occur, as shown in Figure 4.3. Firstly, comes the **concept generation** stage that develops the overall concept for the service or product. The concepts are then **screened** to try to ensure that, in broad terms, they will be a sensible addition to its portfolio and meet the concept as defined. The agreed concept has then to be turned into a **preliminary design** that then goes through a stage of **evaluation and improvement** to see if the concept can be served better, more cheaply or more easily. An agreed design may then be subjected to **prototyping and final design**.

Concept generation
Screening
Preliminary design
Evaluation and improvement
Prototyping and final design

Concept generation

The ideas for new concepts can come from sources outside the organization, such as customers or competitors, and from sources within the organization, such as staff (for example, from sales staff and front-of-house staff) or from the R&D department.

Ideas from customers. Marketing, the function generally responsible for identifying new service or product opportunities, may use many market research tools for gathering data from customers in a formal and structured way, including questionnaires and interviews. These techniques, however, usually tend to be structured in such a way as only to test out ideas or check products or services against predetermined criteria. Listening to the customer, in a less structured way, is sometimes seen as a better means of generating new ideas. **Focus groups**, for example, are one formal but unstructured way of collecting ideas and suggestions from customers. A focus group typically comprises seven to ten participants who are unfamiliar with each other but who have been selected because they have characteristics in common that

Focus groups

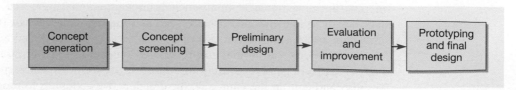

Figure 4.3 The stages of service/product design

relate to the particular topic of the focus group. Participants are invited to 'discuss' or 'share ideas with others' in a permissive environment that nurtures different perceptions and points of view, without pressurizing participants. The group discussion is conducted several times with similar types of participants in order to identify trends and patterns in perceptions. Ideas may also come from customers on a day-to-day basis. They may write to complain about a particular product or service, or make suggestions for its improvement.

Reverse engineering (margin note)

Ideas from competitor activity. All market-aware organizations follow the activities of their competitors. A new idea may give a competitor an edge in the marketplace, even if it is only a temporary one, then competing organizations will have to decide whether to imitate, or alternatively to come up with a better or different idea. Sometimes this involves **reverse engineering**, that is taking apart a product to understand how a competing organization has made it. Some aspects of services may be more difficult to reverse-engineer (especially back-office services) as they are less transparent to competitors. However, by consumer-testing a service, it may be possible to make educated guesses about how it has been created. Many service organizations employ 'testers' to check out the services provided by competitors.

Ideas from staff. The contact staff in a service organization or the salesperson in a product-oriented organization could meet customers every day. These staff may have good ideas about what customers like and do not like. They may have gathered suggestions from customers or have ideas of their own as to how offerings could be developed to meet the needs of their customers more effectively.

Research and development (margin note)

Ideas from research and development. One formal function found in some organizations is **research and development** (R&D). As its name implies, its role is twofold. Research usually means attempting to develop new knowledge and ideas in order to solve a particular problem or to grasp an opportunity. Development is the attempt to try to utilize and operationalize the ideas that come from research. In this chapter we are mainly concerned with the 'development' part of R&D – for example, exploiting new ideas that might be afforded by new materials or new technologies. And although 'development' does not sound as exciting as 'research', it often requires as much creativity and even more persistence. Both creativity and persistence took James Dyson (see the short case earlier) from a potentially good idea to a workable technology. One product has commemorated the persistence of its development engineers in its company name. Back in 1953 the Rocket Chemical Company set out to create a rust-prevention solvent and degreaser to be used in the aerospace industry. Working in their lab in San Diego, California, it took them 40 attempts to get the water-displacing formula worked out. So that is what they called the product. WD-40 literally stands for water displacement, fortieth attempt. Originally used to protect the outer skin of the Atlas missile from rust and corrosion, the product worked so well that employees kept taking cans home to use for domestic purposes. Soon after, the product was launched, with great success, into the consumer market.

Open-sourcing – using a 'development community'[4]

Not all services or products are created by professional, employed designers for commercial purposes. Many of the software applications that we all use, for example, are developed by an open community, including the people who use the products. If you use Google, the Internet search facility, or Wikipedia, the online encyclopaedia, or shop at Amazon, you are using open-source software. The basic concept of open-source software is extremely simple. Large communities of people around the world, who have the ability to write software code, come together and produce software. The finished software is not only available to be used by anyone or any organization for free but is regularly updated to ensure it keeps pace with the necessary improvements. The production of open-source software like its commercial equivalent is continuously supported and maintained. However, unlike its commercial equivalent, it is absolutely free to use. With the maturity open-source software now has to offer, organizations have seen the benefits of using free software to drive down costs. It has been the biggest change in software development for decades and is setting new open standards in the way software is used.

The open nature of this type of development also encourages compatibility between products. BMW, for example, was reported to be developing an open-source platform for vehicle electronics. Using an open-source approach, rather than using proprietary software, BMW can allow providers of 'infotainment' services to develop compatible, plug-and-play applications. *'We were convinced we had to develop an open platform that would allow for open software since the speed in the infotainment and entertainment industry requires us to be on a much faster track'*, said Gunter Reichart, BMW vice-president of driver assistance, body electronics and electrical networks. *'We invite other OEMs to join with us, to exchange with us. We are open to exchange with others.'*

Short case
Square watermelons![5]

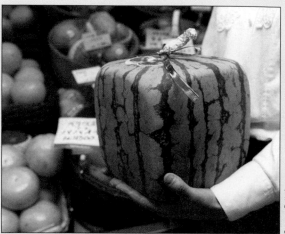

Source: Getty Images

It sounds like a joke, but it is a genuine product innovation motivated by a market need. It's green, it's square and it originally comes from Japan. It's a square watermelon! Why square? Because Japanese grocery stores are not large and space cannot be wasted. A round watermelon does not fit into a refrigerator very conveniently and there is also the problem of trying to cut the fruit when it keeps rolling around. So an innovative farmer from Japan's south-western island of Shikoku solved the problem with the idea of making a cube-shaped watermelon which could easily be packed and stored. There is no genetic modification or clever science involved in growing watermelons. It simply involves placing the young fruit into wooden boxes with clear sides. During its growth, the fruit naturally swells to fill the surrounding shape. Now the idea has spread from Japan. *'Melons are among the most delicious and refreshing fruit around but some people find them a problem to store in their fridge or to cut because they roll around,'* said Damien Sutherland, the exotic fruit buyer from Tesco, the UK supermarket. 'We've seen samples of these watermelons and they literally stop you in their tracks because they are so eye-catching. These square melons will make it easier than ever to eat because they can be served in long strips rather than in the crescent shape.' However, not everyone liked the idea. Comments on news web sites included: *'Where will engineering everyday things for our own unreasonable convenience stop? I prefer melons to be the shape of melons!'*, *'They are probably working on straight bananas next!'*, and *'I would like to buy square sausages, then they would be easier to turn over in the frying pan.'*

Concept screening

Not all concepts which are generated will necessarily be capable of further development into services and products. Designers need to be selective as to which concepts they progress to the next design stage. The purpose of the concept-screening stage is to take the flow of concepts and evaluate them. Evaluation in design means assessing the worth or value of each design option, so that a choice can be made between them. This involves assessing each concept or option against a number of **design criteria**. While the criteria used in any particular design exercise will depend on the nature and circumstances of the exercise, it is useful to think in terms of three broad categories of design criteria:

Design criteria

Feasibility

- The **feasibility** of the design option – can we do it?
  - Do we have the skills (quality of resources)?
  - Do we have the organizational capacity (quantity of resources)?
  - Do we have the financial resources to cope with this option?

Acceptability

- The **acceptability** of the design option – do we want to do it?
  - Does the option satisfy the performance criteria which the design is trying to achieve? (These will differ for different designs.)
  - Will our customers want it?
  - Does the option give a satisfactory financial return?

Vulnerability

- The **vulnerability** of each design option – do we want to take the risk? That is,
  - Do we understand the full consequences of adopting the option?
  - Being pessimistic, what could go wrong if we adopt the option? What would be the consequences of everything going wrong? (This is called the 'downside risk' of an option.)

The design 'funnel'

Design funnel

Applying these evaluation criteria progressively reduces the number of options which will be available further along in the design activity. For example, deciding to make the outside casing of a camera case from aluminium rather than plastic limits later decisions, such as the overall size and shape of the case. This means that the uncertainty surrounding the design reduces as the number of alternative designs being considered decreases. Figure 4.4 shows what is sometimes called the **design funnel**, depicting the progressive reduction of design options from many to one. However, reducing design uncertainty also impacts on the cost of changing one's mind on some detail of the design. In most stages of design the cost of changing a decision is bound to incur some sort of rethinking and recalculation of costs. Early on in the design activity, before too many fundamental decisions have been made, the costs of change are relatively low. However, as the design progresses the interrelated and cumulative decisions already made become increasingly expensive to change.

Critical commentary

Not everyone agrees with the concept of the design funnel. For some it is just too neat and ordered an idea to reflect accurately the creativity, arguments and chaos that sometimes characterize the design activity. Firstly, they argue, managers do not start out with an infinite number of options. No one could process that amount of information – and anyway, designers often have some set solutions in their mind, looking for an opportunity to be used. Secondly, the number of options being considered often *increases* as time goes by. This may actually be a good thing, especially if the activity was unimaginatively specified in the first place. Thirdly, the real process of design often involves cycling back, often many times, as potential design solutions raise fresh questions or become dead ends. In summary, the idea of the design funnel does not describe what actually happens in the design activity. Nor does it necessarily even describe what *should* happen.

Balancing evaluation with creativity

Creativity is important in service/product design

The systematic process of evaluation is important but it must be balanced by the need for design creativity. **Creativity** is a vital ingredient in effective design. The final quality of any design of service or product will be influenced by the creativity of its designers. Increasingly, creativity is seen as an essential ingredient not just in the design of offerings, but also in the design of operations processes. Partly because of the fast-changing nature of many industries, a lack of creativity (and consequently of innovation) is seen as a major risk. For example, '*It has never been a better time to be an industry revolutionary. Conversely, it has never been a more dangerous time to be complacent . . . The dividing line between being a leader and being a laggard is today measured in months or a few days, and not in decades.*' Of course, creativity can be expensive. By its nature it involves exploring sometimes unlikely possibilities.

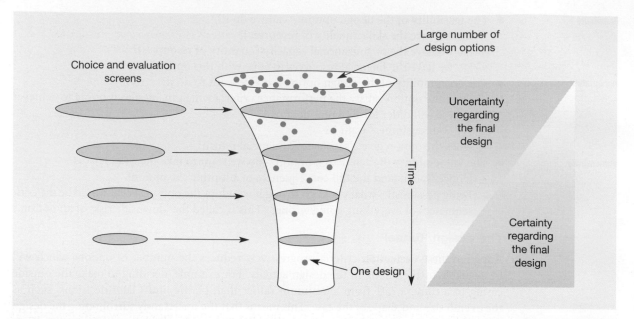

Figure 4.4 The design funnel – progressively reducing the number of possibilities until the final design is reached

Many of these will die as they are proved to be inappropriate. Yet, to some extent, the process of creativity depends on these many seemingly wasted investigations. As Art Fry, the inventor of 3M's Post-it note products, said: *'You have to kiss a lot of frogs to find the prince. But remember, one prince can pay for a lot of frogs.'*

Short case
The Daniel Hersheson Blowdry Bar at Topshop[6]

Even at the chic and stylish end of the hairdressing business, close as it is to the world of changing fashion trends, true innovation and genuinely novel new services are a relative rarity. Yet real service innovation can reap significant rewards as Daniel and Luke Hersheson, the father and son team behind the Daniel Hersheson salons, fully understand. The Hersheson brand has successfully bridged the gaps between salon, photo session and fashion catwalk. The team first put themselves on the fashion map with a salon in London's Mayfair followed by a salon and spa in Harvey Nichols's flagship London store.

Their latest innovation is the 'Blowdry Bar at Topshop'. This is a unique concept that is aimed at customers who want fashionable and catwalk quality styling at an affordable price without the full 'cut and blow-dry' treatment. The Hersheson Blowdry Bar was launched in December 2006 to ecstatic press coverage in Topshop's flagship Oxford Circus store. The four-seater pink pod within the Topshop store is a scissors-free zone dedicated to styling on the go. Originally seen as a walk-in, no-appointment-necessary format, demand has proved to be so high that an

appointment system has been implemented to avoid disappointing customers. Once in the pod, customers can choose from a tailor-made picture menu of nine fashion styles with names like 'The Super Straight', 'The Classic Big and Bouncy' and 'Wavy Gravy'. Typically, the wash and blow-dry takes around 30 minutes. *'It's just perfect for a client who wants to look that bit special for a big night out but who doesn't want a full cut'*, says Ryan Wilkes, one of the stylists at the Blowdry Bar. *'Some clients will "graduate" to become regular customers at the main Daniel Hersheson salons. I have clients who started out using the Blowdry Bar but now also get their hair cut with me in the salon.'*

Partnering with Topshop is an important element in the design of the service, says Daniel Hersheson, *'We are delighted to be opening the UK's first blow-dry bar at Topshop. Our philosophy of constantly relating hair back to fashion means we will be perfectly at home in the most creative store on the British high street.'* Topshop also recognizes the fit. *'The Daniel Hersheson Blowdry Bar is a really exciting service addition to our Oxford Circus flagship and offers the perfect finishing touch to a great shopping experience at Topshop'.*

The new service has not just been a success in the market; it also has advantages for the operation itself.

'It's a great opportunity for young stylists not only to develop their styling skills, but also to develop the confidence that it takes to interact with clients', says George Northwood, Manager of Daniel Hersheson's Mayfair salon. *'You can see a real difference after a trainee stylist has worked in the Blowdry Bar. They learn how to talk to clients, to understand their needs, and to advise them. It's the confidence that they gain that is so important in helping them to become fully qualified and successful stylists in their own right.'*

Preliminary design

Having generated an acceptable, feasible and viable concept the next stage is to create a preliminary design. The objective of this stage is to have a first attempt at both specifying the component products and services in the *package*, and defining the *processes* to create the package.

Specify the components of the package

The first task in this stage of design is to define exactly what will go into the service or product: that is, specifying the components of the package. This will require the collection of information about such things as the *constituent component parts* which make up the package and the **component structure**, the order in which the components of the package have to be put together. For example, the components for a remote mouse for a computer may include, upper and lower casings, a control unit and packaging, which are themselves made up of other components. The product structure shows how these components fit together to make the mouse (see Figure 4.5).

Component structure

Reducing design complexity

Simplicity is usually seen as a virtue amongst designers. The most elegant design solutions are often the simplest. However, when an operation produces a variety of services or products, the range considered as a whole can become complex, which, in turn, increases costs. Designers

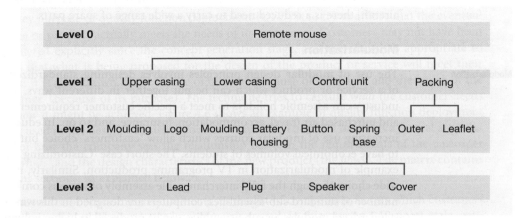

Figure 4.5 The component structure of a remote mouse

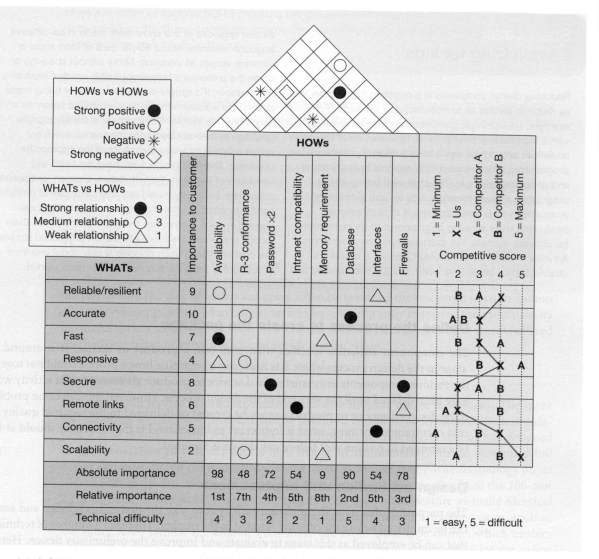

Figure 4.6 A QFD matrix for an information system product

- The competitive scores indicate the relative performance of the product, in this case on a 1 to 5 scale. Also indicated are the performances of two competitor offerings.
- The *hows*, or 'design characteristics' of the product, are the various 'dimensions' of the design which will operationalize customer requirements within the service or product.
- The central matrix (sometimes called the 'relationship matrix') represents a view of the interrelationship between the *whats* and the *hows*. This is often based on value judgements made by the design team. The symbols indicate the strength of the relationship – for example, the relationship between the ability to link remotely to the system and the intranet compatibility of the product is strong. All the relationships are studied, but in many cases, where the cell of the matrix is blank, there is none.
- The bottom box of the matrix is a technical assessment of the product. This contains the absolute importance of each design characteristic. (For example, the design characteristic 'interfaces' has a relative importance of $(9 \times 5) + (1 \times 9) = 54$.) This is also translated into a ranked relative importance. In addition, the degree of technical difficulty to achieve high levels of performance in each design characteristic is indicated on a 1 to 5 scale.
- The triangular 'roof' of the 'house' captures any information the team has about the correlations (positive or negative) between the various design characteristics.

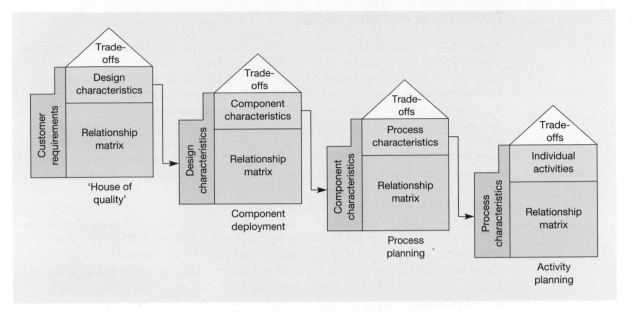

Figure 4.7 QFD matrices can be linked with the 'hows' of one matrix forming the 'whats' of the next

Although the details of QFD may vary between its different variants, the principle is generally common, namely to identify the customer requirements for a service or product (together with their relative importance) and to relate them to the design characteristics which translate those requirements into practice. In fact, this principle can be continued by making the *hows* from one stage become the *whats* of the next. Some experienced users of QFD have up to four linked matrices in this way (see Figure 4.7). If engineering or process trade-offs need to be made at a later stage, the interrelated houses enable the effect on customer requirements to be determined.

Value engineering

Value engineering

The purpose of **value engineering** is to try to reduce costs, and prevent any unnecessary costs, before creating the service or product. Simply put, it tries to eliminate any costs that do not contribute to the value and performance of the service or product. ('Value analysis' is the name given to the same process when it is concerned with cost reduction after the product or service has been introduced.) Value-engineering programmes are usually conducted by project teams consisting of designers, purchasing specialists, operations managers and financial analysts. The chosen elements of the package are subject to rigorous scrutiny, by analysing their function and cost, then trying to find any similar components that could simplify processes do the same job at lower cost. The team may attempt to simplify the service delivery process, reduce the number of components, or use cheaper materials. For example, Motorola used value engineering to reduce the number of parts in its mobile phones from 'thousands' down to 'hundreds' and even less, with a drastic reduction in processing time and cost.

Value engineering requires innovative and critical thinking, but it is also carried out using a formal procedure. The procedure examines the purpose of the service or product, its basic functions and its secondary functions. Taking the example of the remote mouse used previously:

Purpose
Basic functions
Secondary functions

- The **purpose** of the remote mouse is to communicate with the computer.
- The **basic function** is to control presentation slide shows.
- The **secondary function** is to be plug-and-play-compatible with any system.

Team members would then propose ways to improve the secondary functions by combining, revising or eliminating them. All ideas would then be checked for feasibility, acceptability, vulnerability and their contribution to the value and purpose of the service or product.

Prototyping and final design

At around this stage in the design activity it is necessary to turn the improved design into a prototype so that it can be tested. It may be too risky to go into full production of the telephone, or the holiday, before testing it out, so it is usually more appropriate to create a prototype. Service prototypes may also include computer simulations but also the actual implementation of the service on a pilot basis. Product prototypes include everything from clay models to computer simulations. Many retailing organizations pilot new offerings in a small number of stores in order to test customers' reaction to them. Increasingly, it is possible to store the data that define a service or product in a digital format on computer systems, which allows this **virtual prototype** to be tested in much the same way as a physical prototype. This is a familiar idea in some industries such as magazine publishing, where images and text can be rearranged and subjected to scrutiny prior to them existing in any physical form. This allows them to be amended right up to the point of production without incurring high costs. Virtual-reality-based simulations now allow businesses to test new services and products as well as visualize and plan the processes that will create them. Individual component parts can be positioned together virtually and tested for fit or interference. Even virtual workers can be introduced into the prototyping system to check for ease of operating.

Virtual prototype

Computer-aided design (CAD)

CAD

CAD systems provide the computer-aided ability to create and modify designs. These systems allow conventionally used shapes such as points, lines, arcs, circles and text, to be added to a computer-based representation of the design. Once incorporated into the design, these entities can be copied, moved about, rotated through angles, magnified or deleted. The designs thus created can be saved in the memory of the system and retrieved for later use. This enables a library of standardized drawings of parts and components to be built up. The most obvious advantage of CAD systems is that their ability to store and retrieve design data quickly, as well as their ability to manipulate design details, can considerably increase the productivity of the design activity. In addition to this, however, because changes can be made rapidly to designs, CAD systems can considerably enhance the flexibility of the design activity, enabling modifications to be made much more rapidly. Further, the use of standardized libraries of shapes and entities can reduce the possibility of errors in the design.

Skunkworks[8]

Encouraging creativity in design, while at the same time recognizing the constraints of everyday business life, has always been one of the great challenges of industrial design. One well-known approach to releasing the design and development creativity of a group has been called a '**Skunkworks**'. This is usually taken to mean a small team who are taken out of their normal work environment and granted freedom from their normal management activities and constraints. It was an idea that originated in the Lockheed aircraft company in the 1940s, where designers were set up outside the normal organizational structure and given the task of designing a high-speed fighter plane. The experiment was so successful that the company continued with it to develop other innovative products.

Skunkworks

Since that time many other companies have used a similar approach, although 'Skunkworks' is a registered trademark of Lockheed Martin Corporation. Motorola's mobile phone 'Razr' was designed and developed in a Skunkworks-like special laboratory that the company set up, well away from its main Research and Development site in Illinois. Even the décor and layout of the laboratory were different: open-plan and with lots of bright colours. Something similar is reportedly used by Malaysia Airlines to tackle wider business issues, not just 'design' assignments.

The benefits of interactive design

Interactive design

Interactive design can shorten time to market

Earlier we made the point that in practice it is a mistake to separate the design of services and products from the design of the processes which will create them. Operations managers should have some involvement from the initial evaluation of the concept right through to its introduction to the market. Merging the design of services/products and the processes which create them is sometimes called **interactive design**. Its benefits come from the reduction in the elapsed time for the whole design activity, from concept through to market introduction. This is often called the **time to market** (TTM). The argument in favour of reducing time to market is that doing so gives increased competitive advantage. For example, if it takes a company five years to develop a service from concept to market, with a given set of resources, it can introduce a new service only once every five years. If its rival can develop a service in three years, it can introduce its new service, together with its (presumably) improved performance, once every three years. This means that the rival company does not have to make such radical improvements in performance each time it introduces a new service, because it is introducing its new services more frequently. In other words, shorter TTM means that companies get more opportunities to improve the performance of their services or products.

If the development process takes longer than expected (or even worse, longer than competitors') two effects are likely to show. The first is that the costs of development will increase. Having to use development resources, such as designers, technicians, subcontractors, and so on, for a longer development period usually increases the costs of development. Perhaps more seriously, the late introduction of the product or service will delay the revenue from its sale (and possibly reduce the total revenue substantially if competitors have already got to the market with their own services or products). The net effect of this could be not only a considerable reduction in sales but also reduced profitability – an outcome which could considerably extend the time before the company breaks even on its investment in the new service or product. This is illustrated in Figure 4.8.

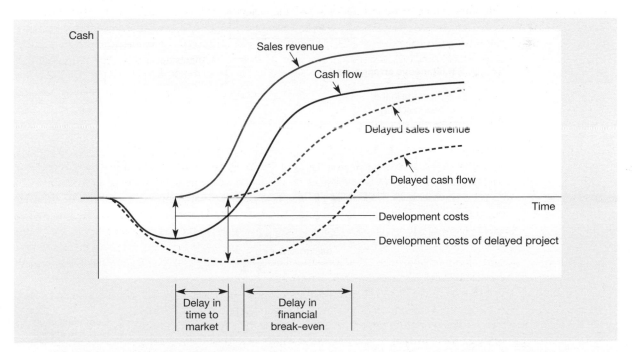

Figure 4.8 Delay in the time to market of new services and products not only reduces and delays revenues, it also increases the costs of development. The combination of both these effects usually delays the financial break-even point far more than the delay in the time to market

A number of factors have been suggested which can significantly reduce time to market for a service or product, including the following:

- simultaneous development of the various stages in the overall process;
- an early resolution of design conflict and uncertainty;
- an organizational structure which reflects the development project.

Simultaneous development

Sequential approach to design

Earlier in the chapter we described the design process as essentially a set of individual, predetermined stages. Sometimes one stage is completed before the next one commences. This step-by-step, or **sequential**, approach has traditionally been the typical form of development. It has some advantages. It is easy to manage and control design projects organized in this way, since each stage is clearly defined. In addition, each stage is completed before the next stage is begun, so each stage can focus its skills and expertise on a limited set of tasks. The main problem of the sequential approach is that it is both time-consuming and costly. When each stage is separate, with a clearly defined set of tasks, any difficulties encountered during the design at one stage might necessitate the design being halted while responsibility moves back to the previous stage. This sequential approach is shown in Figure 4.9(a).

Yet often there is really little need to wait until the absolute finalization of one stage before starting the next. For example, perhaps while generating the concept, the evaluation activity of screening and selection could be started. It is likely that some concepts could be judged as

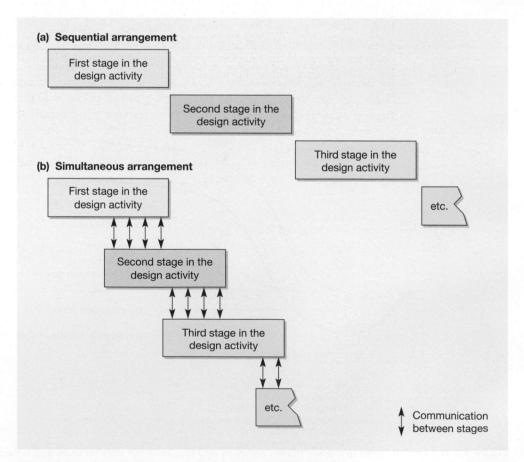

Figure 4.9 (a) Sequential arrangement of the stages in the design activity; (b) simultaneous arrangement of the stages in the design activity

'non-starters' relatively early on in the process of idea generation. Similarly, during the screening stage, it is likely that some aspects of the design will become obvious before the phase is finally complete. Therefore, the preliminary work on these parts of the design could be commenced at that point. This principle can be taken right through all the stages, one stage commencing before the previous one has finished, so there is **simultaneous or concurrent** work on the stages (see Figure 4.9(b)).

Simultaneous or concurrent approach to design

Early conflict resolution

Characterizing the design activity as a whole series of decisions is a useful way of thinking about design. However, a decision, once made, need not totally and utterly commit the organization. For example, if a design team is designing a new vacuum cleaner, the decision to adopt a particular style and type of electric motor might have seemed sensible at the time the decision was made but might have to be changed later, in the light of new information. It could be that a new electric motor becomes available which is clearly superior to the one initially selected. Under those circumstances the designers might very well want to change their decision.

There are other, more avoidable, reasons for designers changing their minds during the design activity, however. Perhaps one of the initial design decisions was made without sufficient discussion among those in the organization who have a valid contribution to make. It may even be that when the decision was made there was insufficient agreement to formalize it, and the design team decided to carry on without formally making the decision. Yet subsequent decisions might be made as though the decision had been formalized. For example, suppose the company could not agree on the correct size of electric motor to put into its vacuum cleaner. It might well carry on with the rest of the design work while further discussions and investigations take place on what kind of electric motor to incorporate in the design. Yet much of the rest of the product's design is likely to depend on the choice of the electric motor. Failure to resolve these conflicts and/or decisions early on in the process can prolong the degree of uncertainty in the total design activity. In addition, if a decision is made (even implicitly) and then changed later on in the process, the costs of that change can be very large. However, if the design team manages to resolve conflict early in the design activity, this will reduce the degree of uncertainty within the project and reduce the extra cost and, most significantly, time associated with either managing this uncertainty or changing decisions already made. Figure 4.10 illustrates two patterns of design changes through the life of the total design, which imply different time-to-market performances.

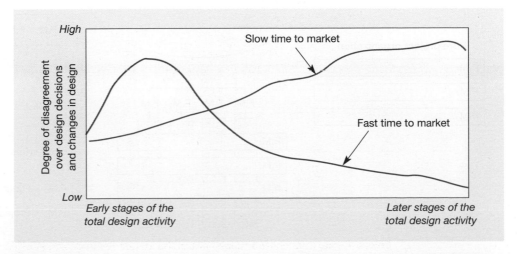

Figure 4.10 Sorting out problems early saves greater disruption later in the design activity

Project-based organization structures

The total process of developing concepts through to market will almost certainly involve personnel from several different areas of the organization. To continue the vacuum cleaner example, it is likely that the vacuum cleaner company would involve staff from its research and development department, engineering, production management, marketing and finance. All these different functions will have some part to play in making the decisions which will shape the final design. Yet any design project will also have an existence of its own. It will have a project name, an individual manager or group of staff who are championing the project, a budget and, hopefully, a clear strategic purpose in the organization. The organizational question is which of these two ideas – the various organizational functions which contribute to the design or the design project itself – should dominate the way in which the design activity is managed?

Functional design organization

Project design organization

Before answering this, it is useful to look at the range of organizational structures which are available – from **pure functional** to **pure project** forms. In a pure functional organization, all staff associated with the design project are based unambiguously in their functional groups. There is no project-based group at all. They may be working full-time on the project but all communications and liaison are carried out through their functional manager. The project exists because of agreement between these functional managers. At the other extreme, all the individual members of staff from each function who are involved in the project could be moved out of their functions and perhaps even physically relocated to a **task force** dedicated

Task force

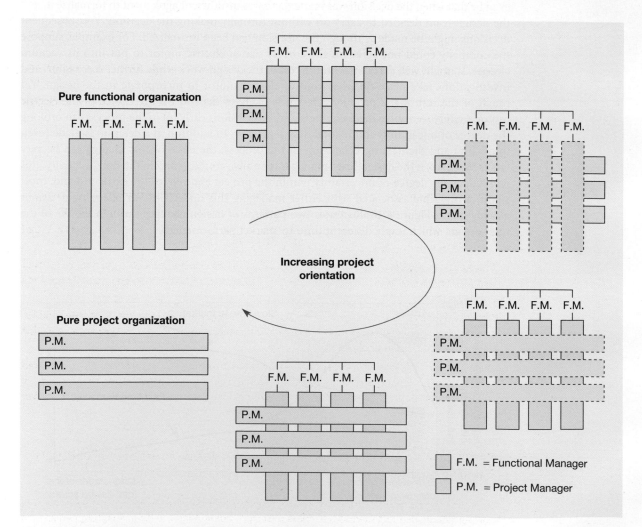

Figure 4.11 Organization structures for the design activity

solely to the project. The task force could be led by a project manager who might hold all the budget allocated to the design project. Not all members of the task force necessarily have to stay in the team throughout the development period, but a substantial core might see the project through from start to finish. Some members of a design team may even be from other companies. In between these two extremes there are various types of **matrix organization** with varying emphasis on these two aspects of the organization (see Figure 4.11). Although the 'task force' type of organization, especially for small projects, can sometimes be a little cumbersome, it seems to be generally agreed that, for substantial projects at least, it is more effective at reducing overall time to market.[9]

Matrix organization

Summary answers to key questions

Check and improve your understanding of this chapter using self-assessment questions and a personalized study plan, audio and video downloads, and an eBook – all at **www.myomlab.com**.

➤ Why is good service and product design important?

■ Good design makes good business sense because it translates customer needs into the shape and form of the product or service and so enhances profitability.

■ Design includes formalizing three particularly important issues: the concept, package and process implied by the design.

■ Design is a process that itself must be designed according to the process design principles described in the previous chapter.

➤ What are the stages in service and product design?

■ *Concept generation* transforms an idea for a service or product into a concept which captures the nature of the product or service and provides an overall specification for its design.

■ *Screening* the concept involves examining its feasibility, acceptability and vulnerability in broad terms to ensure that it is a sensible addition to the company's portfolio.

■ *Preliminary design* involves the identification of all the component parts of the service or product and the way they fit together. Typical tools used during this phase include component structures and flow charts.

■ *Design evaluation and improvement* involve re-examining the design to see if it can be done in a better way, more cheaply or more easily. Typical techniques used here include quality function deployment and value engineering.

■ *Prototyping and final design* involve providing the final details which allow the offering to be delivered or created. The outcome of this stage is a fully developed specification for the package of services and products, as well as a specification for the processes that will make and deliver them to customers.

➤ Why and how should service and product design be considered interactively with process design?

■ Quality of the service or product and of the process can be improved by looking at them in parallel rather than in sequence. It helps a design 'break even' on its investment earlier than would otherwise have been the case.

- Employ *simultaneous development* where design decisions are taken as early as they can be, without necessarily waiting for a whole design phase to be completed.

- Ensure *early conflict resolution* which allows contentious decisions to be resolved early in the design process, thereby not allowing them to cause far more delay and confusion if they emerge later in the process.

- Use a *project-based organizational structure* which can ensure that a focused and coherent team of designers is dedicated to a single design or group of design projects.

Learning exercises

These problems and applications will help to improve your analysis of operations. You can find more practice problems as well as worked examples and guided solutions on MyOMLab at www.myomlab.com.

1 A company is developing a new web site that will allow customers to track the progress of their orders. The website developers charge €10,000 for every development week and it is estimated that the design will take 10 weeks from the start of the design project to the launch of the web site. Once launched, it is estimated that the new site will attract extra business that will generate profits of €5,000 per week. However, if the web site is delayed by more than 5 weeks, the extra profit generated would reduce to €2,000 per week. How will a delay of 5 weeks affect the time when the design will break even in terms of cash flow?

2 How can the concept of modularization be applied to package holidays sold through an online travel agent?

3 One product where a very wide range of product types is valued by customers is that of domestic paint. Most people like to express their creativity in the choice of paints and other home-decorating products that they use in their homes. Clearly, offering a wide range of paint must have serious cost implications for the companies which manufacture, distribute and sell the product. Visit a store which sells paint and get an idea of the range of products available on the market. How do you think paint manufacturers and retailers manage to design their products and services so as to maintain high variety but keep costs under control?

4 Design becomes particularly important at the interface between services or products and the people that use them. This is especially true for internet-based services. Consider two types of website:

(a) those which are trying to sell something such as Amazon.com, and
(b) those which are primarily concerned with giving information, for example bbc.co.uk.

For each of these categories, what seems to constitute 'good design'? Find examples of particularly good and particularly poor web design and explain what makes them good or bad.

Want to know more?

Bangle, C. (2001) The ultimate creativity machine: how BMW turns art into profit, *Harvard Business Review*, Jan, 47–55. A good description of how good aesthetic design translates into business success.

Bruce, M. and Bessant, J. (2002) *Design in Business: Strategic Innovation through Design*, Financial Times Prentice Hall and The Design Council. Probably one of the best overviews of design in a business context available today.

Goldstein, S.M., Johnston, R., Duffy, J. and Raod, J. (2002) The service concept: the missing link in service design research? *Journal of Operations Management*, volume 20, issue 2, April, 121–34. Readable.

The Industrial Designers Society of America (2003) *Design Secrets: Products: 50 Real-Life Projects Uncovered (Design Secrets)*, Rockport Publishers Inc, Gloucester, MA. Very much a practitioner book with some great examples.

Useful websites

www.cfsd.org.uk The Centre for Sustainable Design's site. Some useful resources, but obviously largely confined to sustainability issues.

www.conceptcar.co.uk A site devoted to automotive design. Fun if you like new car designs!

www.betterproductdesign.net A site that acts as a resource for good design practice. Set up by Cambridge University and the Royal College of Art. Some good material that supports all aspects of design.

www.ocw.mit.edu/courses/sloan-school-of-management Good source of open courseware from MIT.

www.design-council.org.uk Site of the UK's Design Council. One of the best sites in the world for design-related issues.

www.nathan.com/ed/glossary/#ED

www.opsman.org Lots of useful stuff.

Now that you have finished reading this chapter, why not visit MyOMLab at *www.myomlab.com* where you'll find more learning resources to help you make the most of your studies and get a better grade.

Chapter 5

Process design

Key questions

➤ What is process design?
➤ How do volume and variety affect process design?
➤ How are processes designed in detail?
➤ What are the human implications for process design?

Introduction

Say you are a 'designer' and most people will assume that you are someone who is concerned with how a product looks. However, the design activity is much broader than that and while there is no universally recognized definition of 'design'. We take it to mean 'the process by which some functional requirement of people is satisfied through the shaping or configuration of the resources and/or activities that compose a service, a product, or the transformation process that creates and delivers them'. All operations managers are designers. When they purchase or rearrange the position of a piece of equipment, or when they change the way of working within a process, it is a design decision because it affects the physical shape and nature of their processes. This chapter examines the design of processes. Figure 5.1 shows where this chapter fits within the overall model of operations management.

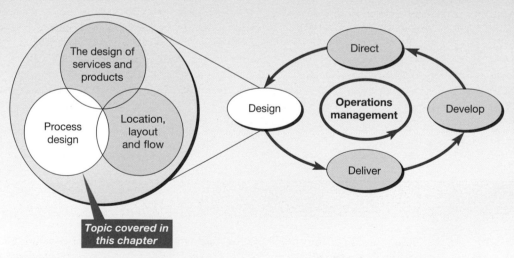

Figure 5.1 This chapter examines process design

Operations in practice Fast-food drive-throughs[1]

The quick-service restaurant (QSR) industry reckons that the very first drive-through dates back to 1928 when Royce Hailey first promoted the drive-through service at his Pig Stand restaurant in Los Angeles. Customers would simply drive by the back door of the restaurant where the chef would come out and deliver the restaurant's famous 'Barbequed Pig' sandwiches. Today, drive-through processes are slicker and faster. They are also more common. In 1975, McDonald's did not have any drive-throughs, but now more than 90 per cent of its US restaurants incorporate a drive-through process. In fact 80 per cent of recent fast-food growth has come through the growing number of drive-throughs. Says one industry specialist, *'There are a growing number of customers for whom fast-food is not fast enough. They want to cut waiting time to the very minimum without even getting out of their car. Meeting their needs depends on how smooth we can get the process.'*

The competition to design the fastest and most reliable drive-through process is fierce. Starbucks' drive-throughs have strategically placed cameras at the order boards so that servers can recognize regular customers and start making their order even before it's placed. Burger King has experimented with sophisticated sound systems, simpler menu boards and see-through food bags to ensure greater accuracy (no point in being fast if you don't deliver what the customer ordered). These details matter. McDonald's reckon that their sales increase one per cent for every six seconds saved at a drive-through, while a single Burger King restaurant calculated that its takings increased by 15,000 dollars a year each time it reduced queuing time by one second.

Source: Getty Images

Menu items must be easy to read and understand. Designing 'combo meals' (burger, fries and a cola), for example, saves time at the ordering stage. Perhaps the most remarkable experiment in making drive-through process times slicker is being carried out by McDonald's in the USA. On California's central coast 150 miles from Los Angeles, a call centre takes orders remotely from 40 McDonald's outlets around the country. The orders are then sent back to the restaurants through the Internet and the food is assembled only a few metres from where the order was placed. It may only save a few seconds on each order, but that can add up to extra sales at busy times of the day. However, not everyone is thrilled by the boom in drive-throughs. People living in the vicinity may complain of the extra traffic they attract and the unhealthy image of fast food combined with a process that does not even make customers get out of their car, is, for some, a step too far.

What is process design?

Design happens before creation

To 'design' is to conceive the looks, arrangement, and workings of something *before it is created*. In that sense it is a conceptual exercise. Yet it is one which must deliver a solution that will work in practice. Design is also an activity that can be approached at different levels of detail. One may envisage the general shape and intention of something before getting down to defining its details. This is certainly true for process design. At the start of the process design activity it is important to understand the design objectives, especially at first, when the overall shape and nature of the process is being decided. The most common way of doing this is by positioning it according to its volume and variety characteristics. Eventually the details of the process must be analysed to ensure that it fulfils its objectives effectively. Yet, it is often only through getting to grips with the detail of a design that the feasibility of its overall shape can be assessed. Don't think of this as a simple sequential process. There may be aspects concerned with the objectives or the broad positioning of the process that will need to be modified following its more detailed analysis.

What objectives should process design have?

The whole point of process design is to make sure that the performance of the process is appropriate for whatever it is trying to achieve. For example, if an operation competed primarily on its ability to respond quickly to customer requests, its processes would need to be designed to give fast throughput times. This would minimize the time between customers requesting a service or product and their receiving it. Similarly, if an operation competed on low price, cost-related objectives would dominate its process design. Some kind of logic should link what the operation as a whole is attempting to achieve and the **performance objectives** of its individual processes. This is illustrated in Table 5.1.

Process design should reflect process objectives

Operations performance objectives translate directly to process design objectives as shown in Table 5.1. As processes are managed at a very operational level, process design also needs to consider a more 'micro' and detailed set of objectives. These are largely concerned with flow through the process. When whatever are being 'processed' enter a process, they will progress through a series of activities where they are 'transformed' in some way. Between these activities they may dwell for some time in inventories, waiting to be transformed by the next activity. This means that the time that a unit spends in the process (its throughput time) will be longer than the sum of all the transforming activities that it passes through. Also the resources that perform the processes activities may not be used all the time because not all units will necessarily require the same activities and the capacity of each resource may not match the demand placed upon it. So neither the units moving through the process, nor the resources performing the activities may be fully utilized.

Table 5.1 The impact of strategic performance objectives on process design objectives and performance

Operations performance objective	Typical process design objectives	Some benefits of good process design
Quality	• Provide appropriate resources, capable of achieving the services or product specification • Error-free processing	• Products and services produced 'on-specification' • Less recycling and wasted effort within the process
Speed	• Minimum throughput time • Output rate appropriate for demand	• Short customer waiting time • Low in-process inventory
Dependability	• Provide dependable process resources • Reliable process output timing and volume	• On-time deliveries of products and services • Less disruption, confusion and rescheduling within the process
Flexibility	• Provide resources with an appropriate range of capabilities • Change easily between processing states (what, how, or how much is being processed)	• Ability to process a wide range of products and services • Low cost/fast product and service change • Low cost/fast volume and timing changes • Ability to cope with unexpected events (e.g. supply or a processing failure)

Cost	• Appropriate capacity to meet demand
	• Eliminate process waste in terms of
	  – excess capacity
	  – excess process capability
	  – in-process delays
	  – in-process errors
	  – inappropriate process inputs
		• Low processing costs
		• Low resource costs (capital costs)
		• Low delay and inventory costs (working capital costs)

Because of this the way that units leave the process is unlikely to be exactly the same as the way they arrive at the process. It is common for more 'micro' performance flow objectives to be used that describe process flow performance. For example:

Throughput rate

- **Throughput rate** (or flow rate) is the rate at which units emerge from the process, i.e. the number of units passing through the process per unit of time.

Throughput time

- **Throughput time** is the average elapsed time taken for inputs to move through the process and become outputs.

Work in process

- The number of units in the process (also called the '**work in process**' or in-process inventory), as an average over a period of time.

Utilization

- The **utilization** of process resources is the proportion of available time that the resources within the process are performing useful work.

Environmentally sensitive design

With the issues of environmental protection becoming more important, both process and service/product designers have to take account of 'green' issues. In many developed countries, legislation has already provided some basic standards which restrict the use of toxic materials, limit discharges to air and water, and protect employees and the public from immediate and long-term harm. Interest has focused on some fundamental issues:

Short case
Ecologically smart[2]

Source: Getty Images

When Daimler-Chrysler started to examine the feasibility of the Smart town car, the challenge was not just to examine the economic feasibility of the product but also to build in environmental sensitivity to the design of the product and the process that was to make it. This is why environmental protection is now a fundamental part of all production activities in its 'Smartville' plant at Hambach near France's border with Germany. The product itself is designed on environmentally compatible principles. Even before assembly starts, the product's disassembly must be considered. In fact the modular construction of the Smart car helps to guarantee economical dismantling at the end of its life. This also helps with the recycling of materials. Over 85 per cent of the Smart's components are recyclable and recycled material is used in its initial construction. For example, the Smart's instrument panel comprises 12 per cent recycled plastic material. Similarly, production processes are designed to be ecologically sustainable. The plant's environmentally friendly painting technique allows less paint to be used while maintaining a high quality of protection. It also involves no solvent emission and no hazardous waste, as well as the recycling of surplus material. It is not only the use of new technology that contributes to the plant's ecological credentials. Ensuring a smooth and efficient movement of materials within the plant also saves time, effort and, above all, energy. So, traffic flow outside and through the building has been optimized, buildings are made accessible to suppliers delivering to the plant, and conveyor systems are designed to be loaded equally in both directions so as to avoid empty runs. The company even claims that the buildings themselves are a model for ecological compatibility. No construction materials contain formaldehyde or CFCs and the outside of the buildings are lined with 'TRESPA', a raw material made from European timber that is quick to regenerate.

- *The sources of inputs* to a service or product. (Will they damage rainforests? Will they use up scarce minerals? Will they exploit the poor or use child labour?)
- *Quantities and sources of energy* consumed in the process. (Do plastic beverage bottles use more energy than glass ones? Should waste heat be recovered and used in fish farming?)
- *The amounts and type of waste material* that are created in the processes. (Can this waste be recycled efficiently, or must it be burnt or buried in landfill sites? Will the waste have a long-term impact on the environment as it decomposes and escapes?)
- *The life of the product itself.* It is argued that if a product has a useful life of, say, twenty years, it will consume fewer resources than one that only lasts five years, which must therefore be replaced four times in the same period. However, the long-life product may require more initial inputs, and may prove to be inefficient in the latter part of its use, when the latest products use less energy or maintenance to run.
- *The end-of-life of the product.* (Will the redundant product be difficult to dispose of in an environmentally friendly way? Could it be recycled or used as a source of energy? Could it still be useful in third-world conditions? Could it be used to benefit the environment, such as old cars being used to make artificial reefs for sea life?)

Designers are faced with complex trade-offs between these factors, although it is not always easy to obtain all the information that is needed to make the 'best' choices. For example, it is relatively straightforward to design a long-life product, using strong material, over-designed components, ample corrosion protection, and so on. However, its production might use more materials and energy and it could create more waste on disposal. To help make more rational decisions in the design activity, some industries are experimenting

Life cycle analysis with **life cycle analysis**. This technique analyses all the production inputs, the life-cycle use of the product and its final disposal, in terms of total energy used (and more recently, of all the emitted wastes such as carbon dioxide, sulphurous and nitrous gases, organic solvents, solid waste, etc.). The inputs and wastes are evaluated at *every* stage in its creation, beginning with the extraction or farming of the basic raw materials. The short case 'Ecologically smart' demonstrates that it is possible to include ecological considerations in all aspects of product and process design.

Process types – the volume–variety effect on process design

In Chapter 1 we saw how processes in operations can range from creating a very high volume of products or services (for example, a food canning factory) to a very low volume (for example, major project consulting engineers). Also they can range from producing a very low variety of products or services (for example, in an electricity utility) to a very high variety (as, for example, in an architects' practice). Usually the two dimensions of volume and variety go together. Low-volume operations processes often have a high variety of services and products, and high-volume operations processes often have a narrow variety of services and products. Thus there is a continuum from low volume and high variety through to high volume and low variety, on which we can position operations. Different operations, even those in the same operation, may adopt different types of processes. In a medical service, compare the approach taken during mass medical treatments, such as large-scale immunization programmes, with that taken for a transplant operation where the treatment is designed specifically to meet the needs of one person. These differences go well beyond their differing technologies or the processing requirements of their products or services. They are explained by the fact that no one type of process design is best for all types

Volume–variety positions of operation in all circumstances. The differences are because of the different **volume–variety positions** of the operations.

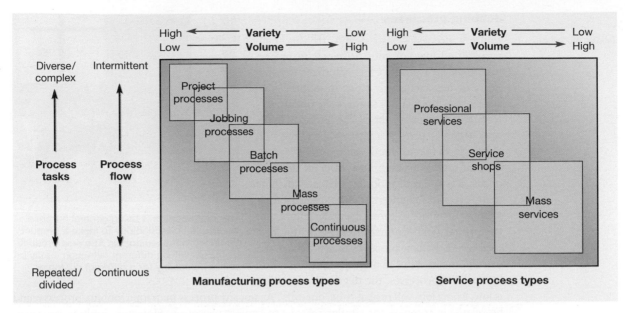

Figure 5.2 Different process types imply different volume–variety characteristics for the process

Process types

Process types

The position of a process on the volume–variety continuum shapes its overall design and the general approach to managing its activities. These 'general approaches' to designing and managing processes are called **process types**. Different terms are sometimes used to identify process types depending on whether they are predominantly manufacturing or service processes, and there is some variation in the terms used. For example, it is not uncommon to find the 'manufacturing' terms used in service industries. Figure 5.2 illustrates how these 'process types' are used to describe different positions on the volume–variety spectrum.

Project processes

Project processes

Project processes are those which deal with discrete, usually highly customized products. Often the timescale of making the product or service is relatively long, as is the interval between the completion of each product or service. So low volume and high variety are characteristics of project processes. The activities involved in making the product can be ill-defined and uncertain, sometimes changing during the production process itself. Examples of project processes include shipbuilding, most construction companies, movie production companies, large fabrication operations such as those manufacturing turbo generators, and installing a computer system. The essence of project processes is that each job has a well-defined start and finish, the time interval between starting

The major construction site shown in this picture is a project process. Each 'product' (project) is different and poses different challenges to those running the process (civil engineers).

different jobs is relatively long and the transforming resources which make the product will probably have been organized especially for each product. The process map for project processes will almost certainly be complex. This is partly because each unit of output is so large with many activities occurring at the same time and partly because the activities in such processes often involve significant discretion to act according to professional judgement.

Jobbing processes

Jobbing processes

Jobbing processes also deal with very high variety and low volumes. Whereas in project processes each product has resources devoted more or less exclusively to it, in jobbing processes each product has to share the operation's resources with many others. The resources of the operation will process a series of products but, although all the products will require the same kind of attention, each will differ in its exact needs. Examples of jobbing processes include many precision engineers such as specialist tool-makers, furniture restorers, bespoke tailors, and the printer who produces tickets for the local social event. Jobbing processes produce more and usually smaller items than project processes but, like project processes, the degree of repetition is low. Many jobs will probably be 'one-offs'. Again, any process map for a jobbing process could be relatively complex for similar reasons to project processes. However, jobbing processes usually produce physically smaller products and, although sometimes involving considerable skill, such processes often involve fewer unpredictable circumstances.

This craftsperson is using general purpose wood-cutting technology to make a product for an individual customer. The next product he makes will be different (although it may be similar), possibly for a different customer.

Source: Corbis

Batch processes

Batch processes

Batch processes can often look like jobbing processes, but batch does not have quite the degree of variety associated with jobbing. As the name implies, each time batch processes produce a product they produce more than one. So each part of the operation has periods when it is repeating itself, at least while the 'batch' is being processed. The size of the batch could be just two or three, in which case the batch process will differ little from jobbing, especially if each batch is a totally novel product. Conversely, if the batches are large, and especially if the products are familiar to the operation, batch processes can be fairly repetitive. Because of this, the batch type of process can be found over a wide range of volume and variety levels. Examples of batch processes include machine tool manufacturing, the production of some special gourmet frozen foods, and the manufacture of most of the component parts which go into mass-produced assemblies such as automobiles.

In this kitchen, food is being prepared in batches. All batches go through the same sequence (preparation, cooking, storing), but each batch is a different dish.

Source: Getty Images

Mass processes

Mass processes

Mass processes are those which produce goods in high volume and relatively narrow variety – narrow, that is, in terms of the fundamentals of the product design. An automobile plant, for example, might produce several thousand variants of car if every option of engine size, colour, extra equipment, etc. is taken into account. Yet essentially it is a mass operation because the different variants of its product do not affect

This automobile plant is everyone's idea of a mass process. Each product is almost (but not quite) the same, and is made in large quantities.

Source: Rex Features

the basic process of production. The activities in the automobile plant, like all mass operations, are essentially repetitive and largely predictable. Examples of mass processes include the automobile plant, a television factory, most food processes and DVD production. Several variants of a product could be produced on a mass process such as an assembly line, but the process itself is unaffected. The equipment used at each stage of the process can be designed to handle several different types of components loaded into the assembly equipment. So, provided the sequence of components in the equipment is synchronized with the sequence of models moving through the process, the process seems to be almost totally repetitive.

Continuous processes

Continuous processes

Continuous processes are one step beyond mass processes insomuch as they operate at even higher volume and often have even lower variety. They also usually operate for longer periods of time. Sometimes they are literally continuous in that their products are inseparable, being produced in an endless flow. Continuous processes are often associated with relatively inflexible, capital-intensive technologies with highly predictable flow. Examples of continuous processes include petrochemical refineries, electricity utilities, steel making and some paper making. There are often few elements of discretion in this type of process and although products may be stored during the process, the predominant characteristic of most continuous

This continuous water treatment process almost never stops (it only stops for maintenance) and performs a narrow range of tasks (filters impurities). Often we only notice the process if it goes wrong!

Source: Alamy Images

processes is of smooth flow from one part of the process to another. Inspections are likely to form part of the process, although the control applied as a consequence of those inspections is often automatic rather than requiring human discretion.

Professional services

Professional services

Professional services are defined as high-contact organizations where customers spend a considerable time in the service process. Such services provide high levels of customization, the service process being highly adaptable in order to meet individual customer needs. A great deal of staff time is spent in the front office and contact staff are given considerable discretion in servicing customers. Professional services tend to be people-based rather than equipment-based, with emphasis placed on the process (how the service is delivered) rather than the 'product' (what is delivered). Professional services include management consultants, lawyers' practices, architects, doctors' surgeries, auditors, health and safety inspectors and some computer field service operations. A typical example would be OEE, a consultancy that sells the problem-solving

Here consultants are preparing to start a consultancy assignment. They are discussing how they might approach the various stages of the assignment, from understanding the real nature of the problem through to the implementation of their recommended solutions. This is a process map, although a very high level one. It guides the nature and sequence of the consultants' activities.

expertise of its skilled staff to tackle clients' problems. Typically, the problem will first be discussed with clients and the boundaries of the project defined. Each 'product' is different, and a high proportion of work takes place at the client's premises, with frequent contact between consultants and the client.

Service shops

Service shops

Service shops are characterized by levels of customer contact, customization, volumes of customers and staff discretion, which position them between the extremes of professional and mass services (see next paragraph). Service is provided via mixes of front- and back-office activities. Service shops include banks, high-street shops, holiday tour operators, car rental companies, schools, most restaurants, hotels and travel agents. For example, an equipment hire and sales organization may have a range of products displayed in front-office outlets, while back-office operations look after purchasing and administration. The front-office staff have some technical training and can advise customers during the process of selling the product. Essentially the customer is buying a fairly standardized product but will be influenced by the process of the sale which is customized to the customer's individual needs.

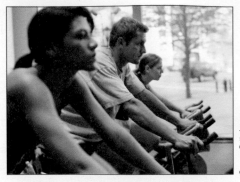

Source: Getty Images

The health club shown in the picture has front-office staff who can give advice on exercise programmes and other treatments. To maintain a dependable service the staff need to follow defined processes every day.

Mass services

Mass services

Mass services have many customer transactions, involving limited contact time and little customization. Such services may be equipment-based and 'product'-oriented, with most value added in the back office and relatively little judgement applied by front-office staff. Staff are likely to have a closely defined division of labour and to follow set procedures. Mass services include supermarkets, a national rail network, an airport, telecommunications services and libraries. For example, rail services such as SNCF in France all move a large number of passengers with a variety of rolling stock on an immense infrastructure of railways. Passengers pick a journey from the range offered. One of the most common types of mass service is the call centres used by almost all companies that deal directly with consumers. Coping with a very high volume of enquiries requires some kind of structuring of the process of communicating with customers. This is often achieved by using a carefully designed enquiry process (sometimes known as a 'script').

Source: © Royal Bank of Scotland Group plc

This is an account management centre for a large retail bank. It deals with thousands of customer requests every day. Although each customer request is different, they are all of the same type – involving customers' accounts.

Critical commentary

Although the idea of process types is useful insomuch as it reinforces the, sometimes important, distinctions between different types of process, it is in many ways simplistic. In reality there is no clear boundary between process types. For example, a specialist camera retailer would normally be categorized as a service shop, yet it also will give, sometimes very specialized, technical advice to customers. It is not a professional service like a consultancy of course, but it does have elements of a professional service process within its design. This is why the volume and variety characteristics of a process are sometimes seen as being a more realistic way of describing processes. The product–process matrix described next adopts this approach.

The product–process matrix

Product–process matrix

Making comparisons between different processes along a spectrum which goes, for example, from shipbuilding at one extreme to electricity generation at the other has limited value. No one grumbles that yachts are so much more expensive than electricity. The real point is that because the different process types overlap, organizations often have a choice of what type of process to employ. This choice will have consequences to the operation, especially in terms of its cost and flexibility. The classic representation of how cost and flexibility vary with process choice is the **product–process matrix** that comes from Professors Hayes and Wheelwright of Harvard University.[3] They represent process choices on a matrix with the volume–variety as one dimension, and process types as the other (our matrix has been updated to incorporate both product and service operations). Figure 5.3 shows their matrix adapted to fit with the terminology used here. Most operations stick to **the 'natural' diagonal** of the matrix, and few, if any, are found in the extreme corners of the matrix. However, because there is some overlap between the various process types, operations might be positioned slightly off the diagonal.

The 'natural' diagonal

The diagonal of the matrix shown in Figure 5.3 represents a 'natural' lowest cost position for an operation. Operations which are on the right of the 'natural' diagonal have processes which would normally be associated with lower volumes and higher variety. This means that their processes are likely to be more flexible than seems to be warranted by their actual volume–variety position. Put another way, they are not taking advantage of their ability to standardize their processes. Therefore, their costs are likely to be higher than they would be with a process that was closer to the diagonal. Conversely, operations that are on the left of the diagonal have adopted processes which would normally be used in a higher-volume and lower-variety situation. Their processes will therefore be 'over-standardized' and probably too inflexible for their volume–variety position. This lack of flexibility can also lead to high costs because the process will not be able to change from one activity to another as efficiently as a more flexible process.

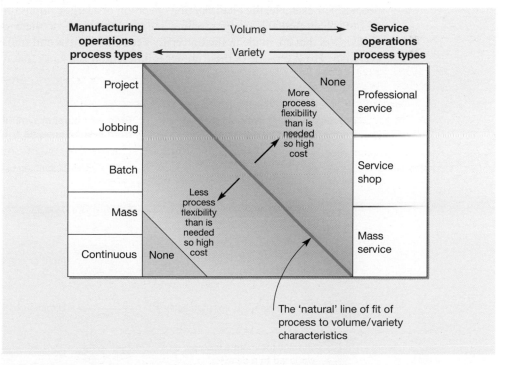

Figure 5.3 Deviating from the 'natural' diagonal on the product–process matrix has consequences for cost and flexibility

Source: Based on Hayes and Wheelwright[4]

Detailed process design

After the overall design of a process has been determined, its individual activities must be configured. At its simplest this detailed design of a process involves identifying all the individual activities that are needed to fulfil the objectives of the process and deciding on the sequence in which these activities are to be performed and who is going to do them. There will, of course, be some constraints on this. Some activities must be carried out before others and some activities can only be done by certain people or machines. Nevertheless, for a process of any reasonable size, the number of alternative process designs is usually large. This means that process design is often done using some simple visual approach such as **process** mapping.

Process mapping

Process mapping

Process mapping simply involves describing processes in terms of how the activities within the process relate to each other. There are many techniques which can be used for *process mapping* (or **process blueprinting**, or **process analysis**, as it is sometimes called). However, all the techniques identify the different *types of* activity that take place during the process and show the flow of materials or people or information through the process.

Process blueprinting
Process analysis

Process mapping symbols

Process mapping symbols

Process mapping symbols are used to classify different types of activity. And although there is no universal set of symbols used all over the world for any type of process, there are some that are commonly used. Most of these derive either from the early days of 'scientific' management around a century ago or, more recently, from information system flowcharting. Figure 5.4 shows the symbols we shall use here.

These symbols can be arranged in order, and in series or in parallel, to describe any process. For example, the retail catering operation of a large campus university has a number of outlets around the campus selling sandwiches. Most of these outlets sell 'standard' sandwiches that are made in the university's central kitchens and transported to each outlet every day. However, one of these outlets is different; it is a kiosk that makes more expensive

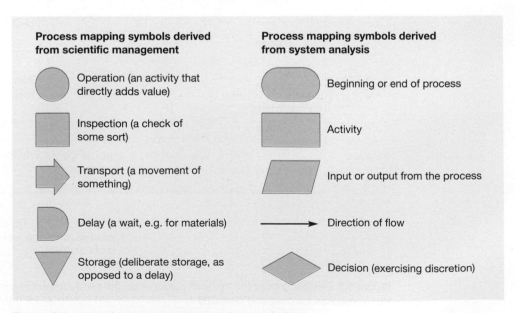

Figure 5.4 Some common process mapping symbols

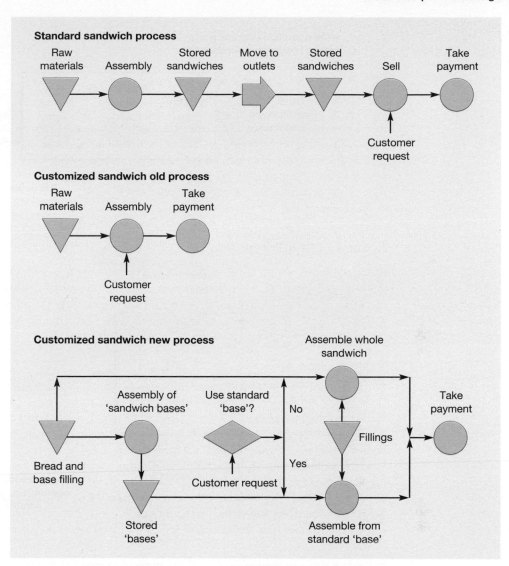

Figure 5.5 Process maps for three sandwich making and selling processes

'customized' sandwiches to order. Customers can specify the type of bread they want and choose from a very wide combination of different fillings. As queues for this customized service are becoming excessive, the catering manager is considering redesigning the process to speed it up. This new process design is based on the findings from a recent student study of the current process which proved that 95 per cent of all customers ordered only two types of bread (soft roll and Italian bread) and three types of protein filling (cheese, ham and chicken). Therefore the six 'sandwich bases' (2 types of bread × 3 protein fillings) could be prepared in advance and customized with salad, mayonnaise, etc. as customers ordered them. The process maps for making and selling the standard sandwiches, the current customized sandwiches and the new customized process are shown in Figure 5.5.

Note how the introduction of some degree of discretion in the new process makes it more complex to map at this detailed level. This is one reason why processes are often mapped at a more aggregated level, called **high-level process mapping**, before more detailed maps are drawn. Figure 5.6 illustrates this for the new customized sandwich operation. At the highest level the process can be drawn simply as an input–transformation–output process with sandwich materials and customers as its input resources and satisfied

High-level process mapping

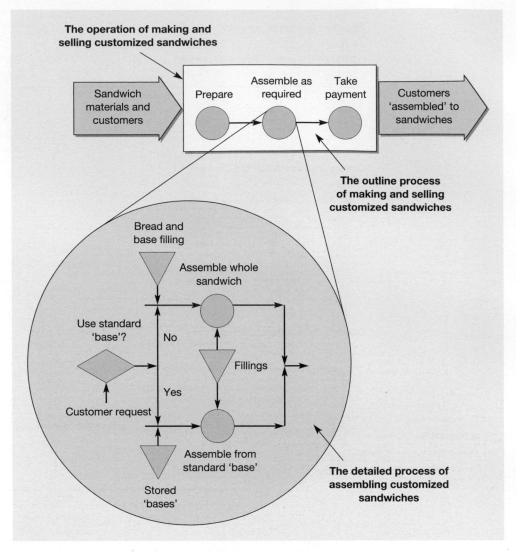

Figure 5.6 The new customized sandwich process mapped at three levels

Outline process map

customers with 'assembled' sandwiches as outputs. No details of how inputs are transformed into outputs are included. At a slightly lower, or more detailed level, what is sometimes called an **outline process map** (or chart) identifies the sequence of activities but only in a general way. So the activity of finding out what type of sandwich a customer wants, deciding if it can be assembled from a sandwich 'base' and then assembling it to meet the customer's request, is all contained in the general activity 'assemble as required'. At the more detailed level, all the activities are shown (we have shown the activities within 'assemble as required').

Using process maps to improve processes

One significant advantage of mapping processes is that each activity can be systematically challenged in an attempt to improve the process. For example, Figure 5.7 shows the flow process chart which Intel Corporation, the computer chip company, drew to describe its method of processing expense reports (claims forms). It also shows the process chart for the same process after critically examining and improving the process. The new process cut the number

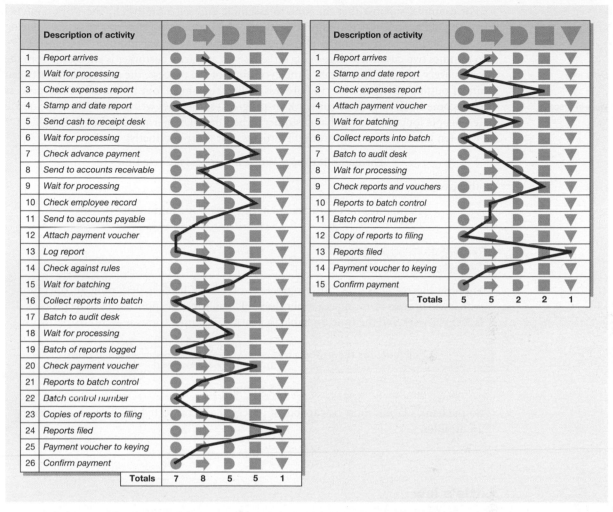

Figure 5.7 Flow process charts for processing expense reports at Intel before and after improving the process

of activities from 26 down to 15. The accounts payable's activities were combined with the cash-receipt's activities of checking employees' past expense accounts (activities 8, 10 and 11) which also eliminated activities 5 and 7. After consideration, it was decided to eliminate the activity of checking items against company rules, because it seemed '*more trouble than it was worth*'. Also, logging the batches was deemed unnecessary. All this combination and elimination of activities had the effect of removing several 'delays' from the process. The end-result was a much-simplified process which reduced the staff time needed to do the job by 28 per cent and considerably speeded up the whole process.

Throughput, cycle time and work-in-process

The new customized sandwich process has one indisputable advantage over the old process: it is faster in the sense that customers spend less time in the process. The additional benefit this brings is a reduction in cost per customer served (because more customers can be served without increasing resources). Note, however, that the total amount of work needed to make and sell a sandwich has not reduced. All the new process has done is to move some of the work to a less busy time. So the **work content** (the total amount of work required to produce a unit of output) has not changed but customer **throughput time** (the time for a unit to move through the process) has improved.

Work content
Throughput time

Cycle time

Work-in-process

For example, suppose that the time to assemble and sell a sandwich (the work content) using the old process was two minutes and that two people were staffing the process during the busy period. Each person could serve a customer every two minutes, therefore every two minutes two customers were being served, so on average a customer is emerging from the process every minute. This is called the **cycle time** of the process, the average time between units of output emerging from the process. When customers join the queue in the process they become **work-in-process** (or work-in-progress) sometimes written as WIP. If the queue is ten people long (including that customer) when the customer joins it, he or she will have to wait ten minutes to emerge from the process. Put more succinctly:

$$\text{Throughput time} = \text{Work-in-process} \times \text{Cycle time}$$

In this case,

$$10 \text{ minutes wait} = 10 \text{ people in the system} \times 1 \text{ minute per person}$$

Worked example

Suppose the regional back-office operation of a large bank is designing an operation which will process its mortgage applications. The number of applications to be processed is 160 per week and the time available to process the applications is 40 hours per week.

$$\text{Cycle time for the process} = \frac{\text{time available}}{\text{number to be processed}} = \frac{40}{160} = \frac{1}{4} \text{ hour}$$

$$= 15 \text{ minutes}$$

So the bank's layout must be capable of processing a completed application once every 15 minutes.

Little's law

Little's law

This mathematical relationship (throughput time = work-in-process × cycle time) is called **Little's law**. It is simple but very useful, and it works for any stable process. For example, suppose it is decided that, when the new process is introduced, the average number of customers in the process should be limited to around ten and the maximum time a customer is in the process should be on average four minutes. If the time to assemble and sell a sandwich (from customer request to the customer leaving the process) in the new process has reduced to 1.2 minutes, how many staff should be serving?

Putting this into Little's law:

$$\text{Throughput time} = 4 \text{ minutes}$$

and

$$\text{Work-in-progress, WIP} = 10$$

So, since

$$\text{Throughput time} = \text{WIP} \times \text{Cycle time}$$

$$\text{Cycle time} = \frac{\text{Throughput time}}{\text{WIP}}$$

$$\text{Cycle time for the process} = \frac{4}{10} = 0.4 \text{ minute}$$

That is, a customer should emerge from the process every 0.4 minute, on average.

Given that an individual can be served in 1.2 minutes,

$$\text{Number of servers required} = \frac{1.2}{0.4} = 3$$

In other words, three servers would serve three customers in 1.2 minutes. Or one customer in 0.4 minute.

Worked example

Mike was totally confident in his judgement, *'You'll never get them back in time'*, he said. *'They aren't just wasting time, the process won't allow them to all have their coffee and get back for 11 o'clock.'* Looking outside the lecture theatre, Mike and his colleague Silvia were watching the 20 business people who were attending the seminar queuing to be served coffee and biscuits. The time was 10.45 and Silvia knew that unless they were all back in the lecture theatre at 11 o'clock there was no hope of finishing his presentation before lunch. *'I'm not sure why you're so pessimistic'*, said Silvia. *'They seem to be interested in what I have to say and I think they will want to get back to hear how operations management will change their lives.'* Mike shook his head. *'I'm not questioning their motivation'*, he said, *'I'm questioning the ability of the process out there to get through them all in time. I have been timing how long it takes to serve the coffee and biscuits. Each coffee is being made fresh and the time between the server asking each customer what they want and them walking away with their coffee and biscuits is taking 48 seconds. Remember that, according to Little's law, throughput equals work-in-process multiplied by cycle time. If the work-in-process is the 20 managers in the queue and cycle time is 48 seconds, the total throughput time is going to be 20 multiplied by 0.8 minute which equals 16 minutes. Add to that sufficient time for the last person to drink their coffee and you must expect a total throughput time of a bit over 20 minutes. You just haven't allowed long enough for the process.'* Silvia was impressed. *'Err . . . what did you say that law was called again?'* *'Little's law'*, said Mike.

Worked example

Every year it was the same. All the workstations in the building had to be renovated (tested, new software installed, etc.) and there was only one week in which to do it. The one week fell in the middle of the August vacation period when the renovation process would cause minimum disruption to normal working. Last year the company's 500 workstations had all been renovated within one working week (40 hours). Each renovation last year took on average 2 hours and 25 technicians had completed the process within the week. This year there would be 530 workstations to renovate but the company's IT support unit had devised a faster testing and renovation routine that would only take on average $1^{1}/_{2}$ hours instead of 2 hours. How many technicians will be needed this year to complete the renovation processes within the week?

Last year:

$$\text{Work-in-progress (WIP)} = 500 \text{ workstations}$$
$$\text{Time available } (T_t) = 40 \text{ hours}$$
$$\text{Average time to renovate} = 2 \text{ hours}$$
$$\text{Therefore throughput rate } (T_r) = {}^{1}/_{2} \text{ hour per technician}$$
$$= 0.5N$$

where $N = \text{Number of technicians}$

Little's law:

$$\text{WIP} = T_t \times T_r$$
$$500 = 40 \times 0.5N$$
$$N = \frac{500}{40 \times 0.5}$$
$$= 25 \text{ technicians}$$

This year:

$$\text{Work-in-progress (WIP)} = 530 \text{ workstations}$$
$$\text{Time available} = 40 \text{ hours}$$
$$\text{Average time to renovate} = 1.5 \text{ hours}$$
$$\text{Throughput rate } (T_r) = 1/1.5 \text{ per technician}$$
$$= 0.67N$$

where
$$N = \text{Number of technicians}$$

Little's law:

$$\text{WIP} = T_t \times T_r$$
$$530 = 40 \times 0.67N$$
$$N = \frac{530}{40 \times 0.67}$$
$$= 19.88 \text{ technicians}$$
$$\approx 20 \text{ technicians}$$

Balancing and bottlenecks

Balancing

One of the most important design decisions in layout is that of **balancing**. Perfect balancing would mean that work content is allocated equally to each stage in the process. This is nearly always impossible to achieve in practice and some imbalance in the work allocation results. Inevitably this will increase the effective cycle time of the process. If it becomes greater than the required cycle time, it may be necessary to devote extra resources, in the shape of a further stage, to compensate for the imbalance. The effectiveness of the balancing activity is

Balancing loss

measured by **balancing loss**. This is the time wasted through the unequal allocation of work as a percentage of the total time invested in processing the product or service. The longest

Bottleneck

stage in the process is called a '**bottleneck**'. It will govern the flow of items through the whole process.

Worked example

In Figure 5.8 the work allocations in a four-stage process are illustrated. The total amount of time invested in creating each service or product is four times the cycle time because, for every unit produced, all four stages have been working for the cycle time. When the work is equally allocated between the stages, the total time invested in each service or product is $4 \times 2.5 = 10$ minutes. However, when work is unequally allocated, as illustrated, the time invested is $3.0 \times 4 = 12$ minutes, i.e. 2.0 minutes of time, 16.67 per cent of the total, is wasted.

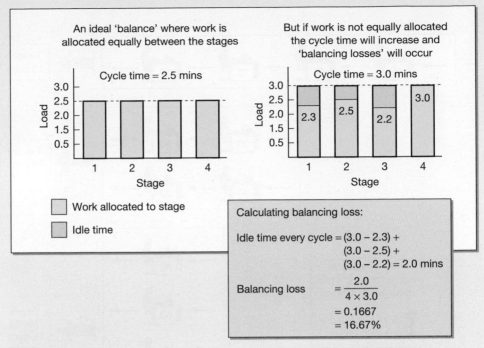

Figure 5.8 Balancing loss is that proportion of the time invested in processing the product or service which is not used productively

'Long thin' on 'short fat' processes

Return to the mortgage-processing process in the earlier worked example. It requires four stages working on the task to maintain a cycle time of one processed application every 15 minutes. The conventional arrangement of the four stages would be to lay them out in one line, each stage having 15 minutes' worth of work. However, nominally, the same output rate could also be achieved by arranging the four stages as two shorter lines, each of two stages with 30 minutes' worth of work each. Alternatively, following this logic to its ultimate conclusion, the stages could be arranged as four parallel stages, each responsible for the whole work content. Figure 5.9 shows these options.

This may be a simplified example, but it represents a genuine issue. Should the process be arranged as a single **long thin** line, as several **short fat** parallel lines, or somewhere in between? (Note that 'long' refers to the number of stages and 'fat' to the amount of work allocated to each stage.) In any particular situation there are usually technical constraints which limit either how 'long and thin' or how 'short and fat' the process can be, but there is usually a range of possible options within which a choice needs to be made.

The advantages of long thin processes include:

- *Controlled flow of materials or customers* – which is easy to manage.
- *Simple materials handling* – especially if a product being manufactured is heavy, large or difficult to move.
- *Lower capital requirements*. If a specialist piece of equipment is needed for one element in the job, only one piece of equipment would need to be purchased; on short fat arrangements every stage would need one.
- *More efficient operation*. If each stage is only performing a small part of the total job, the person at the stage will have a higher proportion of direct productive work as opposed to the non-productive parts of the job, such as picking up tools and materials.

Long thin

Short fat

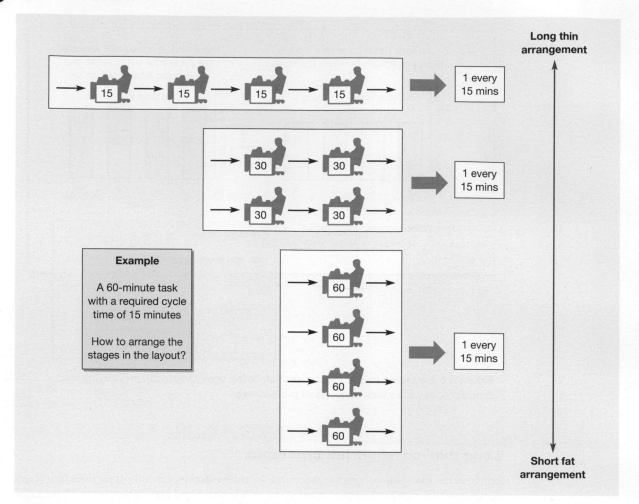

Figure 5.9 The arrangement of stages in product layout can be described on a spectrum from 'long thin' to 'short fat'

The advantages of the short fat processes include:

- *Higher mix flexibility*. If the layout needs to process several types of product or service, each stage or line could specialize in different types.
- *Higher volume flexibility*. As volume varies, stages can simply be closed down or started up as required; long thin processes would need rebalancing each time the cycle time changed.
- *Higher robustness*. If one stage breaks down or ceases operation in some way, the other parallel stages are unaffected; a long thin process would cease operating completely.
- *Less monotonous work*. In the mortgage example, the staff in the short fat arrangement are repeating their tasks only every hour; in the long thin arrangement it is every 15 minutes.

Throughput efficiency

This idea that the throughput time of a process is different from the work content of whatever it is processing has important implications. What it means is that for significant amounts of time no useful work is being done to the materials, information or customers that are progressing through the process. In the case of the simple example of the sandwich process described earlier, customer throughput time is restricted to 4 minutes, but the work content of the task (serving the customer) is only 1.2 minutes. So, the item being processed (the customer) is only being 'worked on' for 1.2/4 = 30 per cent of its time. This is called the **throughput efficiency** of the process.

Throughput efficiency

$$\text{Percentage throughput efficiency} = \frac{\text{Work content}}{\text{Throughput time}} \times 100$$

In this case the throughput efficiency is very high, relative to most processes, perhaps because the 'items' being processed are customers who react badly to waiting. In most material and information transforming processes, throughput efficiency is far lower, usually in single percentage figures.

Worked example

A vehicle licensing centre receives application documents, keys in details, checks the information provided on the application, classifies the application according to the type of licence required, confirms payment and then issues and mails the licence. It is currently processing an average of 5,000 licences every 8-hour day. A recent spot check found 15,000 applications that were 'in progress' or waiting to be processed. The sum of all activities that are required to process an application is 25 minutes. What is the throughput efficiency of the process?

$$\text{Work-in-progress} = 15,000 \text{ applications}$$

$$\text{Cycle time} =$$

$$\frac{\text{Time producing}}{\text{Number produced}} = \frac{8 \text{ hours}}{5,000} = \frac{480 \text{ minutes}}{5,000} = 0.096 \text{ minute}$$

From Little's law,

$$\text{Throughput time} = \text{WIP} \times \text{Cycle time}$$

$$\text{Throughput time} = 15,000 \times 0.096$$

$$= 1,440 \text{ minutes}$$

$$\text{Throughput efficiency} = \frac{\text{Work content}}{\text{Throughput time}} = \frac{25}{1,440} = 1.74 \text{ per cent}$$

Although the process is achieving a throughput time of 24 hours (which seems reasonable for this kind of process) the applications are only being worked on for 1.74 per cent of the time they are in the process.

Value-added throughput efficiency

The approach to calculating throughput efficiency that is described above assumes that all the 'work content' is actually needed. Yet we have already seen from the Intel expense report example that changing a process can significantly reduce the time that is needed to complete the task. Therefore, work content is actually dependent upon the methods and technology used to perform the task. It may be also that individual elements of a task may not be considered 'value-added'. In the Intel expense report example the new method eliminated some steps because they were 'not worth it', that is, they were not seen as adding value. So, **value-added throughput efficiency** restricts the concept of work content to only those tasks that are actually adding value to whatever is being processed. This often eliminates activities such as movement, delays and some inspections.

Value-added throughput efficiency

For example, if in the licensing worked example, of the 25 minutes of work content only 20 minutes were actually adding value, then

$$\text{Value-added throughput efficiency} = \frac{20}{1,440} = 1.39 \text{ per cent}$$

Workflow[5]

When the transformed resource in a process is information (or documents containing information), and when information technology is used to move, store and manage the information, process design is sometimes called 'workflow' or 'workflow management'. It is defined as 'the automation of procedures where documents, information or tasks are passed between participants according to a defined set of rules to achieve, or contribute to, an overall business goal'. Although workflow may be managed manually, it is almost always managed using an IT system. More specifically, workflow is concerned with the following:

- analysis, modelling, definition and subsequent operational implementation of business processes;
- the technology that supports the processes;
- the procedural (decision) rules that move information or documents through processes;
- defining the process in terms of the sequence of work activities, the human skills needed to perform each activity and the appropriate IT resources.

The effects of process variability

So far in our treatment of process design we have assumed that there is no significant variability either in the demand to which the process is expected to respond or in the time taken for the process to perform its various activities. Clearly, this is not the case in reality. So, it is important to take account of variability in process design.

Process variability

There are many reasons why **variability** occurs in processes. These can include: the late or early arrival of material, information or customers, a temporary malfunction or breakdown of process technology within a stage of the process, the recycling of 'mis-processed' materials, information or customers to an earlier stage in the process, and variation in the requirements of items being processed. All these sources of variation interact with each other, but result in two fundamental types of variability.

- Variability in the demand for processing at an individual stage within the process, usually expressed in terms of variation in the inter-arrival times of units to be processed.
- Variation in the time taken to perform the activities (i.e. process a unit) at each stage.

To understand the effect of arrival variability on process performance, it is first useful to examine what happens to process performance in a very simple process as arrival time changes under conditions of no variability. For example, the simple process shown in Figure 5.10 is composed of one stage that performs exactly 10 minutes of work. Units arrive at the process at a constant and predictable rate. If the arrival rate is one unit every 30 minutes, then the process will be utilized for only 33.33% of the time, and the units will never have to wait to be processed. This is shown as point A on Figure 5.10. If the arrival rate increases to one arrival every 20 minutes, the utilization increases to 50%, and again the units will not have to wait to be processed. This is point B on Figure 5.10. If the arrival rate increases to one arrival every 10 minutes, the process is now fully utilized, but, because a unit arrives just as the previous one has finished being processed, no unit has to wait. This is point C on Figure 5.10. However, if the arrival rate ever exceeded one unit every 10 minutes, the waiting line in front of the process activity would build up indefinitely, as is shown as point D in Figure 5.10. So, in a perfectly constant and predictable world, the relationship between process waiting time and utilization is a rectangular function as shown by the red dotted line in Figure 5.10.

However, when arrival and process times are variable, then sometimes the process will have units waiting to be processed, while at other times the process will be idle, waiting for units to arrive. Therefore the process will have both a 'non-zero' average queue and be under-utilized in the same period. So, a more realistic point is that shown as point X in Figure 5.10. If the average arrival time were to be changed with the same variability, the blue *The relationship between average waiting time and process utilization is a particularly important one* line in Figure 5.10 would show **the relationship between average waiting time and process utilization**. As the process moves closer to 100% utilization the higher the average waiting time will become. To put it another way, the only way to guarantee very low waiting times for the units is to suffer low process utilization.

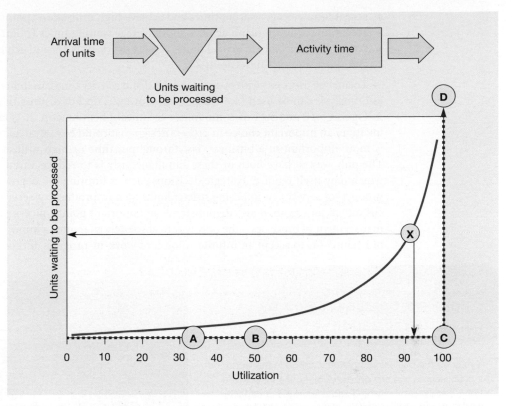

Figure 5.10 The relationship between process utilization and number of units waiting to be processed for constant, and variable, arrival and process times

The greater the variability in the process, the more the waiting time utilization deviates from the simple rectangular function of the 'no variability' conditions that was shown in Figure 5.10. A set of curves for a typical process is shown in Figure 5.11(a). This phenomenon has important implications for the design of processes. In effect it presents three options to process designers wishing to improve the waiting time or utilization performance of their processes, as shown in Figure 5.11(b):

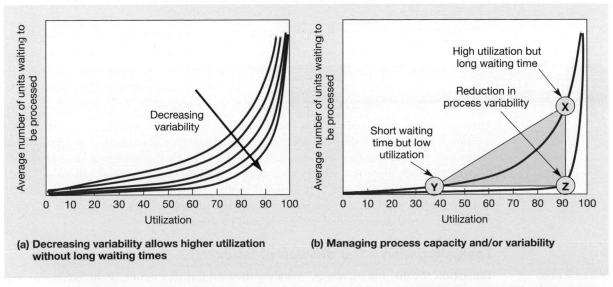

Figure 5.11 The relationship between process utilization and number of units waiting to be processed for variable arrival and activity times

- accept long average waiting times and achieve high utilization (point X);
- accept low utilization and achieve short average waiting times (point Y); or
- reduce the variability in arrival times, activity times, or both, and achieve higher utilization and short waiting times (point Z).

To analyse processes with both inter-arrival and activity time variability, queuing or 'waiting line' analysis can be used (see Chapter 8). However, do not dismiss the relationship shown in Figures 5.10 and 5.11 as some minor technical phenomenon. It is far more than this. It identifies an important choice in process design that could have strategic implications. Which is more important to a business, fast throughput time or high utilization of its resources? The only way to have both of these simultaneously is to reduce variability in its processes, which may itself require strategic decisions such as limiting the degree of customization of products or services, or imposing stricter limits on how products or services can be delivered to customers, and so on. It also demonstrates an important point concerned with the day-to-day management of processes – the only way to absolutely guarantee a hundred per cent utilization of resources is to accept an infinite amount of work-in-progress and/or waiting time.

Short case
Heathrow delays caused by capacity utilization[6]

Source: Alamy Images

It may be the busiest international airport in the world, but it is unlikely to win any prizes for being the most loved. Long delays, overcrowding and a shortage of capacity has meant that Heathrow is often a cause of frustration to harassed passengers. Yet to the airlines it is an attractive hub. Its size and location give it powerful 'network effects'. This means that it can match incoming passengers with outgoing flights to hundreds of different cities. Actually it is its attractiveness to the airlines that is one of its main problems. Heathrow's runways are in such demand that they are almost always operating at, or close to, their maximum capacity. In fact, its runways operate at 99% of capacity. This compares with about 70% at most other large airports. This means that the slightest variability (bad weather or an unscheduled landing such as a plane having to turn back with engine trouble) causes delays, which in turn cause more delays. (See Figure 5.11 for the theoretical explanation of this effect.) The result is that 33% of all flights at Heathrow are delayed by at least 15 minutes. This is poor when compared with other large European airports such as Amsterdam and Frankfurt, which have 21% and 24% of flights delayed respectively.

Human implications for process design

Although we are here dealing with the human implications of process design as the last topic of this chapter, this does not mean that it should be seen as secondary, or unimportant in any way. On the contrary, it is regarded by many as by far the dominant issue of process design. However, there is a whole other field of study – organizational behaviour – that specialises in these issues. Yet, it is included in this chapter in recognition that operations managers are, in practice, the ones who have a significant influence on how people's reactions to their jobs are accommodated in the design of processes.

Task allocation – the division of labour

Division of labour

The idea of the **division of labour** – dividing the total task down into smaller parts, was first formalized as a concept by the economist Adam Smith in his *Wealth of Nations* in 1746.

Perhaps the epitome of the division of labour is the assembly line, where products move along a single path and are built up by operators continually repeating a single task. This is the predominant model of job design in most mass-produced products and in some mass-produced services (fast food, for example). There are some *real advantages* in division of labour:

- *It promotes faster learning.* It is obviously easier to learn how to do a relatively short and simple task than a long and complex one.
- *Automation becomes easier.* Dividing a total task into small parts raises the possibility of automating some of those small tasks.
- *Reduced non-productive work.* This is probably the most important benefit of division of labour. In large, complex tasks the proportion of time spent picking up tools and materials, putting them down again and generally finding, positioning and searching can be very high indeed (called non-productive elements of work). But in shorter, divided, tasks non-productive work can be considerably reduced, which would be very significant to the costs of the operation.

There are also serious drawbacks to highly divided jobs:

- *Monotony.* The shorter the task, the more often operators will need to repeat it. Repeating the same task, for example every 30 seconds, eight hours a day and five days a week, can hardly be called a fulfilling job. As well as any ethical objections, there are other, more obviously practical objections. These include the increased likelihood of absenteeism and staff turnover and the increased likelihood of error.
- *Physical injury.* The continued repetition of a very narrow range of movements can, in extreme cases, lead to physical injury. The over-use of some parts of the body (especially the arms, hands and wrists) can result in pain and a reduction in physical capability. This is sometimes called repetitive strain injury (RSI).
- *Low flexibility.* Dividing a task up into many small parts often gives the job design a rigidity which is difficult to change under changing circumstances.
- *Poor robustness.* Highly divided jobs imply customers, materials or information passing between several stages. If one of these stages is not working correctly, for example because some equipment is faulty, the whole operation is affected.

Scientific management

Scientific management

Related to the division of labour are the ideas of 'scientific' management. The term **scientific management** became established in 1911 with the publication of the book of the same name by Fredrick Taylor (this whole approach to job design is sometimes referred to, pejoratively, as **Taylorism**). In this work he identified what he saw as the basic tenets of scientific management:[7]

Taylorism

- All aspects of work should be investigated on a scientific basis to establish the laws, rules and formulae governing the best methods of working.
- Such an investigative approach to the study of work is necessary to establish what constitutes a 'fair day's work'.
- Workers should be selected, trained and developed methodically to perform their tasks.
- Managers should act as the planners of the work (analysing jobs and standardizing the best method of doing the job) while workers should be responsible for carrying out the jobs to the standards laid down.
- Cooperation should be achieved between management and workers based on the 'maximum prosperity' of both.

The important thing to remember about scientific management is that it is not 'scientific' as such, although it certainly does take an 'investigative' approach to improving operations. Perhaps a better term for it would be 'systematic management'. It gave birth to two separate, but related, fields of study, **method study**, which determines the methods and activities to be included in jobs, and **work measurement**, which is concerned with measuring the time that should be taken for performing jobs. Together, these two fields are often referred to as **work study**.

Method study
Work measurement
Work study

Critical commentary

Even in 1915, criticisms of the scientific management approach were being voiced.[8] In a submission to the United States Commission on Industrial Relations, scientific management is described as:

- being in 'spirit and essence a cunningly devised speeding up and sweating system';
- intensifying the 'modern tendency towards specialization of the work and the task';
- condemning 'the worker to a monotonous routine';
- putting 'into the hands of employers an immense mass of information and methods that may be used unscrupulously to the detriment of workers';
- tending to 'transfer to the management all the traditional knowledge, the judgement and skills of workers';
- greatly intensifying 'unnecessary managerial dictation and discipline';
- tending to 'emphasize quantity of product at the expense of quality'.

Designing the human interface – ergonomic workplace design

Ergonomics

Human factors engineering

Ergonomics is concerned primarily with the physiological aspects of job design. Physiology is about the way the body functions. It involves two aspects: firstly, how a person interfaces with his or her immediate working area; secondly, how people react to environmental conditions. Ergonomics is sometimes referred to as **human factors engineering** or just 'human factors'. Both aspects are linked by two common ideas:

- There must be a fit between people and the jobs they do. To achieve this fit there are only two alternatives. Either the job can be made to fit the people who are doing it, or, alternatively, the people can be made (or perhaps less radically, recruited) to fit the job. Ergonomics addresses the former alternative.
- It is important to take a 'scientific' approach to job design, for example collecting data to indicate how people react under different job design conditions and trying to find the best set of conditions for comfort and performance.

We will explain further some of the aspects of ergonomics in Chapter 6.

Job commitment – behavioural approaches to job design

Behavioural approach

Processes which are designed purely on division of labour, scientific management or even purely ergonomic principles can alienate the people performing them. Process design should also take into account the desire of individuals to fulfil their needs for self-esteem and personal development. This is where motivation theory and its contribution to the **behavioural approach** to process design is important. This achieves two important objectives. Firstly, it provides jobs which have an intrinsically higher quality of working life – an ethically desirable end in itself. Secondly, because of the higher levels of motivation it engenders, it is instrumental in achieving better performance for the operation, in terms of both the quality and the quantity of output.[9] This approach to job design involves two conceptual steps: firstly, exploring how the various characteristics of the job affect people's motivation; secondly, exploring how individuals' motivation towards the job affects their performance at that job.

Some of the job characteristics that are held to have a positive effect on job satisfaction are as follows.

Job rotation

Job rotation

If increasing the number of related tasks in the job is constrained in some way, for example by the technology of the process, one approach may be to encourage **job rotation**. This means moving individuals periodically between different sets of tasks to provide some variety in their activities. When successful, job rotation can increase skill flexibility and make a small contribution to reducing monotony. However, it is not viewed as universally beneficial either by management (because it can disrupt the smooth flow of work) or by the people performing the jobs (because it can interfere with their rhythm of work).

Job enlargement

Job enlargement

The most obvious method of achieving at least some of the objectives of behavioural job design is by allocating a larger number of tasks to individuals. If these extra tasks are broadly of the same type as those in the original job, the change is called **job enlargement**. This may not involve more demanding or fulfilling tasks, but it may provide a more complete and therefore slightly more meaningful job. If nothing else, people performing an enlarged job will not repeat themselves as often, which could make the job less monotonous.

Job enrichment

Job enrichment

Job enrichment, not only means increasing the number of tasks, but also allocating extra tasks which involve more decision making, greater autonomy and greater control over the job. For example, the extra tasks could include maintenance, planning and control, or monitoring quality levels. The effect is both to reduce repetition in the job and to increase autonomy and personal development. So, in the assembly-line example, each operator, as well as being allocated a job which is twice as long as that previously performed could also be allocated responsibility for carrying out routine maintenance and such tasks as record-keeping and managing the supply of materials.

Empowerment

Empowerment

Empowerment is usually taken to mean more than simple autonomy. Whereas autonomy means giving staff the *ability* to change how they do their jobs, empowerment means giving staff the *authority* to make changes to the job itself, as well as how it is performed. This can be designed into jobs to different degrees.[10] At a minimum, staff could be asked to contribute their suggestions for how the operation might be improved. Going further, staff could be empowered to redesign their jobs. Further still, staff could be included in the strategic direction and performance of the whole organization. The *benefits* of empowerment are generally seen as providing fast responses to customer needs, employees who feel better about their jobs and who will interact with customers with more enthusiasm, promoting 'word-of-mouth' advertising and customer retention. However, there are *costs* associated with empowerment, including higher selection and training costs, perceived inequity of service and the possibility of poor decisions being made by employees.

Team-working

Team-based work organization

A development in job design which is closely linked to the empowerment concept is that of **team-based work organization** (sometimes called self-managed work teams). This is where staff, often with overlapping skills, collectively perform a defined task and have a high degree of discretion over how they actually perform the task. The team would typically control such things as task allocation between members, scheduling work, quality measurement and improvement, and sometimes the hiring of staff. To some extent most work has always been a group-based activity. The concept of teamwork, however, is more prescriptive and assumes a shared set of

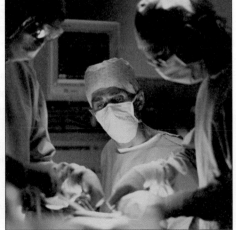

Source: Getty Images

objectives and responsibilities. Groups are described as teams when the virtues of working together are being emphasized, such as the ability to make use of the various skills within the team. Teams may also be used to compensate for other organizational changes such as the move towards flatter organizational structures. When organizations have fewer managerial levels, each manager will have a wider span of activities to control. Teams which are capable of autonomous decision-making have a clear advantage in these circumstances.

Summary answers to key questions

Check and improve your understanding of this chapter using self-assessment questions and a personalized study plan, audio and video downloads, and an eBook – all at **www.myomlab.com.**

➤ What is process design?

■ Process design is the activity which shapes the physical form and purpose of the processes that create and deliver services and products.

■ The overall purpose of process design is to meet the needs of customers through achieving appropriate levels of quality, speed, dependability, flexibility and cost.

■ The design activity must also take account of environmental issues. These include examination of the source and suitability of materials, the sources and quantities of energy consumed, the amount and type of waste material, the life of the product itself, and the end-of-life state of the product.

➤ How do volume and variety affect process design?

■ The overall nature of any process is strongly influenced by the volume and variety of what it has to process.

■ The concept of process types summarizes how volume and variety affect overall process design.

■ In manufacturing, these process types are (in order of increasing volume and decreasing variety) project, jobbing, batch, mass and continuous processes. In service operations, the terms often used (again in order of increasing volume and decreasing variety) are professional services, service shops and mass services.

➤ How are processes designed in detail?

■ Processes are designed initially by breaking them down into their individual activities. Often common symbols are used to represent types of activity. The sequence of activities in a process is then indicated by the sequence of symbols representing activities. This is called 'process mapping'. Alternative process designs can be compared using process maps and improved processes considered in terms of their operations performance objectives.

■ Process performance in terms of throughput time, work-in-progress, and cycle time are related by a formula known as Little's law: throughput time equals work-in-progress multiplied by cycle time.

■ Variability has a significant effect on the performance of processes, particularly the relationship between waiting time and utilization.

➤ What are the human implications for process design?

■ There are many ideas (and a whole field of study – organizational behaviour) that should be taken into account when designing processes. These include the division of labour, ergonomics and more behavioural approaches such as job rotation, job enlargement, job enrichment, empowerment and team-working.

Learning exercises

These problems and applications will help to improve your analysis of operations. You can find more practice problems as well as worked examples and guided solutions on MyOMLab at www.myomlab.com.

1 Read again the description of fast-food drive-through processes at the beginning of this chapter. (a) Draw a process map that reflects the types of process described. (b) What advantage do you think is given to McDonald's through its decision to establish a call centre for remote order-taking for some of its outlets?

2 A regional government office that deals with passport applications is designing a process that will check applications and issue the documents. The number of applications to be processed is 1,600 per week and the time available to process the applications is 40 hours per week. What is the required cycle time for the process?

3 For the passport office, described above, the total work content of all the activities that make up the total task of checking, processing and issuing a passport is, on average, 30 minutes. How many people will be needed to meet demand?

4 The same passport office has a 'clear desk' policy that means that all desks must be clear of work by the end of the day. How many applications should be loaded onto the process in the morning in order to ensure that every one is completed and desks are clear by the end of the day? (Assume a 7.5-hour (450-minute) working day.)

Want to know more?

Chopra, S., Anupindi, R., Deshmukh, S.D., Van Mieghem, J.A. and Zemel, E. (2006) *Managing Business Process Flows*, Prentice-Hall, Englewood Cliffs, NJ. An excellent, although mathematical, approach to process design in general.

Hammer, M. (1990) Reengineering work: don't automate, obliterate, *Harvard Business Review*, July–August. This is the paper that launched the whole idea of business processes and process management in general to a wider managerial audience. Slightly dated but worth reading.

Hopp, W.J. and Spearman, M.L. (2001) *Factory Physics*, 2nd edn, McGraw-Hill, New York. Very technical so don't bother with it if you aren't prepared to get into the maths. However, there is some fascinating analysis, especially concerning Little's law.

Smith, H. and Fingar, P. (2003) *Business Process Management: The Third Wave*, Meghan-Kiffer Press, Tampa, Fl. A popular book on process management from a business process re-engineering perspective.

Useful websites

www.bpmi.org Site of the Business Process Management Initiative. Some good resources including papers and articles.

www.bptrends.com News site for trends in business process management generally. Some interesting articles.

www.bls.gov/oes/ US Department of Labor employment statistics.

www.fedee.com Federation of European Employers guide to employment and job trends in Europe.

www.iienet.org The Global Association of Productivity and Efficiency Professionals site. This is an important professional body for process design and related topics.

www.opsman.org Lots of useful stuff.

www.waria.com A Workflow and Reengineering Association web site. Some useful topics.

Now that you have finished reading this chapter, why not visit MyOMLab at www.myomlab.com where you'll find more learning resources to help you make the most of your studies and get a better grade.

Chapter 6

Location, layout and flow

Introduction

This chapter is about where you put things or, more formally, how operations resources are positioned relative to each other. We shall examine this positioning at three levels from macro to micro. Firstly, we look at how operations locate their sites geographically. Secondly (and this constitutes the majority of the chapter), we look at the layout of resources within operations and processes. Finally, we briefly examine how equipment is positioned within individuals' work areas. This positioning decision is important because it determines the way transformed resources flow through supply networks, operations and processes. Relatively small changes in the position of products in a supermarket, or changing rooms in a sports centre, or the position of a machine in a factory, can affect the flow through the operation which, in turn, affects the costs and general effectiveness of the operation. Figure 6.1 shows where this chapter fits into the overall operations model.

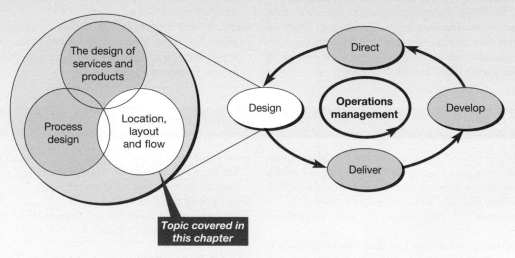

Figure 6.1 This chapter examines location, layout and flow

 *Check and improve your understanding of this chapter using self-assessment questions and a personalized study plan, audio and video downloads, and an eBook – all at* **www.myomlab.com**.

Operations in practice Tesco's store flow processes[1]

Finding, purchasing and developing the sites for its retail stores is a major (and controversial) part of Tesco's activities. In its UK market, the main issue is obtaining permission from local government authorities. The UK's planning regime, once relatively relaxed to encourage retail development and stimulate economic growth, is now far stricter, more complicated and takes longer. Frequently there are local objections to supermarket development. Some are from smaller retailers who fear loss of business, some are from residents wary of traffic congestion, and some from people who dislike the dominance of firms like Tesco. To go through all this effort, Tesco must be convinced that any potential location represents a sound business investment. Location (or, more accurately, layout) within their stores is equally important.

Source: Alamy Images

Successful supermarkets like Tesco also know that the design of their stores has a huge impact on profitability. They must maximize their revenue per square metre and minimize the costs of operating the store, while keeping customers happy. At a basic level, supermarkets have to get the amount of space allocated to the different areas right. Tesco's 'One in front' campaign, for example, tries to avoid long waiting times by opening additional tills if more than one customer is waiting at a checkout. Tesco also uses technology to understand exactly how customers flow through their stores. The 'Smartlane' system from Irisys, a specialist in intelligent infrared technologies, counts the number and type of customers entering the store (in family or other groups known as 'shopping units'), tracks their movement using infrared sensors, and predicts the likely demand at the checkouts up to an hour in advance. The circulation of customers through the store must be right and the right layout can make customers buy more. Some supermarkets put their entrance on the left-hand side of a building with a layout designed to take customers in a clockwise direction around the store. Aisles are made wide to ensure a relatively slow flow of trolleys so that customers pay more attention to the products on display (and buy more). However, wide aisles can come at the expense of reduced shelf space that would allow a wider range of products to be stocked.

The actual location of all the products is a critical decision, directly affecting the convenience to customers, their level of spontaneous purchase and the cost of filling the shelves. Although the majority of supermarket sales are packaged, tinned or frozen goods, the displays of fruit and vegetables are usually located adjacent to the main entrance, as a signal of freshness and wholesomeness, providing an attractive and welcoming point of entry. Basic products that figure on most people's shopping lists, such as flour, sugar and bread, may be located at the back of the store and apart from each other so that customers have to pass higher-margin items as they search. High-margin items are usually put at eye level on shelves (where they are more likely to be seen) and low-margin products lower down or higher up. Some customers also go a few paces up an aisle before they start looking for what they need. Some supermarkets call the shelves occupying the first metre of an aisle 'dead space' – not a place to put impulse-bought goods. The prime site in a supermarket is the 'gondola-end', the shelves at the end of the aisle. Moving products to this location can increase sales 200 or 300 per cent. It's not surprising that suppliers are willing to pay for their products to be located here. The supermarkets themselves are keen to point out that, although they obviously lay out their stores with customers' buying behaviour in mind, it is counterproductive to be too manipulative. Some commonly held beliefs about supermarket layout are not always true. They deny that they periodically change the location of foodstuffs in order to jolt customers out of their habitual shopping patterns so that they are more attentive to other products and end up buying more. Occasionally layouts are changed, they say mainly to accommodate changing tastes and new ranges. At a more micro-level, Tesco will be concerned to make its checkout areas safe and convenient for its staff and customers. Similarly the design of self checkout equipment must be conveniently designed. So positioning, whether it is location, store layout, or workstation design, will have an impact on Tesco's performance.

The location of operations

It was reputedly Lord Sieff, one-time boss of Marks and Spencer, the UK-based retail organization, who said, '*There are three important things in retailing – location, location and location*', and any retailing operation knows exactly what he meant. Get the location wrong and it can have a significant impact on profits. For example, mislocating a fire service station can slow down the average journey time of the fire crews in getting to the fires; locating a factory where there is difficulty attracting labour with appropriate skills will affect the effectiveness of the factory's operations. Location decisions will usually have an effect on an operation's costs as well as its ability to serve its customers (and therefore its revenues). Also, location decisions, once taken, are difficult to undo. The costs of moving an operation can be hugely expensive and the risks of inconveniencing customers very high. No operation wants to move very often.

Reasons for location decisions

Whilst the location of some operations is largely historical, they are implicitly making a decision not to move. Presumably their assumption is that the cost and disruption involved in changing location would outweigh any potential benefits of a new location. Two stimuli often cause organizations to change locations: changes in demand for their services and products, and changes in supply of their inputs.

Changes in demand. A change in location may be prompted by customer demand shifting. For example, as garment manufacturers moved from Europe to Asia, suppliers of zips, threads, etc. started to follow them. Changes in the volume of demand can also prompt relocation. To meet higher demand, an operation could expand its existing site, choose a larger site in another location, or keep its existing location and find a second location for an additional operation; the last two options will involve a location decision. High-visibility operations may not have the choice of expanding on the same site to meet rising demand. A dry cleaning service may attract only marginally more business by expanding an existing site because it offers a local, and therefore convenient, service. Finding a new location for an additional operation is probably its only option for expansion.

Changes in supply. The other stimulus for relocation is changes in the cost or availability of supply of inputs to the operation. For example, a mining or oil company will need to relocate as the minerals it is extracting become depleted. A manufacturing company might choose to relocate its operations to a part of the world where labour costs are low, because the equivalent resources (people) in its original location have become relatively expensive. Sometimes a business might choose to relocate to release funds if the value of the land it occupies is worth more than an alternative, equally good, location.

The objectives of the location decision

The aim of the location decision is to achieve an appropriate balance between three related objectives:

Spatially variable costs
- the **spatially variable costs** of the operation (spatially variable means that something changes with geographical location);
- the service the operation is able to provide to its customers;
- the revenue potential of the operation.

In for-profit organizations the last two objectives are related. The assumption is that the better the service the operation can provide to its customers, the better will be its potential to attract custom and therefore generate revenue. In not-for-profit organizations, revenue

Short case
The Tata Nano finds a new home[2]

Source: Getty Images

Finding a suitable site for any operation can be a political as well as an economic problem. It certainly was when Tata, the Indian company, unveiled its plans for the Nano in 2007. Named the '1 lakh car' (in India one lakh means 100,000), it would be the cheapest car in the world, with the basic model priced at 100,000 rupees, or $2,500, excluding taxes. The price was about half of existing low-cost cars. The site chosen by Tata was equally bold. It was to be made at Singur, in the Indian state of West Bengal, a populous state with Calcutta (now called Kolkata) as its capital. Although the Communist Party had ruled the state for four decades, the West Bengal government was keen to encourage the Nano plant. It would bring much-needed jobs and send a message that the state welcomed inward investment. In fact, it had won the plant against stiff competition from rival states.

Controversially, the state government had expropriated land for the factory using an old law dating from 1894, which requires private owners to sell land for a 'public purpose'. The government justified this action by pointing out that over 13,000 people had some kind of claim to parts of the land required for the new plant. Tata could not be expected to negotiate, one by one, with all of them. Also financial compensation was offered at

significantly above market rates. Unfortunately about 2,250 people refused to accept the offered compensation. The political opposition organized mass protests in support of the farmers who did not want to move. They blocked roads, threatened staff and even assaulted an employee of a Tata supplier. In response, Ratan Tata, chairman of the Tata group, threatened to move the Nano plant from the state if the company really was not wanted, even though the company had already invested 15 billion rupees in the project. Eventually, exasperated with being caught in the 'political crossfire', Tata said it would abandon its factory in the state. Instead, the company selected a location in Gujarat, one of India's most industrialized states, which quickly approved even more land than the West Bengal site.

potential might not be a relevant objective and so cost and customer service are often taken as the twin objectives of location. In making decisions about where to locate an operation, operations managers are concerned with minimizing spatially variable costs and maximizing revenue and customer service. Location affects both of these but not equally for all types of operation. For example, with most products, customers may not care very much where they were made. Location is unlikely to affect the operation's revenues significantly. However, the costs of the operation will probably be very greatly affected by location. Services, on the other hand, often have both costs and revenues affected by location. The location decision for any operation is determined by the relative strength of supply-side and demand-side factors (see Figure 6.2).

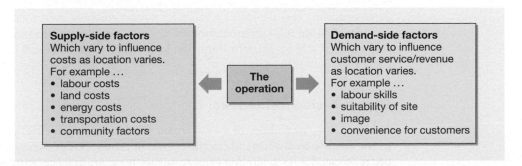

Figure 6.2 Supply-side and demand-side factors in location decisions

Supply-side influences

Labour costs. The costs of employing people with particular skills can vary between different areas in any country, but are likely to be more significant when international comparisons are made. Labour costs can be expressed in two ways. The 'hourly cost' is what firms have to pay workers on average per hour. However, the 'unit cost' is an indication of the labour cost per unit of production. This includes the effects both of productivity differences between countries and of differing currency exchange rates. Exchange rate variation can cause unit costs to change dramatically over time. Yet, labour costs exert a major influence on the location decision, especially in some industries such as clothing, where labour costs as a proportion of total costs are relatively high.

Land costs. The cost of acquiring the site itself is sometimes a relevant factor in choosing a location. Land and rental costs vary between countries and cities. At a more local level, land costs are also important. A retail operation, when choosing 'high-street' sites, will pay a particular level of rent only if it believes it can generate a certain level of revenue from the site.

Energy costs. Operations which use large amounts of energy, such as aluminium smelters, can be influenced in their location decisions by the availability of relatively inexpensive energy. This may be direct, as in the availability of hydroelectric generation in an area, or indirect, such as low-cost coal which can be used to generate inexpensive electricity.

Transportation costs. Transportation costs include both the cost of transporting inputs from their source to the site of the operation, and the cost of transporting goods from the site to customers. Whereas almost all operations are concerned to some extent with the former, not all operations transport goods to customers; rather, customers come to them (for example, hotels). Even for operations that do transport their goods to customers (most manufacturers, for example), we consider transportation as a supply-side factor because as location changes, transportation costs also change. Proximity to sources of *supply* dominates the location decision where the cost of transporting input materials is high or difficult. Food processing and other agriculture-based activities, for example, are often carried out close to growing areas. Conversely, transportation to *customers* dominates location decisions where this is expensive or difficult. Civil engineering projects, for example, are constructed mainly where they will be needed.

Community factors. Community factors are those influences on an operation's costs which derive from the social, political and economic environment of its site. These include:

- local tax rates
- government financial and planning assistance
- political stability, and local attitudes to 'inward investment'
- language
- availability of support services
- history of labour relations and behaviour
- environmental restrictions and waste disposal.

A major influence in where businesses locate is the cost of operating at different locations. Total operating cost depends on more than wage costs, or even total labour costs (which includes allowances for different productivity rates). Figure 6.3 illustrates what makes up the cost of shirts sold in different countries. Remember, the retailer will often sell the item for more than double the cost.[3]

Demand-side influences

Labour skills. The abilities of a local labour force can have an effect on customer reaction to the services or products which the operation produces. For example, 'science parks' are usually located close to universities because they hope to attract companies that are interested in using the skills available at the university.

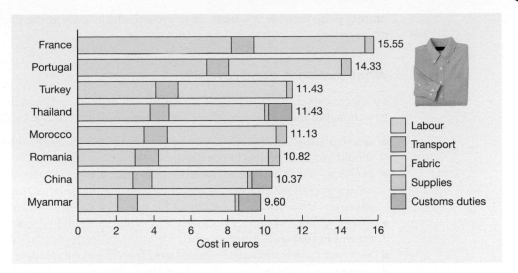

Figure 6.3 The cost of a shirt

The suitability of the site itself. Different sites are likely to have different intrinsic characteristics which can affect an operation's ability to serve customers and generate revenue. For example, the location of a luxury resort hotel which offers up-market holiday accommodation is very largely dependent on the intrinsic characteristics of the site. Located next to the beach, surrounded by waving palm trees and overlooking a picturesque bay, the hotel is very attractive to its customers. Move it a few kilometres away into the centre of an industrial estate and it rapidly loses its attraction.

Image of the location. Some locations are firmly associated in customers' minds with a particular image. Suits from Savile Row (the centre of the up-market bespoke tailoring district in London) may be no better than high-quality suits made elsewhere but, by locating its operation there, a tailor has probably enhanced its reputation and therefore its revenue. The product and fashion design houses of Milan and the financial services in the City of London also enjoy a reputation shaped partly by that of their location.

Convenience for customers. Of all the demand-side factors, this is, for many operations, the most important. Locating a general hospital, for instance, in the middle of the countryside may have many advantages for its staff, and even perhaps for its costs, but it clearly would be very inconvenient to its customers. Those visiting the hospital would need to travel long distances. This means that general hospitals are located close to centres of demand. Similarly with other public services and restaurants, stores, banks, petrol filling stations etc., location determines the effort to which customers have to go in order to use the operation.

What is layout and what are the types used in operations?

The 'layout' of an operation or process means how its transformed resources are positioned relative to each other and how its various tasks are allocated to these transforming resources. Together these two decisions will dictate the pattern of flow for transformed resources as they progress through the operation or process. It is an important decision because, if the layout proves wrong, it can lead to over-long or confused flow patterns, customer queues, long process times, inflexible operations, unpredictable flow and high cost. Also, re-laying out an existing operation can cause disruption, leading to customer dissatisfaction or lost operating time. So, because the **layout decision** can be difficult and expensive, operations managers are reluctant to do it too often. Therefore layout must start with a full appreciation of the objectives that the layout should be trying to achieve. However, this is only the

The layout decision is relatively infrequent but important

starting point of what is a multi-stage process which leads to the final physical layout of the operation.

What makes a good layout?

To a large extent the objectives of any layout will depend on the strategic objectives of the operation, but there are some general objectives which are relevant to all operations:

- *Inherent safety*. All processes which might constitute a danger to either staff or customers should not be accessible to the unauthorized.
- *Length of flow*. The flow of materials, information or customers should be appropriate for the operation. This usually means minimizing the distance travelled by transformed resources. However, this is not always the case (in a supermarket, for example).
- *Clarity of flow*. All flow of customers and materials should be well signposted, clear and evident to staff and customers alike.
- *Staff conditions*. Staff should be located away from noisy or unpleasant parts of the operation.
- *Management coordination*. Supervision and communication should be assisted by the location of staff and communication devices.
- *Accessibility*. All machines and facilities should be accessible for proper cleaning and maintenance.
- *Use of space*. All layouts should use space appropriately. This usually means minimizing the space used, but sometimes can mean achieving an impression of spacious luxury, as in the entrance lobby of a high-class hotel.
- *Long-term flexibility*. Layouts need to be changed periodically. A good layout will have been devised with the possible future needs of the operation in mind.

The basic layout types

Basic layout type

Most practical layouts are derived from only four **basic layout types**. These are:

Fixed-position layout
Functional layout
Cell layout
Line layout

- **fixed-position layout**
- **functional layout**
- **cell layout**
- **line layout (also called product layout)**

Which type of layout is used will (partly) depend on which type of process is being used. Process 'types' (described in Chapter 5) represent the broad approaches to the organization of processes and activities. Layout is a narrower, but related concept. It is the physical mani-

Layout is influenced by process types

festation of a process type, but there is often some overlap between **process types** and the layouts that they could use. As Table 6.1 indicates, a process type does not necessarily imply only one particular basic layout.

Fixed-position layout

Fixed-position layout is in some ways a contradiction in terms, since the transformed resources do not move between the transforming resources. Instead of materials, information or customers flowing through an operation, the recipient of the processing is stationary and the equipment, machinery, plant and people who do the processing move as necessary. This could be because the product or the recipient of the service is too large to be moved conveniently, or it might be too delicate to move, or perhaps it could object to being moved; for example:

- *Motorway construction* – the product is too large to move.
- *Open-heart surgery* – patients are too delicate to move.
- *High-class service restaurant* – customers would object to being moved to where food is prepared.

Table 6.1 The relationship between process types and basic layout types

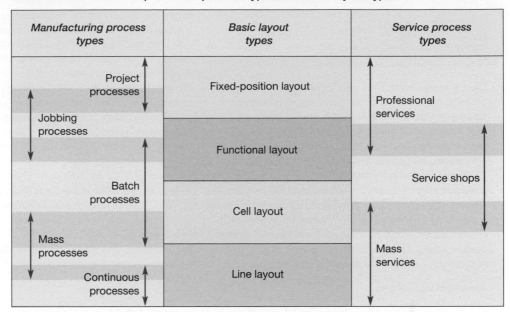

- *Mainframe computer maintenance* – the product is too big and probably also too delicate to move, and the customer might object to bringing it in for repair.

A construction site is typical of a fixed-position layout in that there is a limited amount of space which must be allocated to the various transforming resources. The main problem in designing this layout will be to allocate areas of the site to the various contractors so that they have adequate space, they can receive and store their deliveries of materials, they can have access to their parts of the project without interfering with each other's movements, they minimize movement, and so on.

Functional layout

Functional layout is so called because it conforms to the needs and convenience of the functions performed by the transforming resources within the processes. (Confusingly, functional layout is also referred to as 'process layout' but this term is being superseded.) In functional layout, similar resources or processes are located together. This may be because it is convenient to group them together, or that the utilization of transforming resources is improved. It means that when materials, information or customers flow through the operation, their route is determined according to their needs. Different customers or products will have different needs and therefore take different routes. Usually this makes the flow pattern in the operation very complex. Examples of functional layouts include:

- *Hospital* – some processes (e.g. X-ray machines and laboratories) are required by several types of patient; some processes (e.g. general wards) can achieve high staff- and bed-utilization.
- *Machining the parts which go into aircraft engines* – some processes (e.g. heat treatment) need specialist support (heat and fume extraction); some processes (e.g. machining centres) require the same technical support from specialist setter–operators; some processes (e.g. grinding machines) get high machine utilization as all parts which need grinding pass through a single grinding section.
- *Supermarket* – some products, such as tinned goods, are convenient to restock if grouped together. Some areas, such as those holding frozen vegetables, need the common technology of freezer cabinets. Others, such as the areas holding fresh vegetables, might be together because that way they can be made to look attractive to customers (see the opening short case).

Short case
'Factory flow' helps surgery productivity[4]

Even surgery can be seen as a process, and like any process, it can be improved. Normally patients remain stationary with surgeons and other theatre staff performing their tasks around the patient. However, this idea has been challenged by John Petri, an Italian consultant orthopaedic surgeon at a hospital in Norfolk in the UK. Frustrated by spending time drinking tea while patients were prepared for surgery, he redesigned the process so now he moves continually between two theatres. While he is operating on a patient in one theatre, his anaesthetist colleagues are preparing a patient for surgery in another theatre. After finishing with the first patient, the surgeon 'scrubs up', moves to the second operating theatre, and

begins the surgery on the second patient. While he is doing this the first patient is moved out of the first operating theatre and the third patient is prepared. This method of overlapping operations in different theatres allows the surgeon to work for five hours at a time rather than the previous standard three-and-a-half-hour session. *'If you were running a factory'*, says the surgeon, *'you wouldn't allow your most important and most expensive machine to stand idle. The same is true in a hospital.'* Currently used on hip and knee replacements, this layout would not be suitable for all surgical procedures. Since its introduction the surgeon's waiting list has fallen to zero and his productivity has doubled. *'For a small increase in running costs we are able to treat many more patients'*, said a spokesperson for the hospital management. *'What is important is that clinicians . . . produce innovative ideas and we demonstrate that they are effective.'*

Assembly line surgery

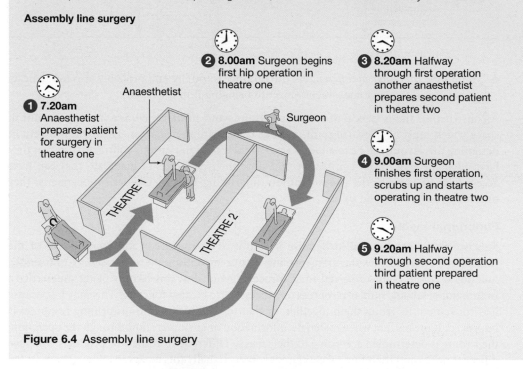

1 7.20am Anaesthetist prepares patient for surgery in theatre one

2 8.00am Surgeon begins first hip operation in theatre one

3 8.20am Halfway through first operation another anaesthetist prepares second patient in theatre two

4 9.00am Surgeon finishes first operation, scrubs up and starts operating in theatre two

5 9.20am Halfway through second operation third patient prepared in theatre one

Figure 6.4 Assembly line surgery

Figure 6.5 shows a functional layout in a university library. The various areas – reference books, enquiry desk, journals, and so on – are located in different parts of the operation. The customer is free to move between the areas depending on his or her requirements. The figure also shows the route taken by one customer on one visit to the library. If the routes for the customers were superimposed on the plan, the pattern of the traffic between the various parts of the operation would be revealed. The density of this traffic flow is an important piece of information in the detailed design of this type of layout. Changing the location of the various areas in the library will change the pattern of flow for the library as a whole.

The detailed design of functional layouts is complex, as is flow in this type of layout. Chief among the factors which lead to this complexity is the very large number of different options. For example, in the very simplest case of just two work centres, there are only two ways of arranging these *relative to each other*. But there are six ways of arranging three centres and 120 ways of arranging five centres. This relationship is a factorial one. For N centres there are factorial N ($N!$) different ways of arranging the centres, where:

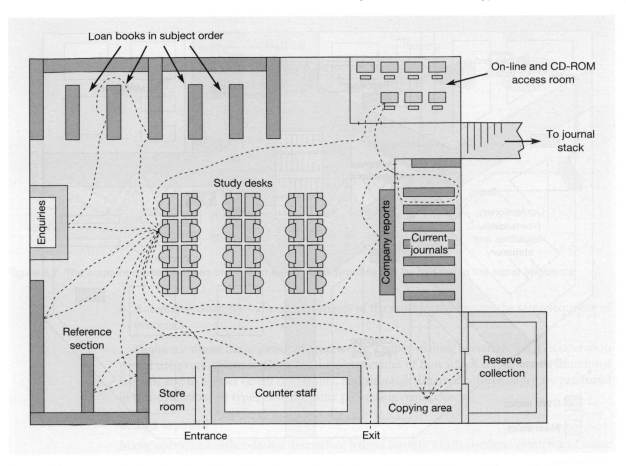

Figure 6.5 An example of a functional layout in a library showing the path of just one customer

$$N! = N \times (N-1) \times (N-2) \times \ldots \times (1)$$

So for a relatively simple functional layout with, say, 20 work centres, there are $20! = 2.433 \times 10^{18}$ **Combinatorial complexity** ways of arranging the operation. This **combinatorial complexity** of functional layouts makes optimal solutions difficult to achieve in practice. Most functional layouts are designed by a combination of intuition, common sense and systematic trial and error.

Cell layout

A cell layout is one where the transformed resources entering the operation are pre-selected (or pre-select themselves) to move to one part of the operation (or cell) in which all the transforming resources, to meet their immediate processing needs, are located. After being processed in the cell, the transformed resources may go on to another cell. In effect, cell layout is an attempt to bring some order to the complexity of flow which characterizes functional layout. Examples of cell layouts include:

- *Maternity unit in a hospital* – customers needing maternity attention are a well-defined group who can be treated together and who are unlikely to need the other facilities of the hospital at the same time that they need the maternity unit.
- *Some laptop assembly* – within a contract manufacturer's factory, the assembly of different laptop brands may be done in a special area dedicated to that one brand that has special requirements such as particularly high quality levels.
- *'Lunch' products area in a supermarket* – some customers use the supermarket just to purchase sandwiches, savoury snacks, etc. for their lunch. These products may be located together so that these customers do not have to search around the store.

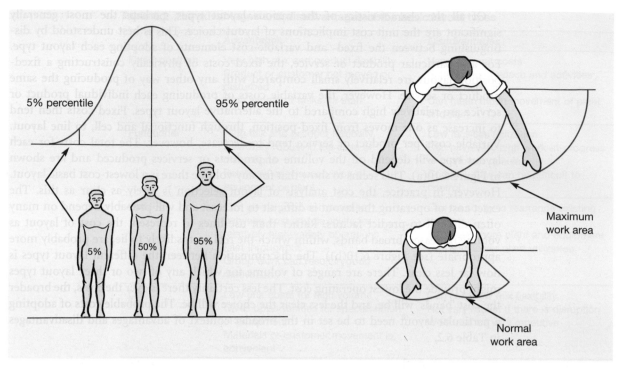

5%   50%   95%

5% percentile   95% percentile

Maximum
work area

Normal
work area

Figure 6.11 The use of anthropometric data in job design

Summary answers to key questions

PEARSON
myomlab

Check and improve your understanding of this chapter using self-assessment questions and a personalized study plan, audio and video downloads, and an eBook – all at **www.myomlab.com.**

➤ Where should operations be located?

■ The stimuli which act on an organization during the location decision can be divided into supply-side and demand-side influences. Supply-side influences are the factors such as labour, land and utility costs which change as location changes. Demand-side influences include such things as the image of the location, its convenience for customers and the suitability of the site itself.

➤ What is layout and what are the types used in operations?

■ The 'layout' of an operation or process means how its transformed resources are positioned relative to each other and how its various tasks are allocated to these transforming resources.

■ There are four basic layout types. They are fixed-position layout, functional layout, cell layout and line layout.

➤ What type of layout should an operation choose?

■ Partly this is influenced by the nature of the process type, which in turn depends on the volume–variety characteristics of the operation. Partly also the decision will depend on the objectives of the operation. Cost and flexibility are particularly affected by the layout decision.

- The fixed and variable costs implied by each layout differ such that, in theory, one particular layout will have the minimum costs for a particular volume level. However, in practice, uncertainty over the real costs involved in layout makes it difficult to be precise on which is the minimum-cost layout.

> ➤ How should items be positioned in a workplace?

- Usually workplace design involves positioning equipment to minimize effort, minimize the risk of injury, and maximize quality of work.

Learning exercises

*These problems and applications will help to improve your analysis of operations. You can find more practice problems as well as worked examples and guided solutions on MyOMLab at **www.myomlab.com**.*

1 Sketch the layout of your local shop, coffee bar or sports hall reception area. Observe the area and draw onto your sketch the movements of people through the area over a sufficient period of time to get over 20 observations. Assess the flow in terms of volume, variety and type of layout.

2 Revisit the opening short case in this chapter that examines some of the principles behind supermarket layout. Then visit a supermarket and observe people's behaviour. You may wish to try and observe which areas they move slowly past and which areas they seem to move past without paying attention to the products. (You may have to exercise some discretion when doing this; people generally don't like to be stalked round the supermarket too obviously.) Try and verify, as far as you can, some of the principles that were outlined in the opening short case. If you were to redesign the supermarket what would you recommend?

3 Draw a rough plan of your (or someone else's) kitchen. Note (or observe) movements around the kitchen during food preparation and cleaning. How could its layout be improved?

Want to know more?

This is a relatively technical chapter and, as you would expect, most books on the subject are technical. Here are a few of the more accessible.

Karlsson, C. (1996) Radically new production systems, *International Journal of Operations and Production Management*, vol. 16, no. 11. An interesting paper because it traces the development of Volvo's factory layouts over the years.

Meyers, F.E. and Stephens, M.P. (2000) *Manufacturing Facilities Design and Material Handling*, Prentice-Hall, Upper Saddle River, NJ. Exactly what it says, thorough.

Meller, R.D. and Kai-Yin Gau (1996) The facility layout problem: recent and emerging trends and perspectives, *Journal of Manufacturing Systems*, vol. 15, issue 5, 351–66. A review of the literature in the area.

Useful websites

www.bpmi.org Site of the Business Process Management Initiative. Some good resources including papers and articles.

www.bptrends.com News site for trends in business process management generally. Some interesting articles.

www.iienet.org The Global Association of Productivity and Efficiency Professionals site. They are an important professional body for process design and related topics.

www.waria.com A Workflow and Reengineering Association website. Some useful topics.

www.opsman.org Lots of useful stuff.

Now that you have finished reading this chapter, why not visit MyOMLab at **www.myomlab.com** where you'll find more learning resources to help you make the most of your studies and get a better grade.

Chapter 7 | Supply network management

Key questions

➤ Why should an organization take a supply network perspective?

➤ What is involved in managing supply networks?

➤ What is involved in designing a supply network?

➤ What are the types of relationships between operations in supply networks?

➤ What is the 'natural' dynamic of a supply network?

➤ How can supply networks be improved?

Introduction

No operation exists in isolation. Every operation is part of a larger and interconnected *supply network*. These networks not only include suppliers and customers, but also suppliers' suppliers and customers' customers, and so on. As operations outsource many of their activities, the way they manage the supply of services and products is hugely important. At a strategic level, operations managers are involved in 'designing' the shape of their network and determining what to do and what to buy. At a more operational level, operations managers must consider the type of relationships they wish to develop with suppliers, understand the dynamics of their network, and improve their supply networks in order to ultimately satisfy end customers. Figure 7.1 shows where this chapter fits into the overall operations model.

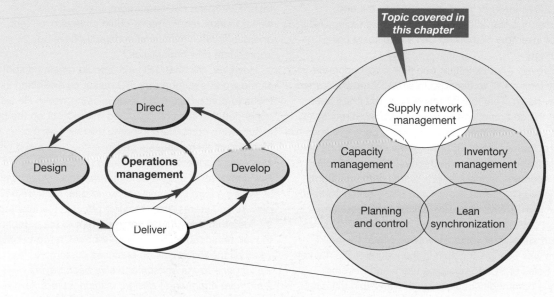

Figure 7.1 This chapter examines supply network management

*Check and improve your understanding of this chapter using self-assessment questions and a personalized study plan, audio and video downloads, and an eBook – all at **www.myomlab.com**.*

Operations in practice Dell: no operating model lasts forever[1]

When he was a student at the University of Texas at Austin, Michael Dell's sideline of buying unused stock of PCs from local dealers, adding components, and re-selling the now higher-specification machines to local businesses was so successful that he quit university and founded a computer company which was to revolutionize the industry's supply network management. His fledgling company was just too small to make its own components. Better, he figured to learn how to manage a network of committed specialist component manufacturers and take the best of what was available in the market. Dell says that his commitment to outsourcing was always done for the most positive of reasons. '*We focus on how we can coordinate our activities to create the most value for customers*'. Yet Dell still faced a cost disadvantage against its far bigger competitors, so they decided to sell its computers direct to its customers, bypassing retailers. This allowed the company to cut out the retailer's (often considerable) margin, which in turn allowed Dell to offer lower prices. Dell also realized that cutting out the link in the supply network between them and the customer also provided them with significant learning opportunities to get to know their customers' needs far more intimately. Most importantly it allowed Dell to learn how to run its supply chain so that products could move through the supply chain to the end-customer in a fast and efficient manner, reducing Dell's level of inventory and giving Dell a significant cost advantage.

However, what is right at one time may become a liability later on. Two decades later Dell's growth started to slow down. The irony of this is that, what had been one of the company's main advantages, its direct sales model using the Internet and its market power to squeeze price reductions from suppliers, were starting to be seen as disadvantages. Although the market had changed, Dell's operating model had not. Some commentators questioned Dell's size. How could a $56 billion company remain lean, sharp, and alert? Other commentators pointed out that Dell's rivals had also now learnt to run efficient supply networks. However, one of the main factors was seen as the shift in the nature of the market itself. Sales of PCs to business users had become largely a commodity business with wafer-thin margins, and this part of the market was growing slowly

Source: Corbis/Gianni Giansanti/Sygma

compared to the sale of computers to individuals. Selling computers to individuals provided slightly better margins than the corporate market, but they increasingly wanted up-to-date computers with a high design value, and most significantly, they wanted to see, touch and feel the products before buying them. This was clearly a problem for a company like Dell which had spent 20 years investing in its telephone- and later, internet-based sales channels. What all commentators agreed on was that in the fast-moving and cut-throat computer business, where market requirements could change overnight, operations resources must constantly develop appropriate new capabilities.

However, Michael Dell said it could regain its spot as the world's number one PC maker by switching its focus to consumers and the developing world. He also conceded that the company had missed out on the boom in supplying computers to home users – who make up just 15% of its revenues – because it was focused on supplying businesses. '*Let's say you wanted to buy a Dell computer in a store nine months ago – you'd have searched a long time and not found one. Now we have over 10,000 stores that sell our products.*' He rejected the idea that design was not important to his company, though he accepted that it had not been a top priority when all the focus was on business customers. '*As we've gone to the consumer we've been paying quite a bit more attention to design, fashion, colors, textures and materials.*'

The supply network perspective

Supply network

Supply side
First-tier suppliers
Second-tier suppliers
Demand side

A **supply network** perspective means setting an operation in the context of all the customers and suppliers that interact with it. Materials, parts, information, ideas and people may all flow through the supply network. On its **supply side**, an operation has its suppliers of materials, information or services. These are often called **first-tier suppliers**. These suppliers themselves have their own **second-tier suppliers** who in turn could also have suppliers, and so on. On the **demand side** the operation has customers. These customers might not be the final consumers of the operation's services or products; they might have their own set of customers. 'First-tier' customers are the main customer group for the operation, who in turn supply 'second-tier' customers.

Figure 7.2 illustrates the simplified supply network for two operations. First is a plastic homeware (kitchen bowls, food containers, etc.) manufacturer. Note that on the demand side the homeware manufacturer supplies some of its basic products to wholesalers which supply retail outlets. However, it also supplies some retailers directly with 'made-to-order' products. The second example, an enclosed shopping mall, also has suppliers and customers that themselves have their own suppliers and customers. Along with the flow of services and products in the network, each link in the network will feed back orders and information to its suppliers. It is a two-way process with goods flowing one way and information flowing the other.

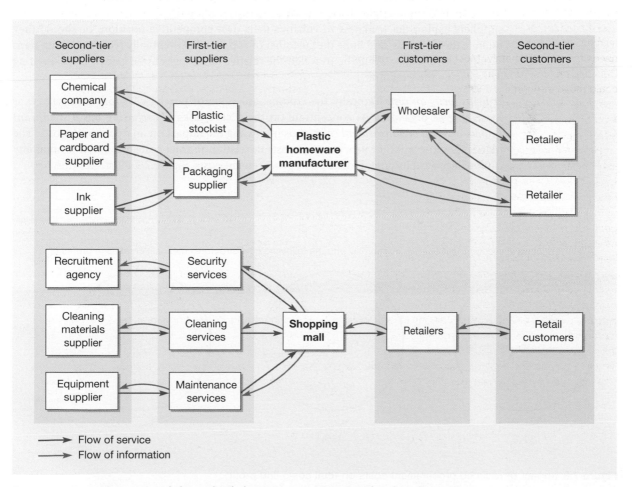

Figure 7.2 Operations network for a plastic homeware company and a shopping mall

Why consider the whole supply network?

There are a number of important reasons for taking a supply network perspective:

It helps an understanding of competitiveness. Immediate customers and immediate suppliers, quite understandably, are the main concern to competitively minded companies. Yet sometimes they need to look beyond these immediate contacts to understand why customers and suppliers act as they do. If it wants to understand its ultimate customers' needs at the end of the network, an operation can and should rely on the intermediate links in the network between itself and its end customers.

It helps identify significant links in the network. The key to understanding supply networks lies in identifying the parts of the network which contribute to those performance objectives valued by end-customers. Any analysis of networks must start, therefore, by understanding the **downstream** end of the network. After this, the **upstream** parts of the network which contribute most to end-customer service will need to be identified. For example, the important end-customers for domestic plumbing appliances are the installers and service companies that deal directly with domestic consumers. They are supplied by 'stock holders' which must have all parts in stock and deliver them fast. Suppliers of parts to the stock holders can best contribute to their end-customers' competitiveness partly by offering a short delivery lead time but mainly through dependable delivery. The key players in this example are the stock holders. The best way of winning end-customer business in this case is to give the stock holder prompt delivery which helps keep costs down while providing high availability of parts.

It helps focus on long-term issues. There are times when circumstances render parts of a supply network weaker than its adjacent links. A major machine breakdown, for example, or a labour dispute might disrupt a whole network. Should its immediate customers and suppliers exploit the weakness to enhance their own competitive position, or should they tolerate the problems, and hope the customer or supplier will eventually recover? A long-term supply-network view would be to weigh the relative advantages to be gained from assisting or replacing the weak link.

It helps focus on cost. Typically the volume and value of purchased goods and services is increasing as organizations concentrate on their 'core tasks'. *Purchasing has a significant impact on total organizational costs*, thus increasing the impact on an operation's costs. The higher the proportion of procurement costs in relation to total costs, the more profitability can be improved through reduction in procurement costs. Figure 7.3 illustrates this.

Downstream
Upstream

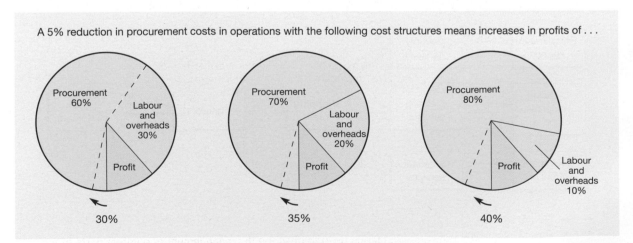

Figure 7.3 Impact of reduced procurement costs on total costs and profit

Designing and managing supply networks

A supply network is all the operations linked together to provide services and products through to the end-customers

A supply chain is a strand of linked operations

Designing and managing **supply networks** is a holistic approach to managing the interconnection of organizations that combine to produce value to the ultimate consumer in the form of services and products. Within supply networks, there can be many hundreds of strands of linked operations, commonly referred to as **supply chains**. An analogy often used to describe supply chains is that of the 'pipeline'. Just as liquids flow through a pipeline, so services and products flow down a supply chain. Long pipelines will, of course, contain more liquid than short ones, so the time taken for liquid to flow all the way through a long pipeline will be longer.

Some of the terms used in supply network management are not universally applied. Furthermore, some of the concepts behind the terminology overlap in the sense that they refer to common parts of the total supply network (Figure 7.4). *Supply network management* (also called supply chain management) coordinates all the operations on the supply side and the demand side. *Purchasing and supply management* deals with the operation's interface with its supply markets. *Physical distribution management* may mean supplying immediate customers, while *logistics* is an extension that often refers to materials and information flow down through a distribution channel, to the retail store or consumers (increasingly common because of the growth of internet-based retailing). The term *third-party logistics* (TPL) indicates outsourcing to a specialist logistics company. *Materials management* is a more limited term and refers to the flow of materials and information only through the immediate supply network.

Performance objectives of supply networks

The key objective in managing supply networks is the satisfaction of the end-customer. All parts of the network must consider the final customer, no matter how far an individual operation is from them. When customers decide to make a purchase, they trigger action across the whole network. All the businesses in the supply network pass on portions of

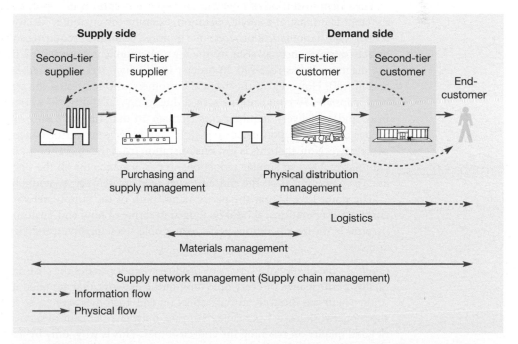

Figure 7.4 Some of the terms used to describe the management of different parts of the supply network

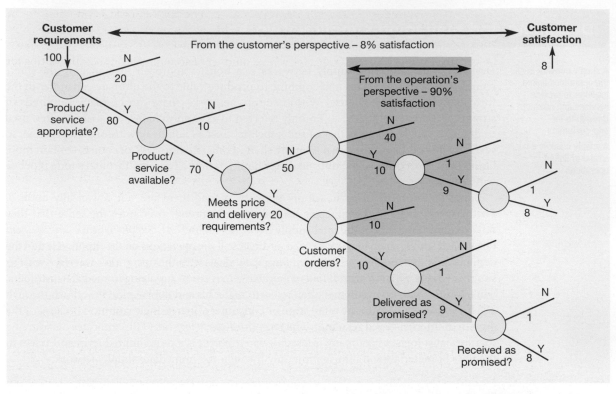

Figure 7.5 Taking a customer perspective of supply network performance can lead to very different conclusions

that end-customer's money to each other, each retaining a margin for the value it has added. Each operation in the network should be satisfying its own customer, but also making sure that eventually the end-customer is satisfied.

For a demonstration of how end-customer perceptions of supply satisfaction can be very different from that of a single operation, examine the customer 'decision tree' in Figure 7.5. It charts the hypothetical progress of a hundred customers requiring service from a business. Supply performance, as seen by the core operation, is represented by the shaded part of the diagram. It has received 20 orders, 18 of which were delivered as promised (on time, and in full). However, of the original customers who requested the service, 20 found it was inappropriate, 10 could not be served due to unavailability, 50 were not satisfied with the price and/or delivery requirements (though 10 did still place an order). So what seems a 90 per cent supply performance is in fact an 8 per cent performance from the customer's perspective. Note that this is just one operation from the operation's perspective. Include the cumulative effect of similar reductions in performance for all the operations in a network, and the probability that the end-customer is adequately served could become remote.

The point here is that the performance both of the supply network as a whole, and its constituent operations, should be judged in terms of how end-customer needs are satisfied, in terms of the five operations performance objectives: quality, speed, dependability, flexibility and cost.

Quality – the quality of a service or product when it reaches the customer is a function of the quality performance of every operation in the network that supplied it. Errors in each stage of the chain can multiply in their effect on end-customer service, so if each of 7 stages in a supply network has a 1 per cent error rate, only 93.2 per cent of services or products will be of good quality on reaching the end-customer. This is why, only by every stage taking some responsibility for its own *and its suppliers'* performance, can a supply network achieve high end-customer quality.

Speed has two meanings in a supply network context. The first is how fast customers can be served. However, fast customer response can be achieved simply by over-resourcing or over-stocking within the network. For example, an accounting firm may be able to respond quickly to customer demand by having a large number of accountants on standby waiting for demand that may (or may not) occur. An alternative perspective on speed is the time taken for services and products to move through the network. So, for example, products that move quickly across a supply network will spend little time as inventory, which in turn reduces inventory-related costs in the network.

Dependability – like speed, one can almost guarantee 'on-time' delivery by keeping excessive resources, such as inventory, within the network. However, dependability of throughput time is a much more desirable aim because it reduces uncertainty. If individual operations do not deliver as promised, there will be a tendency for customers to over-order, or order early, in order to provide some kind of insurance against late delivery. This is why delivery dependability is often measured as 'on time, in full' in supply networks.

Flexibility – in a supply network context, flexibility is usually taken to mean the ability to cope with changes and disturbances. Very often this is referred to as agility. The concept of agility includes previously discussed issues such as focusing on the end-customer and ensuring fast throughput and responsiveness to customer needs. But, in addition, agile supply networks are sufficiently flexible to cope with changes, either in the nature of customer demand or in the supply capabilities of operations within the network.

Cost – in addition to the costs incurred within each operation, the supply network as a whole incurs additional costs that derive from operations doing business with each other. These may include such things as the costs of finding appropriate suppliers, setting up contractual agreements, monitoring supply performance, transporting products between operations, holding inventories, and so on. Many developments in supply network management, such as partnership agreements or reducing the number of suppliers, are attempts to minimize transaction costs.

Short case
Ford Motors' team value management[2]

Purchasing managers are a vital link between an operation and its suppliers. They work best when teamed up with mainstream operations managers who know what the operation really needs, especially if, between them, they take a role that challenges previous assumptions. That is the basis behind Ford Motor Company's 'team value management' (TVM) approach. Reputedly, it all started when Ford's Head of Global Purchasing, David Thursfield, discovered that a roof rack designed for one of Ford's smaller cars was made of plastic-coated aluminium and capable of bearing a 100 kg load. This prompted the questions, *'Why is this rack covered in plastic? Why would anyone want to put 100 kg on the roof of a car that small?'* He found that no one had ever questioned the original specification. When Ford switched to using steel roof racks capable of bearing a smaller weight, they halved the cost. *'It is important'*, he says, *'to check whether the company is getting the best price for parts and raw material that provide the appropriate level of performance without being too expensive.'* The savings in a large company

Source: Getty Images/Getty Images News

such as Ford can be huge. Often in multinationals, each part of the business makes sourcing and design decisions independently and does not exploit opportunities for cross-usage of components. The TVM approach is designed to bring together engineering and purchasing staff and identify where cost can be taken out of purchased parts and where there is opportunity for parts commonality (see Chapter 4) between different models. When a company's global purchasing budget is $75bn like Ford's, the potential for cost savings is significant.

Supply network design

Taking a supply network perspective is useful because it prompts a number of important design decisions. These combine to determine how a supply network can operate and its ability to deliver value to customers. These decisions include:

1 Who should do what in the network? How many steps should there be in the network? What is the role of customers, suppliers, complementors and competitors? This is called the network shape decision.
2 How much of the network should the operation own? This is called the do-or-buy, out-sourcing or vertical integration decision.
3 How should supply networks be configured when operations compete in different ways in different markets? This is called the supply network matching decision.

The network shape decision

Supply base reduction

Reconfiguring a supply network sometimes involves parts of the operation being merged – not necessarily in the sense of a change of ownership of any parts of an operation, but rather in the way responsibility is allocated for carrying out activities. The most common example of network reconfiguration has come through the many companies that have recently reduced the number of direct suppliers. The complexity of dealing with many thousands of suppliers may both be expensive for an operation and (sometimes more important) prevent the operation from developing a close relationship with a supplier. It is not easy to be close to so many different suppliers.

Disintermediation

Disintermediation

Another trend in some supply networks is that of companies within a network bypassing customers or suppliers to make contact directly with customers' customers or suppliers' suppliers. 'Cutting out the middlemen' in this way is called **disintermediation**. An obvious example of this is the way the Internet has allowed some suppliers to 'disintermediate' traditional retailers in supplying services and products to consumers. So, for example, many services in the travel industry that used to be sold through retail outlets (travel agents) are now also available direct from the suppliers. The option of purchasing the individual components of a vacation through the websites of the airline, hotel, car hire company, etc., is now easier for consumers. Of course, they may still wish to purchase an 'assembled' product from retail travel agents which can have the advantage of convenience.

Co-opetition

One approach to thinking about supply networks sees any business as being surrounded by four types of players: suppliers, customers, competitors and complementors. Complementors enable one's services or products to be valued more by customers because they can also have the complementor's products or services, as opposed to when they have yours alone. Competitors are the opposite: they make customers value your service or product less when they can have their product or service, rather than yours alone. Competitors can also be complementors and vice versa. For example, adjacent restaurants may see themselves as competitors for customers' business. A customer standing outside and wanting a meal will choose between the two of them. Yet, in another way they are complementors. Would that customer have come to this part of town unless there was more than one restaurant to choose from? Restaurants, theatres, art galleries and tourist attractions generally, all cluster together in a form of cooperation to increase the total size of their joint market. It is important to distinguish between the way companies cooperate in increasing the total size of a market and the way in which they then compete for a share of that market. In the long term it creates value for the total network to

Co-opetition

find ways of increasing value for suppliers and well as customers. All the players in the supply network, whether they are customers, suppliers, competitors or complementors, can be both friends and enemies at different times. The term used to capture this idea is 'co-opetition'.[3]

The do-or-buy decision

Business process outsourcing (BPO)

No single business does everything that is required to deliver its services and products. Bakers do not grow wheat or even mill it into flour. Banks do not usually do their own credit checking: they retain the services of specialist agencies that have the information systems and expertise to do it better. Although most companies have always outsourced some of their activities, a larger proportion of direct activities are now being bought from suppliers. In addition, many indirect processes are also being outsourced, often referred to as 'business process outsourcing' (BPO). Financial service companies in particular are starting to outsource some of their more routine back-office processes. In a similar way many processes within the human resource function, from payroll services through to more complex training and development processes, are being outsourced to specialist companies. The processes may still be physically located where they were before, but the staff and technology are managed by the outsourcing service provider. The reason for doing this is often primarily to reduce cost. However, there can also be significant gains in the quality and flexibility of service offered. Deciding what to do itself in-house and what to outsource is often called the 'do or buy' decision, when individual components or activities are being considered, or the 'vertical integration decision' when it is the ownership of whole operations that is being decided. Vertical integration can be defined in terms of three factors.[4]

1 *The direction of vertical integration.* Should an operation expand by buying one of its suppliers or by buying one of its customers? The strategy of expanding on the supply side of the network is sometimes called 'backward' or 'upstream' vertical integration, and expanding on the demand side is sometimes called 'forward' or 'downstream' vertical integration.

2 *The extent of vertical integration.* How far should an operation take the extent of its vertical integration? Some organizations deliberately choose not to integrate far, if at all, from their original part of the network. Alternatively, some organizations choose to become very vertically integrated.

3 *The balance among stages.* How exclusive should the relationship be between operations? A totally balanced network relationship is one where an operation produces only for the next stage in the network and totally satisfies its requirements. Less than full balance allows each operation to sell its output to other companies or to buy in some of its supplies from other companies.

Making the do-or-buy decision

Outsourcing is a strategic decision

Whether it is referred to as the do-or-buy, vertical integration or the outsourcing decision, the choice facing operations is rarely simple. Organizations in different circumstances with different objectives are likely to take different decisions. Yet the question itself is relatively simple, even if the decision itself is not: 'Does in-house or outsourced supply in a particular set of circumstances give the appropriate performance objectives that it requires to compete more effectively in its markets?' For example, if the main performance objectives for an operation are dependable delivery and meeting short-term changes in customers' delivery requirements, the key question should be: 'How does in-house or outsourcing give better dependability and delivery flexibility performance?' Table 7.1 summarizes some arguments for in-house supply and outsourcing in terms of each performance objective.

Although the effect of outsourcing on the operation's performance objective is important, there are other factors that companies take into account when deciding if outsourcing an activity is a sensible option. If an activity has long-term **strategic importance** to a company,

Table 7.1 How in-house and outsourced supply may affect an operation's performance objectives

Performance objective	'Do it yourself' in-house supply	'Buy it in' outsourced supply
Quality	The origins of any quality problems are usually easier to trace in-house and improvement can be more immediate but there can be some risk of complacency.	Supplier may have specialized knowledge and more experience, also may be motivated through market pressures, but communication more difficult.
Speed	Can mean synchronized schedules which speeds throughput of materials and information, but if the operation has external customers, internal customers may be low-priority.	Speed of response can be built into the supply contract where commercial pressures will encourage good performance, but there may be significant transport/delivery delays.
Dependability	Easier communications can help dependability, but, if the operation also has external customers, internal customers may be low priority.	Late-delivery penalties in the supply contract can encourage good delivery performance, but organizational barriers may inhibit in communication.
Flexibility	Closeness to real business needs can alert the in-house operation to required changes, but the ability to respond may be limited by the scale and scope of internal operations.	Outsourced suppliers may be larger with wider capabilities and have more ability to respond to changes, but may have to balance conflicting needs of different customers.
Cost	In-house operations do not have to make the margin required by outside suppliers so the business can capture the profits which would otherwise be given to the supplier, but relatively low volumes may mean that it is difficult to gain economies of scale or the benefits of process innovation.	Probably the main reason why outsourcing is so popular. Outsourced companies can achieve economies of scale and they are motivated to reduce their own costs because it directly impacts on their profits, but costs of communication and coordination with supplier need to be taken into account.

it is unlikely to outsource it. For example, a retailer might choose to keep the design and development of its website in-house even though specialists could perform the activity at less cost because it plans to move into web-based retailing at some point in the future. Nor would a company usually outsource an activity where it had specialized skills or knowledge. For example, a company making laser printers may have built up specialized knowledge in the production of sophisticated laser drives. This capability may allow it to introduce product or process innovations in the future. It would be foolish to 'give away' such capability. After these two more strategic factors have been considered, the company's operations performance can be taken into account. Obviously if its operations performance is already superior to any potential supplier, it would be unlikely to outsource the activity. Even if its performance was currently below that of potential suppliers, it may not outsource the activity if it feels that it could significantly improve its performance. Figure 7.6 illustrates this decision logic.

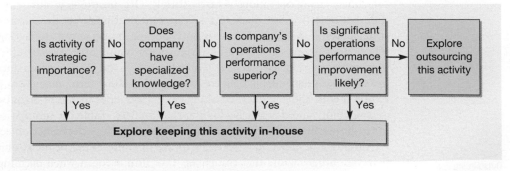

Figure 7.6 The decision logic of outsourcing

Short case
Behind the brand names[5]

Source: Rex Features

The market for notebook computers is a fast-evolving and competitive one. Yet few who buy these products know that the majority of the world's notebooks are made by a small number of Taiwanese and Korean manufacturers. Taiwanese firms alone make around 60 per cent of all notebooks in the world, including most of Dell, Compaq and Apple machines. In a market with unremitting technological innovation and fierce price competition, it makes sense to outsource production to companies that can achieve the economies that come with high-volume manufacture as well as develop the expertise which enables new designs to be put into production without the usual cost overruns and delays. However, the big brand names are keen to defend their products' performance. Dell, for example, admits that a major driver of its outsourcing policy is the requirement to keep costs at a competitive level, but says that it can ensure product quality and performance through

its relationship with its suppliers. *'The production lines are set up by Dell and managed by Dell',* says Tony Bonadero, Director of Product Marketing for Dell's laptop range. Dell also imposes strict quality control and manages the overall design of the product.

Supply network alignment

An important question for supply managers to consider is 'How should supply networks be configured when operations compete in different ways in different markets?' One answer, proposed by Professor Marshall Fisher of Wharton Business School, is to organize the supply network serving those individual markets in different ways.[6] He points out that many companies have seemingly similar products which, in fact, compete in different ways. Shoe manufacturers may produce classics which change little over the years, as well as fashions which last only one or two seasons. Chocolate manufacturers have stable lines which have been sold for 50 years, but also create 'specials' associated with an event or film release, maybe selling only for a few months. Demand for the former products will be relatively stable and predictable, but demand for the latter will be far more uncertain. Also, the profit margin commanded by the innovative product will probably be higher than that of the more functional product. However, the price (and therefore the margin) of the innovative product may drop rapidly once it has become unfashionable in the market.

Efficient supply networks

Responsive supply networks

The supply network policies which are seen to be appropriate for functional services and products and innovative services and products are termed by Fisher **efficient supply network** policies and **responsive supply network** policies, respectively. Efficient supply network policies include keeping inventories low, especially in the downstream parts of the network, so as to maintain fast throughput and reduce the amount of working capital tied up in the inventory. What inventory there is in the network is concentrated mainly in the manufacturing operation, where it can keep utilization high and therefore manufacturing costs low. Information must flow quickly up and down the chain from retail outlets back up to the manufacturer so that schedules can be given the maximum amount of time to adjust efficiently. The network is then managed to make sure that products flow as quickly as possible down the chain to replenish what few stocks are kept in the network. By contrast, responsive supply policies stress high service levels and responsive supply to the end-customer. The inventory in the network will be deployed as closely as possible to the customer. In this way, the network can still supply even when dramatic changes occur in customer demand. Fast throughput from the upstream parts of the network will still be needed to replenish downstream stocks. But

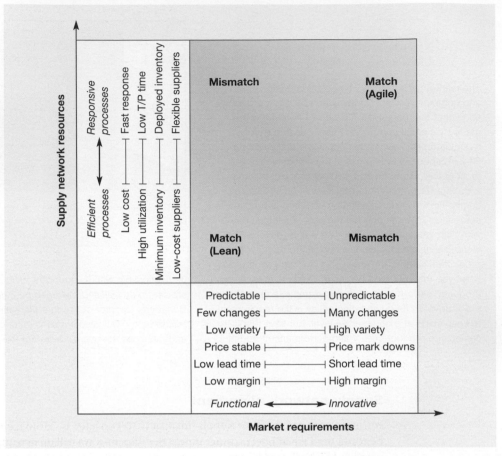

Figure 7.7 Matching the supply network resources with market requirements

Source: Adapted from Fisher, M.C. (1997) What is the right supply chain for your product? *Harvard Business Review*, March–April, 105–16.

those downstream stocks are needed to ensure high levels of availability to end-customers. Figure 7.7 illustrates how the different supply network policies match the different market requirements implied by functional and innovative products.

Types of relationships in supply networks

One of the key issues within a supply network is how relationships with suppliers and customers should be managed. The behaviour of the supply network as a whole is, after all, made up of the relationships which are formed between individual pairs of operations. It is important, therefore, to have some framework which helps us to understand the different ways in which supply relationships can be developed.

Business or consumer relationships?

We can distinguish between relationships that are the final link in the supply network, involving the ultimate consumer, and those involving two commercial businesses (Figure 7.8). So, **business-to-business** (B2B) relationships are by far the most common in a supply network context. **Business-to-consumer** (B2C) relationships include both 'bricks and mortar' retailers

Business to business

Business to consumer

		Relationship – to . . .	
		Business	Consumer (Peer)
Relationship – from . . .	Business	**B2B** *Relationship* • Most common, all but the last link in the supply network *E-commerce examples* • Electronic marketplaces • e.g. b2b Index	**B2C** *Relationship* • Retail operations • Comparison web sites *E-commerce examples* • Online retailers • e.g. Amazon.com
	Consumer (Peer)	**C2B** *Relationship* • Consumers offer, business responds *E-commerce examples* • Usually focused on specialist area • e.g. Google Adsense	**C2C (P2P)** *Relationship* • Originally one of the driving forces behind the modern Internet (ARPANET) *E-commerce examples* • File sharing networks (legal and illegal) • e.g. Napster, Gnutella

Figure 7.8 The business–consumer relationship matrix

Consumer to business

Customer to customer

and online retailers. **Consumer-to-business** (C2B) relationships involve consumers posting their needs on the web (sometimes stating the price they are willing to pay), and companies then deciding whether to offer. **Customer-to-customer** (C2C) or peer-to-peer (P2P) relationships include the online exchange and auction services and file-sharing services. In this chapter we deal almost exclusively with B2B relationships.

Types of business-to-business relationship

A convenient way of categorizing supply relationships is to examine the extent and nature of what a company chooses to buy in from suppliers. Two dimensions are particularly important – *what* the company chooses to outsource, and *who* it chooses to supply it. In terms of what is outsourced, a key question is, 'how many activities are outsourced?' from doing everything in-house at one extreme, to outsourcing everything at the other extreme. In terms of who is chosen to supply products and services, two questions are important, 'how many suppliers will be used by the operation?' and 'how close are the relationships?' Figure 7.9 illustrates this way of characterizing relationships. It also identifies some of the more common types of relationship and shows some of the trends in how supply relationships have moved.

Traditional market supply relationships

Short-term transactional relationships

The very opposite of performing an operation in-house is to purchase services and products from outside in a 'pure' market fashion, often seeking the 'best' supplier every time it is necessary to purchase. Each transaction effectively becomes a separate decision. The **relationship** between buyer and seller, therefore, can be very short-term. Once the services or products are delivered and payment is made, there may be no further trading between the parties. Short-term relationships may be used on a trial basis when new companies are being considered as more regular suppliers. Also, many purchases which are made by operations are

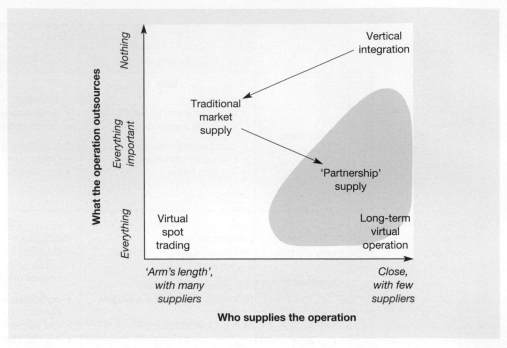

Figure 7.9 Types of supply chain relationship

one-off or very irregular. The advantages of traditional market supplier relationships are usually seen as follows:

- They maintain competition between alternative suppliers. This promotes a constant drive between suppliers to provide best value.
- A supplier specializing in a small number of services or products, but supplying them to many customers, can gain natural economies of scale. This enables the supplier to offer the products and services at a lower price than would be obtained if customers performed the activities themselves.
- There is inherent flexibility in outsourced supplies. If demand changes, customers can simply change the number and type of suppliers. This is a far faster and simpler alternative to having to redirect internal activities.
- Innovations can be exploited no matter where they originate. Specialist suppliers are more likely to come up with innovative products and services which can be bought in faster and cheaper than would be the case if the company were itself trying to innovate.
- They help operations to concentrate on their core activities. One business cannot be good at everything. It is sensible therefore to concentrate on the important activities and outsource the rest.

There are, however, disadvantages in buying in a totally 'free market' manner:

- There may be supply uncertainties. Once an order has been placed, it is difficult to maintain control over how that order is fulfilled. This is a particular problem if the buyer is small relative to the supplier, so lacks power to influence their behaviour.
- Choosing who to buy from takes time and effort. Gathering sufficient information and making decisions continually are, in themselves, activities which need to be resourced.
- There are strategic risks in subcontracting activities to other businesses. An over-reliance on outsourcing can 'hollow out' the company, leaving it with few internal capabilities to exploit in its markets.
- Short-term, price-oriented types of relationship can have a downside in terms of ongoing support and reliability. This may mean that a short-term 'least-cost' purchase decision will lead to long-term high cost.

Short case
Northern Foods wins a slice of the in-flight meals business[7]

The companies that provide airline catering services are in a tough business. Meals must be of a quality that is appropriate for the class and type of flight, yet the airlines that are their customers are always looking to keep costs as low as possible, menus must change frequently and the airlines must respond promptly to customer feedback. If this were not enough, forecasting passenger numbers is difficult. Catering suppliers are advised of the likely numbers of passengers for each flight several days in advance, but the actual minimum number of passengers for each class is only fixed six hours before take-off. Also, flight arrivals are sometimes delayed, putting pressure on everyone to reduce the turnaround time, and upsetting work schedules. Even when a flight lands on time no more than 40 minutes are allowed before the flight is ready for take-off again, so complete preparation and a well-ordered sequence of working is essential. It is a specialized business, and in order to maintain a fast, responsive and agile service, airline caterers have traditionally produced food on, or near, airport sites using their own chefs and staff to cook and tray-set meals. The catering companies' suppliers are also usually airline specialists who themselves are located near the caterers so that they can offer very short response times.

The companies that provide catering services may also provide related services. For example, LSG Sky Chefs (a subsidiary of Deutsche Lufthansa AG) is a provider of tailor-made in-flight services for all types of airlines around the world. Their main areas of service are Airline Catering, In-flight Equipment and Logistics and In-flight Management. They are also large, employing 30,000 people at 200 customer service centres in 49 countries. In 2007 they produced 418 million meals for more than 300 airlines, representing more than 30 per cent of the global airline catering market.

The airline sector has over recent years suffered a series of shocks including 9/11, oil price volatility, financial

Specialized companies have developed that prepare food in specialized factories, often for several airlines.

crises and world recession. This has meant that airlines are reviewing their catering supply solutions. In December 2008 Gate Gourmet, the world's largest independent provider of airline catering lost the contract to supply British Airways' short-haul flights out of Heathrow to new entrants into the airline catering market, a consortium of Northern Foods, a leading food producer, whose normal business is supplying retailers with own-label and branded food, and DHL, a subsidiary of Deutsche Post and the market-leading international express and logistics company. DHL is already a large supplier to 'airside' caterers at Heathrow and already has its own premises at the airport. Northern Foods will make the food at its existing factories and deliver it to DHL, which will assemble onto airline catering trays and transfer them onto aircraft. The new contract is the first time that Northern Foods, whose biggest customer is Marks and Spencer, the UK retail chain, has developed new business outside its normal supermarket customer base.

'Partnership' supply relationships

Partnership relationships   **Partnership relationships** in supply networks are sometimes seen as a compromise between vertical integration on the one hand (owning the resources which supply you) and pure market relationships on the other (having only a transactional relationship with those who supply you). Although to some extent this is true, partnership relationships are not only a simple mixture of vertical integration and market trading, although they do attempt to achieve some of the closeness and coordination efficiencies of vertical integration, but at the same time attempt to achieve a relationship that has a constant incentive to improve. Partnership relationships are defined as: '*relatively enduring inter-firm cooperative agreements, involving flows and linkages that use resources and/or governance structures from autonomous organizations, for the joint accomplishment of individual goals linked to the corporate mission of each* *sponsoring firm*.[8] What this means is that suppliers and customers are expected to cooperate, even to the extent of sharing skills and resources, to achieve joint benefits beyond those they could have achieved by acting alone. At the heart of the concept of partnership lies the issue of the *closeness* of the relationship. Partnerships are close relationships, the degree of which is influenced by a number of factors:

- *Sharing success.* An attitude of shared success means that both partners work together in order to increase the total amount of joint benefit they receive, rather than manoeuvring to maximize their own individual contribution.
- *Long-term expectations.* Partnership relationships imply relatively long-term commitments, but not necessarily permanent ones.
- *Multiple points of contact.* Communication between partners is not only through formal channels, but may take place between many individuals in both organizations.
- *Joint learning.* Partners in a relationship are committed to learn from each other's experience and perceptions of the other operations in the chain.
- *Few relationships.* Although partnership relationships do not necessarily imply single sourcing by customers, they do imply a commitment on the part of both parties to limit the number of customers or suppliers with whom they do business. It is difficult to maintain close relationships with many different trading partners.
- *Joint coordination of activities.* As there are fewer relationships, it becomes possible jointly to coordinate activities such as the flow of materials or service, payment, and so on.
- *Information transparency.* An open and efficient information exchange is seen as a key element in partnerships because it helps to build confidence between the partners.
- *Joint problem-solving.* Although partnerships do not always run smoothly, jointly approaching problems can increase closeness over time.
- *Trust.* This is probably the key element in partnership relationships. In this context, trust means the willingness of one party to relate to the other on the understanding that the relationship will be beneficial to both, even though that cannot be guaranteed. Trust is widely held to be both the key issue in successful partnerships, but also, by far, the most difficult element to develop and maintain.

Virtual operations

Virtual operation

An extreme form of outsourcing operational activities is that of the **virtual operation**. Virtual operations do relatively little themselves, but rely on a network of suppliers that can provide services and products on demand. A network may be formed for only one project and then disbanded once that project ends. For example, some software and Internet companies are virtual in the sense that they buy in all the services needed for a particular development. This may include not only the specific software development skills but also such things as project management, testing, applications prototyping, marketing, physical production, and so on. Much of the Hollywood film industry also operates in this way. A production company may buy and develop an idea for a movie, but it is created, edited and distributed by a loose network of agents, actors, technicians, studios and distribution companies. The advantage of virtual operations is their flexibility and the fact that the risks of investing in production facilities are far lower than in a conventional operation. However, without any solid base of resources, a company may find it difficult to hold onto and develop a unique core of technical expertise. The resources used by virtual companies will almost certainly be available to competitors. In effect, the core competence of a virtual operation lies in the way it is able to manage its supply network.

Selecting suppliers

Choosing appropriate suppliers should involve trading off alternative attributes. Rarely are potential suppliers so clearly superior to their competitors that the decision is self-evident.

Table 7.2 Factors for rating alternative suppliers

Short-term ability to supply	Longer-term ability to supply
Range of services or products provided	Potential for innovation
Quality of services or products	Ease of doing business
Responsiveness	Willingness to share risk
Dependability of supply	Long-term commitment to supply
Delivery and volume flexibility	Ability to transfer knowledge as well as products and services
Total cost of being supplied	Technical capability
Ability to supply in the required quantity	Operations capability
	Financial capability
	Managerial capability

Most businesses find it best to adopt some kind of supplier 'scoring' or assessment procedure. This should be capable of rating alternative suppliers in terms of factors such as those in Table 7.2.

Supplier selection

Selecting suppliers should involve evaluating the relative importance of all these factors. So, for example, a business might choose a supplier that, although more expensive than alternative suppliers, has an excellent reputation for on-time delivery, or because the high level of supply dependability allows the business to hold lower stock levels. Other trade-offs may be more difficult to calculate. For example, a potential supplier may have high levels of technical capability, but may be financially weak, with a small but finite risk of going out of business. Other suppliers may have little track record of supplying the products or services required, but show the managerial talent and energy for potential customers to view developing a supply relationship as an investment in future capability.

Worked example

A hotel chain has decided to change its supplier of cleaning supplies because its current supplier has become unreliable in its delivery performance. The two alternative suppliers that it is considering have been evaluated, on a 1–10 scale, against the criteria shown in Table 7.3. That also shows the relative importance of each criterion, also on a 1–10 scale. Based on this evaluation, Supplier B has the superior overall score.

Table 7.3 Weighted supplier selection criteria for the hotel chain

Factor	Weight	Supplier A score	Supplier B score
Cost performance	10	8 (8 × 10 = 80)	5 (5 × 10 = 50)
Quality record	10	7 (7 × 10 = 70)	9 (9 × 10 = 90)
Delivery speed promised	7	5 (5 × 7 = 35)	5 (5 × 7 = 35)
Delivery speed achieved	7	4 (4 × 7 = 28)	8 (8 × 7 = 56)
Dependability record	8	6 (6 × 8 = 48)	8 (8 × 8 = 64)
Range provided	5	8 (8 × 5 = 40)	5 (5 × 5 = 25)
Innovation capability	4	6 (6 × 4 = 24)	9 (9 × 4 = 36)
Total weighted score		325	356

Single-sourcing
Multi-sourcing

An important decision facing most purchasing managers is whether to source each individual product or service from one or more than one supplier, known, respectively, as **single-sourcing** and **multi-sourcing**. Some of the advantages and disadvantages of single- and multi-sourcing are shown in Table 7.4.

Table 7.4 Advantages and disadvantages of single- and multi-sourcing

	Single-sourcing	Multi-sourcing
Advantages	• Potentially better quality because more supplier quality assurance possibilities • Strong relationships which are more durable • Greater dependency encourages more commitment and effort • Better communication • Easier to cooperate on new innovation • More scale economies • Higher confidentiality	• Purchaser can drive price down by competitive tendering • Reduces dependency on individual suppliers • Can switch sources in case of supply failure • Wide sources of knowledge and expertise to tap
Disadvantages	• More vulnerable to disruption if a failure to supply occurs • Individual supplier more affected by volume fluctuations • Supplier might exert upward pressure on prices if no alternative supplier is available	• Difficult to encourage commitment by supplier • Less easy to develop effective SQA • More effort needed to communicate • Suppliers less likely to invest in new processes • More difficult to obtain scale economies

It may seem as though companies that multi-source do so exclusively for their own short-term benefit. However, this is not always the case: multi-sourcing can bring benefits to both supplier and purchaser in the long term. For example, Robert Bosch GmbH, the German automotive components business, required that subcontractors do no more than 20 per cent of their total business with them. This was to prevent suppliers becoming too dependent and allow volumes to be fluctuated without pushing the supplier into bankruptcy. However, there has been a trend for purchasing functions to reduce the number of companies supplying any one part or service.

Dual sourcing
Parallel sourcing

Dual sourcing or **parallel sourcing** is often seen as a way to balance the relative merits of single and multi-sourcing. This involves using two suppliers for similar goods or services. Whilst dual suppliers are usually required to cooperate, an element of competition may also be encouraged by adjusting the percentage of the contract awarded to each supplier based on previous performance.

Global sourcing

Global sourcing

One of the major developments of recent years has been the expansion in the proportion of services and products which businesses source from outside their home country; this is called **global sourcing**. Traditionally, even companies that exported their goods and services all over the world (that is, they were international on their demand side) still sourced the majority of their supplies locally. There are a number of factors promoting global sourcing:

● The formation of trading blocs in different parts of the world has lowered tariff barriers, at least within those blocs. For example, the single market developments within the European Union (EU), the North American Free Trade Agreement (NAFTA) and the South American Trade Group (MERCOSUR) have all made it easier to trade internationally within the regions.
● Transportation infrastructures are considerably more sophisticated and cheaper than they once were. Super-efficient port operations in Rotterdam and Singapore, for example, integrated road–rail systems, jointly developed autoroute systems, and cheaper air freight have all reduced some of the cost barriers to international trade.
● Perhaps most significantly, far tougher world competition has forced companies to look to reducing their total costs. Given that in many industries bought-in items are the largest single part of operations costs, an obvious strategy is to source from wherever is cheapest.

There are, of course, challenges to global sourcing. Suppliers that are further away need to transport their products across long distances. The risks of delays and hold-ups can be far greater than when sourcing locally. Also, negotiating with suppliers whose native language is different from one's own makes communication more difficult and can lead to misunderstandings over contract terms. Therefore global sourcing decisions require businesses to balance cost, performance, service and risk factors, not all of which are obvious. These factors are important in global sourcing because of non-price or 'hidden' cost factors such as cross-border freight and handling fees, complex inventory stocking and handling requirements, more complex administrative, documentation and regulatory requirements, and increased operational risk caused by geopolitical factors.

Supply network dynamics

The bullwhip effect

The 'bullwhip effect' is used to describe how a small disturbance at the downstream end of a supply network causes increasingly large disturbances, errors, inaccuracies and volatility as it works its way upstream. Its main cause is an understandable desire by the different links in the supply network to manage their production rates and inventory levels sensibly. To demonstrate this, examine the production rate and stock levels for the supply network shown in Table 7.5. This is a four-stage supply network where the focal operation is served by three tiers of suppliers. The demand from the market has been running at a rate of 100 items per period, but in period 2 demand reduces to 95 items. All stages in the supply chain work on the principle that they will keep in stock one period's demand (a simplification but not a gross one). The 'stock' column shows the starting stock at the beginning, and the finish stock at the end, of the period. At the beginning of period 2, the focal operation has

Table 7.5 Fluctuations of production levels along supply chain in response to small change in end-customer demand

Period	Third-tier supplier Prodn.	Third-tier supplier Stock	Second-tier supplier Prodn.	Second-tier supplier Stock	First-tier supplier Prodn.	First-tier supplier Stock	Focal operation Prodn.	Focal operation Stock	Demand
1	100	100	100	100	100	100	100	100	100
		100		100		100		100	
2	20	100	60	100	80	100	90	100	95
		60		80		90		95	
3	180	60	120	80	100	90	95	95	95
		120		100		95		95	
4	60	120	90	100	95	95	95	95	95
		90		95		95		95	
5	100	90	95	95	95	95	95	95	95
		95		95		95		95	
6	95	95	95	95	95	95	95	95	95
		95		95		95		95	

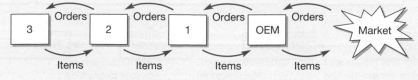

(Note all operations keep one period's inventory.)

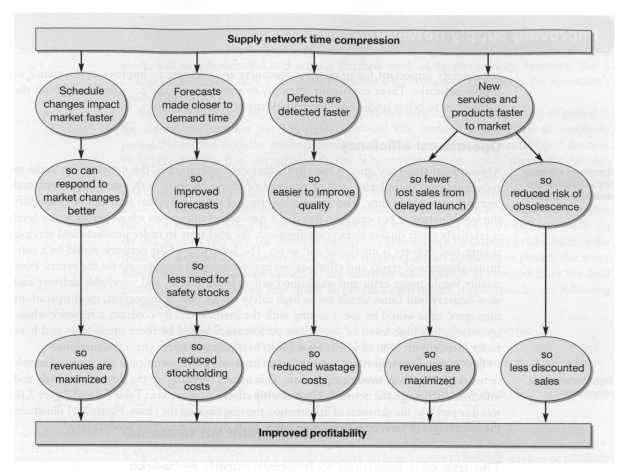

Figure 7.11 Supply network time compression can both reduce costs and increase revenues
Source: Based on Towill

e-business on three important aspects of supply network management – business and market information flow, product and service flow, and the cash flow.

E-procurement

E-procurement

E-procurement is the generic term used to describe the use of electronic methods in every stage of the purchasing process from identification of requirement through to payment, and potentially to contract management.[10] For some years, electronic means have been used by businesses to confirm purchased orders and ensure payment to suppliers. The rapid development of the Internet, however, opened up the potential for far more fundamental changes in purchasing behaviour. Partly this was as the result of supplier information made available through the Internet. By making it easier to search for alternative suppliers, the Internet has changed the economies of the search process and offers the potential for wider searches. It also changed the economies of scale in purchasing. For example, purchasers requiring relatively low volumes find it easier to group together in order to create orders of sufficient size to warrant lower prices. However, whilst the cost savings from purchased goods and services may be the most visible advantage of e-procurement, some managers say that it is just the tip of the iceberg. It can also be far more efficient because purchasing staff are no longer chasing purchase orders and performing routine administrative tasks. Much of the advantage and time savings comes from the decreased need to re-enter information, from streamlining the interaction with suppliers and from having a central repository for data with everything contained in one system. Purchasing staff can negotiate with vendors faster and more effectively. Online auctions can compress negotiations from months to one or two hours, or even minutes.

E-procurement has grown largely because of the development over the last ten years of electronic marketplaces (also sometimes called infomediaries or cybermediaries). These intermediaries allow buyers and sellers in a B2B context to exchange information about prices and offerings. They can be categorized as consortium, private or third party.

- A private e-marketplace is where buyers or sellers conduct business in the market only with their partners and suppliers by previous arrangement.
- The consortium e-marketplace is where several large businesses combine to create an e-marketplace controlled by the consortium.
- A third-party e-marketplace is where an independent party creates an unbiased, market-driven e-marketplace for buyers and sellers in an industry.

The Internet is an important source of purchasing information, even if the purchase itself is made using more traditional methods. Also, even though many businesses have gained advantages by using e-procurement, it does not mean that everything should be bought electronically. When businesses purchase very large amounts of strategically important products or services, they will negotiate multimillion-euro deals, which involve months of discussion, arranging for deliveries up to a year ahead. In such environments, e-procurement may add little value.

Logistics and the Internet

In supply networks dealing with physical assets, transportation is required. Internet communications in this area of supply management have had two major effects. The first is to make information more readily available along the **distribution chain**. This means that the transport companies, warehouses, suppliers and customers that make up the network can share knowledge of where things are at any given time. This allows the operations within the network to coordinate their activities more readily, with potentially significant cost savings. For example, an important issue for transportation companies is **back-loading**. When the company is contracted to transport goods from A to B, its vehicles may have to return from B to A empty. Back-loading means finding a potential customer that wants their goods transported from B to A in the right time frame. Companies which can fill their vehicles on both the outward and return journeys will have significantly lower costs per distance travelled than those whose vehicles are empty for half the total journey.

The second impact of the Internet on logistics has been in the 'business to consumer' part of the supply network. While the last few years have seen an increase in the number of goods bought by consumers online, most goods still have to be physically transported to the customer. Often early e-retailers ran into major problems in the **order fulfilment** task of actually supplying their customers. Partly this was because many traditional warehouse and distribution operations were not designed for e-commerce fulfilment. Supplying a conventional retail operation requires relatively large vehicles to move relatively large quantities of goods from warehouses to shops. Distributing to individual customers requires a large number of smaller deliveries.

Information-sharing

One of the reasons for the fluctuations in output described in the bullwhip example earlier was that each operation in the network reacted to the orders placed by its immediate customer. None of the operations had an overview of what was happening throughout the chain. If information had been available and **shared throughout the chain**, it is unlikely that such wild fluctuations would have occurred. It is sensible therefore to try to transmit information throughout the chain so that all the operations can monitor true demand, free of these distortions. An obvious improvement is to make information on end-customer demand

Distribution chain

Back-loading

Order fulfilment

Information sharing helps improve supply chain performance

Short case
TDG serving the whole supply chain[11]

Source: TDG Logistics

TDG are specialists in providing *third-party* logistics services to the growing number of manufacturers and retailers that choose not to do their own distribution. Instead they outsource to companies like TDG, which have operations spread across 250 sites that cover the UK, Ireland, France, Spain, Poland and Holland, employ 8,000 people and use 1,600 vehicles.

'There are a number of different types of company providing distribution services', says David Garman, Chief Executive Officer of TDG, *'each with different propositions for the market. At the simplest level, there are the "haulage" and "storage" businesses. These companies either move goods around or they store them in warehouses. Clients plan what has to be done and it is done to order. One level up from the haulage or storage operations are the physical distribution companies, who bring haulage and storage together. These companies collect clients' products, put them into storage facilities and deliver them to the end-customer as and when required. After that there are the companies who offer contract logistics. As a contract logistics service provider, you are likely to be dealing with the more sophisticated clients who are looking for better quality facilities and management and the capability to deal with more complex operations. One level further up is the market for supply chain management services. To do this you have to be able to manage supply chains from end to end, or at least some significant part of the whole chain. Doing this requires a much greater degree of*
analytical and modelling capability, business process reengineering and consultancy skills.'

TDG, along with other prominent logistics companies, describes itself as a 'lead logistics provider'. This means that they can provide the consultancy-led, analytical and strategic services integrated with a sound base of practical experience in running successful 'on-the-road' operations. *'In 1999 TDG was a UK distribution company'*, says David Garman, *'now we are a European contract logistics provider with a vision to becoming a full supply chain management company. Providing such services requires sophisticated operations capability, especially in terms of information technology and management dynamism. Because our sites are physically dispersed with our vehicles at any time spread around the motorways of Europe, IT is fundamental to this industry. It gives you visibility of your operation. We need the best operations managers, supported by the best IT.'*

available to upstream operations. Electronic point-of-sale (EPOS) systems used by many retailers attempt to do this. Sales data from checkouts or cash registers are consolidated and transmitted to the warehouses, transportation companies and supplier manufacturing operations that form their supply network. Similarly, electronic data interchange (EDI) helps to share information (see the short case on Seven-Eleven Japan). EDI can also affect the economic order quantities shipped between operations in the supply chain.

Channel alignment

Channel alignment focuses on harmonizing the network

Channel alignment means the adjustment of scheduling, material movements, stock levels, pricing and other sales strategies so as to bring all the operations in the network into line with each other. This goes beyond the provision of information. It means that the systems and methods of planning and control decision-making are harmonized through the network. For example, even when using the same information, differences in forecasing methods or purchasing practices can lead to fluctuations in orders between operations in the chain. One way of avoiding this is to allow an upstream supplier to manage the inventories of its downstream customer. This is known as **vendor-managed inventory** (VMI). So, for example, a packaging supplier could take responsibility for the stocks of packaging materials held by a food manufacturing customer. In turn, the food manufacturer takes responsibility for the stocks of its products which are held in its customer's, the supermarket's warehouses.

Vendor-managed inventory

Short case
Seven-Eleven Japan's agile supply chain[12]

Source: Getty Images

Seven-Eleven Japan (SEJ) is Japan's largest and most successful retailer. The average amount of stock in an SEJ store is between 7 and 8.4 days of demand, a remarkably fast stock turnover for any retailer. Industry analysts see SEJ's agile supply management as being the driving force behind its success. It is an agility that is supported by a fully integrated information system that provides visibility of the whole supply network and ensures fast replenishment of goods in its stores customized exactly to the needs of individual stores. As a customer comes to the checkout counter the assistant first keys in the customer's gender and approximate age and then scans the bar codes of the purchased goods. This sales data is transmitted to the Seven-Eleven headquarters through its own high-speed lines. Simultaneously, the store's own computer system records and analyzes the information so that store managers and headquarters have immediate point-of-sale information. This allows both store managers and headquarters to, hour by hour, analyze sales trends, any stock-outs, types of customer buying certain products, and so on. The headquarter's computer aggregates all this data by region, product and time so that all parts of the supply network, from suppliers through to the stores, have the information by the next morning. Every Monday, the company chairman and top executives review all performance information for the previous week and develop plans for the up-coming week. These plans are presented on Tuesday morning to SEJ's 'operations field counsellors' each of which is responsible for facilitating performance improvement in around eight stores. On Tuesday afternoon the field counsellors for each region meet to decide how they will implement the overall plans

for their region. On Tuesday night the counsellors fly back to their regions and by next morning are visiting their stores to deliver the messages developed at headquarters which will help the stores implement their plans. SEJ's physical distribution is also organized on an agile basis. The distribution company maintains radio communications with all drivers and SEJ's headquarters keeps track of all delivery activities. Delivery times and routes are planned in great detail and published in the form of a delivery time-table. On average each delivery takes only one and a half minutes at each store, and drivers are expected to make their deliveries within ten minutes of scheduled time. If a delivery is late by more than thirty minutes the distribution company has to pay the store a fine equivalent to the gross profit on the goods being delivered. The agility of the whole supply system also allows SEJ headquarters and the distribution company to respond to disruptions. For example, on the day of the Kobe earthquake, SEJ used 7 helicopters and 125 motor cycles to rush through a delivery of 64,000 rice balls to earthquake victims.

The SCOR model

The Supply Chain Operations Reference model (SCOR) is a broad, but highly structured and systematic, framework for improving supply networks. The framework uses a methodology, diagnostic and benchmarking tools that are increasingly widely accepted for evaluating and comparing supply activities and their performance. Just as important, the SCOR model allows its users to improve, and communicate management practices within and between all interested parties in their supply network by using a standard language and a set of structured definitions. Companies that have used the model include BP, AstraZeneca, Shell, SAP AG, Siemens AG and Bayer. Claimed benefits from using the SCOR model include improved process understanding and performance, improved supply network performance, increased customer satisfaction and retention, a decrease in required capital, better profitability and return on investment, and increased productivity. The model uses three individual techniques turned into an integrated approach. These are:

- Business process modelling.
- Benchmarking performance.
- Best practice analysis.

Business process modelling

SCOR does not represent organizations or functions, but rather processes. Each basic 'link' in the supply network is made up of five types of process, each process being a 'supplier–customer' relationship, see Figure 7.12.

- 'Source' is the procurement, delivery, receipt and transfer of raw material items, sub-assemblies, and/or services.
- 'Make' is the transformation process of adding value to products and services through mixing operations processes.
- 'Deliver' processes perform all customer-facing order management and fulfilment activities including outbound logistics.
- 'Plan' processes manage each of these customer–supplier links and balance the activity of the supply network. They are the supply and demand reconciliation process, which includes prioritization when needed.
- 'Return' processes look after the reverse logistics flow of moving material back from end-customers upstream in the supply chain because of product defects, post-delivery customer support, or recycling (end-of-life reverse supply).

All these processes are modelled at increasingly detailed levels from level 1 through to level 3.

Benchmarking performance

Performance metrics in the SCOR model are also structured by level. Level 1 metrics are the yardsticks by which an organization can measure how successful it is in achieving its desired positioning within the competitive environment, as measured by the performance of a particular supply chain. These level 1 metrics are the key performance indicators (KPIs) of the chain and are created from lower-level diagnostic metrics (called level 2 and level 3 metrics) which are calculated on the performance of lower-level processes.

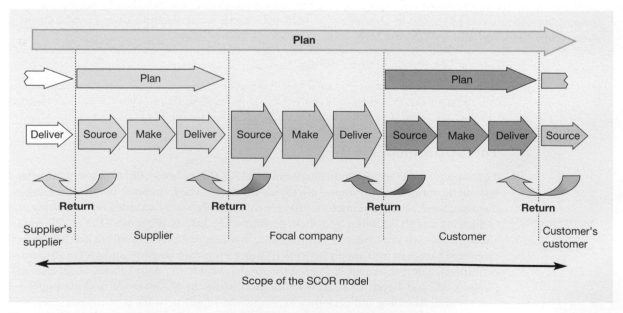

Figure 7.12 Matching the operations resources in the supply network with market requirements

Best practice analysis

Best practice analysis follows the benchmarking activity that should have measured the performance of the supply network processes and identified the main performance gaps. Best practice analysis identifies the activities that need to be performed to close the gaps. The definition of a 'best practice' in the SCOR model is one that:

- Is current – neither untested (emerging) nor outdated.
- Is structured – it has clearly defined goals, scope and processes.
- Is proven – there has been some clearly demonstrated success.
- Is repeatable – it has been demonstrated to be effective in various contexts.
- Has an unambiguous method – the practice can be connected to business processes, operations strategy, technology, supply relationships, and information or knowledge management systems.
- Has a positive impact on results – operations improvement can be linked to KPIs.

The SCOR roadmap

The SCOR model can be implemented by using a five-phase project 'roadmap'. Within this roadmap lies a collection of tools and techniques that both help to implement and support the SCOR framework. In fact many of these tools are commonly used management decision tools such as Pareto charts, cause–effect diagrams, maps of material flow and brainstorming.

Phase 1: Discover – Involves supply-network definition and prioritization where a 'Project Charter' sets the scope for the project. This identifies logic groupings of supply network within the scope of the project. The priorities, based on a weighted rating method, determine which supply network should be dealt with first. This phase also identifies the resources that are required, identified and secured through business process owners or actors.

Phase 2: Analyse – Using data from benchmarking and competitive analysis, the appropriate level of performance metrics are identified; that will define the strategic requirements of each supply network.

Phase 3: Material flow design – In this phase the project teams have their first go at creating a common understanding of how processes can be developed. The current state of processes is identified and an initial analysis attempts to see where there are opportunities for improvement.

Phase 4: Work and information flow design – The project teams collect and analyse the work involved in all relevant processes (plan, source, make, deliver and return) and map the productivity and yield of all transactions.

Phase 5: Implementation planning – This is the final and preparation phase for communicating the findings of the project. Its purpose is to transfer the knowledge of the SCOR team(s) to individual implementation or deployment teams.

Summary answers to key questions

Check and improve your understanding of this chapter using self-assessment questions and a personalized study plan, audio and video downloads, and an eBook – all at www.myomlab.com.

➤ Why should an organization take a supply network perspective?

■ The main advantage is that it helps any operation to understand how it can compete effectively within the network. This is because a supply network approach requires operations managers to think about their suppliers and their customers *as operations*. It can also help to identify particularly significant links within the network and hence identify long-term strategic changes which will affect the operation.

➤ What is involved in managing supply networks?

■ Managing supply networks involves understanding and influencing the various linkages between upstream and downstream operations with the objective of delivering better performance to the end-customer.

■ Key activities include designing the supply network, determining the type of supply relationships, understanding supply dynamics and improving supply networks.

➤ What is involved in designing a supply network?

■ Deciding the 'shape' of the supply network: This may involve reducing the number of suppliers to the operation so as to develop closer relationships, bypassing or disintermediating operations in the network, and co-opetition.

■ Deciding what to do and what to buy: This concerns the nature of the ownership of the operations within a supply network. The direction of vertical integration refers to whether an organization wants to own operations on its supply side or demand side (backwards or forwards integration). The extent of vertical integration relates to whether an organization wants to own a wide span of the supply network. The balance of integration refers to whether operations can trade with only their vertically integrated partners or with organizations as well.

■ Deciding how to align supply and demand in the network: Marshall Fisher distinguishes between functional markets and innovative markets. He argues that functional markets, which are relatively predictable, require efficient supply networks, whereas innovative markets, which are less predictable, require responsive supply networks.

➤ What are the types of relationship between operations in supply networks?

■ Supply networks are made up of individual pairs of buyer–supplier relationships. Business-to-business (B2B) relationships are of the most interest to operations managers. They can be characterized on two dimensions – what is outsourced to a supplier, and the number and closeness of the relationships.

■ Traditional market supplier relationships are where a purchaser chooses suppliers on an individual periodic basis. No long-term relationship is usually implied by such 'transactional' relationships, but it makes it difficult to build internal capabilities.

■ Partnership supplier relationships involve customers forming long-term relationships with suppliers. In return for the stability of demand, suppliers are expected to commit to high levels of service. True partnerships are difficult to sustain and rely heavily on the degree of trust which is allowed to build up between partners.

- Virtual operations are an extreme form of outsourcing where an operation does relatively little itself and subcontracts almost all its activities.
- Selecting suppliers involves deciding whether to source from one (single), two (dual or parallel) or many (multi) suppliers. One must then consider the relative merits of alternative suppliers.

➤ What is the 'natural' dynamic of a supply network?

- Supply networks exhibit a dynamic behaviour known as the 'bullwhip' effect. This shows how small changes at the demand end of a supply chain are progressively amplified for operations further back in the network.
- Common causes of the bullwhip effect include errors in forecasting, long and variable lead-times, order batching, demand volatility, panic ordering, and bounded rationality.

➤ How can supply networks be improved?

- To reduce the 'bullwhip' effect, operations can adopt some mixture of coordination strategies:
  - operational efficiency: this means eliminating sources of inefficiency or ineffectiveness in the network; of particular importance is 'time compression', which attempts to increase the throughput speed of the operations in the network;
  - e-business: new IT applications have transformed supply networks, enabling improvements in flows of services, information, and products;
  - information-sharing: the efficient distribution of information throughout the chain can reduce demand fluctuations along the chain by linking all operations to the source of demand;
  - channel alignment: this means adopting the same or similar decision-making processes throughout the chain to coordinate how and when decisions are made.
- The Supply Chain Operations Reference model (SCOR) is a highly structured framework for supply network improvement using business process modelling, benchmarking and best practice analysis in an integrated approach.

Learning exercises

These problems and applications will help to improve your analysis of operations. You can find more practice problems as well as worked examples and guided solutions on MyOMLab at www.myomlab.com.

1 Visit sites on the Internet that offer (legal) downloadable music using MP3 or other compression formats. Consider the music business supply network, **(a)** for the recordings of a well-known popular music artist, and **(b)** for a less well-known (or even largely unknown) artist struggling to gain recognition. How might the transmission of music over the Internet affect each of these artists' sales? What implications does electronic music transmission have for record shops?

2 'Look, why should we waste our time dealing with suppliers who can merely deliver good product, on time, and in full? There are any number of suppliers who can do that. What we are interested in is developing a set of suppliers who will be able to supply us with suitable components for the generation of products that comes after the next products we launch. It's the underlying capability of suppliers that we are really interested in.'

(a) Devise a set of criteria that this manager could use to evaluate alternative suppliers.
(b) Suggest ways in which she could determine how to weight each criterion.

3 The example of the bullwhip effect shown in Table 7.5 shows how a simple 5 per cent reduction in demand at the end of the supply network causes fluctuations that increase in severity the further back an operation is placed in the chain.

(a) Using the same logic and the same rules (i.e. all operations keep one period's inventory), what would the effect on the chain be if demand fluctuated period by period between 100 and 95? That is, period 1 has a demand of 100, period 2 has a demand of 95, period 3 a demand of 100, period 4 a demand of 95, and so on?

(b) What happens if all operations in the supply network decided to keep only half of the period's demand as inventory?

4 Visit a C2C auction site (for example eBay) and analyse the function of the site in terms of the way it facilitates transactions. What does such a site have to get right to be successful?

Want to know more?

Carmel, E. and Tjia, P. (2005) *Offshoring Information Technology: Sourcing and Outsourcing to a Global Workforce*, Cambridge University Press, Cambridge. An academic book on outsourcing.

Chopra, S. and Meindl, P. (2001) *Supply Chain Management: Strategy, Planning and Operations*, Prentice Hall, Upper Saddle River, NJ. A good textbook that covers both strategic and operations issues.

Fisher, M.L. (1997) What is the right supply chain for your product?, *Harvard Business Review*, vol. 75, no. 2.

A particularly influential article that explores the issue of how supply networks are not all the same.

Harrison, A. and van Hoek, R. (2002) *Logistics Management and Strategy*, Financial Times Prentice Hall, Harlow. A short but readable book that explains many of the modern ideas in supply network management including lean supply networks and agile supply networks.

Vashistha, A. and Vashistha, A. (2006) *The Offshore Nation: Strategies for Success in Global Outsourcing and Offshoring*, McGraw-Hill Higher Education. A topical book on outsourcing.

Useful websites

www.cio.com/topic/3207/supply_chain_management Site of CIO's Supply Chain Management Research Center. Topics include procurement and fulfilment, with case studies.

www.gsb.stanford.edu/scforum/ Stanford University's supply chain forum. Interesting debate.

www.rfidc.com/ Site of the RFID Centre that contains RFID demonstrations and articles to download.

www.spychips.com/ Vehemently anti-RFID site. If you want to understand the nature of some activists' concern over RFID, this site provides the arguments.

www.cips.org/ The Chartered Institute of Purchasing and Supply (CIPS) is an international organization, serving the purchasing and supply profession and dedicated to promoting best practice. Some good links.

www.opsman.org Lots of useful stuff.

Now that you have finished reading this chapter, why not visit MyOMLab at www.myomlab.com where you'll find more learning resources to help you make the most of your studies and get a better grade.

Chapter 8

Capacity management

Key questions

➤ What is capacity management?
➤ How are demand and capacity measured?
➤ What are the alternative ways of coping with demand fluctuation?
➤ How can operations manage their capacity level?
➤ How can queuing theory be used to plan capacity?

Introduction

Providing the capability to satisfy current and future demand is a fundamental responsibility of operations management. Get the balance between capacity and demand right and the operation can satisfy its customers cost-effectively. Get it wrong and it will fail to satisfy demand, and have excessive costs. Capacity management is also sometimes referred to as *aggregate planning*. This is because, at this level, demand and capacity calculations are usually performed on an aggregated basis which does not discriminate between the different services and products that an operation might offer. The essence of the task is to reconcile, at a general and aggregated level, the supply of capacity with the level of demand which it must satisfy. Figure 8.1 shows where this chapter fits into the overall operations model.

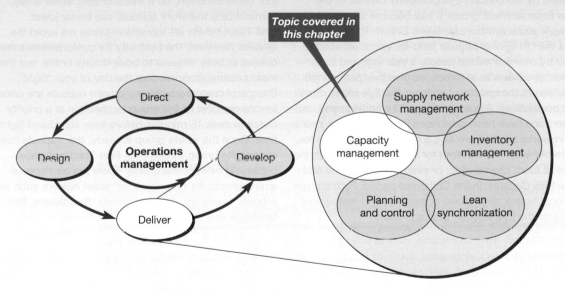

Topic covered in this chapter

Figure 8.1 This chapter examines capacity management

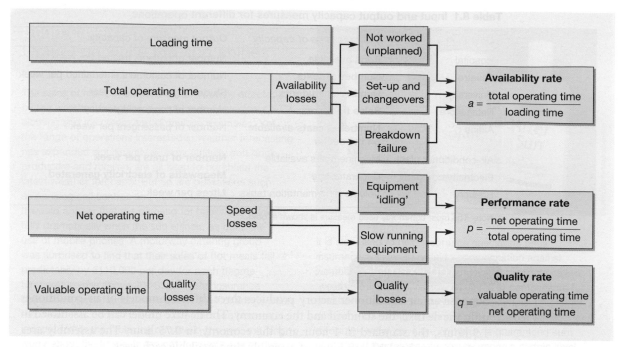

Figure 8.5 Operating equipment effectiveness

Finally, not everything processed by a piece of equipment will be error-free. So some capacity is lost through quality losses (see Figure 8.5).

Taking the notation in Figure 8.5,

$$OEE = a \times p \times q$$

For equipment to operate effectively, it needs to achieve high levels of performance against all three of these dimensions. Viewed in isolation, these individual metrics are important indicators of performance, but they do not give a complete picture of *overall* effectiveness. This can only be understood by looking at the combined effect of the three measures, calculated by multiplying the three individual metrics together. All these losses to the OEE performance can be expressed in terms of units of time – the design cycle time to deliver one unit. In effect, this means that an OEE represents the valuable operating time as a percentage of the design capacity.

Worked example

In a typical 7-day period, the planning department programmes a particular machine to work for 150 hours – its loading time. Changeovers and set-ups take an average of 10 hours and breakdown failures average 5 hours every 7 days. The time when the machine cannot work because it is waiting for material to be delivered from other parts of the process is 5 hours on average and during the period when the machine is running, it averages 90 per cent of its rated speed. Three per cent of the parts processed by the machine are subsequently found to be defective in some way.

$$\text{Maximum time available} = 7 \times 24 \text{ hours}$$
$$= 168 \text{ hours}$$
$$\text{Loading time} = 150 \text{ hours}$$
$$\text{Availability losses} = 10 \text{ hours (set-ups)} + 5 \text{ hrs (breakdowns)}$$
$$= 15 \text{ hours}$$

So, Total operating time = Loading time − Availability

$$= 150 \text{ hours} - 15 \text{ hours}$$

$$= 135 \text{ hours}$$

Speed losses = 5 hours (idling) + $((135 - 5) \times 0.1)$(10% of remaining time)

$$= 18 \text{ hours}$$

So, Net operating time = Total operating time − Speed losses

$$= 135 - 18$$

$$= 117 \text{ hours}$$

Quality losses = 117 (Net operating time) × 0.03 (Error rate)

$$= 3.51 \text{ hours}$$

So, Valuable operating time = Net operating time − Quality losses

$$= 117 - 3.51$$

$$= 113.49 \text{ hours}$$

Therefore, availability rate = $a = \dfrac{\text{Total operating time}}{\text{Loading time}}$

$$= \frac{135}{150} = 90\%$$

and, performance rate = $p = \dfrac{\text{Net operating time}}{\text{Total operating time}}$

$$= \frac{117}{135} = 86.67$$

and quality rate = $q = \dfrac{\text{Valuable operating time}}{\text{Net operating time}}$

$$= \frac{113.49}{117} = 97\%$$

OEE $(a \times p \times q) = 75.6\%$

The alternative capacity plans

With an understanding of both demand and capacity, the next step is to consider the alternative methods of responding to demand fluctuations. There are three 'pure' options available for coping with such variation:

Level capacity plan
Chase demand plan
Demand management

- Ignore the fluctuations and keep activity levels constant (**level capacity plan**).
- Adjust capacity to reflect the fluctuations in demand (**chase demand plan**).
- Attempt to change demand to fit capacity availability (**demand management**).

In practice, most organizations will use a mixture of all of these 'pure' plans, although often one plan might dominate. The Short case 'Seasonal salads' describes how one operation pursues some of these options.

Level capacity plan

In a level capacity plan, the processing capacity is set at a uniform level throughout the planning period, regardless of the fluctuations in forecast demand. This means that the same

Critical commentary

To many, the idea of fluctuating the workforce to match demand, either by using part-time staff or by hiring and firing, is more than just controversial. It is regarded as unethical. It is any business's responsibility, they argue, to engage in a set of activities which are capable of sustaining employment at a steady level. Hiring and firing merely for seasonal fluctuations, which can be predicted in advance, is treating human beings in a totally unacceptable manner. Even hiring people on a short-term contract, in practice, leads to them being offered poorer conditions of service and leads to a state of permanent anxiety as to whether they will keep their jobs. On a more practical note, it is pointed out that, in an increasingly global business world where companies may have sites in different countries, those countries that allow hiring and firing are more likely to have their plants 'downsized' than those where legislation makes this difficult.

'city break' vacation packages in the months when fewer business visitors are expected. Skiing and camping holidays are cheapest at the beginning and end of the season and are particularly expensive during school vacations. Discounts are given by photo-processing firms during winter periods, but never around summer holidays. Ice cream is 'on offer' in many supermarkets during the winter. The objective is invariably to stimulate off-peak demand and to constrain peak demand, in order to smooth demand as much as possible. Organizations can also attempt to increase demand in low periods by appropriate advertising. For example, turkey growers in the UK and the USA make vigorous attempts to promote their products at times other than Christmas and Thanksgiving.

Short case
Working by the year[3]

One method of fluctuating capacity as demand varies throughout the year without many of the costs associated with overtime or hiring temporary staff is called the Annual Hours Work Plan. This involves staff contracting to work a set number of hours per year rather than a set number of hours per week. The advantage of this is that the amount of staff time available to an organization can be varied throughout the year to reflect the real state of demand. Annual hours plans can also be useful when supply varies throughout the year. For example, a UK cheese factory of Express Foods, like all cheese factories, must cope with processing very different quantities of milk at different times of the year. In spring and during early summer, cows produce large quantities of milk, but in late summer and autumn the supply of milk slows to a trickle. Before the introduction of annualized hours, the factory had relied on overtime and

hiring temporary workers during the busy season. Now the staff are contracted to work a set number of hours a year with rotas agreed more than a year in advance and after consultation with the union. This means that at the end of July staff broadly know what days and hours they will be working up to September of the following year. If an emergency should arise, the company can call in people from a group of 'super crew' who work more flexible hours in return for higher pay but can do any job in the factory.

However, not all experiments with annualized hours have been as successful as that at Express Foods. In cases where demand is very unpredictable, staff can be asked to come in to work at very short notice. This can cause considerable disruption to social and family life. For example, at one news-broadcasting company, the scheme caused problems. Journalists and camera crew who went to cover a foreign crisis found that they had worked so many hours they were asked to take the whole of one month off to compensate. Since they had no holiday plans, many would have preferred to work.

Alternative offerings

Alternative offerings

Sometimes, a more radical approach is required to fill periods of low demand such as developing offerings which can be delivered using existing processes, but have different demand patterns throughout the year (see the Short case 'Getting the message' for an example of this approach). Most universities fill their accommodation and lecture theatres with conferences and company meetings during vacations. Ski resorts provide organized mountain activity holidays in the summer. Some garden tractor companies in the US now make snow movers in the autumn and winter. The apparent benefits of filling capacity in this way must be weighted against the risks of damaging the core service or product, and the operation must be fully capable of serving both markets. Some universities have been criticized for providing sub-standard, badly decorated accommodation which met the needs of impecunious undergraduates, but which failed to impress executives at a trade conference.

Mixed plans

Each of the three 'pure' plans is applied only where its advantages strongly outweigh its disadvantages. For many organizations, however, these 'pure' approaches do not match their required combination of competitive and operational objectives. Most operations managers are required simultaneously to reduce costs and inventory, to minimize capital investment, and yet to provide a responsive and customer-oriented approach at all times. For this reason, most choose to follow a mixture of the three approaches. This can be best illustrated by the woollen knitwear company example (see Figure 8.10). Here some of the peak demand has been brought forward by the company offering discounts to selected retail customers (manage demand plan). Capacity has also been adjusted at two points in the year to reflect the broad changes in demand (chase demand plan). Yet the adjustment in capacity is not sufficient to totally avoid the build-up of inventories (level capacity plan).

Yield management

Yield management

In operations which have relatively fixed capacities, such as airlines and hotels, it is important to use the capacity of the operation for generating revenue to its full potential. One approach used by such operations is called **yield management**.[4] This is really a collection of methods, some of which we have already discussed, which can be used to ensure that an operation maximizes its potential to generate profit. Yield management is especially useful where:

- capacity is relatively fixed;
- the market can be fairly clearly segmented;
- the service cannot be stored in any way;

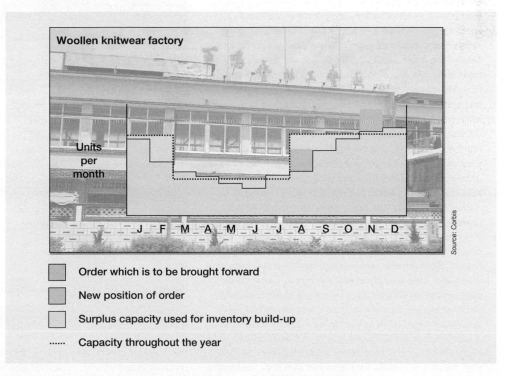

Figure 8.10 A mixed capacity plan for the woollen knitwear factory

- the services are sold in advance;
- the marginal cost of making a sale is relatively low.

Airlines, for example, fit all these criteria. They adopt a collection of methods to try to maximize the yield (i.e. profit) from their capacity. These include the following:

- *Over-booking capacity.* Not every passenger who has booked a place on a flight will actually show up for the flight. If the airline did not fill this seat it would lose the revenue from it. Because of this, airlines regularly book more passengers onto flights than the capacity of the aircraft can cope with. If they over-book by the exact number of passengers who fail to show up, they have maximized their revenue under the circumstances. Of course, if more passengers show up than they expect, the airline will have a number of upset passengers to deal with (although they may be able to offer financial inducements for the passengers to take another flight). If they fail to over-book sufficiently, they will have empty seats. By studying past data on flight demand, airlines try to balance the risks of over-booking and under-booking.

- *Price discounting.* At quiet times, when demand is unlikely to fill capacity, airlines will also sell heavily discounted tickets to agents who themselves take the risk of finding customers for them. In effect, this is using the price mechanism to affect demand.

- *Varying service types.* Discounting and other methods of affecting demand are also adjusted depending on the demand for particular types of service. For example, the relative demand for first-, business- and economy-class seats varies throughout the year. There is no point discounting tickets in a class for which demand will be high. Yield management also tries to adjust the availability of the different classes of seat to reflect their demand. They will also vary the number of seats available in each class by upgrading or even changing the configuration of airline seats.

Short case
Getting the message[5]

Companies which traditionally operate in seasonal markets can demonstrate some considerable ingenuity in their attempts to develop counter-seasonal products. One of the most successful industries in this respect has been the greetings card industry. Mother's Day, Father's Day, Halloween, Valentine's Day and other occasions have all been promoted as times to send (and buy) appropriately designed cards. Now, having run out of occasions to promote, greetings card manufacturers have moved on to 'non-occasion' cards, which can be sent at any time. These have the considerable advantage of being less seasonal, thus making the companies' seasonality less marked.

Hallmark Cards, the market leader in North America, has been the pioneer in developing non-occasion cards. Their cards include those intended to be sent from a parent to a child with messages such as 'Would a hug help?', 'Sorry I made you feel bad' and 'You're perfectly wonderful – it's your room that's a mess'. Other cards deal with more serious adult themes such as friendship ('You're more than a friend, you're just like family') or even alcoholism ('This is hard to say, but I think you're a much neater person when you're not drinking'). Now Hallmark Cards has founded a 'loyalty marketing group' that 'helps companies communicate with their customers at an emotional level'. It promotes the use of greetings

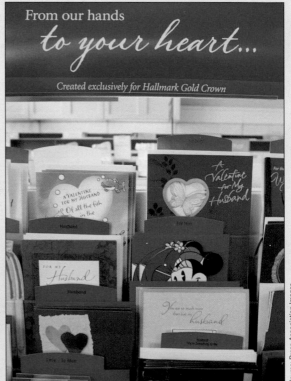

Source: Press Association Images

cards for corporate use, to show that customers and employees are valued. Whatever else these products may be, they are not seasonal!

Choosing a capacity management approach

Before an operation can decide which of the capacity plans to adopt, it must be aware of the consequences of adopting each plan in its own set of circumstances. Two methods are particularly useful in helping to assess the consequences of adopting particular capacity plans:

Cumulative
representations
Queuing theory

● cumulative representations of demand and capacity;
● queuing theory.

Cumulative representations

Figure 8.11 shows the forecast aggregated demand for a chocolate factory which makes confectionery products. Demand for its products in the shops is greatest at Christmas. To meet this demand and allow time for the products to work their way through the distribution system, the factory must supply a demand which peaks in September, as shown. One method of assessing whether a particular level of capacity can satisfy the demand would be to calculate the degree of over-capacity below the graph which represents the capacity levels (areas A and C) and the degree of under-capacity above the graph (area B). If the total over-capacity is greater than the total under-capacity for a particular level of capacity, then that capacity could be regarded as adequate to satisfy demand fully, the assumption being that inventory has been accumulated in the periods of over-capacity. However, there are two problems with this approach. The first is that each month shown in Figure 8.11 may not have the same amount of productive time. Some months (August, for example) may contain vacation periods which reduce the availability of capacity. The second problem is that a capacity level which seems adequate may only be able to supply products *after* the demand for them has occurred. For example, if the period of under-capacity occurred at the beginning of the year, no inventory could have accumulated to meet demand. A far superior way of assessing capacity plans is first to plot demand on a *cumulative* basis. This is shown as the blue line in Figure 8.12.

The cumulative representation of demand immediately reveals more information. First, it shows that although total demand peaks in September, because of the restricted number of available productive days, the peak demand per productive day occurs a month earlier in August. Second, it shows that the fluctuation in demand over the year is even greater than it seemed. The ratio of monthly peak demand to monthly lowest demand is 6.5:1, but the ratio of peak to lowest demand per productive day is 10:1. Demand per productive day is more relevant to operations managers, because productive days represent the time element of capacity.

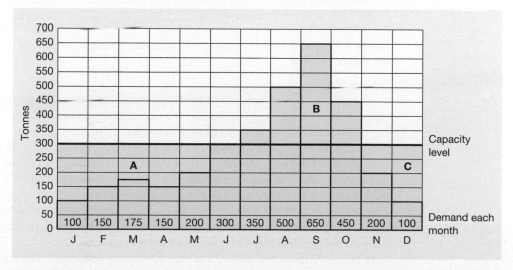

Figure 8.11 If the over-capacity areas (A+C) are greater than the under-capacity area (B), the capacity level seems adequate to meet demand. This may not necessarily be the case, however

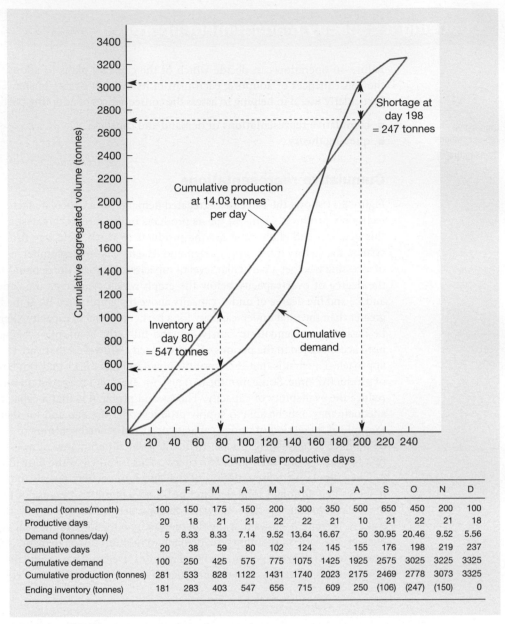

Figure 8.12 A level capacity plan which produces shortages in spite of meeting demand at the end of the year

The most useful consequence of plotting demand on a cumulative basis is that, by plotting capacity on the same graph, the feasibility and consequences of a capacity plan can be assessed. Figure 8.12 also shows a level capacity plan which produces at a rate of 14.03 tonnes per productive day. This meets cumulative demand by the end of the year. It would also pass our earlier test of total over-capacity being the same as or greater than under-capacity.

However, if one of the aims of the plan is to supply demand when it occurs, the plan is inadequate. Up to around day 168, the line representing cumulative production is above that representing cumulative demand. This means that at any time during this period, more product has been produced by the factory than has been demanded from it. In fact the vertical distance between the two lines is the level of inventory at that point in time. So by day 80, 1,122 tonnes have been produced but only 575 tonnes have been demanded. The surplus of production above demand, or inventory, is therefore 547 tonnes. When the cumulative demand line lies above the cumulative production line, the reverse is true. The vertical distance between the two lines now indicates the shortage, or lack of supply. So by day 198, 3,025 tonnes have been demanded but only 2,778 tonnes produced. The shortage is therefore 247 tonnes.

For any capacity plan to meet demand as it occurs, its cumulative production line must always lie above the cumulative demand line. This makes it a straightforward task to judge the adequacy of a plan, simply by looking at its cumulative representation. An impression of the inventory implications can also be gained from a cumulative representation by judging the area between the cumulative production and demand curves. This represents the amount of inventory carried over the period. Figure 8.13 illustrates an adequate level capacity plan for the chocolate manufacturer, together with the costs of carrying inventory. It is assumed that

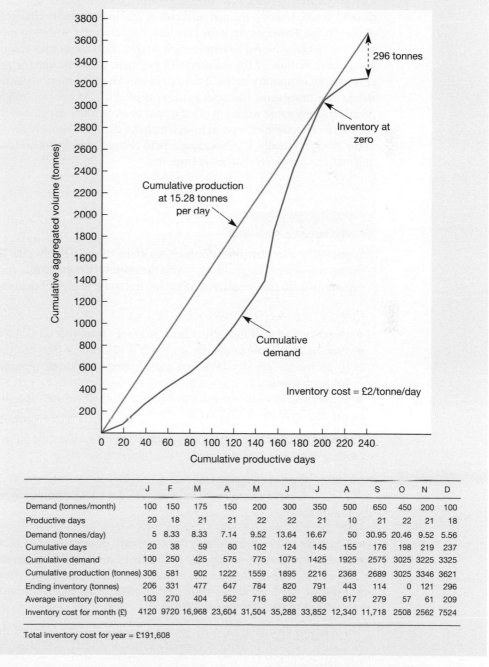

	J	F	M	A	M	J	J	A	S	O	N	D
Demand (tonnes/month)	100	150	175	150	200	300	350	500	650	450	200	100
Productive days	20	18	21	21	22	22	21	10	21	22	21	18
Demand (tonnes/day)	5	8.33	8.33	7.14	9.52	13.64	16.67	50	30.95	20.46	9.52	5.56
Cumulative days	20	38	59	80	102	124	145	155	176	198	219	237
Cumulative demand	100	250	425	575	775	1075	1425	1925	2575	3025	3225	3325
Cumulative production (tonnes)	306	581	902	1222	1559	1895	2216	2368	2689	3025	3346	3621
Ending inventory (tonnes)	206	331	477	647	784	820	791	443	114	0	121	296
Average inventory (tonnes)	103	270	404	562	716	802	806	617	279	57	61	209
Inventory cost for month (£)	4120	9720	16,968	23,604	31,504	35,288	33,852	12,340	11,718	2508	2562	7524

Total inventory cost for year = £191,608

Figure 8.13 A level capacity plan which meets demand at all times during the year

inventory costs £2 per tonne per day to keep in storage. The average inventory each month is taken to be the average of the beginning- and end-of-month inventory levels, and the inventory-carrying cost each month is the product of the average inventory, the inventory cost per day per tonne and the number of days in the month.

Comparing plans on a cumulative basis

Chase demand plans can also be illustrated on a cumulative representation. Rather than the cumulative production line having a constant gradient, it would have a varying gradient representing the output rate at any point in time. If a pure demand chase plan was adopted, the cumulative production line would match the cumulative demand line. The gap between the two lines would be zero and hence inventory would be zero. Although this would eliminate inventory-carrying costs, as we discussed earlier, there would be costs associated with changing capacity levels. Usually, the marginal cost of making a capacity change increases with the size of the change. For example, if the chocolate manufacturer wishes to increase capacity by 5 per cent, this can be achieved by requesting its staff to work overtime – a simple, fast and relatively inexpensive option. If the change is 15 per cent, overtime cannot provide sufficient extra capacity and temporary staff will need to be employed – a more expensive solution which also would take more time. Increases in capacity of above 15 per cent might only be achieved by subcontracting some work out. This would be even more expensive. The cost of the change will also be affected by the point from which the change is being made, as well as the direction of the change. Usually, it is less expensive to change capacity towards what is regarded as the 'normal' capacity level than away from it.

Worked example

Suppose the chocolate manufacturer, which has been operating the level capacity plan as shown in Figure 8.13, is unhappy with the inventory costs of this approach. It decides to explore two alternative plans, both involving some degree of demand chasing.

Plan 1

- Organize and staff the factory for a 'normal' capacity level of 8.7 tonnes per day.
- Produce at 8.7 tonnes per day for the first 124 days of the year, then increase capacity to 29 tonnes per day by heavy use of overtime, hiring temporary staff and some subcontracting.
- Produce at 29 tonnes per day until day 194, then reduce capacity back to 8.7 tonnes per day for the rest of the year.

The costs of changing capacity by such a large amount (the ratio of peak to normal capacity is 3.33:1) are calculated by the company as being:

Cost of changing from 8.7 tonnes/day to 29 tonnes/day = £110,000
Cost of changing from 29 tonnes/day to 8.7 tonnes/day = £60,000

Plan 2

- Organize and staff the factory for a 'normal' capacity level of 12.4 tonnes per day.
- Produce at 12.4 tonnes per day for the first 150 days of the year, then increase capacity to 29 tonnes per day by overtime and hiring some temporary staff.
- Produce at 29 tonnes/day until day 190, then reduce capacity back to 12.4 tonnes per day for the rest of the year.

The costs of changing capacity in this plan are smaller because the degree of change is smaller (a peak to normal capacity ratio of 2.34:1), and they are calculated by the company as being:

Cost of changing from 12.4 tonnes/day to 29 tonnes/day = £35,000
Cost of changing from 29 tonnes/day to 12.4 tonnes/day = £15,000

Figure 8.14 illustrates both plans on a cumulative basis. Plan 1, which envisaged two drastic changes in capacity, has high capacity change costs but, because its production levels are close to demand levels, it has low inventory carrying costs. Plan 2 sacrifices some of the inventory cost advantage of Plan 1 but saves more in terms of capacity change costs.

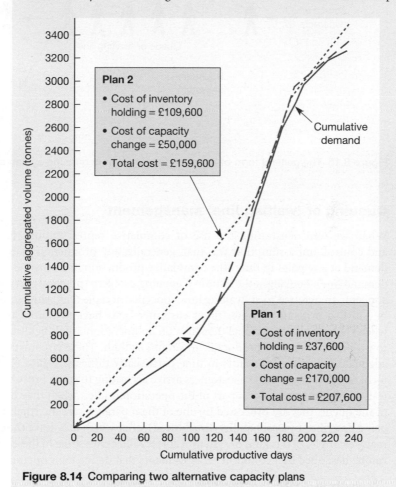

Figure 8.14 Comparing two alternative capacity plans

Capacity planning as a queuing problem

Cumulative representations of capacity plans are useful where the operation has the ability to store its finished goods as inventory. However, for operations where it is not possible to produce products and services *before* demand for them has occurred, a cumulative representation would tell us relatively little. The cumulative 'production' could never be above the cumulative demand line. At best, it could show when an operation failed to meets its demand. So the vertical gap between the cumulative demand and production lines would indicate the amount of demand unsatisfied. Some of this demand would look elsewhere to be satisfied, but some would wait. This is why, for operations which, by their nature, cannot store their output, such as most service operations, capacity planning and control is best considered

Queuing theory using waiting or **queuing theory**.

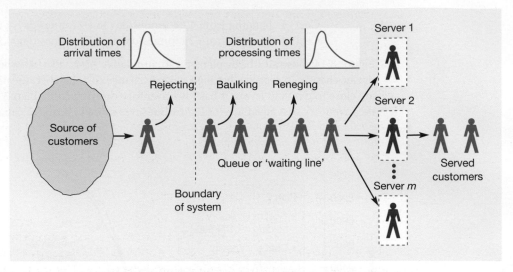

Figure 8.15 The general form of the capacity decision in queuing systems

Queuing or 'waiting line' management

When we were illustrating the use of cumulative representations for capacity planning and control, our assumption was that, generally, any production plan should aim to meet demand at any point in time (the cumulative production line must be above the cumulative demand line). Looking at the issue as a queuing problem (in many parts of the world queuing concepts are referred to as 'waiting line' concepts) accepts that, while sometime demand may be satisfied instantly, at other times customers may have to wait. This is particularly true when the arrival of individual demands on an operation are difficult to predict, or the time to produce a service or product is uncertain, or both. These circumstances make providing adequate capacity at all points in time particularly difficult. Figure 8.15 shows the general form of this capacity issue. Customers arrive according to some probability distribution and wait to be processed (unless part of the operation is idle); when they have reached the front of the queue, they are processed by one of the n parallel 'servers' (their processing time also being described by a probability distribution), after which they leave the operation. There are many examples of this kind of system. Table 8.2 illustrates some of these. All of these examples can be described by a common set of elements that define their queuing behaviour.

Calling population   *The source of customers* – sometimes called the **calling population** – is the source of supply of customers. In queue management 'customers' are not always human. 'Customers' could for example be trucks arriving at a weighbridge, orders arriving to be processed or machines waiting to be serviced, etc. The source of customers for queuing system can be either *finite*

Table 8.2 Examples of operations which have parallel processors

Operation	Arrivals	Processing capacity
Bank	Customers	Tellers
Supermarket	Shoppers	Checkouts
Hospital clinic	Patients	Doctors
Graphic artist	Commissions	Artists
Custom cake decorators	Orders	Cake decorators
Ambulance service	Emergencies	Ambulances with crews
Telephone switchboard	Calls	Telephonists
Maintenance department	Breakdowns	Maintenance staff

or *infinite*. A finite source has a known number of possible customers. For example, if one maintenance person serves four assembly lines, the number of customers for the maintenance person is known, i.e. four. There will be a certain probability that one of the assembly lines will break down and need repairing. However, if one line really does break down the probability of another line needing repair is reduced because there are now only three lines to break down. So, with a finite source of customers the probability of a customer arriving depends on the number of customers already being serviced. By contrast, an infinite customer source assumes that there is a large number of potential customers so that it is always possible for another customer to arrive no matter how many are being serviced. Most queuing systems that deal with outside markets have infinite, or 'close-to-infinite', customer sources.

Balancing capacity and demand

The dilemma in managing the capacity of a queuing system is how many servers to have available at any point in time in order to avoid unacceptably long queuing times or unacceptably low utilization of the servers. Because of the probabilistic arrival and processing times, only rarely will the arrival of customers match the ability of the operation to cope with them. Sometimes, if several customers arrive in quick succession and require longer-than-average processing times, queues will build up in front of the operation. At other times, when customers arrive less frequently than average and also require shorter-than-average processing times, some of the servers in the system will be idle. So even when the average capacity (processing capability) of the operation matches the average demand (arrival rate) on the system, both queues and idle time will occur.

If the operation has too few servers (that is, capacity is set at too low a level), queues will build up to a level where customers become dissatisfied with the time they are having to wait, although the utilization level of the servers will be high. If too many servers are in place (that is, capacity is set at too high a level), the time which customers can expect to wait will not be long but the utilization of the servers will be low. This is why the capacity management problem for this type of operation is often presented as a trade-off between customer waiting time and system utilization. What is certainly important in making capacity decisions is being able to predict both of these factors for a given operation.

Variability in demand or supply

Variability reduces effective capacity

The variability, either in demand or capacity, as discussed above, will reduce the ability of an operation to process its inputs. That is, it will **reduce its effective capacity**. This effect was explained in Chapter 5 when the consequences of variability in individual processes were discussed. As a reminder, the greater the variability in arrival time or activity time at a process the more the process will suffer both high throughput times and reduced utilization. This principle holds true for whole operations, and because long throughput times mean that queues will build up in the operation, high variability also affects inventory levels. This is illustrated in Figure 8.16. The implication of this is that the greater the variability, the more extra capacity will need to be provided to compensate for the reduced utilization of available capacity. Therefore, operations with high levels of variability will tend to set their base level of capacity relatively high in order to provide this extra capacity.

Customer perceptions of queuing

If the 'customers' waiting in a queue are real human customers, an important aspect of how they judge the service they receive from a queuing system is how they perceive the time spent queuing. It is well known that if you are told that you'll be waiting in a queue for fifteen minutes and you are actually serviced in ten minutes, your perception of the queuing experience will be more positive than if you were told that you would be waiting five minutes but the queue actually took ten minutes. Because of this, the management of queuing systems

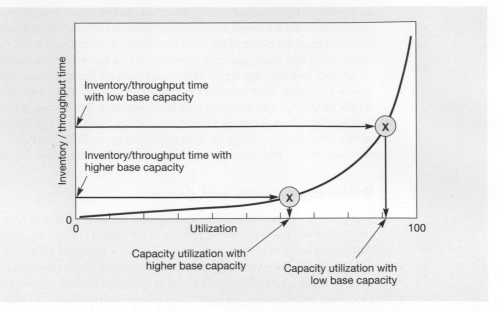

Figure 8.16 The effect of variability on the utilization of capacity

usually involves attempting to manage customers' perceptions and expectations in some way (see the Short case on Madame Tussaud's for an example of this). There are a number of principles that influence how customers perceive waiting times:[6]

Short case
Managing queues at Madame Tussaud's, Amsterdam

A short holiday in Amsterdam would not be complete without a visit to Madame Tussaud's, located on four upper floors of the city's most prominent department store in Dam Square. With 600,000 visitors each year, this is one of the most popular tourist attractions in Amsterdam. On busy days in the summer, the centre can just manage to handle 5,000 visitors. On a wet day in January, however, there may only be 300 visitors throughout the whole day. The centre is open for admission, seven days a week, from 10.00 am to 5.30 pm. In the streets outside, orderly queues of expectant tourists snake along the pavement, looking in at the displays in the store windows. In this public open space, Tussaud's can do little to entertain the visitors, but entrepreneurial buskers and street artists are quick to capitalize on a captive market. On reaching the entrance lobby, individuals, families and groups purchase their admission tickets. The lobby is in the shape of a large horseshoe, with the ticket sales booth in the centre. On winter days or at quiet spells, there will only be one sales assistant, but on busier days, visitors can pay at either side of the ticket booth, to speed up the process. Having paid, the visitors assemble in the

lobby outside the two lifts. While waiting in this area, a photographer wanders around offering to take photos of the visitors standing next to life-sized wax figures of famous people. They may also be entertained by living look-alikes of famous personalities who act as guides to groups of visitors in batches of around 25 customers (the capacity of each of the two lifts which takes visitors up to the facility). The lifts arrive every four minutes and customers simultaneously disembark, forming one group of about 50 customers, who stay together throughout the session.

- Time spent idle is perceived as longer than time spent occupied.
- The wait before a service starts is perceived as more tedious than a wait within the process.
- Anxiety and/or uncertainty heightens the perception that time spent waiting is long.
- A wait of unknown duration is perceived as more tedious than a wait of known duration.
- An unexplained wait is perceived as more tedious than a wait that is explained.
- The higher the value of the service for the customer, the longer the waiting tolerance.
- Waiting on one's own is more tedious than waiting in a group (unless you really don't like the others in the group).

Summary answers to key questions

Check and improve your understanding of this chapter using self-assessment questions and a personalized study plan, audio and video downloads, and an eBook – all at **www.myomlab.com**.

➤ What is capacity management?

- It is the way operations organize the level of value-added activity which they can achieve under normal operating conditions over a period of time.

- It is usual to distinguish between long-, medium- and short-term capacity decisions. Medium- and short-term capacity management, where the capacity level of the organization is adjusted within the fixed limits which are set by long-term capacity decisions, is sometimes called aggregate planning and control.

- Almost all operations have some kind of fluctuation in demand (or seasonality) caused by some combination of climatic, festive, behavioural, political, financial or social factors.

➤ How are demand and capacity measured?

- Either by the availability of its input resources or by the output which is created. Which of these measures is used partly depends on how stable the mix of outputs is. If it is difficult to aggregate the different types of output from an operation, input measures are usually preferred.

- The usage of capacity can be measured by overall equipment effectiveness (OEE).

➤ What are the alternative ways of coping with demand fluctuation?

- Output can be kept level, in effect ignoring demand fluctuations. This will result in under-utilization of capacity where outputs cannot be stored, or the build-up of inventories where output can be stored or queues when they can't be stored.

- Output can chase demand by fluctuating the output level through some combination of over-time, varying the size of the workforce, using part-time staff and subcontracting.

- Demand can be changed, either by influencing the market through such measures as advertising and promotion, or by developing alternative products with a counter-seasonal demand pattern.

- Most operations use a mix of all these three 'pure' strategies.

> ➤ **How can operations manage their capacity level?**

■ Representing demand and output in the form of cumulative representations allows the feasibility of alternative capacity plans to be assessed.

■ In many operations, especially service operations, a queuing approach can be used to explore capacity strategies.

> ➤ **How can queuing theory be used to plan capacity?**

■ By considering the capacity decision as a dynamic decision which periodically updates the decisions and assumptions upon which decisions are based.

Learning exercises

These problems and applications will help to improve your analysis of operations. You can find more practice problems as well as worked examples and guided solutions on MyOMLab at www.myomlab.com.

1   A local government office issues hunting licences. Demand for these licences is relatively slow in the first part of the year but then increases after the middle of the year before slowing down again towards the end of the year. The department works a 220-day year on a 5-days-a-week basis. Between working days 0 and 100, demand is 25 per cent of demand during the peak period which lasts between day 100 and day 150. After 150 demand reduces to about 12 per cent of the demand during the peak period. In total, the department processes 10,000 applications per year. The department has 2 permanent members of staff who are capable of processing 15 licence applications per day. If an untrained temporary member of staff can only process 10 licences per day, how many temporary staff should the department recruit between days 100 and 150?

2   In the example above, if a new computer system is installed that allows experienced staff to increase their work rate to 20 applications per day, and untrained staff to 15 applications per day, (a) does the department still need 2 permanent staff, and (b) how many temporary members of staff will be needed between days 100 and 150?

3   A field service organization repairs and maintains printing equipment for a large number of customers. It offers one level of service to all its customers and employs 30 staff. The operation's marketing vice-president has decided that in future the company will offer 3 standards of service, platinum, gold and silver. It is estimated that platinum-service customers will require 50 per cent more time from the company's field service engineers than the current service. The current service is to be called 'the gold service'. The silver service is likely to require about 80 per cent of the time of the gold service. If future demand is estimated to be 20 per cent platinum, 70 per cent gold and 10 per cent silver service, how many staff will be needed to fulfil demand?

4   Look again at the principles which govern customers' perceptions of the queuing experience. For the following operations, apply the principles to minimize the perceived negative effects of queuing.

(a) A cinema

(b) A doctor's surgery

(c) Waiting to board an aircraft.

Want to know more?

Hopp, W.J. and Spearman, M.L. (2000) *Factory Physics*, 2nd edn, McGraw-Hill, New York, NY. Very mathematical indeed, but includes some interesting maths on queuing theory.

Olhager, J., Rudberg, M. and Wikner, J. (2001) Long-term capacity management: linking the perspectives from manufacturing strategy and sales and operations planning, *International Journal of Production Economics*, vol. 69, issue 2, 215–25. Academic article, but interesting.

Vollmann, T., Berry, W., Whybark, D.C. and Jacobs, F.R. (2004) *Manufacturing Planning and Control Systems for Supply Chain Management: The Definitive Guide for Professionals*, McGraw-Hill Higher Education, New York. The latest version of the 'bible' of manufacturing planning and control. It's exhaustive in its coverage of all aspects of planning and control including aggregate planning.

Useful websites

www.bis.gov.uk/employment Website which has developed a framework for employers and employees to promote a skilled and flexible labour market founded on principles of partnership.

www.worksmart.org.uk/index.php This site is from the Trades Union Congress. Its aim is 'to help today's working people get the best out of the world of work'.

www.opsman.org Lots of useful stuff.

www.equalityhumanrights.com This web site aims to provide a resource for legal advisers and representatives who are conducting claims on behalf of applicants in sex discrimination and equal pay cases in England and Wales. This site covers employment-related sex discrimination only.

www.dol.gov/index.htm US Department of Labor's site with information regarding using part-time employees.

www.downtimecentral.com/ Lots of information on operational equipment efficiency (OEE).

Now that you have finished reading this chapter, why not visit MyOMLab at www.myomlab.com where you'll find more learning resources to help you make the most of your studies and get a better grade.

Chapter 9

Inventory management

Key questions

➤ What is inventory?
➤ What are the reasons for holding inventory and what are the disadvantages?
➤ How much inventory should an operation hold?
➤ When should an operation replenish its inventory?
➤ How can inventory be managed?

Introduction

Operations managers often have an ambivalent attitude towards inventories. On the one hand, they are costly, sometimes tying up considerable amounts of working capital. They are also risky because items held in stock could deteriorate, become obsolete or just get lost, and, furthermore, they take up valuable space in the operation. This risk is also seen when inventory is in the form of customers who rarely enjoy waiting. On the other hand, inventories provide some security in an uncertain environment that one can deliver items in stock or work on customers in process should demand materialize. This is the dilemma of inventory management: in spite of the cost and the other disadvantages associated with inventories, they do facilitate the smoothing of supply and demand. In fact they only exist because supply and demand are not exactly in harmony with each other. Figure 9.1 shows where this chapter fits into the overall operations model.

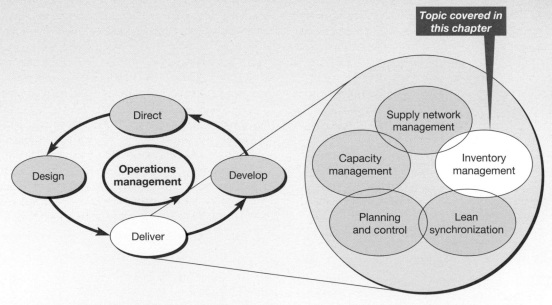

Figure 9.1 This chapter examines inventory management

Check and improve your understanding of this chapter using self-assessment questions and a personalized study plan, audio and video downloads, and an eBook – all at www.myomlab.com.

Operations in practice **The UK's National Blood Service**[1]

No inventory manager likes to run out of stock. But for blood services, such as the UK's National Blood Service (NBS) the consequences of running out of stock can be particularly serious. Many people owe their lives to transfusions that were made possible by the efficient management of blood, stocked in a supply network that stretches from donation centres through to hospital blood banks. The NBS supply chain has three main stages:

1 *Collection*, which involves recruiting and retaining blood donors, encouraging them to attend donor sessions (at mobile or fixed locations) and transporting the donated blood to their local blood centre.
2 *Processing*, which breaks blood down into its constituent parts (red cells, platelets and plasma) as well over twenty other blood-based 'products'.
3 *Distribution*, which transports blood from blood centres to hospitals in response to both routine and emergency requests. Of the Service's 200,000 deliveries a year, about 2,500 are emergency deliveries.

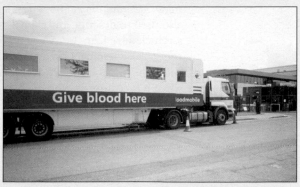

Source: Alamy/Van Hilversum

Inventory accumulates at all three stages, and in individual hospitals' blood banks. Within the supply chain, around 11.5 per cent of donated red blood cells donated are lost. Much of this is due to losses in processing, but around 5 per cent is not used because it has 'become unavailable', mainly because it has been stored for too long. Part of the Service's inventory control task is to keep this 'time-expired' loss to a minimum. In fact, only small losses occur within the NBS, most blood being lost when it is stored in hospital blood banks that are outside its direct control. However, it does attempt to provide advice and support to hospitals to enable them to use blood efficiently.

Blood components and products need to be stored under a variety of conditions, but will deteriorate over time. This varies depending on the component; platelets have a shelf life of only five days and demand can fluctuate significantly. This makes stock control particularly difficult. Even red blood cells that have a

shelf life of 35 days may not be acceptable to hospitals if they are close to their 'use-by date'. Stock accuracy is crucial. Giving a patient the wrong type of blood can be fatal.

At a local level demand can be affected significantly by accidents. For example, one serious accident involving a cyclist used 750 units of blood, which completely exhausted the available supply (miraculously, he survived). Large-scale accidents usually generate a surge of offers from donors wishing to make immediate donations. There is also a more predictable seasonality to the donating of blood, however, with a low period during the summer vacation. Yet there is always an unavoidable tension between maintaining sufficient stocks to provide a very high level of supply dependability to hospitals and minimizing wastage. Unless blood stocks are controlled carefully, they can easily go past the 'use-by date' and be wasted. But avoiding outdated blood products is not the only inventory objective at NBS. It also measures the percentage of requests that it was able to meet in full, the percentage emergency requests delivered within two hours, the percentage of units banked to donors bled, the number of new donors enrolled, and the number of donors waiting longer than 30 minutes before they are able to donate. The traceability of donated blood is also increasingly important. Should any problems with a blood product arise, its source can be traced back to the original donor.

What is inventory?

Inventory

Inventory, or 'stock' as it is more commonly called in some countries, is defined here as the *stored accumulation of resources in a transformation system*. Sometimes the term 'inventory' is also used to describe any capital-transforming resource, such as rooms in a hotel, or cars in a vehicle-hire firm, but we will not use that definition here. Usually the term refers only to *transformed resources*. So a manufacturing company will hold stocks of materials, a tax office will hold stocks of information, and a theme park will hold stocks of customers. Note that when it is customers who are being processed we normally refer to these 'stocks' as 'queues'. This chapter will deal particularly with inventories of materials.

Revisiting operations objectives; the roles of inventory

Inventory can influence all performance objectives

Most of us are accustomed to keeping inventory for use in our personal lives, but often we don't think about it. For example, most families have some stocks of food and drinks, so that they don't have to go out to the shops before every meal. Holding a variety of food ingredients in stock in the kitchen cupboard or freezer gives us the ability to respond quickly (with *speed*) in preparing a meal whenever unexpected guests arrive. It also allows us the *flexibility* to choose a range of menu options without having to go to the time and trouble of purchasing further ingredients. We may purchase some items because we have found something of exceptional *quality*, but intend to save it for a special occasion. Many people buy multiple packs to achieve lower *costs* for a wide range of goods. In general, our inventory planning protects us from critical stock-outs; so this approach gives a level of *dependability* of supplies.

It is, however, entirely possible to manage our inventory differently. For example, some people are short of available cash and/or space, and so cannot 'invest' in large inventories of goods. They may shop locally for much smaller quantities. They forfeit the cost benefits of bulk-buying, but do not have to transport heavy or bulky supplies. They also reduce the risk of forgetting an item in the cupboard and letting it go out of date. Essentially, they purchase against specific known requirements (the next meal). However, they may find that the local shop is temporarily out of stock of a particular item, forcing them, for example, to drink coffee without their usual milk. How we control our own supplies is therefore a matter of choice which can affect their quality (e.g. freshness), availability or speed of response, dependability of supply, flexibility of choice, and cost. It is the same for most organizations. Significant levels of inventory can be held for a range of sensible and pragmatic reasons but it must also be tightly controlled for other equally good reasons.

Why is inventory necessary?

No matter what is being stored as inventory, or where it is positioned in the operation, it will be there because there is a difference in the timing or rate of supply and demand. If the supply of any item occurred exactly when it was demanded, the item would never be stored. A common analogy is the water tank shown in Figure 9.2. If, over time, the rate of supply of water to the tank differs from the rate at which it is demanded, a tank of water (inventory) will be needed if supply is to be maintained. When the rate of supply exceeds the rate of demand, inventory increases; when the rate of demand exceeds the rate of supply, inventory decreases. So if an operation can match supply and demand rates, it will also succeed in reducing its inventory levels.

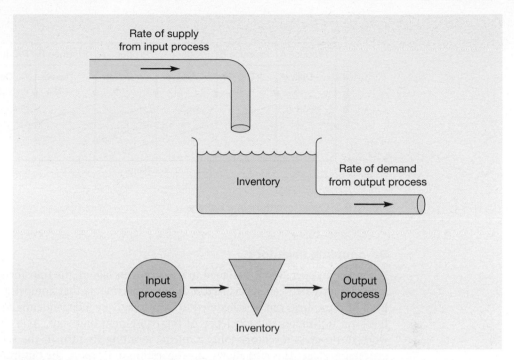

Figure 9.2 Inventory is created to compensate for the differences in timing between supply and demand

Types of inventory

The various reasons for an imbalance between the rates of supply and demand at different points in any supply network lead to the different types of inventory. There are five of these: buffer inventory, cycle inventory, de-coupling inventory, anticipation inventory and pipeline inventory.

Buffer inventory

Buffer inventory is also called **safety inventory**. Its purpose is to compensate for the unexpected fluctuations in supply and demand. For example, a retail operation can never forecast demand perfectly, even when it has a good idea of the most likely demand level. It will order goods from its suppliers such that there is always a certain amount of most items in stock. This minimum level of inventory is there to cover against the possibility that demand will be greater than expected during the time taken to deliver the goods. It can also compensate for the uncertainties in the process of the supply of goods into the store, perhaps because of the unreliability of certain suppliers or transport firms.

Buffer inventory
Safety inventory

Cycle inventory

Cycle inventory occurs because one or more stages in the process cannot supply all the items it produces simultaneously. For example, suppose a baker makes three types of bread, each of which is equally popular with its customers. Because of the nature of the mixing and baking process, only one kind of bread can be produced at any time. The baker would have to produce each type of bread in batches as shown in Figure 9.3. The batches must be large enough to satisfy the demand for each kind of bread between the times when each batch is ready for sale. So even when demand is steady and predictable, there will always be some inventory to compensate for the intermittent supply of each type of bread. Cycle inventory only results from the need to produce products in batches, and the amount of it depends on volume decisions which are described in a later section of this chapter.

Cycle inventory

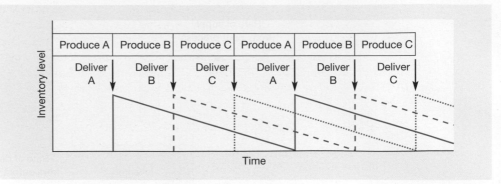

Figure 9.3 Cycle inventory in a bakery

De-coupling inventory

De-coupling inventory

Wherever an operation is designed to use a process layout, the transformed resources move intermittently between specialized areas or departments that comprise similar operations. Each of these areas can be scheduled to work relatively independently in order to maximize the local utilization and efficiency of the equipment and staff. As a result, each batch of work-in-progress inventory joins a queue, awaiting its turn in the schedule for the next processing stage. This also allows each operation to be set to the optimum processing speed (cycle time), regardless of the speed of the steps before and after. Thus **de-coupling inventory** creates the opportunity for independent scheduling and processing speeds between process stages.

Anticipation inventory

Anticipation inventory

In Chapter 8 we saw how anticipation inventory can be used to cope with seasonal demand. Rather than trying to make the product (such as chocolate) only when it was needed, it was produced throughout the year ahead of demand and put into inventory until it was needed. **Anticipation inventory** is most commonly used when demand fluctuations are large but relatively predictable. It might also be used when supply variations are significant, such as in the canning or freezing of seasonal foods.

Pipeline inventory

Pipeline inventory

Pipeline inventory exists because material cannot be transported instantaneously between the point of supply and the point of demand. If a retail store orders a consignment of items from one of its suppliers, the supplier will allocate the stock to the retail store in its own warehouse, pack it, load it onto its truck, transport it to its destination, and unload it into the retailer's inventory. From the time that stock is allocated (and therefore it is unavailable to any other customer) to the time it becomes available for the retail store, it is pipeline inventory. Pipeline inventory also exists within processes where the layout is geographically spread out. For example, a large European manufacturer of specialized steel regularly moves cargoes of part-finished materials between its two mills in the UK and Scandinavia using a dedicated vessel that shuttles between the two countries every week. All the thousands of tonnes of material in transit are pipeline inventory.

The position of inventory

Not only are there several reasons for supply–demand imbalance, there could also be several points where such imbalance exists between different stages in the operation. Perhaps the simplest level is the single-stage inventory system, such as a retail store, which will have only one stock of goods to manage. An automotive parts distribution operation will have a central

Raw materials inventory
Components inventory

Work-in-progress
Finished goods inventory

depot and various local distribution points which contain inventories. In many manufacturers of standard items, there are three types of inventory. The **raw material** and **components inventories** (sometimes called input inventories) receive goods from the operation's suppliers; the raw materials and components work their way through the various stages of the production process but spend considerable amounts of time as **work-in-progress** (or work-in-process) (WIP) before finally reaching the **finished goods inventory**.

Some disadvantages of holding inventory

Although inventory plays an important role in many operations performance, there are a number of negative aspects of inventory:

- Inventory ties up money, in the form of working capital, which is therefore unavailable for other uses, such as reducing borrowings or making investment in productive fixed assets.
- Inventory incurs storage costs (leasing space, maintaining appropriate conditions, etc.).
- Inventory may become obsolete as alternatives become available.
- Inventory can be damaged, or deteriorate.
- Inventory could be lost, or be expensive to retrieve, as it gets hidden amongst other inventory.
- Inventory might be hazardous to store (for example flammable solvents, explosives, chemicals and drugs), requiring special facilities and systems for safe handling.
- Inventory uses space that could be used to add value.
- Inventory involves administrative and insurance costs.

Day-to-day inventory decisions

At each point in the inventory system, operations managers need to manage the day-to-day tasks of running the system. Orders will be received from internal or external customers; these will be dispatched and demand will gradually deplete the inventory. Orders will need to be placed for replenishment of the stocks; deliveries will arrive and require storing. In managing the system, operations managers are involved in three major types of decision:

- *How much to order*. Every time a replenishment order is placed, how big should it be (sometimes called the *volume decision*)?
- *When to order*. At what point in time, or at what level of stock, should the replenishment order be placed (sometimes called the *timing decision*)?
- *How to control the system*. What procedures and routines should be installed to help make these decisions? Should different priorities be allocated to different stock items? How should stock information be stored?

The rest of this chapter examines the three key decisions.

The volume decision – how much to order

To illustrate this decision, consider again the example of the food and drinks we keep at our home. In managing this inventory we implicitly make decisions on *order quantity*, which is how much to purchase at one time. In making this decision we are balancing two sets of costs: the costs associated with going out to purchase the food items and the costs associated with holding the stocks. The option of holding very little or no inventory of food and purchasing each item only when it is needed has the advantage that it requires little money since purchases are made only when needed. However, it would involve purchasing provisions several times a day, which is inconvenient. At the very opposite extreme,

As before:

$$\text{Total cost} = \text{holding cost} + \text{order cost}$$

$$C_t = \frac{C_h Q(P - D)}{2P} + \frac{C_o D}{Q}$$

$$\frac{dC_t}{dQ} = \frac{C_h(P - D)}{2P} - \frac{C_o D}{Q^2}$$

Again, equating to zero and solving Q gives the minimum-cost order quantity EBQ:

$$\text{EBQ} = \sqrt{\frac{2C_o D}{C_h(1 - (D/P))}}$$

Worked example

The manager of a bottle-filling plant which bottles soft drinks needs to decide how long a 'run' of each type of drink to process. Demand for each type of drink is reasonably constant at 80,000 per month (a month has 160 production hours). The bottling lines fill at a rate of 3,000 bottles per hour, but take an hour to clean and reset between different drinks. The cost (of labour and lost production capacity) of each of these changeovers has been calculated at £100 per hour. Stock-holding costs are counted at £0.1 per bottle per month.

$$D = 80,000 \text{ per month}$$

$$= 500 \text{ per hour}$$

$$\text{EBQ} = \sqrt{\frac{2C_o D}{C_h(1 - (D/P))}}$$

$$= \sqrt{\frac{2 \times 100 \times 80,000}{0.1(1 - (500/3,000))}}$$

$$\text{EBQ} = 13,856$$

The staff who operate the lines have devised a method of reducing the changeover time from 1 hour to 30 minutes. How would that change the EBQ?

$$\text{New } C_o = £50$$

$$\text{New EBQ} = \sqrt{\frac{2 \times 50 \times 80,000}{0.1(1 - (500/3,000))}}$$

$$= 9,798$$

Critical commentary

The approach to determining order quantity which involves optimizing costs of holding stock against costs of ordering stock, typified by the EOQ and EBQ models, has always been subject to criticisms. Originally these concerned the validity of some of the assumptions of the model; more recently they have involved the underlying rationale of the approach itself. The criticisms fall into four broad categories, all of which we shall examine further:

- The assumptions included in the EOQ models are simplistic.
- The real costs of stock in operations are not as assumed in EOQ models.
- The models are really descriptive, and should not be used as prescriptive devices.
- Cost minimization is not an appropriate objective for inventory management.

Responding to the criticisms of EOQ

In order to keep EOQ-type models relatively straightforward, it was necessary to make assumptions. These concerned such things as the stability of demand, the existence of a fixed and identifiable ordering cost, that the cost of stock holding can be expressed by a linear function, shortage costs which were identifiable, and so on. While these assumptions are rarely strictly true, most of them can approximate to reality. Furthermore, the shape of the total cost curve has a relatively flat optimum point which means that small errors will not significantly affect the total cost of a near-optimum order quantity. However, at times the assumptions do pose severe limitations to the models. For example, the assumption of steady demand is untrue for a wide range of inventory problems.

Cost of stock

Other questions surround some of the assumptions made concerning the nature of stock-related costs. For example, placing an order with a supplier as part of a regular and multi-item order might be relatively inexpensive, whereas asking for a special one-off delivery of an item could prove far more costly. Similarly with stock-holding costs – although many companies make a standard percentage charge on the purchase price of stock items, this might not be appropriate. The marginal costs of increasing stock-holding levels might be merely the cost of the working capital involved. On the other hand, it might necessitate the lease of a whole new stock-holding facility such as a warehouse. Operations managers using an EOQ-type approach must check that the decisions implied by the use of the formulae do not exceed the boundaries within which the cost assumptions apply. And it is useful at this stage to examine the effect on an EOQ approach of regarding inventory as being more costly than previously believed. Increasing the slope of the holding cost line increases the level of total costs of *any* order quantity, but more significantly, shifts the minimum cost point substantially to the left, in favour of a lower economic order quantity. In other words, the less willing an operation is to hold stock on the grounds of cost, the more it should move towards smaller, more frequent ordering.

Using EOQ models as prescriptions

Perhaps the most fundamental criticism of the EOQ approach comes from the 'lean' and JIT philosophies. The EOQ tries to optimize order decisions. Implicitly the costs involved are taken as fixed, in the sense that the task of operations managers is to find out what are the true costs rather than to change them in any way. EOQ is essentially a reactive approach. Some critics would argue that it fails to ask the right question. Rather than asking the EOQ question of 'What is the optimum order quantity?', operations managers should really be asking, 'How can I change the operation in some way so as to reduce the overall level of inventory I need to hold?' The EOQ approach may be a reasonable description of stock-holding costs but should not necessarily be taken as a strict prescription over what decisions to take. For example, many organizations have made considerable efforts to reduce the effective cost of placing an order. Often they have done this by working to reduce changeover times on machines. This means that less time is taken changing over from one product to the other, and therefore less operating capacity is lost, which in turn reduces the cost of the changeover. Under these circumstances, the order cost curve in the EOQ formula reduces and, in turn, reduces the effective economic order quantity. Figure 9.8 shows the EOQ formula represented graphically with increased holding costs (*see* the previous discussion) and reduced order costs. The net effect of this is to significantly reduce the value of the EOQ.

Should the cost of inventory be minimized?

Many organizations (such as supermarkets and wholesalers) make the most of their revenue and profits simply by holding and supplying inventory. Because their main investment is in the inventory it is critical that they make a good return on this capital, by ensuring that it has the highest possible 'stock turn' (defined later in this chapter) and/or gross profit

Operations in practice Joanne manages the schedule[1]

Joanne Cheung is the Senior Service Adviser at a premier BMW dealership. She and her team act as the interface between customers who want their cars serviced and repaired, and the 16 technicians who carry out the work in their state-of-the-art workshop. *'There are three types of work that we have to organize'*, says Joanne. *'The first is performing repairs on customers' vehicles. They usually want this doing as soon as possible. The second type of job is routine servicing. It is usually not urgent so customers are generally willing to negotiate a time for this. The remainder of our work involves working on the pre-owned cars which our buyer has bought-in to sell on to customers. Before any of these cars can be sold they have to undergo extensive checks. To some extent we treat these categories of work slightly differently. We have to give good service to our internal car buyers, but there is some flexibility in planning these jobs. At the other extreme, emergency repair work for customers has to be fitted into our schedule as quickly as possible. If someone is desperate to have their car repaired at very short notice, we sometimes ask them to drop their car in as early as they can and pick it up as late as possible. This gives us the maximum amount of time to fit it into the schedule.*

'There are a number of service options open to customers. We can book short jobs in for a fixed time and do it while they wait. Most commonly, we ask the customer to leave the car with us and collect it later. To help customers we have ten loan cars which are booked out on a first-come first-served basis. Alternatively, the vehicle can be collected from the customer's home and delivered back there when it is ready. Our four drivers who do this are able to cope with up to twelve jobs a day.

'Most days we deal with fifty to eighty jobs, taking from half-an-hour up to a whole day. To enter a job into our process all Service Advisers have access to the computer-based scheduling system. On-screen it shows the total capacity we have day-by-day, all the jobs that are booked in, the amount of free capacity still available, the number of loan cars available, and so on. We use this to see when we have the capacity to book a customer in, and then enter all the customer's details. BMW have

Source: © BMW Group

Joanne has to balance the needs of customers and the constraints of the workshop

issued "standard times" for all the major jobs. However, you have to modify these standard times a bit to take account of circumstances. That is where the Service Adviser's experience comes in.

'We keep all the most commonly used parts in stock, but if a repair needs a part which is not in stock, we can usually get it from the BMW parts distributors within a day. Every evening our planning system prints out the jobs to be done the next day and the parts which are likely to be needed for each job. This allows the parts staff to pick out the parts for each job so that the technicians can collect them first thing the next morning without any delay.

'Every day we have to cope with the unexpected. A technician may find that extra work is needed, customers may want extra work doing, and technicians are sometimes ill, which reduces our capacity. Occasionally parts may not be available so we have to arrange with the customer for the vehicle to be rebooked for a later time. Every day up to four or five customers just don't turn up. Usually they have just forgotten to bring their car in so we have to rebook them in at a later time. We can cope with most of these uncertainties because our technicians are flexible in terms of the skills they have and also are willing to work overtime when needed. Also, it is important to manage customers' expectations. If there is a chance that the vehicle may not be ready for them, it shouldn't come as a surprise when they try and collect it.'

Planning and control is concerned with the reconciliation between what the market requires and what the operation's resources can deliver. **Planning and control** activities provide the systems, procedures and decisions which bring different aspects of supply and demand together. The purpose is always the same – to make a connection between supply and demand that will ensure that the operation's processes run effectively and efficiently and produce products and services as required by customers. Consider, for example, the way in which routine surgery is organized in a hospital. When a patient arrives and is admitted to the hospital, much of the planning for the surgery will already have happened. The operating theatre will have been reserved, and the doctors and nurses who staff the operating theatre will have been provided with all the information regarding the patient's condition. Appropriate preoperative and postoperative care will have been organized. All this will involve staff and facilities in different parts of the hospital. All must be given the same information and their activities coordinated. Soon after the patient arrives, he or she will be checked to make sure that their condition is as expected. Blood, if required, will be cross-matched and reserved, and any medication will be made ready. Any last-minute changes may require some degree of replanning. For example, if the patient shows unexpected symptoms, observation may be necessary before the surgery can take place. Not only will this affect the patient's own treatment, but other patients' treatment may also have to be rescheduled. All these activities of scheduling, coordination and organization are concerned with the planning and control of the hospital.

Planning and control reconciles supply and demand

The difference between planning and control

We have chosen to treat planning and control together. This is because the division between planning and control is not always clear. However, there are some general features that help to distinguish between the two. **Planning** is a formalization of what is intended to happen at some time in the future. But a plan does not guarantee that an event will actually happen. Customers change their minds about what they want and when they want it. Suppliers may not always deliver on time, machines may fail, or staff may be absent through illness. **Control** is the process of coping with changes. It may mean that plans need to be redrawn. It may also mean that an 'intervention' will need to be made in the operation to bring it back 'on track' – for example, finding a new supplier that can deliver quickly, repairing the machine which failed, or moving staff from another part of the operation to cover for the absentees. Control makes the adjustments which allow the operation to achieve the objectives that the plan has set, even when the assumptions on which the plan was based do not hold true.

Planning concerns what should happen in the future

Control copes with changes

Long-, medium- and short-term planning and control

The nature of planning and control activities changes over time. In the very long term, operations managers make plans concerning what they intend to do, what resources they need, and what objectives they hope to achieve. The emphasis is on planning rather than control, because there is little to control as such. They will use forecasts of likely demand which are described in aggregated terms. For example, a hospital will make plans for '2,000 patients' without necessarily going into the details of the individual needs of those patients. Similarly, the hospital might plan to have 100 nurses and 20 doctors but again without deciding on the specific attributes of the staff. Operations managers will be concerned mainly to achieve financial targets. Budgets will be put in place which identify its costs and revenue targets.

Medium-term planning and control is more detailed. It looks ahead to assess the overall demand which the operation must meet in a partially disaggregated manner. By this time, for example, the hospital must distinguish between different types of demand. The number of patients coming as accident and emergency cases will need to be distinguished from those requiring routine operations. Similarly, different categories of staff will have been identified

(say) a bottled cola manufacturer or other mass producer. The equivalent in the conference market would be a conference centre which schedules a series of events and conferences, programmed in advance and open to individual customers to book into or even turn up on the day. Cinemas and theatres usually work in this manner. Their performances are produced and supplied irrespective of the level of actual demand. Operations of this type will require **make-to-stock** planning and control.

Make-to-stock

P:D ratios[3]

P:D ratio

Another way of characterizing the graduation between resource-to-order and make-to-stock is by using a *P:D ratio*. This contrasts the total length of time customers have to wait between asking for the service and receiving it, demand time, D, and the total throughput time, P. Throughput time is how long the operation takes to obtain the resources, and produce and deliver the service.

P and D times depend on the operation

Make-to-stock operations produce their services and products in advance of any demand. For example, in an operation making consumer durables, demand time, D, is the sum of the times for transmitting the order to the company's warehouse or stock point, picking and packing the order and physically transporting it to the customer. Behind this visible order cycle, however, lie other cycles. Reduction in the finished goods stock will eventually trigger the decision to manufacture a replenishment batch. This 'produce' cycle involves scheduling work in the manufacturing process. Behind the 'produce' cycle lies the 'obtain resources' cycle – the time for obtaining the input stocks. So, for this type of operation, the 'demand' time which the customer sees is very short compared with the total 'throughput' cycle. Contrast this with a resource-to-order operation. Here, D is the same as P. Both include the 'obtain resources', 'produce' and 'delivery' cycles. The produce-to-order operation lies in between these two (see Figure 10.4).

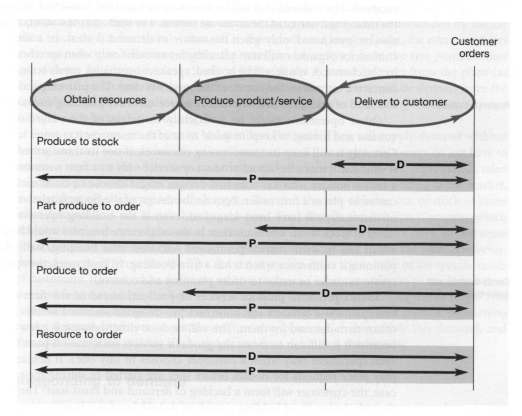

Figure 10.4 P and D for the different types of planning and control

P:D ratios indicate the degree of speculation

Reducing total throughput time *P* will have varying effects on the time the customer has to wait for demand to be filled. In resource-to-order operations, *P* and *D* are the same. Speeding up any part of *P* will reduce customer's waiting time, *D*. On the other hand, in 'produce-to-stock' operations, customers would only see reduced *D* time if the 'deliver' part of *P* were reduced. Also, in Figure 10.4, *D* is always shown as being smaller than *P*, which is the case for most companies. How much smaller *D* is than *P* is important because it indicates the proportion of the operation's activities which are speculative, that is, carried out on the expectation of eventually receiving a firm order for its efforts. The larger *P* is compared with *D*, the higher the proportion of speculative activity in the operation and the greater the risk the operation carries. The speculative element in the operation is there because demand cannot be forecast perfectly. With exact or close to exact forecasts, risk would be non-existent or very low, no matter how much bigger *P* was than *D*. Expressed another way: when *P* and *D* are equal, no matter how inaccurate the forecasts are, speculation is eliminated because everything is resourced and made to a firm order (although bad forecasting will lead to other problems). Reducing the *P:D* ratio becomes, in effect, a way of taking some of the risk out of operations planning and control.

Planning and control activities

There are four overlapping activities: loading, sequencing, scheduling, and monitoring and control that together form the planning and control task (see Figure 10.5). Some caution is needed when using these terms. Different organizations may use them in different ways, and even textbooks in the area adopt different definitions. For example, some authorities describe what we have called 'planning and control' as 'operations scheduling'. However, the terminology of planning and control is less important than understanding the basic ideas.

Loading

Loading

Loading is the amount of work that is allocated to a part of an operation. For example, a machine on the shop floor of a manufacturing business is available, in theory, 168 hours

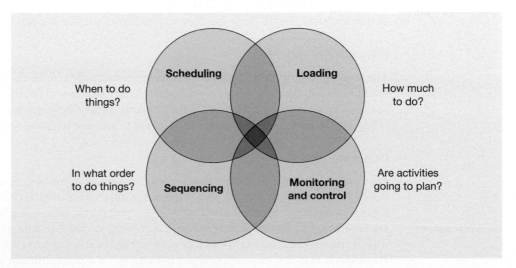

Figure 10.5 Planning and control activities

a week. However, this does not necessarily mean that 168 hours of work can be loaded onto that machine. For some periods the machine cannot be worked; for example, it may not be available on statutory holidays and weekends. Therefore, the load put onto the machine must take this into account. Of the time that the machine is available for work, other losses further reduce the available time. For example, time may be lost while changing over from making one component to another. If the machine breaks down, it will not be available. If there is machine reliability data available, this must also be taken into account. Sometimes the machine may be waiting for parts to arrive or be 'idling' for some other reason. Other losses could include an allowance for the machine being run below its optimum speed (for example, because it has not been maintained properly) and an allowance for the 'quality losses' or defects which the machine may produce. Likewise, in a service-dominant operation it may not be appropriate to schedule workers for 8 hours per day. Loading will need to take into account rest breaks, idle time, changing from one task to another, and boredom reducing actual time available, for example. Of course, many of these losses should be small or non-existent in a well-managed operation. However, the **valuable operating time** available for productive working, even in the best operations, can be significantly below the maximum time available.

Valuable operating time

Sequencing

Sequencing

When work arrives at any part of an operation decisions must be taken on the order in which the work will be tackled. This activity is termed **sequencing**. The priorities given to work in an operation are often determined by some predefined set of rules, some of which are summarized below.

Customer priority

Customer priority sequencing

Operations will sometimes use **customer priority sequencing**, which allows an important or aggrieved customer (or item) to be 'processed' prior to others, irrespective of the order of arrival. This approach is typically used by operations whose customer base is skewed, containing a mass of small customers and a few large, very important customers. Some banks, for example, give priority to important customers. The emergency services often have to use their judgement in prioritizing the urgency of requests for service. For example, in the priority system used by police forces the operators receiving emergency and other calls are trained to grade the calls into priority categories. The response by the police is then organized to match the level of priority. The triage system in hospitals operates in a similar way (see short case). However, customer priority sequencing, although giving a high level of service to some customers, may erode the service given to many others. This may lower the overall performance of the operation if work flows are disrupted to accommodate important customers.

Physical constraints

The physical nature of the materials being processed may determine the priority of work. For example, in an operation using paints or dyes, lighter shades will be sequenced before darker shades. On completion of each batch, the colour is slightly darkened for the next batch. This is because darkness of colour can only be added to and not removed from the colour mix.

Due date (DD)

Due date sequencing

Prioritizing by due date means that work is sequenced according to when it is 'due' for delivery, irrespective of the size of each job or the importance of each customer. For example, a support service in an office block, such as a reprographic unit, will often ask when copies are required, and then sequence the work according to that due date. **Due date sequencing** usually improves the delivery reliability of an operation and improves average delivery speed. However, it may not provide optimal productivity, as a more efficient sequencing of work may reduce total costs.

Short case
The hospital triage system[4]

One of the hospital environments that is most difficult to
sequence is the Accident and Emergency department,
where patients arrive at random, without any prior warning,
throughout the day. It is up to the hospital's reception and
the medical staff to devise very rapidly a schedule which
meets most of the necessary criteria. In particular, patients
who arrive having had very serious accidents, or presenting
symptoms of a serious illness, need to be attended to
urgently. Therefore, the hospital will sequence these
cases first. Less urgent cases – perhaps patients who are
in some discomfort, but whose injuries or illnesses are not
life-threatening – will have to wait until the urgent cases
are treated. Routine non-urgent cases will have the lowest
priority of all. In many circumstances, these patients will
have to wait for the longest time, which may be many
hours, especially if the hospital is busy. Sometimes these
non-urgent cases may even be turned away if the hospital
is too busy with more important cases. In situations where
hospitals expect sudden influxes of patients, they have
developed what is known as a triage system, whereby

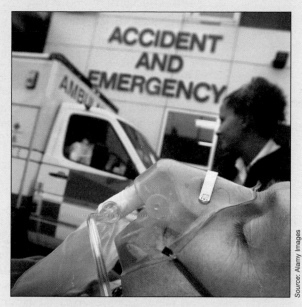

Source: Alamy Images

medical staff hurriedly sort through the patients who have
arrived to determine which category of urgency each patient
fits into. In this way a suitable schedule for the various
treatments can be devised in a short period of time.

Last-in first-out (LIFO)

Last-in first-out
sequencing

Last-in first-out (LIFO) is a method of sequencing usually selected for practical reasons.
For example, unloading an elevator is more convenient on a LIFO basis, as there is only one
entrance and exit. However, it is not an equitable approach. Patients at hospital clinics may
be infuriated if they see newly arrived patients examined first.

First-in first-out (FIFO)

First-in first-out
sequencing

Some operations serve customers in exactly the sequence they arrive in. This is called **first-in
first-out sequencing** (FIFO), or sometimes 'first come, first served' (FCFS). For example,
passport offices receive mail, and sort it according to the day when it arrived. They work through
the mail, opening it in sequence, and process the passport applications in order of arrival.

Longest operation time (LOT)

Longest operation time
sequencing

Operations may feel obliged to sequence their longest jobs first in the system called **longest
operation time sequencing**. This has the advantage of occupying work centres for long periods.
By contrast, relatively small jobs progressing through an operation will take up time at each
work centre because of the need to change over from one job to the next. However, although
longest operation time sequencing keeps utilization high, this rule does not take into account
delivery speed, reliability or flexibility.

Shortest operation time first (SOT)

Shortest operation time
sequencing

Most operations at some stage become cash-constrained. Larger jobs that take more time will
not enable the business to invoice as quickly. In these situations, the sequencing rules may be
adjusted to tackle short jobs first in the system, called **shortest operation time sequencing**.
These jobs can then be invoiced and payment received to ease cash-flow problems. This
has an effect of improving delivery performance, if the unit of measurement is delivery of
jobs. However, it may adversely affect total productivity and can damage service to larger
customers.

Judging sequencing rules

All five performance objectives, or some variant of them, could be used to judge the effectiveness of sequencing rules. However, the objectives of dependability, speed and cost are particularly important. So, for example, the following performance objectives are often used:

- Meeting 'due date' promised to customer (dependability);
- Minimizing the time the job spends in the process, also known as 'flow time' (speed);
- Minimizing work-in-progress inventory (an element of cost);
- Minimizing idle time of work centres (another element of cost).

Scheduling

Scheduling

Having determined the sequence that work is to be tackled in, some operations require a detailed timetable showing at what time or date jobs should start and when they should end – this is **scheduling**. Schedules are familiar statements of volume and timing in many consumer environments. For example, a bus schedule shows that more buses are put on routes at more frequent intervals during rush-hour periods. The bus schedule shows the time each bus is due to arrive at each stage of the route. Schedules of work are used in operations where some planning is required to ensure that customer demand is met. Other operations, such as rapid-response service operations where customers arrive in an unplanned way, cannot schedule the operation in a short-term sense. They can only respond at the time demand is placed upon them.

The complexity of scheduling[5]

The scheduling activity is one of the most complex tasks in operations management. Firstly, schedulers must deal with several different types of resource simultaneously. Machines will have different capabilities and capacities; staff will have different skills. More importantly, the number of possible schedules increases rapidly as the number of activities and processes increases. For example, suppose one machine has five different jobs to process. Any of the five jobs could be processed first and, following that, any one of the remaining four jobs, and so on. This means that there are:

$$5 \times 4 \times 3 \times 2 = 120 \text{ different schedules possible}$$

More generally, for n jobs there are $n!$ (factorial n) different ways of scheduling the jobs through a single process. We can now consider what impact there would be if, in the same situation, there was more than one type of machine. If we were trying to minimize the number of set-ups on two machines, there is no reason why the sequence on machine 1 would be the same as the sequence on machine 2. If we consider the two sequencing tasks to be independent of each other, for two machines there would be:

$$120 \times 120 = 14,400 \text{ possible schedules of the two machines and five jobs.}$$

A general formula can be devised to calculate the number of possible schedules in any given situation, as follows:

$$\text{Number of possible schedules} = (n!)m$$

where n is the number of jobs and m is the number of machines. In practical terms, this means that there are often many millions of feasible schedules, even for relatively small operations. This is why scheduling rarely attempts to provide an 'optimal' solution but rather satisfies itself with an 'acceptable' feasible one.

Forward and backward scheduling

Forward scheduling
Backward scheduling

Forward scheduling involves starting work as soon as it arrives. **Backward scheduling** involves starting jobs at the last possible moment to prevent them from being late. For example, assume that it takes six hours for a contract laundry to wash, dry and press a batch of overalls. If the work is collected at 8.00 am and is due to be picked up at 4.00 pm, there are more than six hours available to do it. Table 10.1 shows the different start times of each job, depending on whether they are forward- or backward-scheduled.

Table 10.1 The effects of forward and backward scheduling

Task	Duration	Start time (backwards)	Start time (forwards)
Press	1 hour	3.00 pm	1.00 pm
Dry	2 hours	1.00 pm	11.00 am
Wash	3 hours	10.00 am	8.00 am

The choice of backward or forward scheduling depends largely upon the circumstances. Table 10.2 lists some advantages and disadvantages of the two approaches.

Table 10.2 Advantages of forward and backward scheduling

Advantages of forward scheduling	Advantages of backward scheduling
High labour utilization – workers always start work to keep busy	Lower material costs – materials are not used until they have to be, therefore delaying added value until the last moment
Flexible – the time slack in the system allows unexpected work to be loaded	Less exposed to risk in case of schedule change by the customer Tends to focus the operation on customer due dates

Gantt charts

Gantt chart

The most common method of scheduling is by use of the **Gantt chart**. This is a simple device which represents time as a bar, or channel, on a chart. The start and finish times for activities can be indicated on the chart and sometimes the actual progress of the job is also indicated. The advantages of Gantt charts are that they provide a simple visual representation both of what should be happening and of what actually is happening in the operation. Furthermore, they can be used to 'test out' alternative schedules. It is a relatively simple task to represent alternative schedules (even if it is a far from simple task to find a schedule which fits all the resources satisfactorily). Figure 10.6 illustrates a Gantt chart for a specialist software developer. It indicates the progress of several jobs as they are expected to progress through five stages of the process. Gantt charts are not an optimizing tool, they merely facilitate the development of alternative schedules by communicating them effectively.

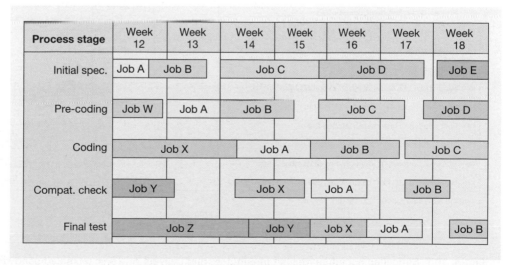

Figure 10.6 Gantt chart showing the schedule for jobs at each process stage

Short case
The life and times of a chicken salad sandwich[6]

Pre-packed sandwiches are a growth product around the world as consumers put convenience and speed above relaxation and cost. But if you have recently consumed a pre-packed sandwich, think about the schedule of events which has gone into its making. For example, take a chicken salad sandwich. Less than 5 days ago, the chicken was on the farm unaware that it would never see another weekend. The Gantt chart schedule shown in Figure 10.7 tells the story of the sandwich, and (posthumously), of the chicken.

From the forecast, orders for non-perishable items are placed for goods to arrive up to a week in advance of their use. Orders for perishable items will be placed daily, a day or two before the items are required. Tomatoes, cucumbers and lettuces have a three-day shelf life so may be received up to three days before production. Stock is held on a strict first-in-first-out (FIFO) basis. If today is Wednesday, vegetables are processed that have been received during the last three days. This morning the bread arrived from a local bakery and the chicken arrived fresh,

cooked and in strips ready to be placed directly in the sandwich during assembly. Yesterday (Tuesday) it had been killed, cooked, prepared and sent on its journey to the factory. By midday orders for tonight's production will have been received on the Internet. From 2.00 pm until 10.00 pm the production lines are closed down for maintenance and a very thorough cleaning. During this time the production planning team is busy planning the night's production run. Production for delivery to customers furthest away from the factory will have to be scheduled first. By 10 pm production is ready to start. Sandwiches are made on production lines. The bread is loaded onto a conveyor belt by hand and butter is spread automatically by a machine. Next the various fillings are applied at each stage according to the specified sandwich 'design', see Figure 10.8. After the filling has been assembled the top slice of bread is placed on the sandwich and machine-chopped into two triangles, packed and sealed by machine. It is now early Thursday morning and by 2.00 am the first refrigerated lorries are already departing on their journeys to various customers. Production continues through until 2.00 pm on the Thursday, after which once again the maintenance and cleaning teams move in. The last sandwiches are dispatched by 4.00 pm on the Thursday. There is no finished goods stock.

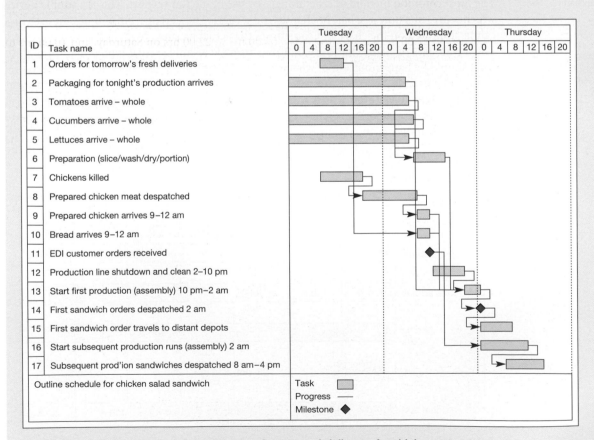

Figure 10.7 Simplified schedule for the manufacture and delivery of a chicken salad sandwich

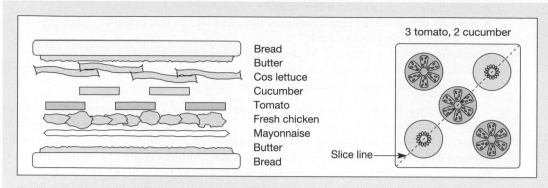

Figure 10.8 Design for a chicken salad sandwich

Scheduling work patterns

Where the dominant resource in an operation is its staff, then the schedule of work times effectively determines the capacity of the operation itself. The main task of scheduling, therefore, is to make sure that sufficient numbers of people are working at any point in time to provide a capacity appropriate for the level of demand at that point in time. This is often called **staff rostering**. Operations such as call centres, postal delivery, policing, holiday couriers, retail shops and hospitals will all need to schedule the working hours of their staff with demand in mind. This is a direct consequence of these operations having relatively high 'visibility'. Such operations cannot store their outputs in inventories and so must respond directly to customer demand. For example, Figure 10.9 shows the scheduling of shifts for a small technical 'hot line' support service for a small software company. It gives advice to customers on their technical problems. Its service times are 04.00 hrs to 20.00 hrs on Monday, 04.00 hrs to 22.00 hrs Tuesday to Friday, 06.00 hrs to 22.00 hrs on Saturday, and 10.00 hrs to 20.00 hrs on Sunday. Demand is heaviest Tuesday to Thursday, starts to decrease on Friday, is low over the weekend and starts to increase again on Monday.

The scheduling task for this kind of problem can be considered over different timescales, two of which are shown in Figure 10.9. During the day, working hours need to be agreed with individual staff members. During the week, days off need to be agreed. During the year, vacations, training periods and other blocks of time where staff are unavailable need to be agreed. All this has to be scheduled such that:

- capacity matches demand;
- the length of each shift is neither excessively long nor too short to be attractive to staff;

Staff rostering (margin note)

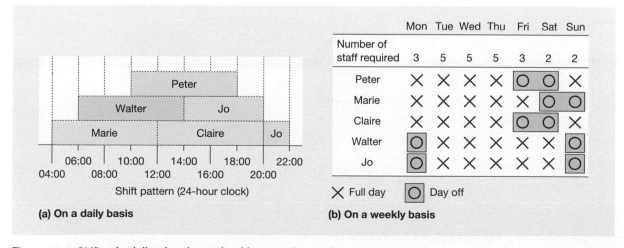

(a) On a daily basis

(b) On a weekly basis

Figure 10.9 Shift scheduling in a home-banking enquiry service

- working at unsocial hours is minimized;
- days off match agreed staff conditions (for example) in this example – staff prefer two consecutive days off every week;
- vacation and other 'time-off' blocks are accommodated;
- sufficient flexibility is built into the schedule to cover for unexpected changes in supply (staff illness) and demand (surge in customer calls).

Scheduling staff times is one of the most complex of scheduling problems. In the relatively simple example shown in Figure 10.9 we have assumed that all staff have the same level and type of skill. In very large operations with many types of skill to schedule and uncertain demand (for example a large hospital) the scheduling problem becomes extremely complex. Some mathematical techniques are available but most scheduling of this type is, in practice, solved using heuristics (rules of thumb), some of which are incorporated into commercially available software packages.

Monitoring and controlling the operation

Having created a plan for the operation through loading, sequencing and scheduling, each part of the operation has to be monitored to ensure that planned activities are indeed happening. Any deviation from the plans can then be rectified through some kind of intervention in the operation, which itself will probably involve some replanning. Figure 10.10 illustrates a simple view of control. The output from a work centre is monitored and compared with the plan which indicates what the work centre is supposed to be doing. Deviations from this plan are taken into account through a replanning activity and the necessary interventions made to the work centre which will ensure that the new plan is carried out. Eventually, some further deviation from planned activity will be detected and the cycle is repeated.

Push and pull control

One element of control is periodic intervention into the activities of the operation. An important decision is how this intervention takes place. The key distinction is between

Push control
Pull control

intervention signals which **push** work through the processes within the operation and those which **pull** work only when it is required. In a push system of control, activities are scheduled by means of a central system and completed in line with central instructions, such as an ERP system (see later). Each work centre pushes out work without considering whether the succeeding work centre can make use of it. Work centres are coordinated by means of the

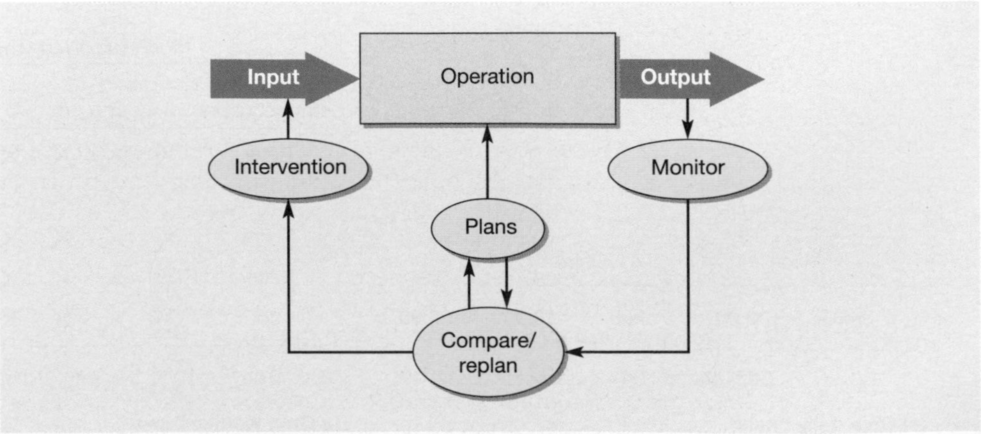

Figure 10.10 A simple model of control

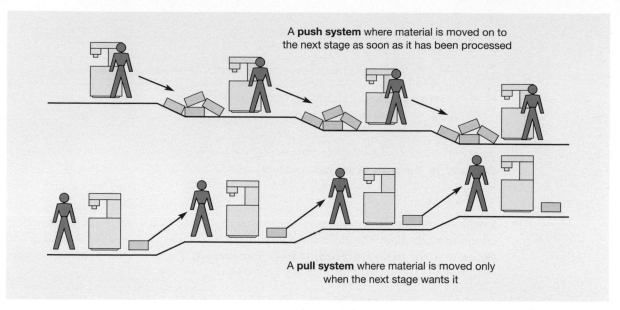

Figure 10.11 Push versus pull: the gravity analogy

central operations planning and control system. In practice, however, there are many reasons why actual conditions differ from those planned. As a consequence, idle time, queues and inventory often characterize push systems. By contrast, in a pull system of control, the pace and specification of what is done are set by the 'customer' workstation, which 'pulls' work from the preceding (supplier) workstation. The customer acts as the only 'trigger' for movement. If a request is not passed back from the customer to the supplier, the supplier cannot do anything. A request from a customer not only triggers activity at the supplying stage, but also prompts the supplying stage to request a further delivery from its own suppliers. In this way, demand is transmitted back through the stages from the original point of demand by the original customer.

Understanding the differing principles of push and pull is important because they have different effects in terms of their propensities to accumulate inventory in the operation. Pull systems are far less likely to result in inventory build-up and are therefore favoured by lean operations (see Chapter 11).

Drum, buffer, rope

Drum, buffer, rope
Theory of constraints

The **drum, buffer, rope** concept comes from the **theory of constraints** (TOC) originally described by Eli Goldratt in his novel *The Goal*.[7] It is an idea that helps to decide exactly *where* in a process control should occur. Most operations do not have the same amount of work loaded onto each separate work centre (that is, they are not perfectly balanced). This means there is likely to be a part of the process which is acting as a bottleneck on the work flowing through the process. Goldratt argued that the bottleneck in the process should be the control point of the whole process. It is called the *drum* because it sets the 'beat' for the rest of the process to follow. Because it does not have sufficient capacity, a bottleneck is (or should be) working all the time. Therefore, it is sensible to keep a *buffer* of inventory in front of it to make sure that it always has something to work on. Because it constrains the output of the whole process, any time lost at the bottleneck will affect the output from the whole process. Therefore, it is not worthwhile for the parts of the process before the bottleneck to work to their full capacity. All they would do is produce work which

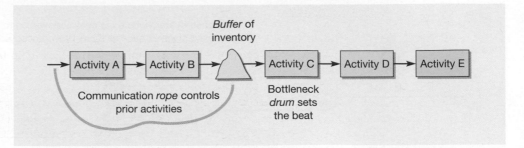

Figure 10.12 The drum, buffer, rope concept

would accumulate further along in the process up to the point where the bottleneck is constraining the flow. Therefore, some form of communication between the bottleneck and the input to the process is needed to make sure that activities before the bottleneck do not overproduce. This is called the *rope* (see Figure 10.12).

Critical commentary

Most of the perspectives on control taken in this chapter are simplifications of a far more messy reality. They are based on models used to understand mechanical systems such as car engines. But anyone who has worked in real organizations knows that organizations are not machines. They are social systems, full of complex and ambiguous interactions. Simple models such as these assume that operations objectives are always clear and agreed, yet organizations are political entities where different and often conflicting objectives compete. Local government operations, for example, are overtly political. Furthermore, the outputs from operations are not always easily measured. A university may be able to measure the number and qualifications of its students, for example, but it cannot measure the full impact of its education on their future happiness. Also, even if it is possible to work out an appropriate intervention to bring an operation back into 'control', most operations cannot perfectly predict what effect the intervention will have. Even the largest burger bar chain does not know *exactly* how a new shift allocation system will affect performance. Also, some operations never do the same thing more than once anyway. Most of the work done by construction operations is one-offs. If every output is different, how can 'controllers' ever know what is supposed to happen? Their plans themselves are mere speculation.

Enterprise resource planning (ERP)

One of the most important issues in planning and controlling operations is managing the sometimes vast amounts of information generated by the activity. It is not just the operations function that is the author and recipient of this information – almost every other function of a business will be involved. So, it is important that all relevant information that is spread throughout the organization is brought together. Then it can inform planning and control decisions such as when activities should take place, where they should happen, who should be doing them, how much capacity will be needed, and so on. This is what enterprise resource planning (ERP) does.

What is ERP?

Enterprise resource
planning

An easy way of thinking about **enterprise resource planning** (ERP) is to imagine that you have decided to hold a party in two weeks' time and expect about 40 people to attend. As well as drinks, you decide to provide sandwiches and snacks. You will probably do some simple calculations, estimating guests' preferences and how much people are likely to drink and eat. You may already have some food and drink in the house which you will use, so you will take that into account when making your shopping list. If any of the food is to be cooked from a recipe, you may have to multiply up the ingredients to cater for 40 people. Also, you may also wish to take into account the fact that you will prepare some of the food the week before and freeze it, while you will leave the rest to either the day before or the day of the party. So, you will need to decide when each item is required so that you can shop in time. In fact, planning a party requires a series of interrelated decisions about the volume (quantity) and timing of the *materials* needed. This is the basis of the foundation concept for ERP called **materials requirement planning** (MRP). It is a process that helps companies make volume and timing calculations (similar to those in the party, but on a much larger scale, and with a greater degree of complexity). But your planning may extend beyond 'materials'. You may want to hire in a sound system from a local supplier – you will have to plan for this. The party also has financial implications. You may have to agree a temporary increase to your credit card limit. Again, this requires some forward planning and calculations of how much it is going to cost, and how much extra credit you require. Both the equipment and financial implications may vary if you increase the number of guests. But, if you postpone the party for a month, these arrangements will change. Also, there are also other implications of organizing the party. You will need to give friends, who are helping with the organization, an idea of when they should come and for how long. This will depend on the timing of the various tasks to be done (making sandwiches etc.).

Materials requirement
planning

So, even for this relatively simple activity, the key to successful planning is how we generate, integrate and organize all the information on which planning and control depends. Of course, in business operations it is more complex than this. Companies usually sell many different services and products to many hundreds of customers with constantly changing demands. This is a bit like organizing 200 parties one week, 250 the next and 225 the following week, all for different groups of guests with different requirements who keep changing their minds about what they want to eat and drink. This is what ERP does, it helps companies 'forward-plan' these types of decisions and understand all the implications of any changes to the plan.

How did ERP develop?

Enterprise resource planning is the latest, and the most significant, development of the original materials requirements planning (MRP) philosophy. The large companies which have grown almost exclusively on the basis of providing ERP systems include SAP and Oracle. Yet to understand ERP, it is important to understand the various stages in its development, summarized in Figure 10.13. The original MRP became popular during the 1970s, although the planning and control logic that underlies it had, by then, been known for some time. What popularized MRP was the availability of computer power to drive the basic planning and control mathematics.

Manufacturing Resource
Planning

Manufacturing Resource Planning (MRP II) expanded out of MRP during the 1980s. Again, it was a technology innovation that allowed the development. Local-area networks (LANs), together with increasingly powerful desktop computers, allowed a much higher degree of processing power and communication between different parts of a business. Also MRP II's extra sophistication allowed the forward modelling of 'what-if' scenarios. The strength of MRP and MRP II lay always in the fact that it could explore the *consequences* of any changes to what an operation was required to do. So, if demand changed, the MRP system would calculate all the 'knock-on' effects and issue instructions accordingly. This

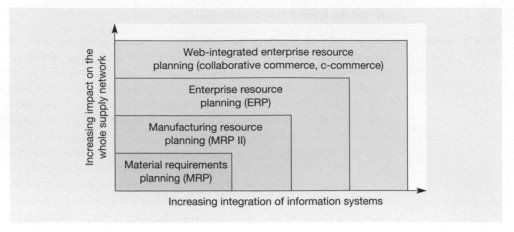

Figure 10.13 The development of ERP

Enterprise resource
planning

same principle also applies to ERP, but on a much wider basis. **Enterprise resource planning** (ERP) has been defined as,

> '*a complete enterprise wide business solution. The ERP system consists of software support modules such as: marketing and sales, field service, product design and development, production and inventory control, procurement, distribution, industrial facilities management, process design and development, manufacturing, quality, human resources, finance and accounting, and information services. Integration between the modules is stressed without the duplication of information.*'[8]

So, ERP systems allow decisions and databases from all parts of the organization to be integrated so that the consequences of decisions in one part of the organization are reflected in the planning and control systems of the rest of the organization (see Figure 10.14). ERP is the equivalent of the organization's central nervous system, sensing information about the condition of different parts of the business and relaying the information to other parts of

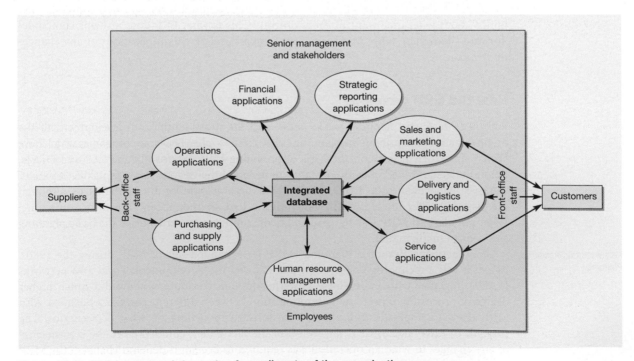

Figure 10.14 ERP integrates information from all parts of the organization

the business that need it. The information is updated in real time by those who use it and yet is always available to everyone connected to the ERP system.

Also, the potential of web-based communication has provided a further boost to ERP development. Many companies have suppliers, customers and other businesses with whom they collaborate who themselves have ERP-type systems. An obvious development is to allow these systems to communicate across supply networks. However, the technical, as well as organizational and strategic consequences of this can be formidable. Nevertheless, many authorities believe that the true value of ERP systems is only fully exploited when such **web-integrated ERP** (known by some people as 'collaborative commerce', or c-commerce) becomes widely implemented.

Web-integrated ERP

Summary answers to key questions

Check and improve your understanding of this chapter using self-assessment questions and a personalized study plan, audio and video downloads, and an eBook – all at **www.myomlab.com.**

➤ What is planning and control?

■ Planning and control is the reconciliation of the potential of the operation to supply services and products, with the demands of its customers on the operation. It is the set of day-to-day activities that run the operation.

■ A plan is a formalization of what is intended to happen at some time in the future. Control is the process of coping with changes to the plan and the operation to which it relates. Although planning and control are theoretically separable, they are usually treated together.

■ The balance between planning and control changes over time. Planning dominates in the long term and is usually done on an aggregated basis. At the other extreme, in the short term, control usually operates within the resource constraints of the operation but makes interventions into the operation in order to cope with short-term changes in circumstances.

➤ How do supply and demand affect planning and control?

■ The degree of uncertainty in demand affects the balance between planning and control. The greater the uncertainty, the more difficult it is to plan, and greater emphasis must be placed on control.

■ This idea of uncertainty is linked with the concepts of dependent and independent demand. Dependent demand is relatively predictable because it is dependent on some known factor. Independent demand is less predictable because it depends on the chances of the market or customer behaviour.

■ The different ways of responding to demand can be characterized by differences in the *P:D* ratio of the operation. The *P:D* ratio is the ratio of total throughput time of goods or services to demand time.

➤ What are the activities of planning and control?

■ In planning and controlling the volume and timing of activity in operations, four distinct activities are necessary:
  - loading, which dictates the amount of work that is allocated to each part of the operation;
  - sequencing, which decides the order in which work is tackled within the operation;

- scheduling, which determines the detailed timetable of activities and when activities are started and finished;
- monitoring and control, which involve detecting what is happening in the operation, replanning if necessary, and intervening in order to impose new plans. Two important types are 'pull' and 'push' control. Pull control is a system whereby demand is triggered by requests from a work centre's (internal) customer. Push control is a centralized system whereby decisions are issued to work centres which are then required to perform the task and supply the next workstation.

➤ How can enterprise resource planning (ERP) help planning and control?

- ERP is an enterprise-wide information system that integrates all the information from many functions, that is needed for planning and controlling operations activities. This integration around a common database allows for transparency.

- ERP can be seen as the latest development from the original planning and control approach known as materials requirements planning (MRP).

- Although ERP is becoming increasingly competent at the integration of internal systems and databases, there is the even more significant potential of integration with other organizations' ERP (and equivalent) systems.

Learning exercises

*These problems and applications will help to improve your analysis of operations. You can find more practice problems as well as worked examples and guided solutions on MyOMLab at **www.myomlab.com**.*

1 Re-read the 'operations management in practice' at the beginning of the chapter, 'Joanne manages the schedule', and also the short case on Air France. What are the differences and what are the similarities between the planning and control tasks in these two operations?

2 A specialist sandwich retailer must order sandwiches at least 8 hours before they are delivered. When they arrive in the shop, they are immediately displayed in a temperature-controlled cabinet. The average time that the sandwiches spend in the cabinet is 6 hours. What is the *P:D* ratio for this retail operation?

3 *Step 1* – Make a list of all the jobs you have to do in the next week. Include in this list jobs relating to your work and/or study, jobs relating to your domestic life, in fact all the things you have to do.

Step 2 – Prioritize all these jobs on a 'most important' to 'least important' basis.

Step 3 – Draw up an outline schedule of exactly when you will do each of these jobs.

Step 4 – At the end of the week compare what your schedule said you *would* do with what you actually *have* done. If there is a discrepancy, why did it occur?

Step 5 – Draw up your own list of planning and control rules from your experience in this exercise in personal planning and control.

4 From your own experience of making appointments at your general practitioner's surgery, or by visiting whoever provides you with primary medical care, reflect on how patients are scheduled to see a doctor or nurse.

(a) What do you think planning and control objectives are for a general practitioner's surgery?
(b) How could your own medical practice be improved?

Want to know more?

Goldratt, E.Y. and Cox, J. (1984) *The Goal*, North River Press, Great Barrington, MA. Don't read this if you like good novels but do read it if you want an enjoyable way of understanding some of the complexities of scheduling. It particularly applies to the drum, buffer, rope concept described in this chapter.

Kehoe, D.F. and Boughton, N.J. (2001) New paradigms in planning and control across manufacturing supply chains – the utilization of Internet technologies, *International Journal of Operations and Production Management*, vol. 21, issue 5/6, 582–93.

Vollmann, T., Berry, W., Whybark, D.C. and Jacobs, F.R. (2004) *Manufacturing Planning and Control Systems for Supply Chain Management: The Definitive Guide for Professionals*, McGraw-Hill Higher Education, New York. The latest version of the 'bible' of planning and control.

Useful websites

www.bpic.co.uk/ Some useful information on general planning and control topics.

www.apics.org The American professional and education body that has its roots in planning and control activities.

www.opsman.org Lots of useful stuff.

Now that you have finished reading this chapter, why not visit MyOMLab at www.myomlab.com where you'll find more learning resources to help you make the most of your studies and get a better grade.

Chapter 11

Lean synchronization

Key questions

➤ What is lean synchronization?
➤ How does lean synchronization eliminate waste?
➤ How does lean synchronization apply throughout the supply network?

Introduction

This chapter examines an approach that we call 'lean synchronization' or just 'lean'. It was originally called 'just-in-time' (JIT) when it started to be adopted outside its birthplace, Japan. It is both a philosophy and a method of operations planning and control. Lean synchronization aims to meet demand instantaneously, with perfect quality and no waste. This involves supplying services and products in perfect synchronization with the demand for them. These principles were once a radical departure from traditional operations practice, but have now become orthodox in promoting the synchronization of flow through processes, operations and supply networks. Although we will focus on planning and control issues, in practice the 'lean' concept has much wider implications for improving operations performance. Figure 11.1 shows where this chapter fits into the overall operations model.

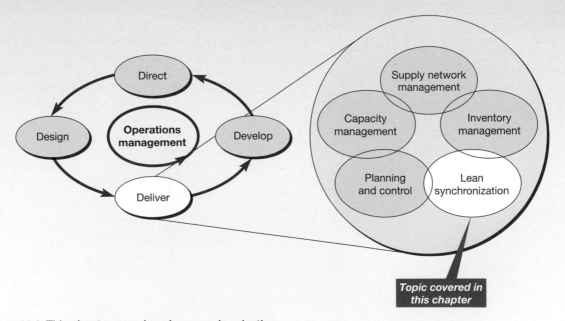

Figure 11.1 This chapter examines lean synchronization

 *Check and improve your understanding of this chapter using self-assessment questions and a personalized study plan, audio and video downloads, and an eBook – all at **www.myomlab.com**.*

Operations in practice Toyota

Seen as the leading practitioner and the main originator of the lean approach, the Toyota Motor Company has progressively synchronized all its processes simultaneously to give high-quality, fast throughput and exceptional productivity. It has done this by developing a set of practices that has largely shaped what we now call 'lean' or 'just-in-time' but which Toyota calls the Toyota Production System (TPS). The TPS has two themes, 'just-in-time' and 'jidoka'. Just-in-time is defined as the rapid and coordinated movement of parts throughout the production system and supply network to meet customer demand. It is operationalized by means of *heijunka* (levelling and smoothing the flow of items), *kanban* (signalling to the preceding process that more parts are needed) and *nagare* (laying out processes to achieve smoother flow of parts throughout the production process). *Jidoka* is described as 'humanizing the interface between operator and machine'. Toyota's philosophy is that the machine is there to serve the operator's purpose. The operator should be left free to exercise his or her judgement. Jidoka is operationalized by means of fail-safeing (or machine jidoka), line-stop authority (or human jidoka) and visual control (at-a-glance status of production processes and visibility of process standards).

Source: Corbis/Denis Balibouse

Toyota believes that both just-in-time and jidoka should be applied ruthlessly to the elimination of waste, where waste is defined as 'anything other than the minimum amount of equipment, items, parts and workers that are absolutely essential to production'. Fujio Cho of Toyota identified seven types of waste that must be eliminated from all operations processes. They are: waste from over-production, waste from waiting time, transportation waste, inventory waste, processing waste, waste of motion and waste from product defects. Beyond this, authorities on Toyota claim that its strength lies in understanding the differences between the tools and practices used with Toyota operations and the overall philosophy of their approach

to lean synchronization. This is what some have called the apparent paradox of the Toyota production system: 'namely, that activities, connections and production flows in a Toyota factory are rigidly scripted, yet at the same time Toyota's operations are enormously flexible and adaptable. Activities and processes are constantly being challenged and pushed to a higher level of performance, enabling the company to continually innovate and improve.'

One influential study of Toyota identified four rules that guide the design, delivery, and development activities within the company.[1]

- *Rule one* – all work shall be highly specified as to content, sequence, timing, and outcome.
- *Rule two* – every customer–supplier connection must be direct and there must be an unambiguous yes or no method of sending requests and receiving responses.
- *Rule three* – the route for every product and service must be simple and direct.
- *Rule four* – any improvement must be made in accordance with the scientific method, under the guidance of a teacher, and at the lowest possible level in the organization.

What is lean synchronization?

Synchronization

Synchronization means that the flow of products and services always delivers exactly what customers want (perfect quality), in exact quantities (neither too much nor too little), exactly when needed (not too early or too late), and exactly where required (not to the wrong location). *Lean* synchronization is to do all this at the lowest possible cost. It results in items flowing rapidly and smoothly through processes, operations and supply networks.

The benefits of synchronized flow

Lean
Just-in-time

When first introduced, the lean synchronization (or 'lean' or 'just-in-time') approach was relatively radical, even for large and sophisticated companies. Now the lean, just-in-time approach is being adopted outside its traditional automotive, high-volume and manufacturing roots. But wherever it is applied, the principles remain the same. The best way to understand how lean synchronization differs from more traditional approaches to managing flow is to contrast the two simple processes in Figure 11.2. The traditional approach assumes that each stage in the process will place its output in an inventory that 'buffers' that stage from the next one downstream in the process. The next stage down will then take outputs from the inventory, process them, and pass them through to the next buffer inventory. These buffers are there to insulate each stage from its neighbours, making each stage relatively independent so that if, for example, stage A stops operating for some reason, stage B can continue, at least for a time. The larger the buffer inventory, the greater the degree of insulation between the stages. This insulation has to be paid for in terms of inventory and slow throughput times because items will spend time waiting in the buffer inventories.

But, the main argument against this traditional approach lies in the very conditions it seeks to promote, namely the insulation of the stages from one another. When a problem occurs at one stage, the problem will not immediately be apparent elsewhere in the system. The responsibility for solving the problem will be centred largely on the people within that stage, and the consequences of the problem will be prevented from spreading to the whole system. However, contrast this with the pure lean synchronized process illustrated in Figure 11.2b.

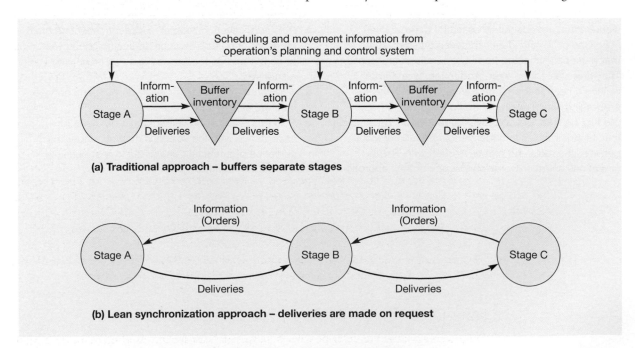

Figure 11.2 (a) Traditional and (b) lean synchronized flow between stages

Here items are processed and then passed directly to the next stage 'just-in-time' for them to be processed further. Problems at any stage have a very different effect in such a system. Now if stage A stops processing, stage B will notice immediately and stage C very soon after. Stage A's problem is now quickly exposed to the whole process, which is immediately affected by the problem. This means that the responsibility for solving the problem is no longer confined to the staff at stage A. It is now shared by everyone, considerably improving the chances of the problem being solved, if only because it is now too important to be ignored. In other words, by preventing items accumulating between stages, the operation has increased the chances of the intrinsic efficiency of the plant being improved.

Non-synchronized approaches seek to encourage efficiency by protecting each part of the process from disruption. The lean synchronized approach takes the opposite view. Exposure of the system to problems can both make them more evident and change the 'motivation structure' of the whole system towards solving the problems. Lean synchronization sees accumulations of inventory as a 'blanket of obscurity' that lies over the system and prevents problems being noticed. This same argument can be applied when, instead of queues of material, or information, an operation has to deal with queues of customers. Table 11.1 shows how certain aspects of inventory are analogous to certain aspects of queues.

Table 11.1 Inventories of materials, information or customers have similar characteristics

	Inventory		
	Of material (queue of material)	Of information (queue of information)	Of customers (queue of people)
Cost	Ties up working capital	Less current information and so worth less	Wastes customers' time
Space	Needs storage space	Needs memory capacity	Needs waiting area
Quality	Defects hidden, possible damage	Defects hidden, possible data corruption	Gives negative perception
De-coupling	Makes stages independent	Makes stages independent	Promotes job specialization/ fragmentation
Utilization	Stages kept busy by work-in-progress	Stages kept busy by work in data queues	Servers kept busy by waiting customers
Coordination	Avoids need for synchronization	Avoids need for straight-through processing	Avoids having to match supply and demand

Source: Adapted from Fitzsimmons, J.A. (1990) Making continual improvement: a competitive strategy for service firms, in Bowen, D.E., Chase, R.B., Cummings, T.G. and Associates (eds) *Service Management Effectiveness*, Copyright © 1990 Jossey-Bass. Reproduced with permission of John Wiley & Sons Inc.

The river and rocks analogy

The idea of obscuring effects of inventory is often illustrated diagrammatically, as in Figure 11.3. The many problems of the operation are shown as rocks in a river bed that cannot be seen because of the depth of the water. The water in this analogy represents the inventory in the operation. Yet, even though the rocks cannot be seen, they slow the progress of the river's flow and cause turbulence. Gradually reducing the depth of the water (inventory) exposes the worst of the problems which can be resolved, after which the water is lowered further, exposing more problems, and so on. The same argument will also apply for the flow between whole processes, or whole operations. For example, stages A, B and C in Figure 11.2 could be a supplier operation, a focal operation and a customer's operation, respectively.

Synchronization, 'lean' and 'just-in-time'

Different terms are used to describe what here we call 'lean synchronization'. Our definition – '*lean synchronization aims to meet demand instantaneously, with perfect quality and no*

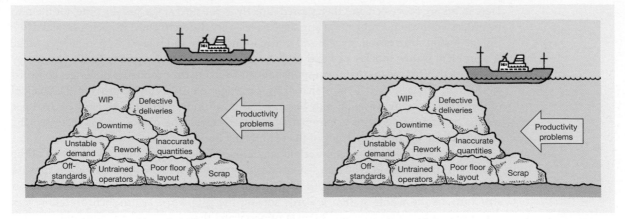

Figure 11.3 Reducing the level of inventory (water) allows operations management (the ship) to see the problems in the operation (the rocks) and work to reduce them

waste' – could also be used to describe the general concept of 'lean', or 'just-in-time' (JIT). The concept of 'lean' stresses the elimination of waste, while 'just-in-time' emphasizes the idea of producing items only when they are needed. But all three concepts overlap to a large degree, and no definition fully conveys the full implications for operations practice. Here we use the term 'lean synchronization' because it best describes the impact of these ideas on flow and delivery.

Lean synchronization and capacity utilization

Lean synchronization has many benefits but these come at the cost of capacity utilization. Return to the process shown in Figure 11.2. When stoppages occur in the traditional system, the buffers allow each stage to continue working and thus achieve high-capacity utilization. The high utilization does not necessarily make the process as a whole produce more. Often extra 'production' goes into buffer inventories. In a lean process, any stoppage will affect the whole process. This will necessarily lead to lower-capacity utilization, at least in the short term. However, there is no point in producing output just for its own sake. Unless the output is useful and allows the operation as a whole to produce saleable products or to process customers satisfactorily, there is no point in doing it anyway. In fact, working just to keep utilization high is not only pointless, it is counter-productive, because the extra inventory produced (or queues created in the case of customer-processing operations) merely serves to make improvements less likely. Figure 11.4 illustrates the two approaches to capacity utilization.

The lean philosophy

Lean synchronization can be viewed in different ways: as a broad philosophy of operations management, as a set of useful prescriptions of how to manage day-to-day operations, or a collection of tools and techniques for improving operations performance. Some of these tools and techniques are well known outside the lean sphere and relate to activities covered in other chapters of this book. As a philosophy, lean synchronization is founded on smoothing flow through processes by doing all the simple things well, on gradually doing them better and (above all) on squeezing out waste every step of the way. Three key issues define the lean philosophy: the involvement of staff in the operation, the drive for continuous improvement, and the elimination of waste. We will look at the first two issues briefly, but devote a whole section to the central idea of the elimination of waste.

The involvement of everyone

Lean philosophy is often put forward as a 'total' system. Its aim is to provide guidelines which embrace everyone and every process in the organization. An organization's culture is seen

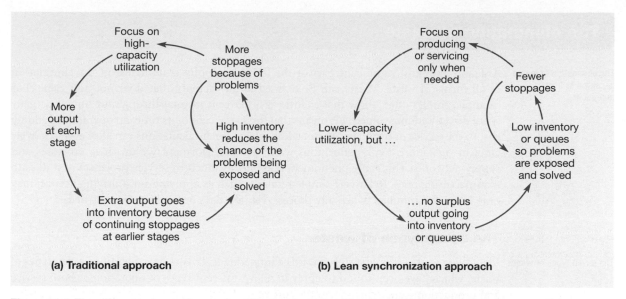

Figure 11.4 The different views of capacity utilization in (a) traditional and (b) JIT approaches to operations

as being important in supporting these objectives through an emphasis on involving all of the organization's staff. This culture is sometimes seen as synonymous with 'total quality' and is discussed in detail in Chapter 12. The lean approach to people management has also been called the **respect-for-humans** system. It encourages (and often requires) team-based problem-solving, job enrichment (by including maintenance and set-up tasks in operators' jobs), job rotation and multi-skilling. The intention is to encourage a high degree of personal responsibility, engagement and 'ownership' of the job.

Respect for humans

Critical commentary

Not all commentators see JIT-influenced people-management practices as entirely positive. The JIT approach to people management can be viewed as patronizing. It may be, to some extent, less autocratic than some Japanese management practice dating from earlier times. However, it is certainly not in line with some of the job design philosophies which place a high emphasis on contribution and commitment. Even in Japan the approach of JIT is not without its critics. Kamata wrote an autobiographical description of life as an employee at a Toyota plant called *Japan in the Passing Lane*.[2] His account speaks of 'the inhumanity and the unquestioning adherence' of working under such a system. Similar criticisms have been voiced by some trade union representatives.

Continuous improvement

Lean objectives are often expressed as ideals, such as our definition: 'to meet demand instantaneously with perfect quality and no waste'. While any operation's current performance may be far removed from such ideals, a fundamental lean belief is that it is possible to get closer to them over time. Without such beliefs to drive progress, lean proponents claim improvement is more likely to be transitory than continuous. This is why the concept of continuous improvement is such an important part of the lean philosophy. If its aims are set in terms of ideals which individual organizations may never fully achieve, then the emphasis must be on the way in which an organization moves closer to the ideal state. The Japanese word for continuous improvement is **kaizen**, and it is a key part of the lean philosophy. It is explained fully in Chapter 13.

Kaizen

The elimination of waste

The elimination of waste is central to lean approaches

Arguably the most significant part of the lean philosophy is its focus on the **elimination of all forms of waste**. Waste can be defined as any activity that does not add value. For example, studies often show that as little as 5 per cent of total throughput time is actually spent directly adding value. This means that for 95 per cent of its time, an operation is adding cost to the service or product, but not adding value. Such calculations can alert even relatively efficient operations to the enormous waste which is dormant within their processes and supply networks. This same phenomenon applies as much to service processes as it does to manufacturing ones. Relatively simple requests, such as applying for a driving licence, may only take a few minutes to actually process, yet take days or weeks to be returned.

The seven types of waste

The seven types of waste

Identifying waste is the first step towards eliminating it. Toyota have identified **seven types of waste**, which have been found to apply in many different types of operations – both service and production – and which form the core of lean philosophy:

1 *Over-production.* Producing more than is immediately needed by the next process in the operation is the greatest source of waste according to Toyota.
2 *Waiting time.* Equipment efficiency and labour efficiency are two popular measures which are widely used to measure equipment and labour waiting time, respectively. Less obvious is the amount of waiting time of items, disguised by operators who are kept busy doing things that are not needed at the time.
3 *Transport.* Moving items or customers around the operation often does not add value. Layout changes which bring processes closer together, improvements in transport methods and workplace organization can all reduce waste.
4 *Process.* The process itself may be a source of waste. Some operations may only exist because of poor product or service design, or poor maintenance, and so could be eliminated.
5 *Inventory.* All inventory should become a target for elimination. However, it is only by tackling the causes of inventory that it can be reduced.
6 *Motion.* An operator may look busy but sometimes no value is being added by the work. Simplification of work is a rich source of reduction in the waste of motion.
7 *Defectives.* Quality waste is often very significant in operations. Total costs of quality are much greater than has traditionally been considered, and it is therefore more important to attack the causes of such costs. This is discussed further in Chapter 12.

Between them, these seven types of waste contribute to four barriers to any operation achieving lean synchronization. They are: waste from irregular (non-streamlined) flow, waste from inexact supply, waste from inflexible response, and waste from variability. We will examine each of these barriers to achieving lean synchronization.

Eliminate waste through streamlined flow

The smooth flow of materials, information and people in the operation is a central idea of lean synchronization. Long process routes provide opportunities for delay and inventory build-up, add no value, and slow down throughput time. So, the first contribution any operation can make to streamlining flow is to reconsider the basic layout of its processes. Primarily, reconfiguring the layout of a process to aid lean synchronization involves moving it down the 'natural diagonal' of process design that was discussed in Chapter 5. Broadly speaking, this means moving from functional layouts towards cell-based layouts, or from cell-based layouts towards line layouts. Either way, it is necessary to move towards a layout that brings more systematization and control to the process flow. At a more detailed level, typical layout techniques include: placing workstations close together so that inventory of materials or customers just cannot build up because there is no space for it to do so, and arranging workstations in such a way that all those who contribute to a common activity are in sight of each other and can provide mutual help, for example by facilitating movement between workstations to balance capacity.

Examine all elements of throughput time

Throughput time is often taken as a surrogate measure for waste in a process. The longer that items being processed are held in inventory, moved, checked, or subject to anything else that does not add value, the longer they take to progress through the process. So, looking at exactly what happens to items within a process is an excellent method of identifying sources of waste.

Value stream mapping

Value stream mapping (also known as 'end-to-end' system mapping) is a simple but effective approach to understanding the flow of material, customers and information as value is added as it progresses through a process, operation, or supply network. It visually maps a product or services path from start to finish. In doing so it records, not only the direct activities of creating products and services, but also the 'indirect' information systems that support the direct process. It is called 'value stream' mapping because it focuses on value-adding activities and distinguishes between value-adding and non-value-adding activities. It is similar to process mapping (see Chapter 5) but different in four ways:

- It uses a broader range of information than most process maps.
- It is usually at a higher level (5–10 activities) than most process maps.
- It often has a wider scope, frequently spanning the whole supply network.
- It can be used to identify where to focus future improvement activities.

A value stream perspective involves working on and improving the 'big picture', rather than just optimizing individual processes. Value stream mapping is seen by many practitioners as a starting point to help recognize waste and identify its causes. It is a four-step technique that identifies waste and suggests ways in which activities can be streamlined. Firstly, it involves identifying the value stream (the process, operation or supply chain) to map. Secondly, it involves physically mapping a process, then above it mapping the information flow that enables the process to occur. This is the so-called 'current state' map. Thirdly, problems are diagnosed and changes suggested, making a future state map that represents the improved process, operation or supply chain. Finally, the changes are implemented. Figure 11.5 shows a value stream map for an air conditioning installation service. The service process itself is broken down into five relatively large stages and various items of data for each stage are marked on the chart. The type of data collected here does vary, but all types of value stream map compare the total throughput time with the amount of value-added time within the larger process. In this case, only 8 of the 258 hours of the process is value-adding.

Worked example[3]

An ordinary flight, just a trip to Amsterdam for two or three days. Breakfast was a little rushed but left the house at 6.15. Had to return a few minutes later, forgot my passport. Managed to find it and leave (again) by 6.30. Arrived at the airport 7.00, dropped Angela off with bags at terminal and went to the long-term car park. Eventually found a parking space after 10 minutes. Waited 8 minutes for the courtesy bus. Six minute journey back to the terminal, we start queuing at the check-in counters by 7.24. Twenty minute wait. Eventually get to check-in and find that we have been allocated seats at different ends of the plane. Staff helpful but takes 8 minutes to sort it out. Wait in queue for security checks for 10 minutes. Security decide I look suspicious and search bags for 3 minutes. Waiting in lounge by 8.05. Spend 1 hour and 5 minutes in lounge reading computer magazine and looking at small plastic souvenirs. Hurrah, flight is called 9.10, takes 2 minutes to rush to the gate and queue for further 5 minutes at gate. Through the gate and on to air bridge

→

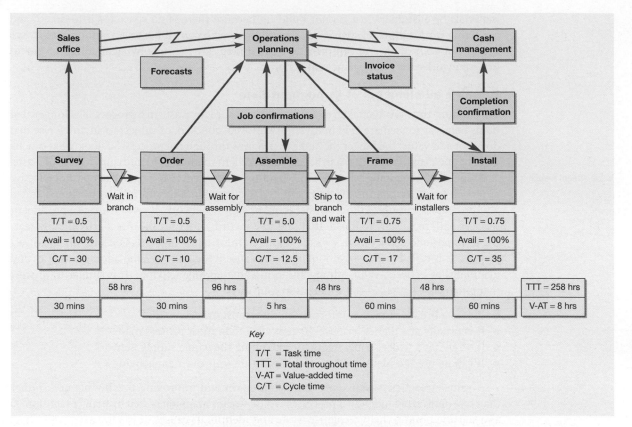

Figure 11.5 Value stream map for an industrial air conditioning installation service

which is continuous queue going onto plane, takes 4 minutes but finally in seats by 9.21. Wait for plane to fill up with other passengers for 14 minutes. Plane starts to taxi to runway at 9.35. Plane queues to take-off for 10 minutes. Plan takes off 9.45. Smooth flight to Amsterdam, 55 minutes. Stacked in queue of planes waiting to land for 10 minutes. Touch down at Schipol Airport 10.50. Taxi to terminal and wait 15 minutes to disembark. Disembark at 11.05 and walk to luggage collection (calling at lavatory on way), arrive luggage collection 11.15. Wait for luggage 8 minutes. Through customs (not searched by Netherlands security who decide I look trustworthy) and to taxi rank by 11.26. Wait for taxi 4 minutes. In to taxi by 11.30, 30 minutes ride into Amsterdam. Arrive hotel 12.00.

Analysis

How much of all this time was value-added? The total elapsed time, or throughput time, for the whole process was between 6.15 and 12.00, i.e. 5 hours 45 minutes. A detailed analysis of what was happening to the items being processed (Angela and me) indicates the following breakdown.

Time waiting in queue for check-in, luggage, etc. = 59 minutes
Time being 'served' at end of queue = 11 minutes
Waiting in lounge/plane etc. = 1 hour 55 minutes
Generally non-value-added moving about in airports, car parks etc. = 31 minutes
Quality error because I forgot my passport = 15 minutes
Value-added travelling time in car + plane + taxi = 1 hour 55 minutes.

So, only 1 hour 55 minutes of a total throughput time of 5 hours 45 minutes was spent in value-added activity. That is, 33.3 per cent value-added. Note, this was a smooth flight with no appreciable problems or delays.

Ensure visibility

Visibility

Appropriate layout also includes the extent to which all movement is transparent to everyone within the process. High **visibility** of flow makes it easier to recognize potential improvements to flow. It also promotes quality within a process because the more transparent the operation or process, the easier it is for all staff to share in its management and improvement. Problems are more easily detectable and information becomes simple, fast and visual. Visibility measures include the following.

- Clearly indicated process routes using signage.
- Performance measures clearly displayed in the workplace.
- Coloured lights used to indicate stoppages.
- An area is devoted to displaying samples of one's own and competitors' process outputs, together with samples of good and defective output.
- Visual control systems (e.g. kanbans, discussed later).

An important technique used to ensure flow visibility is the use of simple, but highly visual signals to indicate that a problem has occurred, together with operational authority to stop the process. For example, on an assembly line, if an employee detects some kind of quality problem, he or she could activate a signal that illuminates a light (called an 'andon' light) above the workstation and stops the line. Although this may seem to reduce the efficiency of the line, the idea is that this loss of efficiency in the short term is less than the accumulated losses of allowing defects to continue on in the process. Unless problems are tackled immediately, they may never be corrected.

Use small-scale simple process technology

Several small units instead of one large unit

There may also be possibilities to encourage smooth streamlined flow through the use of small-scale technologies. That is, using several small units of process technology rather than one large unit. Small machines have several advantages over large ones. First, they can process different products and services simultaneously. For example, in Figure 11.6 one large machine produces a batch of A, followed by a batch of B, and followed by a batch of C. However, if three smaller machines are used they can each produce A, B or C simultaneously. The system is also more robust. If one large machine breaks down, the whole system ceases to operate. If one of the three smaller machines breaks down, it is still operating at two-thirds effectiveness. Small machines are also easily moved, so that layout flexibility is enhanced, and the risks of making errors in investment decisions are reduced. However, investment in capacity may increase in total because parallel facilities are needed, so utilization may be lower.

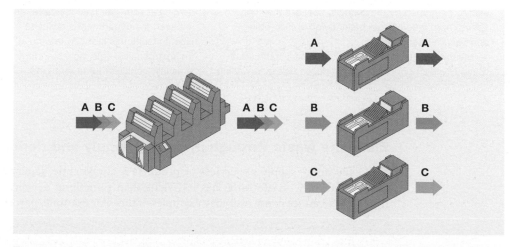

Figure 11.6 Using several small machines rather than one large one, allows simultaneous processing, is more robust, and is more flexible

Short case
Lean hospitals[4]

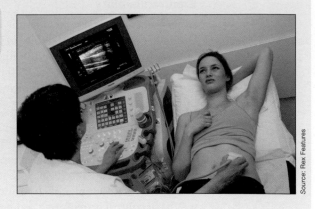

Source: Rex Features

One of the increasing number of health-care services to adopt lean principles, the Bolton Hospitals National Health Service Trust in the north of England, has reduced its hospitals' mortality rate in one injury by more than a third. David Fillingham, chief executive of Bolton Hospitals NHS Trust said, '*We had far more people dying from fractured hips than should have been dying.*' Then the trust greatly reduced its mortality rate for fractured neck of femur by redesigning the patient's stay in hospital to reduce or remove the waits between 'useful activity'. The mortality rate fell from 22.9% to 14.6%, which is the equivalent of 14 more patients surviving every six months. At the same time, average length of stay fell by a third from 34.6 days to 23.5 days. The trust held five 'rapid improvement events', involving employees from across the organization who spent several days examining processes and identifying alternative ways to improve them. Some management consultants were also used but strictly in an advisory role. In addition third-party experts were brought in. These included staff from the Royal Air Force, who had been applying lean principles to running aircraft carriers. The value of these outsiders was not only their expertise, '*They asked all sorts of innocent, naïve questions*', said Mr Fillingham, '*to which, often, no member of staff has an answer.*' Other lean-based improvement initiatives included examining the patient's whole experience from start to finish so that delays (some of which could prove fatal) could be removed on their journey to the operating theatre, speeding up the radiology process and eliminating unnecessary paperwork. Cutting the length of stay and reducing process complications should also start to reduce costs, although Mr Fillingham says that it could take several years for the savings to become substantial. Not only that, but staff are also said to be helped by the changes because they can spend more time helping patients rather than doing non-value-added activities.

Meanwhile at Salisbury district hospital in the south of the UK, lean principles have reduced delays in waiting for the results of tests from the ultrasound department. Waiting lists have been reduced from 12 weeks to between 2 weeks and zero after an investigation showed that 67% of demand was coming from just 5% of possible ultrasound tests: abdominal, gynaecological and urological. So all work was streamed into routine 'green' streams and complex 'red' ones. This is like having different traffic lanes on a motorway dedicated to different types of traffic with fast cars in one lane and slow trucks in another. Mixing both types of work is like mixing fast cars and slow-moving trucks in all lanes. The department then concentrated on doing the routine 'green' work more efficiently. For example, the initial date scan used to check the age of a foetus took only two minutes, so a series of five-minute slots were allocated just for these. '*The secret is to get the steady stream of high-volume, low-variety chugging down the ultrasound motorway*', says Kate Hobson, who runs the department. Streaming routine work in this way has left more time to deal with the more complex jobs, yet staff are not overloaded. They are more likely to leave work on time and also believe that the department is doing a better job, all of which has improved morale, says Kate Hobson, '*I think people feel their day is more structured now. It's not that madness, opening the doors and people coming at you.*' Nor has this more disciplined approach impaired the department's ability to treat really urgent jobs. In fact it has stopped leaving space in its schedule for emergencies – the, now standard, short waiting time is usually sufficient for urgent jobs.

Eliminate waste through matching supply and demand exactly

The value of the supply of services or products is always time-dependent. Something that is delivered early or late often has less value than something delivered exactly when it is needed. We can see many everyday examples of this. For example, parcel delivery companies charge more for guaranteed faster delivery. This is because our real need for the delivery is often for it to be as fast as possible. The closer to instantaneous delivery we can get the more value the delivery has for us and the more we are willing to pay for it. In fact delivery of information earlier than it is required can be even more harmful than late delivery because it results in information inventories that serve to confuse flow through the process. For example, an Australian tax office used to receive applications by mail, open the mail and send it through to the relevant department which, after processing it, sent it to the next department. This led to piles of unprocessed applications building up within its processes, causing problems in tracing applications, and losing them, sorting through and prioritizing applications, and worst of all, long throughput times. Now they only open mail when the stages in front can process it. Each department requests more work only when they have processed previous work.

Pull control

The exact matching of supply and demand is often best served by using 'pull control' wherever possible (discussed in Chapter 10). At its simplest, consider how some fast-food restaurants cook and assemble food and place it in the warm area only when the customer-facing server has sold an item. Production is being triggered only by real customer demand. Similarly supermarkets usually replenish their shelves only when customers have taken sufficient products off the shelf. The movement of goods from the 'back-office' store to the shelf is triggered only by the 'empty-shelf' demand signal. Some construction companies make it a rule to call for material deliveries to their sites, only the day before those items are actually needed. This not only reduces clutter and the chances of theft, it speeds up throughput time and reduces confusion and inventories. The essence of pull control is to let the downstream stage in a process, operation, or supply network, pull items through the system rather than have them 'pushed' to them by the supplying stage. As Richard Hall, an authority on lean operations put it, '*Don't send nothing nowhere, make 'em come and get it.*'[5]

Kanbans

Kanbans

The use of kanbans is one method of operationalizing pull control. **Kanban** is the Japanese for card or signal. It is sometimes called the 'invisible conveyor' that controls the transfer of items between the stages of an operation. In its simplest form, it is a card used by a customer stage to instruct its supplier stage to send more items. Kanbans can also take other forms. In some Japanese companies, they are solid plastic markers or even coloured ping-pong balls. Whichever kind of kanban is being used, the principle is always the same: the receipt of a kanban triggers the movement, production or supply of one unit. If two kanbans are received, this triggers the movement, production or supply of two units and so on. Kanbans are the only means by which movement, production or supply can be authorized. Some companies use 'kanban squares'. These are marked spaces on the shop floor or bench that are drawn to fit one or more work pieces or containers. Only the existence of an empty square triggers production at the stage that supplies the square. As one would expect, at Toyota the key control tool is its kanban system. The kanban is seen as serving three purposes:

● It is an instruction for the preceding process to send more work.
● It is a visual control tool to show up areas of over-production and lack of synchronization.
● It is a tool for kaizen (continuous improvement). Toyota's rules state that 'the number of kanbans should be reduced over time'.

> ### Critical commentary
>
> Just-in-time principles can be taken to an extreme. When lean ideas first started to have an impact on operations practice in the West, some authorities advocated the reduction of between-process inventories to zero. While in the long term this provides the ultimate in motivation for operations managers to ensure the efficiency and reliability of each process stage, it does not admit the possibility of some processes always being intrinsically less than totally reliable. An alternative view is to allow inventories (albeit small ones) around process stages with higher than average uncertainty. This at least allows some protection for the rest of the system. The same ideas apply to just-in-time delivery between factories. The Toyota Motor Corp., often seen as the epitome of lean, has suffered from its low inter-plant inventory policies. Both the Kobe earthquake and fires in supplier plants have caused production at Toyota's main factories to close down for several days because of a shortage of key parts. Even in the best-regulated networks, one cannot always account for such events.

Eliminate waste through flexible processes

Responding exactly and instantaneously to customer demand implies that operations resources need to be sufficiently flexible to change both what they do and how much they do of it without incurring high cost or long delays. In fact, flexible processes (often with flexible technologies) can significantly enhance smooth and synchronized flow. For example, new publishing technologies allow professors to assemble printed and e-learning course material customized to the needs of individual courses or even individual students. In this case flexibility is allowing customized, small batches to be delivered 'to order'. In another example, a firm of lawyers used to take ten days to prepare its bills for customers. This meant that customers were not asked to pay until ten days after the work had been done. Now they use a system that, every day, updates each customer's account. So, when a bill is sent it includes all work up to the day before the billing date. The principle here is that process inflexibility also delays cash flow.

Reduce set-up times

Set-up time reduction

For many technologies, increasing process flexibility, means reducing set-up times; defined as the time taken to change over the process from one activity to the next. Compare the time it takes you to change the tyre on your car with the time taken by a Formula 1 team. **Set-up reduction** can be achieved by a variety of methods such as cutting out time taken to search for tools and equipment, the pre-preparation of tasks which delay changeovers, and the constant practice of set-up routines. The other common approach to set-up time reduction is to convert work which was previously performed while the machine was stopped (called internal work) to work that is performed while the machine is running (called external work). There are three major methods of achieving the transfer of internal set-up work to external work:[6]

- Pre-prepare equipment instead of having to do it while the process is stopped. Preferably, all adjustment should be carried out externally.
- Make equipment capable of performing all required tasks so that changeovers become a simple adjustment.
- Facilitate the change of equipment, for example by using simple devices such as roller conveyors.

Fast changeovers are particularly important for airlines because they can't make money from aircraft that are sitting idle on the ground. It is called 'running the aircraft hot' in the industry. For many smaller airlines, the biggest barrier to running hot is that their markets are not large enough to justify passenger flights during the day and night. So, in order to avoid aircraft being idle over night, they must be used in some other way. That was the motive behind Boeing's 737 'Quick Change' (QC) aircraft. With it, airlines have the flexibility to use it for passenger flights during the day and, with less than a one-hour changeover (set-up) time, use it as a cargo aircraft throughout the night. Boeing engineers designed frames that hold entire rows of seats that could smoothly glide on and off the aircraft, allowing twelve seats to be rolled into place at once. When used for cargo, the seats are simply rolled out and replaced by special cargo containers designed to fit the curve of the fuselage and prevent damage to the interior. Before reinstalling the seats the sidewalls are thoroughly cleaned so that, once the seats are in place, passengers cannot tell the difference between a QC aircraft and a normal 737. Some airlines particularly value the aircraft's flexibility. It allows them to provide frequent reliable services in both passenger and cargo markets.

Eliminate waste through minimizing variability

One of the biggest causes of the variability that will disrupt flow and prevent lean synchronization is variation in the quality of items. This is why a discussion of lean synchronization should always include an evaluation of how quality conformance is ensured within processes. In particular, the principles of statistical process control (SPC) can be used to understand quality variability. Chapter 12 examines this subject, so in this section we shall focus on other causes of variability. The first of these is variability in the mix of products and services moving through processes, operations, or supply networks.

Level schedules as much as possible

Heijunka

Levelled scheduling (or **heijunka**) means keeping the mix and volume of flow between stages even over time. For example, instead of producing 500 parts in one batch, which would cover the needs for the next three months, levelled scheduling would require the process to make only one piece per hour regularly. Thus, the principle of levelled scheduling is very straightforward. However, the requirements to put it into practice are quite severe. The move from conventional to levelled scheduling is illustrated in Figure 11.7. Conventionally, if a mix of products were required in a time period (usually a month), a batch size would be calculated for each product and the batches produced in some sequence. Figure 11.7(a) shows three products that are produced in a 20-day time period in a production unit.

Quantity of product A required = 3,000
Quantity of product B required = 1,000
Quantity of product C required = 1,000

Batch size of product A = 600
Batch size of product B = 200
Batch size of product C = 200

Starting at day 1, the unit commences producing product A. During day 3, the batch of 600 As is finished and dispatched to the next stage. The batch of Bs is started but is not finished until day 4. The remainder of day 4 is spent making the batch of Cs and both batches are dispatched at the end of that day. The cycle then repeats itself. The consequence of using large batches is, first, that relatively large amounts of inventory accumulate within and between the units, and second, that most days are different from one another in terms of what they are expected to produce (in more complex circumstances, no two days would be the same).

Now suppose that the flexibility of the unit could be increased to the point where the batch sizes for the products were reduced to a quarter of their previous levels without loss of capacity (see Fig. 11.7(b)):

Batch size of product A = 150
Batch size of product B = 50
Batch size of product C = 50

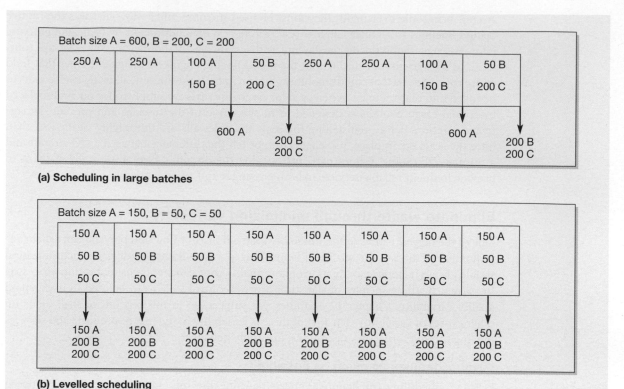

Figure 11.7 Levelled scheduling equalizes the mix of products made each day

A batch of each product can now be completed in a single day, at the end of which the three batches are dispatched to their next stage. Smaller batches of inventory are moving between each stage, which will reduce the overall level of work-in-progress in the operation. Just as significant, however, is the effect on the regularity and rhythm of production at the unit. Now every day in the month is the same in terms of what needs to be produced. This makes planning and control of each stage in the operation much easier. For example, if on day 1 of the month the daily batch of As was finished by 11.00 am, and all the batches were successfully completed in the day, then the following day the unit will know that, if it again completes all the As by 11.00 am, it is on schedule. When every day is different, the simple question 'Are we on schedule to complete our production today?' requires some investigation before it can be answered. However, when every day is the same, everyone in the unit can tell whether production is on target by looking at the clock. Control becomes visible and transparent to all, and the advantages of regular, daily schedules can be passed to upstream suppliers.

Level delivery schedules

A similar concept to levelled scheduling can be applied to many transportation processes. For example, a chain of convenience stores may need to make deliveries of all the different types of products it sells every week. Traditionally it may have dispatched a truck loaded with one particular product around all its stores so that each store received the appropriate amount of the product that would last them for one week. This is equivalent to the large batches discussed in the previous example. An alternative would be to dispatch smaller quantities of all products in a single truck more frequently. Then, each store would receive smaller deliveries more frequently, inventory levels would be lower and the system could respond to trends in demand more readily because more deliveries means more opportunity to change the quantity delivered to a store. This is illustrated in Figure 11.8.

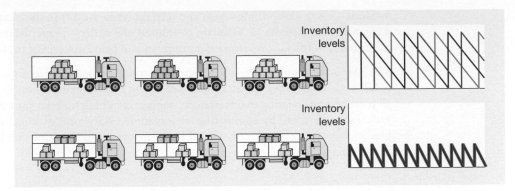

Figure 11.8 Delivering smaller quantities more often can reduce inventory levels

Adopt mixed modelling where possible

The principle of levelled scheduling can be taken further to give mixed modelling; that is, a repeated mix of outputs. Suppose that the machines in the production unit can be made so flexible that they achieve the JIT ideal of a batch size of one. The sequence of individual products emerging from the unit could be reduced progressively as illustrated in Figure 11.9. This would produce a steady stream of each product flowing continuously from the unit. However, the sequence of products does not always fall as conveniently as in Figure 11.9. The unit production times for each product are not usually identical and the ratios of required volumes are less convenient. For example, if a process is required to produce products A, B and C in the ratio 8:5:4, it could produce 800 of A, followed by 500 of B, followed by 400 of A, or 80A, 50B, and 40C. But ideally, sequencing the products as smoothly as possible, it would produce in the order . . . BACABACABACABACAB . . . repeated . . . repeated . . . etc. Doing this achieves relatively smooth flow (but does rely on significant process flexibility).

Keep things simple – the 5 Ss

The 5 Ss

The **5-S terminology** came originally from Japan, and although the translation into English is approximate, they are generally taken to represent the following.

1 **Sort** (*Seiri*) – eliminate what is not needed and keep what is needed.
2 **Straighten** (*Seiton*) – position things in such a way that they can be easily reached whenever they are needed.

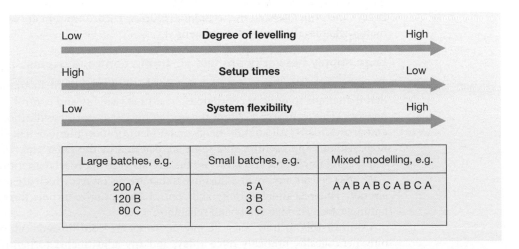

Figure 11.9 Levelled scheduling and mixed modelling: mixed modelling becomes possible as the batch size approaches one

3 **Shine** (*Seiso*) – keep things clean and tidy; no refuse or dirt in the work area.
4 **Standardize** (*Seiketsu*) – maintain cleanliness and order – perpetual neatness.
5 **Sustain** (*Shitsuke*) – develop a commitment and pride in keeping to standards.

The 5 Ss can be thought of as a simple housekeeping methodology to organize work areas that focuses on visual order, organization, cleanliness and standardization. It helps to eliminate all types of waste relating to uncertainty, waiting, searching for relevant information, creating variation, and so on. By eliminating what is unnecessary, and making everything clear and predictable, clutter is reduced, needed items are always in the same place and work is made easier and faster.

Lean synchronization applied throughout the supply network

Lean supply networks

Although most of the concepts and techniques discussed in this chapter are devoted to the management of stages *within* processes and processes *within* an operation, the same principles can apply to the whole supply network. In this context, the stages in a process are the whole businesses, operations or processes between which services and products flow. And as any business starts to approach lean synchronization it will eventually come up against the constraints imposed by the lack of lean synchronization of the other operations in its supply network. So, achieving further gains must involve trying to spread lean synchronization practice outward to its partners in the network; a far more demanding task than doing the same within a single process. And it becomes more complex as more of the supply network embraces the lean philosophy. The nature of the interaction between whole operations is far more complex than between individual stages within a process. To make a **supply network lean** means more than making each operation lean. A collection of localized lean operations rarely leads to an overall lean network. Rather one needs to apply the lean synchronization philosophy to the supply network as a whole. And essentially the principles of lean synchronization are the same for a supply network as they are for a process. Fast throughput throughout the whole supply network is still valuable and will save cost. Lower levels of inventory will still make it easier to achieve lean synchronization. Waste is just as evident (and even larger) at the level of the supply network and reducing waste is still a worthwhile task. Streamline flow, exact matching of supply and demand, enhanced flexibility, and minimizing variability are all still tasks that will benefit the whole network. The principles of pull control can work between whole operations in the same way as they can between stages within a single process. In fact, the principles and the techniques of lean synchronization are essentially the same no matter what level of analysis is being used.

Lean supply networks are like air traffic control systems[7]

The concept of the lean supply network has been likened to an air traffic control system, in that it attempts to provide continuous, 'real-time visibility and control' to all elements in the network. This is the secret of how the world's busiest airports handle thousands of departures and arrivals daily. All aircraft are given an identification number that shows up on a radar map. Aircraft approaching an airport are detected by the radar and contacted using radio. The control tower precisely positions the aircraft in an approach pattern which it coordinates. The radar detects any small adjustments that are necessary, which are communicated to the aircraft. This real-time visibility and control can optimize airport throughput while maintaining extremely high safety and reliability.

Contrast this to how most supply networks are coordinated. Information is captured only periodically, probably once a day, and any adjustments to logistics, output levels at the various operations in the supply network are adjusted, and plans rearranged. But imagine what would happen if this was how the airport operated, with only a 'radar snapshot' once a day. Coordinating aircraft with sufficient tolerance to arrange take-offs and landings every two minutes would be out of the question. Aircraft would be jeopardized, or alternatively, if aircraft were spaced further apart to maintain safety, throughput would be drastically reduced. Yet this is how most supply networks have traditionally operated. They use a daily 'snapshot' from their ERP systems (see Chapter 10 for an explanation of ERP). This limited visibility means operations must either space their work out to avoid 'collisions' (i.e. missed customer orders) thereby reducing output, or they must 'fly blind' thereby jeopardizing reliability.

Lean service

Any attempt to consider how lean ideas apply throughout a whole supply network must also confront the fact that these networks include service operations. So how can lean principles be applied in these parts of the network? The idea of lean factory operations is relatively easy to understand. Waste is evident in over-stocked inventories, excess scrap, badly sited machines and so on. In services it is less obvious, inefficiencies are more difficult to see. Yet most of the principles and techniques of lean synchronization, although often described in the context of manufacturing operations, are also applicable to service settings. In fact, some of the philosophical underpinning to lean synchronization can also be seen as having its equivalent in the service sector. Take, for example, the role of inventory. The comparison between manufacturing systems that hold large stocks of inventory between stages and those that did not centred on the effect which inventory had on improvement and problem-solving. Exactly the same argument can be applied when, instead of queues of material (inventory), an operation has to deal with queues of information or customers. With its customer focus, standardization, continuous quality improvement, smooth flow and efficiency, lean thinking has direct application in all operations, manufacturing or service. Bradley Staats and David Upton of Harvard Business School[8] have studied how lean ideas can be applied in service operations. They make three main points:

1 In terms of operations and improvements, the service industries in general are a long way behind manufacturing.
2 Not all lean manufacturing ideas translate from factory floor to office cubicle. For example, tools such as empowering manufacturing workers to 'stop the line' when they encounter a problem is not directly replicable when there is no line to stop.
3 Adopting lean operations principles alters the way a company learns through changes in problem solving, coordination through connections, and pathways and standardization.

Examples of lean service

Many of the examples of lean philosophy and lean techniques in service industries are directly analogous to those found in manufacturing industries because physical items are being moved or processed in some way. Consider the following examples.

- Supermarkets usually replenish their shelves only when customers have taken sufficient products off the shelf. The movement of goods from the 'back-office' store to the shelf is triggered only by the 'empty-shelf' demand signal. *Principle: pull control.*
- An Australian tax office used to receive applications by mail, open the mail and send it through to the relevant department which, after processing it, sent it to the next department. Now they only open mail when the stages in front can process it. Each department requests more work only when they have processed previous work. *Principle: don't let inventories build up, use pull control.*
- One construction company makes a rule of only calling for material deliveries to its sites the day before materials are needed. This reduces clutter and the chances of theft. *Principle: pull control reduces confusion.*

- Many fast-food restaurants cook and assemble food and place it in the warm area only when the customer-facing server has sold an item. *Principle: pull control reduces throughput time.*

Other examples of lean concepts and methods apply even when most of the service elements are intangible.

- Some web sites allow customers to register for a reminder service that automatically e-mails reminders for action to be taken, for example, the day before a partner's birthday, in time to prepare for a meeting, etc. *Principle: the value of delivered information, like delivered items, can be time-dependent; too early and it deteriorates (you forget it), too late and it's useless (because it's too late).*

- A firm of lawyers used to take ten days to prepare its bills for customers. This meant that customers were not asked to pay until ten days after the work had been done. Now they use a system that, every day, updates each customer's account. So, when a bill is sent it includes all work up to the day before the billing date. *Principle: process delays also delay cash flow, fast throughput improves cash flow.*

- New publishing technologies allow professors to assemble printed and e-learning course material customized to the needs of individual courses or even individual students. *Principle: flexibility allows customization and small batch sizes delivered 'to order'.*

Summary answers to key questions

Check and improve your understanding of this chapter using self-assessment questions and a personalized study plan, audio and video downloads, and an eBook – all at www.myomlab.com.

➤ What is lean synchronization?

- Lean synchronization is an approach to operations which tries to meet demand instantaneously with perfect quality and no waste. It is an approach which differs from traditional operations practices insomuch as it stresses waste elimination and fast throughput, both of which contribute to low inventories.

- The ability to deliver just-in-time not only saves working capital (through reducing inventory levels) but also has a significant impact on the ability of an operation to improve its intrinsic efficiency.

- The lean synchronization philosophy can be summarized as concerning three overlapping elements, (a) the elimination of waste in all its forms, (b) the inclusion of all staff of the operation in its improvement, and (c) the idea that all improvement should be on a continuous basis.

➤ How does lean synchronization eliminate waste?

- The most significant part of the lean philosophy is its focus on the elimination of all forms of waste, defined as any activity that does not add value.

- Lean synchronization identifies seven types of waste that, together, form four barriers to achieving lean synchronization. They are: waste from irregular (non-streamlined) flow, waste from inexact supply, waste from inflexible response, and waste from variability.

> ➤ **How does lean synchronization apply throughout the supply network?**

- Most of the concepts and techniques of lean synchronization, although usually described as applying to individual processes and operations, also apply to the whole supply networks.

- The concept of the lean supply network has been likened to an air traffic control system, in that it attempts to provide continuous, 'real-time visibility and control' to all elements in the network.

- Most of the ideas of lean synchronization are directly applicable to all the service operations in the supply network.

Learning exercises

These problems and applications will help to improve your analysis of operations. You can find more practice problems as well as worked examples and guided solutions on MyOMLab at www.myomlab.com.

1 Revisit the worked example earlier in the chapter that analysed a journey in terms of value-added time (actually going somewhere) and non-value-added time (the time spent queuing etc.). Calculate the value-added time for a recent journey that you have taken.

2 A production process is required to produce 1,400 of product X, 840 of product Y and 420 of product Z in a 4-week period. If the process works 7 hours per day and 5 days per week, devise a mixed model schedule in terms of the number of each products required to be produced every hour, that would satisfy demand.

3 Revisit the 'Operations in action' at the beginning of this chapter, and (a) list all the different techniques and practices which Toyota adopts. (b) How are operations objectives (quality, speed, dependability, flexibility, cost) influenced by the practices which Toyota adopts?

4 Consider how set-up reduction principles can be used on the following:

(a) changing a tyre at the side of the road (following a puncture);

(b) cleaning out an aircraft and preparing it for the next flight between an aircraft on its inbound flight landing and disembarking its passengers, and the same aircraft being ready to take-off on its outbound flight;

(c) the time between the finish of one surgical procedure in a hospital's operating theatre, and the start of the next one;

(d) the 'pitstop' activities during a Formula One race (how does this compare to (a) above?).

Want to know more?

Ahlstrom, P. (2004) Lean service operations: translating lean production principles to service operations, *International Journal of Services, Technology and Management*, vol. 5, nos 5/6. Explains how lean can be used in services.

Bicheno, J. and Holweg, M. (2009) *The Lean Toolbox: The Essential Guide to Lean Transformation*, 4th edn, Piscie Press, Buckingham. A manual of lean techniques, very much a 'how to do it' book, and none the worse for it.

Holweg, M. (2007) The genealogy of lean production, *Journal of Operations Management*, vol. 25, 420–37. An excellent overview of how lean ideas developed.

Spear, S. and Bowen, H.K. (1999) Decoding the DNA of the Toyota Production System, *Harvard Business Review*, September–October. Revisits the leading company as regards JIT practice and re-evaluates the underlying philosophy behind the way it manages its operations. Recommended.

Womack, J.P. and Jones, D.T. (1996) *Lean Thinking: Banish Waste and Create Wealth in Your Corporation*, Simon and Schuster, New York. Some of the lessons from *The Machine that Changed the World* but applied in a broader context.

Womack, J.P., Jones, D.T. and Roos, D. (1990) *The Machine that Changed the World*, Rawson Associates, New York. Arguably the most influential book on operations management practice of the last fifty years. Firmly rooted in the automotive sector but did much to establish lean.

Useful websites

www.lean.org/ Site of the lean enterprise unit, set up by one of the founders of the lean thinking movement.

www.theiet.org/index.cfm The site of the Institution Electrical Engineers (which includes manufacturing engineers surprisingly) has material on this and related topics as well as other issues covered in this book.

www.mfgeng.com The manufacturing engineering site.

www.opsman.org Lots of useful stuff.

Now that you have finished reading this chapter, why not visit MyOMLab at www.myomlab.com where you'll find more learning resources to help you make the most of your studies and get a better grade.

Chapter 12

Quality management

Key questions

➤ What is quality and why is it so important?

➤ How can quality problems be diagnosed?

➤ What steps lead towards conformance to specification?

➤ What is total quality management (TQM)?

Introduction

Quality is the only one of the five operations performance criteria to have its own dedicated chapter in this book. There are two reasons for this. Firstly, in some organizations a separate function is devoted exclusively to the management of quality. Secondly, quality is a key concern of almost all organizations. High-quality offerings can give an organization a considerable competitive edge. Good quality reduces the costs of rework, waste, complaints and returns and, most importantly, generates satisfied customers. Some operations managers believe that, in the long run, quality is the most important single factor affecting an organization's performance relative to its competitors. Figure 12.1 shows where this chapter fits into the overall operations model.

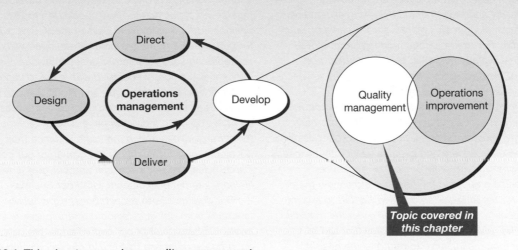

Figure 12.1 This chapter examines quality management

Check and improve your understanding of this chapter using self-assessment questions and a personalized study plan, audio and video downloads, and an eBook – all at www.myomlab.com.

Operations in practice Quality at the Four Seasons Canary Wharf[1]

The first Four Seasons Hotel opened over 45 years ago. Since then the company has grown to 81 properties in 34 countries. Famed for its quality of service, the hotel group has won countless awards including the prestigious Zagat survey and numerous AAA Five Diamond Awards, and it is also one of only 14 organizations that have been on the *Fortune* magazine's list of '100 Best Companies to Work For' every year since it launched in 1998, thus ranking as 'top hotel chain' internationally. From its inception the group has had the same guiding principle, 'to make the quality of our service our competitive advantage'. The company has what it calls its Golden Rule: 'Do to others (guests and staff) as you would wish others to do to you.' It is a simple rule, but it guides the whole organization's approach to quality.

Source: Four Seasons Hotels, Photographer Robert Miller

'*Quality service is our distinguishing edge and the company continues to evolve in that direction. We are always looking for better, more creative and innovative ways of serving our guests*', says Michael Purtill, the General Manager of the Four Seasons Hotel Canary Wharf in London. '*We have recently refined all of our operating standards across the company, enabling us to further enhance the personalized, intuitive service that all our guests receive. All employees are empowered to use their creativity and judgement in delivering exceptional service and making their own decisions to enhance our guests' stay. For example, one morning an employee noticed that a guest had a flat tyre on their car and decided of his own accord to change it for them, which was very much appreciated by the guest.*

'*The golden rule means that we treat our employees with dignity, respect and appreciation. This approach encourages them to be equally sensitive to our guests' needs and offer sincere and genuine service that exceeds expectations. Just recently one of our employees accompanied a guest to the hospital and stayed there with him for the entire afternoon. He wanted to ensure that the guest wasn't alone and was given the medical attention he needed. The following day that same employee took the initiative to return to the hospital (even though it was his day off) to visit and made sure that the guest's family in America was kept informed about his progress. We ensure that we have an ongoing focus on recognizing these successes and publicly praise and celebrate all individuals who deliver these warm, spontaneous, thoughtful touches.*

'*At Four Seasons we believe that our greatest asset and strength is our people. We pay a great deal of attention to selecting the right people with an attitude that takes great pride in delivering exceptional service. We know that motivated and happy employees are essential to our service culture and are committed to developing our employees to*

their highest potential. Our extensive training programmes and career development plans are designed with care and attention to support the individual needs of our employees as well as operational and business demands. In conjunction with traditional classroom-based learning, we offer tailor-made internet-based learning featuring exceptional quality courses for all levels of employee. Such importance is given to learning and development that the hotel has created two specialized rooms, designated for learning and development. One is intended for group learning and the other is equipped with private computer stations for internet-based individual learning. There is also a library equipped with a broad variety of hospitality-related books, CDs and DVDs that can be taken home at any time. This encourages our employees to learn and develop at an individual pace. This is very motivating for our employees and in the same instance their development is invaluable to the growth of our company. Career-wise, the sky is the limit and our goal is to build lifelong, international careers with Four Seasons.

'*Our objective is to exceed guest expectations and feedback from our guests and our employees is an invaluable barometer of our performance. We have created an in-house database that is used to record all guest feedback (whether positive or negative). We also use an online guest survey and guest comment cards which are all personally responded to and analysed to identify any potential service gaps. We continue to focus on delivering individual personalized experiences and our Guest History database remains vital in helping us to achieve this. All preferences and specific comments about service experience are logged on the database. Every comment and every preference is discussed and planned for, for every guest, for every visit. It is our culture that sets Four Seasons apart: the drive to deliver the best service in the industry that keeps our guests returning again and again.*'

What is quality and why is it so important?

It is worth revisiting some of the arguments which were presented in Chapter 3 regarding the benefits of high quality. This will explain why quality is seen as being so important by most operations. There are ways in which quality improvements can affect other aspects of operations performance. Revenues can be increased by better sales and enhanced prices in the market. At the same time, costs can be brought down by improved efficiencies, productivity and the use of capital. So, a key task of the operations function must be to ensure that it provides quality services and goods, to both its internal and external customers.

The operation's view of quality

There are many definitions of quality

There are many definitions of **quality**; here we define it as *'consistent conformance to customers' expectations'*. The use of the word 'conformance' implies that there is a need to meet a clear specification. Ensuring a service or product conforms to specification is a key operations task. 'Consistent' implies that conformance to specification is not an *ad hoc* event but that the service or product meets the specification because quality requirements are used to design and run the processes that create services and products. The use of 'customers' expectations' recognizes that the service or product must take the views of customers into account, which may be influenced by price. Also note the use of the word 'expectations' in this definition, rather than 'needs' or 'wants'.

Customers' view of quality

Past experiences, individual knowledge and history will all shape customers' expectations. Furthermore, customers may each *perceive* a service or product in different ways. One person may perceive a long-haul flight as an exciting part of a holiday; the person on the next seat may see it as a necessary chore to get to a business meeting. So quality needs to be understood from a customer's point of view because, to the customer, the quality of a particular offering is whatever he or she perceives it to be. If the passengers on a skiing charter flight perceive it to be of good quality, despite long queues at check-in or cramped seating and poor meals, then the flight really is of good perceived quality.[2] Also customers may be unable to judge the 'technical' specification of the service or product and so use surrogate measures as a basis for their perception of quality.[3] For example, a customer may find it difficult to judge the technical quality of dental treatment, except insofar as it does not give any more trouble. The customer may therefore perceive quality in terms of the attire and demeanour of the dentist and technician, décor of the surgery, and how they were treated.

Reconciling the operation's and the customer's views of quality

Customer expectations

Customer perception

A customer's view of quality is shaped by the gap between perception and expectation

The operation's view of quality is concerned with trying to meet **customer expectations**. The customer's view of quality is what he or she *perceives* the service or product to be. To create a unified view, quality can be defined as the degree of fit between customers' expectations and **customer perception** of the service or product.[4] Using this idea allows us to see the customers' view of quality of the service or product as the result of the customers comparing their expectations of performance with their perception of performance. If the service or product experience was better than expected then the customer is satisfied and quality is perceived to be high. If the service or product was less than his or her expectations then quality is low and the customer may be dissatisfied. If the service or product matches expectations then the perceived quality of the product or service is seen to be **acceptable**. These relationships are summarized in Figure 12.2.

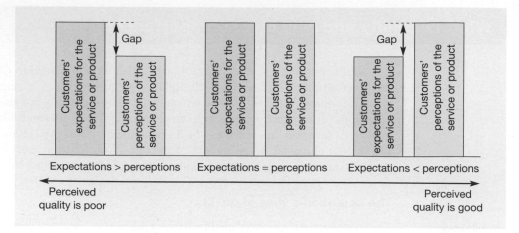

Perceived quality is poor ← → Perceived quality is good

Figure 12.2 Perceived quality is governed by the magnitude and direction of the gap between customers' expectations and their perceptions of the service or product

Short case
Tea and Sympathy[5]

Defining quality in terms of perception and expectation can sometimes reveal some surprising results. For example, Tea and Sympathy is a British restaurant and café in the heart of New York's West Village. Over the last ten years it has become a fashionable landmark in a city with one of the broadest range of restaurants in the world. Yet it is tiny, around a dozen tables packed into an area little bigger than the average British sitting room. Not only expatriate Brits but also native New Yorkers and celebrities queue to get in. As the only British restaurant in New York, it has a novelty factor, but also it has become famous for the unusual nature of its service. *'Everyone is treated in the same way'*, says Nicky Perry, one of the two ex-Londoners who run it, *'We have a firm policy that we don't take any shit.'* This robust attitude to the treatment of customers is reinforced by 'Nicky's Rules' which are printed on the menu.

1 Be pleasant to the waitresses – remember Tea and Sympathy girls are always right.
2 You will have to wait outside the restaurant until your entire party is present – no exceptions.
3 Occasionally, you may be asked to change tables so that we can accommodate all of you.
4 If we don't need the table you may stay all day, but if people are waiting it's time to naff off.

Source: Corbis

5 These rules are strictly enforced. Any argument will incur Nicky's wrath. You have been warned.

Most of the waitresses are also British and enforce Nicky's Rules strictly. If customers object they are thrown out. Nicky says that she has had to train 'her girls' to toughen up. *'I've taught them that when people cross the line they can tear their throats out as far as I'm concerned. What we've discovered over the years is that if you are really sweet, people see it as a weakness. People get thrown out of the restaurant about twice a week and yet customers still queue for the genuine shepherd's pie, a real cup of tea, and of course the service.'*

Both customers' expectations and perceptions are influenced by a number of factors, some of which cannot be controlled by the operation and some of which, to a certain extent, can be managed. Figure 12.3 shows some of the factors that will influence the gap between expectations and perceptions. This model of customer-perceived quality can help us understand how operations can manage quality and identifies some of the problems in so doing. The bottom part of the diagram represents the operation's 'domain' of quality and the top part the customer's 'domain'. These two domains meet in the actual service or product, which is provided by the

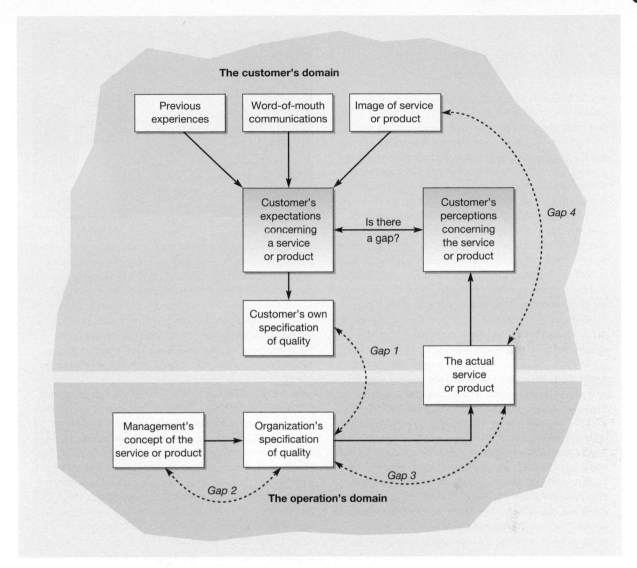

Figure 12.3 The customer's domain and the operations domain in determining the perceived quality, showing how the gap between customers' expectations and their perception of a service or product could be explained by one or more gaps elsewhere in the model

Source: Adapted from Parasuraman, A. *et al.* (1985) A conceptual model of service quality and implications for future research, *Journal of Marketing*, vol. 49, Fall, pp. 41–50. Reproduced with permission from the American Marketing Association.

organization and experienced by the customer. Within the operation's domain, management is responsible for designing the service or product and providing a specification of the quality to which the service or product has to be created. Within the customer's domain, his or her expectations are shaped by such factors as previous experiences with the particular service or product, the marketing image provided by the organization and word-of-mouth information from other users. These expectations are internalized as a set of quality characteristics.

Diagnosing quality problems[6]

Figure 12.3 shows how quality problems can be diagnosed. If the perceived quality gap is such that customers' perceptions of the offering fail to match their expectations of it, then the reason (or reasons) must lie in other gaps elsewhere in the model as follows.

Short case
Quality at Magic Moments

Source: Alamy Images

Magic Moments is a small, but successful wedding photography business. Its owner, Richard Webber, has seen plenty of changes over the last twenty years. *'In the past, my job involved taking a few photos during the wedding ceremony and then formal group shots outside. I was rarely at a wedding for more than two hours. Clients would select around 30 photos to go in a standard wedding album. It was important to get the photos right, because that was really the only thing I was judged on. Now it's different. I usually spend all day at a wedding, and sometimes late into the evening as well. This creates a very different dynamic with the wedding party, as you're almost like another guest. Whilst the bride and groom are still my primary concern, other guests at the wedding are also important. The challenge is to find the right balance between getting the best photos possible whilst being as discreet as possible. I could spend hours getting the perfect picture, but annoy everyone in the process. It's difficult, because clients judge you on both the technical quality of your work and the way you interact with everyone on the day. The product has changed too. Clients receive a CD or memory stick with around 500 photos taken during the day. Also I can give them a choice of 10 albums in different sizes, ranging from 30 to 100 photos. This year, I have started offering photo books which allow a much greater level of customization and have proved popular for younger couples. For the future, I'm considering offering albums with wedding items such as invitations, confetti and menus, and individual paintings created from photographs. Obviously I would have to outsource the paintings. I'm also going to upgrade our* web site, so wedding guests can order photos and related products online. This will generate revenue and act as a good marketing tool. My anxiety is that advertising this additional service at the wedding will be seen as being too commercial, even if it's actually of benefit to guests.

One of the biggest problems for the business is the high level of demand in the summer months. Weekends in June, July and August are often booked up two years in advance. One option is to take on additional photographers during busy periods. However, the best ones are busy themselves. The concern is that the quality of the service I offer would deteriorate. A large part of the business is about how one relates to clients and that's hard to replicate. Having been to so many weddings, I often offer clients advice on various aspects of their wedding, such as locations, bands, caterers and florists. However, with development, wedding planning is clearly an area that could be profitable to the business. Of course, another option is to move beyond weddings into other areas, such as school photos, birthdays, celebrations, or studio work.'

Gap 1: The customer's specification–operation's specification gap. Perceived quality could be poor because there may be a mismatch between the organization's own internal quality specification and the specification which is expected by the customer. For example, a car may be designed to need servicing every 10,000 kilometres but the customer may expect 15,000-kilometre service intervals.

Gap 2: The concept–specification gap. Perceived quality could be poor because there is a mismatch between the concept (see Chapter 4) and the way the organization has specified quality internally. For example, the concept of a car might have been for an inexpensive, energy-efficient means of transportation, but the inclusion of a climate control system may have both added to its cost and made it less energy-efficient.

Gap 3: The quality-specification–actual-quality gap. Perceived quality could be poor because there is a mismatch between actual quality and the internal quality specification (often called 'conformance to specification'). For example, the internal quality specification for a car may be that the gap between its doors and body, when closed, must not exceed 7 mm. However, because of inadequate equipment, the gap in reality is 9 mm.

Gap 4: The actual-quality–communicated-image gap. Perceived quality could be poor because there is a gap between the organization's external communications or market image and the actual quality delivered to the customer. This may be because the marketing function has set unachievable expectations or operations is not capable of the level of quality expected by the customer. For example, an advertising campaign for an airline might show a cabin attendant offering to replace a customer's shirt on which food or drink has been spilt, whereas such a service may not in fact be available should this happen.

Conformance to specification

Conformance to specification means producing a product or providing a service to its design specification. It is usually seen as the most important contribution that operations management can make to the customer's perception of quality. Achieving conformance can be summarized in six sequential steps.

Step 1   Define the quality characteristics of the service or product.
Step 2   Decide how to measure each quality characteristic.
Step 3   Set quality standards for each quality characteristic.
Step 4   Control quality against those standards.
Step 5   Find and correct causes of poor quality.
Step 6   Continue to make improvements.

Step 1 – Define the quality characteristics

Much of the 'quality' of an offering will have been specified in its design. But not all the design details are useful in controlling quality. For example, the design of a television may specify that its outer cabinet is made with a particular veneer. Each television is not checked, however, to make sure that the cabinet is indeed made from that particular veneer. Rather it is the *consequences* of the design specification which are examined – the appearance of the cabinet, for example. These consequences for quality planning and control of the design

Quality characteristics

are called the **quality characteristics** of the offering. Table 12.1, overleaf, shows a list of the quality characteristics which are generally useful.

Step 2 – Decide how to measure each characteristic

These characteristics must be defined in such a way as to enable them to be measured and then controlled. This involves taking a very general quality characteristic such as 'appearance' and breaking it down, as far as one can, into its constituent elements. 'Appearance' is difficult to measure as such, but 'colour match', 'surface finish' and 'number of visible scratches' are all capable of being described in a more objective manner. They may even be quantifiable. Other quality characteristics pose more difficulty. The 'courtesy' of airline staff, for example, has no objective quantified measure. Yet operations with high customer contact, such as airlines, place a great deal of importance on the need to ensure courtesy in their staff. In cases like this, the operation will have to attempt to measure customer *perceptions* of courtesy.

Variables and attributes

Variables
Attributes

The measures used by operations to describe quality characteristics are of two types: **variables** and **attributes**. Variable measures are those that can be measured on a continuously variable scale (for example, length, diameter, weight or time). Attributes are those which are assessed by judgement and are dichotomous, i.e. have two states (for example, right or wrong, works or does not work, looks OK or not OK). Table 12.2 categorizes some of the measures which might be used for the quality characteristics of the car and the airline journey.

Table 12.1 Quality characteristics for a car, a bank loan and an air journey

Quality characteristic	Car (material transformation process)	Bank loan (information transformation process)	Air journey (customer transformation process)
Functionality – how well the product or service does its job	Speed, acceleration, fuel consumption, ride quality, road-holding, etc.	Interest rate, terms and conditions	Safety and duration of journey, onboard meals and drinks, car and hotel booking services
Appearance – the sensory characteristics of the product or service: its aesthetic appeal, look, feel, etc.	Aesthetics, shape, finish, door gaps, etc.	Aesthetics of information, web site, etc.	Décor and cleanliness of aircraft, lounges and crew
Reliability – the consistency of the product's or service's performance over time	Mean time to failure	Keeping promises (implicit and explicit)	Keeping to the published flight times
Durability – the total useful life of the product or service	Useful life (with repair)	Stability of terms and conditions	Keeping up with trends in the industry
Recovery – the ease with which problems with the product or service can be resolved	Ease of repair	Resolution of service failures	Resolution of service failures
Contact – the nature of the person-to-person contact which might take place	Knowledge and courtesy of sales staff	Knowledge and courtesy of branch and call centre staff	Knowledge, courtesy and sensitivity of airline staff

Table 12.2 Variable and attribute measures for quality characteristics

Quality characteristic	Car		Airline journey	
	Variable	Attribute	Variable	Attribute
Functionality	Acceleration and braking characteristics from test bed	Is the ride quality satisfactory?	Number of journeys which actually arrived at the destination (i.e. didn't crash!)	Was the food acceptable?
Appearance	Number of blemishes visible on car	Is the colour to specification?	Number of seats not cleaned satisfactorily	Is the crew dressed smartly?
Reliability	Average time between faults	Is the reliability satisfactory?	Proportion of journeys which arrived on time	Were there any complaints?
Durability	Life of the car	Is the useful life as predicted?	Number of times service innovations lagged competitors	Generally, is the airline updating its services in a satisfactory manner?
Recovery	Time from fault discovered to fault repaired	Is the serviceability of the car acceptable?	Proportion of service failures resolved satisfactorily	Do customers feel that staff deal satisfactorily with complaints?
Contact	Level of help provided by sales staff (1 to 5 scale)	Did customers feel well served (yes or no)?	The extent to which customers feel well treated by staff (1 to 5 scale)	Did customers feel that the staff were helpful (yes or no)?

Step 3 – Set quality standards

When operations managers have identified how any quality characteristic can be measured, they need a quality standard against which it can be checked; otherwise they will not know whether it indicates good or bad performance. The quality standard is that level of quality which defines the boundary between acceptable and unacceptable. Such standards may well be constrained by operational factors such as the state of technology in the factory, and the cost limits of making the product. At the same time, however, they need to be appropriate to the expectations of customers. But quality judgements can be difficult. If one airline passenger out of every 10,000 complains about the food, is that good because 9,999 passengers out of 10,000 are satisfied? Or is it bad because, if one passenger complains, there must be others who, although dissatisfied, did not bother to complain? And if that level of complaint is similar for other airlines, should it regard its quality as satisfactory?

Step 4 – Control quality against those standards

After setting up appropriate standards, the operation will then need to check that the services or products conform to those standards: doing things right, first time, every time. This involves three decisions:

1　Where in the operation should they check that it is conforming to standards?
2　Should they check everything or take a sample?
3　How should the checks be performed?

Where should the checks take place?

At the start of the process incoming resources may be inspected to make sure that they are to the correct specification. For example, a university will screen applicants to try to ensure that they have a high chance of getting through the programme. A car manufacturer will check that components are of the right specification. During the process, checks may take place before a particularly costly process, prior to 'difficult to check', immediately after a process with a high defective rate, before potential damage or distress might be caused, and so on. Checks may also take place after the process itself to ensure that customers do not experience non-conformance.

Check everything or take a sample?

Quality sampling

While it might seem ideal to check every single service or product, a **sample** may be more practical for a number of reasons.

● It might be dangerous to inspect everything. A doctor, for example, checks just a small sample of blood rather than taking all of a patient's blood! The characteristics of this sample are taken to represent those of the rest of the patient's blood.
● Checking everything might destroy the product or interfere with the service. Not every light bulb is checked for how long it lasts – it would destroy every bulb. Waiters do not check that customers are enjoying the meal every 30 seconds.
● Checking everything can be time-consuming and costly. It may not be feasible to check the feelings of every bus commuter every day or to check all output from a high-volume machine.

Also 100 per cent checking may not guarantee that all defects will be identified. Sometimes it is intrinsically difficult. For example, although a physician may undertake the correct testing procedure, he or she may not necessarily diagnose a disease. Nor is it easy to notice everything. For example, try counting the number of 'e's on this page. Count them again and see if you get the same score!

Type I and type II errors

Although it reduces checking time, using a sample to make a decision about quality does have its own inherent problems. Like any decision activity, we may get the decision wrong. Take the example of a pedestrian waiting to cross a street. He or she has two main decisions: whether to continue waiting or to cross. If there is a satisfactory break in the traffic and the pedestrian crosses then a correct decision has been made. Similarly, if that person continues to wait because the traffic is too dense then he or she has again made a correct decision. There are two types of incorrect decisions or errors, however. One incorrect decision would be if he or she decides to cross when there is not an adequate break in the traffic, resulting in an accident – this is referred to as a type I error. Another incorrect decision would occur if he or she decides not to cross even though there was an adequate gap in the traffic – this is called a type II error. In crossing the road, therefore, there are four outcomes, which are summarized in Table 12.3.

Table 12.3 Type I and type II errors for a pedestrian crossing the road

| Decision | Road conditions | |
	Unsafe	Safe
Cross	Type I error	Correct decision
Wait	Correct decision	Type II error

Type I errors are those which occur when a decision was made to do something and the situation did not warrant it. Type II errors are those which occur when nothing was done, yet a decision to do something should have been taken as the situation did indeed warrant it. For example, if a school's inspector checks the work of a sample of 20 out of 1,000 pupils and all 20 of the pupils in the sample have failed, the inspector might draw the conclusion that all the pupils have failed. In fact, the sample just happened to contain 20 out of the 50 students who had failed the course. The inspector, by assuming a high fail rate would be making a type I error. Alternatively, if the inspector checked 20 pieces of work all of which were of a high standard, he or she might conclude that all the pupils' work was good despite having been given, or having chosen, the only pieces of good work in the whole school. This would be a type II error. Although these situations are not likely, they are possible. Therefore any sampling procedure has to be aware of these risks (see the short case on 'Surgical statistics').

Short case
Surgical statistics[7]

Understanding the nature of type I and type II errors is an essential part of any surgeon's quality planning. Take the well-known appendectomy operation, for example. This is the removal of the appendix when it becomes infected or inflamed. Removal is necessary because of the risk of the appendix bursting and causing peritonitis, a potentially fatal poisoning of the blood. The surgical procedure itself is a relatively simple operation with expected good results but there is always a small risk associated with any invasive surgery needing a general anaesthetic. In addition, like any surgical procedure, it is expensive. The cost of the USA's approximately quarter-of-a-million appendectomies averages out to around $4,500 per operation. Unfortunately, appendicitis is difficult to diagnose accurately. Using standard X-ray procedures a definite diagnosis can only be obtained about 10 per cent of the time. But now a new technique, developed in the Massachusetts General Hospital in Boston, claims to be able to identify 100 per cent of true appendicitis cases before surgery is carried out.

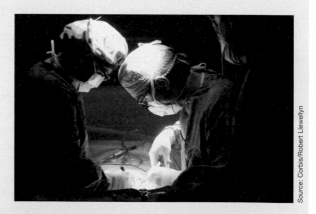

Source: Corbis/Robert Llewellyn

The new technique (Focused Appendix Computed Tomography) uses spiral X-ray images together with a special dye. It scans only the relevant part of the body, so exposure to radiation is not as major an issue as with conventional X-ray techniques. The technique can also help in providing an alternative diagnosis when an appendectomy is not needed. Most significantly, the potential cost savings are very great. The test itself costs less than $250, which means that one single avoided surgery pays for around 20 tests.

How should the checks be performed?

In practice most operations will use some form of sampling to check the quality of their services or products. The decision then is what kind of sample procedure to adopt. By far the best known method of doing this is the procedure called **statistical process control** (SPC). SPC is concerned with sampling the process during the production of the goods or the delivery of service. Based on this sample, decisions are made as to whether the process is 'in control', that is, operating as it should be. The value of SPC is not just to make checks of a single sample but to monitor the quality over a period of time. It does this by using **control charts** to see if the process seems to be performing as it should, or alternatively if it is 'out of control'. If the process does seem to be going out of control, then steps can be taken *before* there is a problem. Actually, most operations chart their quality performance in some way. Figure 12.4, or something like it, could be found in almost any operation. The chart could, for example, represent the percentage of customers in a sample of 1,000 who, each month, were dissatisfied with the restaurant's cleanliness. While the amount of dissatisfaction may be acceptably small, management should be concerned that it has been steadily increasing over time and may wish to investigate why this is so. In this case, the control chart is plotting an attribute measure of quality (satisfied or not). Looking for trends is an important use of control charts. If the trend suggests the process is getting steadily worse, then it will be worth investigating the process. If the trend is steadily improving, it may still be worthy of investigation to try to identify what is happening that is making the process better.

Statistical process control *(margin note)*

Control charts *(margin note)*

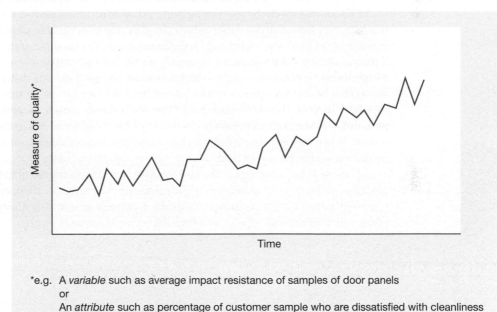

*e.g. A *variable* such as average impact resistance of samples of door panels
or
An *attribute* such as percentage of customer sample who are dissatisfied with cleanliness

Figure 12.4 Charting trends in quality measures

Common causes of variability

The processes charted in Figure 12.4 showed an upwards trend. But the trend was neither steady nor smooth: it varied, sometimes up, sometimes down. All processes vary to some extent. People perform tasks slightly differently each time. No machine will give precisely the same result each time it is used. Given this, it is not surprising that the measure of quality will also vary. Variations which derive from these *common causes* can never be entirely eliminated (although they can be reduced). For example, if a machine is filling boxes with rice, it will not place *exactly* the same weight of rice in every box it fills. Usually this type of variation can be described by a normal distribution with 99.7 per cent of the variation lying within ±3 standard deviations. The obvious question for any operations manager would be:

Common causes *(margin note)*

'Is this variation in the process performance acceptable?' The answer will depend on the acceptable range of weights which can be tolerated by the operation. This range is called the **specification range**. If the weight of rice in the box is too small then the organization might infringe labelling regulations; if it is too large, the organization is 'giving away' too much of its product for free.

Assignable causes of variation

Not all variation in processes is the result of common causes. There may be something wrong with the process which is assignable to a particular and preventable cause. An untrained person may not be following prescribed procedures. Machinery may have worn or been set up badly. The causes of such variation are called *assignable causes*. The question is whether the results from any particular sample, when plotted on the control chart, simply represent the variation due to common causes or due to some specific and correctable *assignable* cause. Figure 12.5, for example, shows the control chart for the average impact resistance of samples of door panels taken over time. Like any process the results vary, but the last three points seem to be lower than usual. So, is this natural (common cause) variation, or the symptom of some more serious (assignable) cause?

To help make this decision, **control limits** can be added to the control chart (the red dashed lines) which indicates the expected extent of 'common-cause' variation. If any points lie outside these control limits (the shaded zone) then the process can be deemed out of control in the sense that variation is likely to be due to assignable causes. These control limits could be set intuitively by examining past variation during a period when the process was thought to be free of any variation which could be due to assignable causes. But control limits can also be set in a more statistically revealing manner. For example, if the process which tests door panels had been measured to determine the normal distribution which represents its common-cause variation, then control limits can be based on this distribution. Figure 12.5 also shows how control limits can be added; here they are put at ±3 standard deviations (of the population of sample means) away from the mean of sample averages. It shows that the probability of the final point on the chart being influenced by an assignable cause is very high indeed. When the process is exhibiting behaviour which is outside its normal 'common-cause' range, it is said to be 'out of control'. Yet there is a small but finite chance that the (seemingly out of limits) point is just one of the rare but natural results at the tail of the distribution which describes perfectly normal behaviour. Stopping the process under these circumstances would represent a type I error because the process is actually in control. Alternatively, ignoring a result which in reality is due to an assignable cause is a type II error.

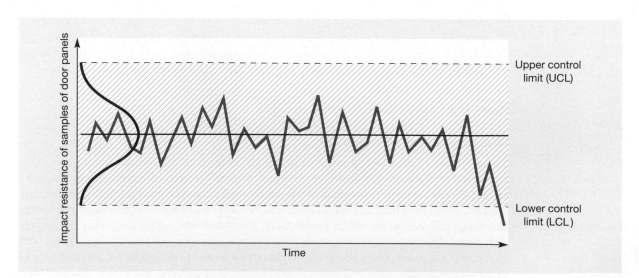

Figure 12.5 Control chart for the impact resistance of door panels, together with control limits

Why variability is a bad thing

Assignable variation is a signal that something has changed in the process which therefore must be investigated. But normal variation is itself a problem because it masks any changes in process behaviour. Figure 12.6 shows the performance of two processes both of which are subjected to a change in their process behaviour at the same time. The process on the left has such a wide natural variation that it is not immediately apparent that any change has taken place. Eventually it will become apparent because the likelihood of process performance violating the lower (in this case) control limit has increased, but this may take some time. By contrast, the process on the right has a far narrower band of natural variation. Because of this, the same change in average performance is more easily noticed (both visually and statistically). So, the narrower the natural variation of a process, the more obvious are changes in the behaviour of that process. And the more obvious are process changes, the easier it is to understand how and why the process is behaving in a particular way. Accepting any variation in any process is, to some degree, admitting to ignorance of how that process works.

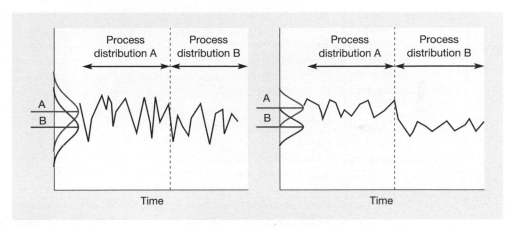

Figure 12.6 Low process variation allows changes in process performance to be readily detected

Steps 5 and 6 – Find and correct causes of poor quality and continue to make improvements

The final two steps in our list of quality management activities are, in some ways, the most important yet also the most difficult. They also blend into the general area of operations improvement covered in the next chapter. Nevertheless, there is an aspect of quality management that has been particularly important in shaping how quality is improved and the improvement activity made self-sustaining. This is total quality management (TQM).

Total quality management (TQM)

Total quality management

Total quality management (TQM) was one of the earliest of the current wave of management 'fashions'. Its peak of popularity was in the late 1980s and early 1990s. As such it has suffered from something of a backlash in recent years and there is little doubt that many companies adopted TQM in the simplistic belief that it would transform their operations performance overnight. Yet the general precepts and principles that constitute TQM are still the dominant mode of organizing operations improvement. The approach we take here is to stress the importance of the 'total' in total quality management and how it can guide the agenda for improvement.

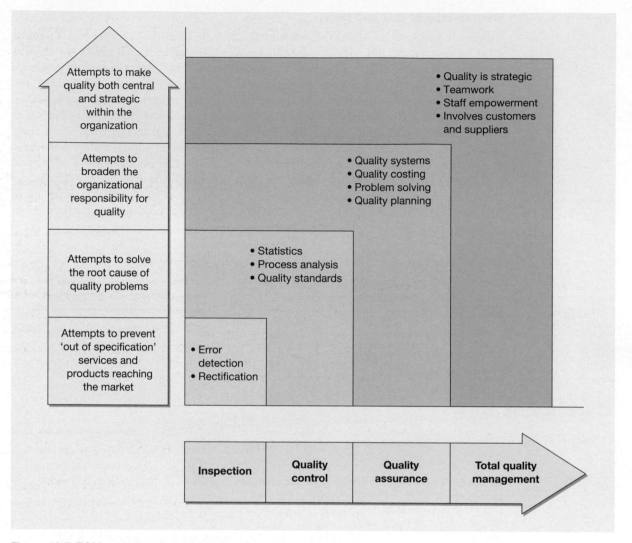

Figure 12.7 TQM as an extension

TQM as an extension of previous practice

Inspection
Quality control
Quality assurance

TQM can be viewed as a logical extension of the way in which quality-related practice has progressed (see Figure 12.7). Originally quality was achieved by **inspection** – screening out defects before they were noticed by customers. The **quality control** (QC) concept developed a more systematic approach to not only detecting, but also treating quality problems. **Quality assurance** (QA) widened the responsibility for quality to include functions other than direct operations. It also made increasing use of more sophisticated statistical quality techniques. TQM included much of what went before but developed its own distinctive themes. We will use some of these themes to describe how TQM represents a clear shift from traditional approaches to quality.

What is TQM?

TQM is a philosophy of how to approach the organization of quality improvement

TQM is 'an effective system for integrating the quality development, quality maintenance and quality improvement efforts of the various groups in an organization so as to enable production and service at the most economical levels which allow for full customer satisfaction'.[8] However, it was the Japanese who first made the concept work on a wide scale and subsequently popularized the approach and the term 'TQM'. It was then developed further by several, so-called, 'quality gurus'. Each 'guru' stressed a different set of issues, from which emerged the TQM approach. It is best thought of as a philosophy of how to approach quality improvement. This philosophy, above everything, stresses the 'total' of TQM. It is an approach that puts quality at the heart of everything that is done by an operation and includes all activities within an operation. This totality can be summarized by the way TQM lays particular stress on the following:

- meeting the needs and expectations of customers;
- covering all parts of the organization;
- including every person in the organization;
- examining all costs which are related to quality, especially failure costs and getting things 'right first time';
- developing the systems and procedures which support quality and improvement;
- developing a continuous process of improvement (this will be treated in the broader context of improvement, in Chapter 13).

TQM means meeting the needs and expectations of customers

Earlier in this chapter we defined quality as 'consistent conformance to customers' expectations'. Therefore any approach to quality management must necessarily include the customer perspective. In TQM this customer perspective is particularly important. It may be referred to as '**customer-centricity**' or the '**voice of the customer**'. However, the term TQM stresses the importance of starting with an insight into customer needs, wants, perceptions and preferences. This can then be translated into quality objectives and used to drive quality improvement.

Customer-centricity
Voice of the customer

TQM means covering all parts of the organization

For an organization to be truly effective, every single part of it, each department, each activity, and each person must work properly together, because of the affect they have on one another. One of the most powerful concepts that has emerged from various improvement approaches is the concept of the **internal customer or supplier**. This is recognition that everyone is a customer within the organization and consumes services or products provided by other internal suppliers, and everyone is also an internal supplier for other internal customers. The implication of this is that errors in the service provided within an organization will eventually affect the service or product which reaches the external customer.

Internal customer or supplier

Service-level agreements

Some organizations bring a degree of formality to the internal customer concept by encouraging different parts of the operation to agree **service-level agreements** (SLAs) with each other. SLAs are formal definitions of the dimensions of service and the relationship between two parts of an organization. The type of issues which would be covered by such an agreement could include response times, the range of services, dependability of service supply, and so on. Boundaries of responsibility and appropriate performance measures could also be agreed. For example, an SLA between an information systems support unit and a research unit in the laboratories of a large company could define such performance measures as:

Service-level agreements

- the types of information network services which may be provided as 'standard';
- the range of special information services which may be available at different periods of the day;
- the minimum 'up-time', i.e. the proportion of time the system will be available at different periods of the day;

- the maximum response time and average response time to get the system fully operational should it fail;
- the maximum response time to provide 'special' services, and so on.

TQM means including every person in the organization

Every person in the organization has the potential to contribute to quality. Although it may be necessary to develop some specialists to assist with maintaining quality levels, TQM was amongst the first approaches to stress the centrality of harnessing everyone's impact on quality and therefore their potential contribution to quality. There is scope for creativity and innovation even in relatively routine activities, claim TQM proponents. The shift in attitude which is needed to view employees as the most valuable intellectual and creative resource which the organization possesses can still prove difficult for some organizations. When TQM practices first began to migrate from Japan in the late 1970s, the ideas seemed even more radical. Some Japanese industrialists even thought (mistakenly) that companies in Western economies would never manage to change.

TQM means all costs of quality are considered

The costs of controlling quality may not be small, whether the responsibility lies with each individual or a dedicated quality control department. It is therefore necessary to examine all the costs and benefits associated with quality (in fact 'cost of quality' is usually taken to refer to both costs and benefits of quality). These costs of quality are usually categorized as *prevention costs*, *appraisal costs*, *internal failure costs* and *external failure costs*.

Prevention costs

Prevention costs are those costs incurred in trying to prevent problems, failures and errors from occurring in the first place. They include such things as:

- identifying potential problems and putting the process right before poor quality occurs;
- designing and improving the design of services, products and processes to reduce quality problems;
- training and development of personnel in the best way to perform their jobs;
- process control through SPC.

Appraisal costs

Appraisal costs are those costs associated with controlling quality to check to see if problems or errors have occurred during and after the creation of the product or service. They might include such things as:

- the setting up of statistical acceptance sampling plans;
- the time and effort required to inspect inputs, processes and outputs;
- obtaining processing inspection and test data;
- investigating quality problems and providing quality reports;
- conducting customer surveys and quality audits.

Internal failure costs

Internal failure costs are failure costs associated with errors which are dealt with inside the operation. These costs might include such things as:

- the cost of scrapped parts and material;
- reworked parts and materials;
- the lost production time as a result of coping with errors;
- lack of concentration due to time spent troubleshooting rather than improvement.

External failure costs

External failure costs are those which are associated with an error going out of the operation to a customer. These costs include such things as:

- loss of customer goodwill affecting future business;
- aggrieved customers who may take up time;

- litigation (or payments to avoid litigation);
- guarantee and warranty costs;
- the cost to the company of providing excessive capability (too much coffee in the pack or too much information to a client).

The relationship between quality costs

In traditional quality management it was assumed that failure costs reduce as the money spent on appraisal and prevention increases. Furthermore, it was assumed that there is an *optimum* amount of quality effort to be applied in any situation, which minimizes the total costs of quality. The argument is that there must be a point beyond which diminishing returns set in – that is, the cost of improving quality gets larger than the benefits which it brings. Figure 12.8(a) sums up this idea. As quality effort is increased, the costs of providing the effort – through extra quality controllers, inspection procedures, and so on – increases proportionally. At the same time, however, the cost of errors, faulty products, and so on, decreases because there are fewer of them. However, TQM proponents believe that this logic is flawed. Firstly, it implies that failure and poor quality are acceptable. Why, TQM proponents argue, should any operation accept the *inevitability* of errors? Some occupations seem to be able to accept a zero-defect standard. No one accepts that pilots are allowed to crash a certain proportion of their aircraft, or that nurses will drop a certain proportion of the babies they deliver. Secondly, it assumes that costs are known and measurable. In fact putting realistic figures to the cost of quality is not a straightforward matter. Thirdly, it is argued that failure costs in the traditional model are greatly underestimated. In particular, all the management time wasted by failures and the loss of concentration it causes are rarely accounted for. Fourthly, it implies that prevention costs are inevitably high because it involves expensive inspection. But why shouldn't quality be an integral part of everyone's work rather than employing extra people to inspect. Finally, the 'optimum-quality level' approach, by accepting compromise, does little to challenge operations managers and staff to find ways of improving quality. Put these corrections into the optimum-quality effort calculation and the picture looks very different (see Figure 12.8b). If there is an 'optimum', it is a lot further to the right, in the direction of putting more effort (but not necessarily cost) into quality.

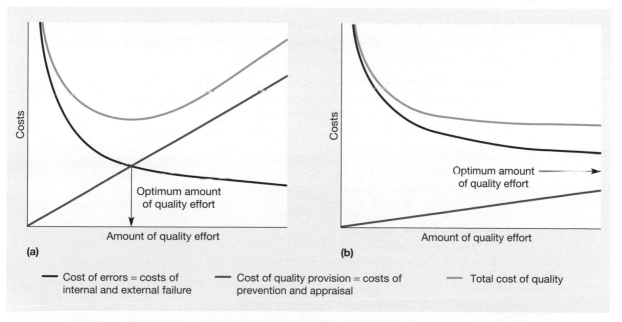

Figure 12.8 (a) The traditional cost of quality model, and (b) the traditional cost of quality model with adjustments to reflect TQM criticisms

Short case
Deliberate defectives

A story which illustrates the difference in attitude between a TQM and a non-TQM company has become almost a legend among TQM proponents. It concerns a plant in Ontario, Canada, of IBM, the computer company. It ordered a batch of components from a Japanese manufacturer and specified that the batch should have an acceptable quality level (AQL) of three defective parts per thousand. When the parts arrived in Ontario they were accompanied by a letter which expressed the supplier's bewilderment at being asked to supply defective parts as well as good ones. The letter also explained that they had found it difficult to make parts which were defective, but had indeed managed it. These three defective parts per thousand had been included and were wrapped separately for the convenience of the customer!

The TQM quality cost model

TQM rejects the optimum-quality level concept and strives to reduce all known and unknown failure costs by preventing errors and failure taking place. Rather than looking for 'optimum' levels of quality effort, TQM stresses the relative balance between different types of quality cost. Of the four cost categories, two (costs of prevention and costs of appraisal) are open to managerial influence, while the other two (internal costs of failure and external costs of failure) show the consequences of a lack of prevention and appraisal. So, rather than placing most emphasis on appraisal (so that 'bad products and service don't get through to the customer') TQM emphasizes prevention (to stop errors happening in the first place). That is because the more effort that is put into error prevention, the more internal and external failure costs are reduced. Then, once confidence has been firmly established, appraisal costs can be reduced. Eventually even prevention costs can be stepped down in absolute terms, though prevention remains a significant cost in relative terms. Figure 12.9 illustrates this idea. Initially total quality costs may rise as investment in some aspects of prevention – mainly training – is increased. However, a reduction in total costs can quickly follow.

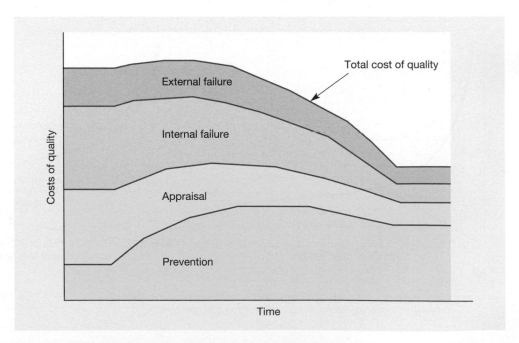

Figure 12.9 Increasing the effort spent on preventing errors occurring in the first place brings a more than equivalent reduction in other cost categories

Getting things 'right first time'

Accepting the relationships between categories of quality cost as illustrated in Figure 12.9 has a particularly important implication for how quality is managed. It shifts the emphasis from *reactive* (waiting for something to happen) to *proactive* (doing something before anything happens). This change in the view of quality costs has come about with a movement from an inspect-in (appraisal-driven) approach to a design-in (**getting it right first time**) approach.

Getting it right first time

Developing the systems and procedures which support quality and improvement

The emphasis on highly formalized systems and procedures to support TQM has declined in recent years, yet one aspect is still active for many companies. This is the adoption of the ISO 9000 standard. And although ISO 9000 can be regarded as a stand-alone issue, it is very closely associated with TQM.

ISO 9000

The **ISO 9000** series is a set of worldwide standards that establishes requirements for companies' quality management systems. ISO 9000 is being used worldwide to provide a framework for quality assurance. Registration requires a third-party assessment of a company's quality standards and procedures and regular audits are made to ensure that the systems do not deteriorate. Rather than using different standards for different functions within a business it takes a 'process' approach that focuses on outputs from any operation's process rather than detailed procedures. This process orientation requires operations to define and record core processes and sub-processes (in a manner very similar to the 'hierarchy of processes' principle that was outlined in Chapter 1). In addition, processes are documented using the process mapping approach that was described in Chapter 5.

ISO 9000 is seen as providing benefits both to the organizations adopting it (because it gives them detailed guidance on how to design their control procedures) and especially to customers (who have the assurance of knowing that the services and products they purchase are produced by an operation working to a defined standard). It may also provide a useful discipline to stick to 'sensible' process-oriented procedures which lead to error reduction, reduced customer complaints and reduced costs of quality, and may even identify existing procedures which can be eliminated. Moreover, gaining the certificate demonstrates that the company takes quality seriously; it therefore has a marketing benefit.

Critical commentary

Notwithstanding its widespread adoption (and its revision to take into account some of its perceived failings), ISO 9000 is not seen as beneficial by all authorities, and is still subject to some specific criticisms. These include the following:

- The use of standards and procedures encourages 'management by manual' and over-systematized decision-making.
- The whole process of documenting processes, writing procedures, training staff and conducting internal audits is expensive and time-consuming.
- Similarly, the time and cost of achieving and maintaining ISO 9000 registration are excessive.
- It is too formulaic. It encourages operations to substitute a 'recipe' for a more customized and creative approach to managing operations improvement.

Summary answers to key questions

 *Check and improve your understanding of this chapter using self-assessment questions and a personalized study plan, audio and video downloads, and an eBook – all at www.myomlab.com.*

➤ What is quality and why is it so important?

- The definition of quality used in this book defines quality as 'consistent conformance to customers' expectations'.
- High quality offerings are a key driver of competitive advantage for organizations.

➤ How can quality problems be diagnosed?

- At a broad level, quality is best modelled as the gap between customers' expectations concerning the service or product and their perceptions concerning the service or product.
- Modelling quality this way will allow the development of a diagnostic tool which is based around the perception–expectation gap. Such a gap may be explained by four other gaps:
  - the gap between a customer's specification and the operation's specification;
  - the gap between the concept and the way the organization has specified it;
  - the gap between the way quality has been specified and the actual delivered quality;
  - the gap between the actual delivered quality and the way the offering has been described to the customer.

➤ What steps lead towards conformance to specification?

- There are six steps:
  - define quality characteristics;
  - decide how to measure each of the quality characteristics;
  - set quality standards for each characteristic;
  - control quality against these standards;
  - find and correct the causes of poor quality;
  - continue to make improvements.
- Most quality planning and control involves sampling the operations performance in some way. Sampling can give rise to erroneous judgements which are classed as either type I or type II errors. Type I errors involve making corrections where none are needed. Type II errors involve not making corrections where they are in fact needed.
- Statistical process control (SPC) involves using control charts to track the performance of one or more quality characteristics in the operation. The power of control charting lies in its ability to set control limits derived from the statistics of the natural variation of processes. These control limits are often set at ± 3 standard deviations of the natural variation of the process samples.

➤ What is total quality management (TQM)?

- TQM is 'an effective system for integrating the quality development, quality maintenance and quality improvement efforts of the various groups in an organization so as to enable production and service at the most economical levels which allow for full customer satisfaction'.

- It is best thought of as a philosophy that stresses the 'total' of TQM and puts quality at the heart of everything that is done by an operation.
- 'Total' in TQM means the following:
  - meeting the needs and expectations of customers;
  - covering all parts of the organization;
  - including every person in the organization;
  - examining all costs which are related to quality, and getting things 'right first time';
  - developing the systems and procedures which support quality and improvement;
  - developing a continuous process of improvement.

Learning exercises

These problems and applications will help to improve your analysis of operations. You can find more practice problems as well as worked examples and guided solutions on MyOMLab at www.myomlab.com.

1 Find two products, one a manufactured food item (for example, a pack of breakfast cereals, packet of biscuits, etc.) and the other a domestic electrical item (for example, electric toaster, coffee maker, etc.).

  (a) Identify the important quality characteristics for these two products.
  (b) How could each of these quality characteristics be specified?
  (c) How could each of these quality characteristics be measured?

2 Many organizations check up on their own level of quality by using 'mystery shoppers'. This involves an employee of the company acting the role of a customer and recording how they are treated by the operation. Choose two or three high-visibility operations (for example, a cinema, a department store, the branch of a retail bank, etc.) and discuss how you would put together a mystery shopper approach to testing their quality. This may involve you determining the types of characteristics you would wish to observe, the way in which you would measure these characteristics, an appropriate sampling rate, and so on. Try out your mystery shopper plan by visiting these operations.

3 Re-read the short case 'Quality at Magic Moments'. What does 'quality' mean for Richard Webber's service? How might his customers' expectations and perceptions influence perceived quality?

4 Find any website selling clothes. How would you judge the quality of its services?

Want to know more?

Dale, B.G. (ed.) (2003) *Managing Quality*, Blackwell, Oxford. This latest version of a long-established, comprehensive and authoritative text.

Garvin, D.A. (1988) *Managing Quality*, The Free Press, New York. Somewhat dated now but relates to our discussion at the beginning of this chapter.

George, M.L., Rowlands, D. and Kastle, B. (2003) *What Is Lean Six Sigma?* McGraw-Hill, New York. Very much a quick introduction on what Lean Six Sigma is and how to use it.

Pande, P.S., Neuman, R.P. and Kavanagh, R.R. (2000) *The Six Sigma Way*, McGraw-Hill, New York. There are many books written by consultants for practising managers on the now fashionable Six Sigma Approach. This is as readable as any.

Useful websites

www.bqf.org.uk/ The British Quality Foundation is a not-for-profit organization promoting business excellence.

www.juran.com The Juran Institute's mission statement is to provide clients with the concepts, methods and guidance for attaining leadership in quality.

www.asq.org/ The American Society for Quality site. Good professional insights.

www.opsman.org Lots of useful stuff.

www.nist.gov/baldrige American Quality Assurance Institute. Well-established institution for all types of business quality assurance.

www.gslis.utexas.edu/~rpollock/tqm.html Non-commercial site on total quality management with some good links.

www.iso.org/iso/home.htm Site of the International Standards Organization that runs the ISO 9000 and ISO 14000 families of standards. ISO 9000 has become an international reference for quality management requirements.

Now that you have finished reading this chapter, why not visit MyOMLab at www.myomlab.com where you'll find more learning resources to help you make the most of your studies and get a better grade.

Chapter 13

Operations improvement

Key questions

➤ Why is improvement so important in operations management?

➤ What are the key elements of operations improvement?

➤ What are the broad approaches to managing improvement?

➤ What techniques can be used for improvement?

Introduction

Even when an operation is designed and its activities delivered, the operations manager's task is not finished. All operations, no matter how well managed, are capable of improvement. In fact, in recent years the emphasis has shifted markedly towards making improvement one of the main responsibilities of operations managers. We treat three aspects of improvement. Firstly, we look at the elements commonly found in various improvement approaches. Secondly, we examine four of the more widely used approaches. Thirdly, we illustrate some of the techniques which can be adopted to improve the operation. Figure 13.1 shows where this chapter fits into the overall operations model.

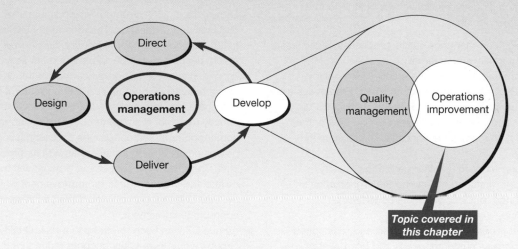

Figure 13.1 This chapter examines operations improvement

Operations in practice Taxing quality[1]

Operations effectiveness is just as important an issue in public-sector operations as it is for commercial companies. People have the right to expect that their taxes are not wasted on inefficient or inappropriate public processes. This is especially true of the tax collecting system itself. It is never a popular organization in any country, and taxpayers can be especially critical when the tax collection process is not well managed. This was very much on the minds of the Aarhus Region Customs and Tax unit (Aarhus CT) when they developed their award-winning quality initiative. The Aarhus Region is the largest of Denmark's twenty-nine local customs and tax offices. It acts as an agent for central government in collecting taxes in a professional and efficient manner while being able to respond to taxpayers' queries. Aarhus CT must, *'keep the user (customer) in focus'*, they say, *'Users must pay what is due – no more, no less and on time. But users are entitled to fair control and collection, fast and efficient case work, service and guidance, flexible employees, polite behaviour and a professional telephone service.'* The Aarhus CT approach to managing its quality initiative was built around a number of key points.

Source: Rex Features

- A recognition that poor-quality processes cause waste both internally and externally.
- A determination to adopt a practice of regularly surveying the satisfaction of its users. Employees were also surveyed, both to understand their views on quality and to check that their working environment would help to instil the principles of high-quality service.
- Although a not-for-profit organization, quality measures included measuring the organization's adherence to financial targets as well as error reporting.
- Internal processes were redefined and redesigned to emphasize customer needs and internal staff requirements. For example, Aarhus CT was the only tax region in Denmark to develop an independent information process that was used to analyse customers' needs and prevent misunderstanding in users' perception of legislation.

- Internal processes were designed to allow staff the time and opportunity to develop their own skills, exchange ideas with colleagues and take on greater responsibility for management of their own work processes.
- The organization set up what it called its 'Quality Organization' (QO) structure which spanned all divisions and processes. The idea of the QO was to foster staff commitment to continuous improvement and to encourage the development of ideas for improving process performance. Within the QO was the Quality Group (QG). This consisted of four managers and four process staff, and reported directly to senior management. It also set up a number of improvement groups and suggestion groups consisting of managers as well as process staff. The role of the suggestion groups was to collect and process ideas for improvement which the improvement groups would then analyse and if appropriate implement.
- Aarhus CT was keen to stress that their Quality Groups would eventually become redundant if they were to be successful. In the short term they would maintain a stream of improvement ideas, but in the long term they should have fully integrated the idea of quality improvement into the day-to-day activities of all staff.

Why improvement is so important

At one time the focus of most operations management was seen as the planning and control or delivery activity. Operations managers were expected to get on with running the operation on a day-by-day and month-by-month basis (but rarely thinking in the longer term). Design activities such as process design, layout, etc. were often the domain of specialists, and changes in process design would happen relatively infrequently. Similarly, improvement was organized separately from mainstream operations management and again was often the province of specialists. Operations strategy was rarely considered at all. This has changed radically. Two things have happened. Firstly, all four activities (strategy, design, delivery, and improvement) are seen as interrelated and interdependent. Secondly, the locus of the operations management job has moved from planning and control (important though this still is) to **improvement**. Operations managers are judged not only on how they meet their ongoing responsibilities of delivering services and products to acceptable levels of quality, speed, dependability, flexibility and cost, but also on how they improve the performance of the operations function overall.

Improvement is now seen as the imperative for operations managers

The Red Queen effect

The scientist Leigh Van Valen was looking to describe a discovery that he had made while studying marine fossils. He had established that, no matter how long a family of animals had already existed, the probability that the family will become extinct is unaffected. In other words, the struggle for survival never gets easier. However well a species fits with its environment it can never relax. The analogy that Van Valen drew came from *Alice's Adventures through the Looking Glass*, by Lewis Carroll. In the book, Alice had encountered living chess pieces and, in particular, the Red Queen.

> 'Well, in our country', said Alice, still panting a little, 'you'd generally get to somewhere else – if you ran very fast for a long time, as we've been doing.' 'A slow sort of country!' said the Queen. 'Now, here, you see, it takes all the running you can do, to keep in the same place. If you want to get somewhere else, you must run at least twice as fast as that!'[2]

In many respects this is like business. Improvements and innovations may be imitated or countered by competitors. For example, in the automotive sector, the quality of most firms' products is very significantly better than it was two decades ago. This reflects the improvement in those firms' operations processes. Yet their relative competitive position has in many cases not changed. Those firms that have improved their competitive position have improved their operations **performance** *more than* **competitors**. Where improvement has simply matched competitors, survival has been the main benefit. The implications for operations improvement are clear. It is even more important, especially when competitors are actively improving their operations.

Generally, improvement is needed just to maintain relative performance

Elements of improvement

There are many approaches to improvement. Some have been used for over a century (for example some come from the 'scientific management' movement of the early 20th century), others are relatively recent (for example, Six Sigma, explained later). However, do not think that these approaches to improvement are different in all respects. There are many elements that are common to several approaches. Think of these 'elements' as the building blocks of the various improvement approaches. Furthermore, as these approaches develop over time, they may acquire elements from elsewhere. So the Six Sigma approach has developed beyond its process control roots (explained in Chapter 12) to encompass many other elements. This section explains some of these elements. We will then show how these elements are combined to form different improvement approaches.

Radical or breakthrough change

Breakthrough improvement

Radical **breakthrough improvement** (or 'innovation'-based improvement as it is sometimes called) is a philosophy that assumes that the main vehicle of improvement is major and dramatic change in the way the operation works. The introduction of a new, more efficient machine in a factory, the total redesign of a computer-based hotel reservation system, and the introduction of an improved degree programme at a university are all examples of breakthrough improvement. The impact of these improvements is relatively sudden and represents a step change in practice (and hopefully performance). Such improvements are rarely inexpensive, usually calling for high investment of capital, often disrupting the ongoing workings of the operation, and frequently involving changes in the product/service or process technology. The bold line in Figure 13.2(a) illustrates the pattern of performance with several breakthrough improvements. The improvement pattern illustrated by the dashed line in Figure 13.2(a) is regarded by some as being more representative of what really occurs when operations rely on pure breakthrough improvement. Breakthrough improvement places a high value on creative solutions. It encourages free thinking and individualism. It is a radical philosophy insomuch as it fosters an approach to improvement which does not accept many constraints on what is possible. 'Starting with a clean sheet of paper', 'going back to first principles' and 'completely rethinking the system' are all typical breakthrough improvement principles.

Continuous improvement

Continuous improvement

Continuous improvement, as the name implies, adopts an approach to improving performance which assumes many small incremental improvement steps. For example, modifying

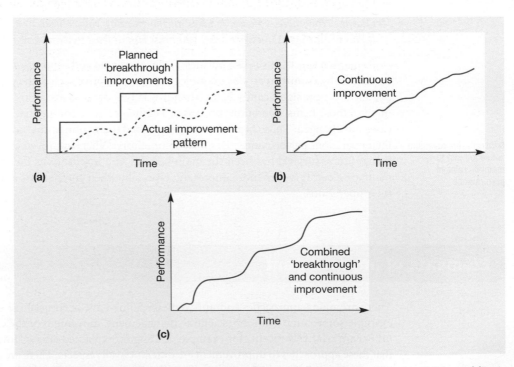

Figure 13.2 (a) 'Breakthrough' improvement, (b) 'continuous' improvement and (c) combined improvement patterns

the way a product is fixed to a machine to reduce changeover time, simplifying the question sequence when taking a hotel reservation, and rescheduling the assignment completion dates on a university course so as to smooth the students' workload are all examples of incremental improvements. While there is no guarantee that such small steps towards better performance will be followed by other steps, the whole philosophy of continuous improvement attempts to ensure that they will be. Continuous improvement is not concerned with promoting small improvements *per se*. It does see small improvements, however, as having one significant advantage over large ones – they can be followed relatively painlessly by other small improvements (see Figure 13.2(b)). Continuous improvement is also known as **kaizen**. **Kaizen** is a Japanese word, the definition of which is given by Masaaki Imai[3] (who has been one of the main proponents of continuous improvement) as follows. *'Kaizen means improvement. Moreover, it means improvement in personal life, home life, social life and work life. When applied to the workplace, kaizen means continuing improvement involving everyone – managers and workers alike.'* In continuous improvement it is not the *rate* of improvement which is important; it is the *momentum* of improvement. It does not matter if successive improvements are small; what does matter is that every month (or week, or quarter, or whatever period is appropriate) some kind of improvement has actually taken place.

Kaizen

Improvement cycles

An important element within some improvement approaches is the use of a literally never-ending process of repeatedly questioning and re-questioning the detailed working of a process or activity. This repeated and cyclical questioning is usually summarized by the idea of the **improvement cycle**, of which there are many, but two are widely used models – the PDCA cycle (sometimes called the Deming cycle, named after the famous quality 'guru', W.E. Deming) and the DMAIC (pronounced de-make) cycle, made popular by the Six Sigma approach (see later). The **PDCA cycle** model is shown in Figure 13.3(a). It starts with the P (for plan) stage, which involves an examination of the current method or the problem area being studied. This involves collecting and analysing data so as to formulate a plan of action which is intended to improve performance. Once a plan for improvement has been agreed, the next step is the D (for do) stage. This is the implementation stage during which the plan is tried out in the operation. This stage may itself involve a mini-PDCA cycle as the problems of implementation are resolved. Next comes the C (for check) stage where the new implemented solution is evaluated to see whether it has resulted in the expected performance improvement. Finally, at least for this cycle, comes the A (for act) stage. During this stage the change is consolidated or standardized if it has been successful. Alternatively, if the change

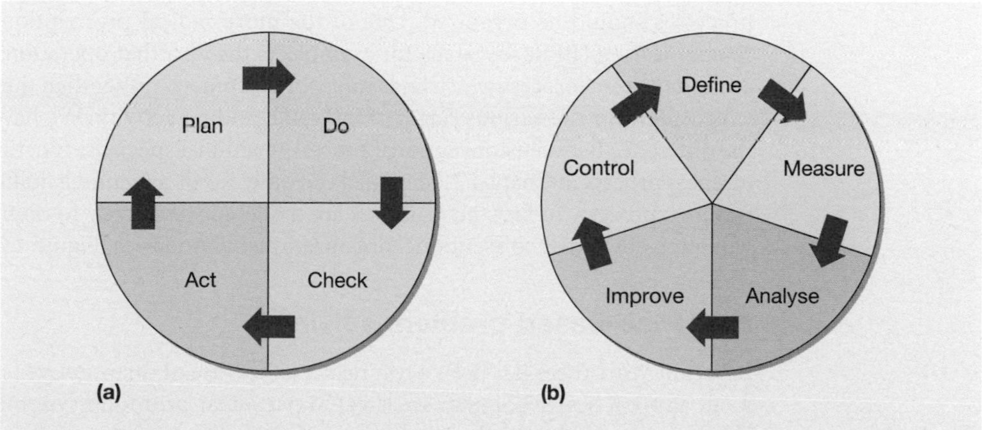

Improvement cycle

PDCA cycle

Figure 13.3 (a) The plan–do–check–act, or Deming improvement cycle, and (b) the define–measure–analyse–improve–control, or DMAIC Six Sigma improvement cycle

has not been successful, the lessons learned from the 'trial' are formalized before the cycle starts again.

DMAIC cycle

The DMAIC cycle is in some ways more intuitively obvious than the PDCA cycle insomuch as it follows a more 'experimental' approach. The **DMAIC cycle** starts with defining the problem or problems, partly to understand the scope of what needs to be done and partly to define exactly the requirements of the process improvement. Often at this stage a formal goal or target for the improvement is set. After definition comes the measurement stage. This stage involves validating the problem to make sure that it really is a problem worth solving, using data to refine the problem and measuring exactly what is happening. Once these measurements have been established, they can be analysed. The analysis stage is sometimes seen as an opportunity to develop hypotheses as to what the root causes of the problem really are. Such hypotheses are validated (or not) by the analysis and the main root causes of the problem identified. Once the causes of the problem are identified, work can begin on improving the process. Ideas are developed to remove the root causes of problems, solutions are tested and those solutions that seem to work are implemented and formalized and results measured. The improved process needs then to be continually monitored and controlled to check that the improved level of performance is sustaining. After this point the cycle starts again and defines the problems which are preventing further improvement. Remember though, it is the last point about both cycles that is the most important – the cycle starts again. It is only by accepting that in a continuous improvement philosophy these cycles quite literally never stop that improvement becomes part of every person's job.

A process perspective

Even if some improvement approaches do not explicitly or formally include the idea that taking a process perspective should be central to operations improvement, almost all do so implicitly. This has two major advantages. Firstly, it means that improvement can be focused on what actually happens rather than on which part of the organization has responsibility for what happens. In other words, if improvement is not reflected in the process of creating products and services, then it is not really improvement as such. Secondly, as we have mentioned before, all parts of the business manage processes. This is what we call operations, an activity rather than operations as a function. So, if improvement is described in terms of how processes can be made more effective, those messages will have relevance for all the other functions of the business in addition to the operations function.

End-to-end processes

Some improvement approaches take the process perspective further and prescribe exactly how processes should be organized. One of the more radical prescriptions of business process re-engineering (BPR, see later), for example, is the idea that operations should be organized around the total process which adds value for customers, rather than the functions or activities which perform the various stages of the value-adding activity. We have already pointed out the difference between conventional processes within a specialist function, and an end-to-end business process in Chapter 1. Identified customer needs are entirely fulfilled by an 'end-to-end' business process. In fact the processes are designed specifically to do this, which is why they will often cut across conventional organizational boundaries. Figure 13.4 illustrates this idea.

Evidence-based problem-solving

In recent years there has been a resurgence of the use of quantitative techniques in improvement approaches. Six Sigma (see later) in particular promotes systematic use of (preferably quantitative) evidence. Yet Six Sigma is not the first of the improvement approaches to use quantitative methods (some of the TQM gurus promoted statistical process control for example) although it has done a lot to emphasize the use of quantitative evidence. In fact,

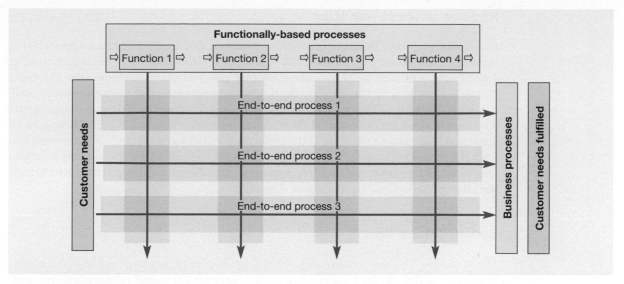

Figure 13.4 BPR advocates reorganizing (re-engineering) micro-operations to reflect the natural customer-focused business processes

much of the considerable training required by Six Sigma consultants is devoted to mastering quantitative analytical techniques. However, the statistical methods used in improvement activities do not always reflect conventional academic statistical knowledge as such. They emphasize observational methods of collecting data and the use of experimentation to examine hypotheses. Techniques include graphical methods, analysis of variance, and two-level factorial experiment design. Underlying the use of these techniques is an emphasis on the scientific method, responding only to hard evidence, and using statistical software to facilitate analysis.

Customer-centricity

There is little point in improvement unless it meets the requirements of the customers. However, in most improvement approaches, meeting the expectations of customers means more than this. It involves the whole organization in understanding the central importance of customers to its success and even to its survival. Customers are seen not as being external to the organization but as the most important part of it. However, the idea of being customer-centric does not mean that customers must be provided with everything that they want. Although 'What's good for customers' may frequently be the same as 'What's good for the business', it is not always. Operations managers are always having to strike a balance between what customers would like and what the operation can afford (or wants) to do.

Systems and procedures

Improvement is not something that happens simply by getting everyone to 'think improvement'. Some type of system that supports the improvement effort may be needed. An improvement system (sometimes called a 'quality system') is defined as:

'the organizational structure, responsibilities, procedures, processes and resources for implementing quality management'.[4]

It should

'define and cover all facets of an organization's operation, from identifying and meeting the needs and requirements of customers, design, planning, purchasing, manufacturing, packaging, storage, delivery and service, together with all relevant activities carried out within these functions. It deals with organization, responsibilities, procedures and processes. Put simply [it] is good management practice.'[5]

Reduce process variation

Processes change over time, as does their performance. Some aspect of process performance (usually an important one) is measured periodically (either as a single measurement or as a small sample of measurements). These are then plotted on a simple timescale. This has a number of advantages. The first is to check that the performance of the process is, in itself, acceptable (capable). They can also be used to check if process performance is changing over time, and to check on the extent of the variation in process performance. In Chapter 12 we illustrated how random variation in the performance of any process could obscure what was really happening within the process. So a potentially useful method of identifying improvement opportunities is to try and identify the sources of random variation in process performance. Statistical process control is one way of doing this.

Synchronized flow

This is another idea that we have seen before – in Chapter 11, as part of the lean philosophy. Synchronized flow means that items in a process, operation or supply network flow smoothly and with even velocity from start to finish. This is a function of how inventory accumulates within the operation. Whether inventory is accumulated in order to smooth differences between demand and supply, or as a contingency against unexpected delays, or simply to batch for purposes of processing or movement, it all means that flow becomes asynchronous. It waits as inventory rather than progressing smoothly on. Once this state of perfect synchronization of flow has been achieved, it becomes easier to expose any irregularities of flow which may be the symptoms of more deep-rooted underlying problems.

Emphasize education and training

Several improvement approaches stress the idea that structured training and organization of improvement should be central to improvement. Not only should the techniques of improvement be fully understood by everyone engaged in the improvement process, the business and organizational context of improvement should also be understood. After all, how can one improve without knowing what kind of improvement would best benefit the organization and its customers? Furthermore, education and training have an important part to play in motivating all staff towards seeing improvement as a worthwhile activity. Some improvement approaches in particular place great emphasis on formal education. Six Sigma for example (see later) and its proponents often mandate a minimum level of training (measured in hours) that they deem necessary before improvement projects should be undertaken.

Perfection is the goal

Almost all organization-wide improvement programmes will have some kind of goal or target that the improvement effort should achieve. While targets can be set in many different ways, some improvement authorities hold that measuring process performance against some kind of absolute target does most for encouraging improvement. By an 'absolute target' one literally means the theoretical level of perfection, for example, zero errors, instant delivery, delivery absolutely when promised, infinite flexibility, zero waste, etc. Of course, in reality such perfection may never be achievable. That is not the point. What is important is that current performance can be calibrated against this target of perfection in order to indicate how much more improvement is possible. Improving (for example) delivery accuracy by five per cent may seem good until it is realized that only an improvement of thirty per cent would eliminate all late deliveries.

Waste identification

All improvement approaches aspire to eliminate waste. In fact, any improvement implies that some waste has been eliminated, where waste is any activity that does not add value. But the identification and elimination of waste is sometimes a central feature. For example, as we discussed in Chapter 11, it is arguably the most significant part of the lean philosophy.

Include everybody

Harnessing the skills and enthusiasm of every person and all parts of the organization seems an obvious principle of improvement. The phrase 'quality at source' is sometimes used, stressing the impact that each individual has on improvement. The contribution of all individuals in the organization may go beyond understanding their contribution to 'not make mistakes'. Individuals are expected to bring something positive to improving the way they perform their jobs. The principles of 'empowerment' are frequently cited as supporting this aspect of improvement. When Japanese improvement practices first began to migrate in the late 1970s, this idea seemed even more radical. Yet now it is generally accepted that individual creativity and effort from all staff represents a valuable source of development. However, not all improvement approaches have adopted this idea. Some authorities believe that a small number of internal improvement consultants or specialists offer a better method of organizing improvement. However, these two ideas are not incompatible. Even with improvement specialists used to lead improvement efforts, the staff who actually operate the process can still be used as a valuable source of information and improvement ideas.

Develop internal customer–supplier relationships

One of the best ways to ensure that external customers are satisfied is to establish the idea that every part of the organization contributes to external customer satisfaction by satisfying its own internal customers. It means stressing that each process in an operation has a responsibility to manage these internal customer–supplier relationships. They do this primarily by defining as clearly as possible what their own and their customers' *requirements* are. In effect this means defining what constitutes 'error-free' service – the quality, speed, dependability and flexibility required by internal customers.

Approaches to Improvement

Many of the elements described above are present in one or more of the commonly used approaches to improvement. Some of these approaches have already been described. For example, both lean and TQM have been discussed in some detail. In this section we will briefly re-examine TQM and lean, specifically from an improvement perspective and also add two further approaches – business process re-engineering (BPR) and Six Sigma.

Total quality management as an improvement approach

Total quality management was one of the earliest management 'fashions'. Yet the general precepts and principles that constitute TQM are still hugely influential. Few, if any, managers have not heard of TQM and its impact on improvement. Indeed, TQM has come to be seen as an approach to the way operations and processes should be managed and improved, generally. It is best thought of as a philosophy of how to approach improvement. This philosophy, above everything, stresses the 'total' of TQM. It is an approach that puts quality (and indeed improvement generally) at the heart of everything that is done by an operation. As a reminder, this totality can be summarized by the way TQM lays particular stress on the following elements:

- Meeting the needs and expectations of customers;
- Improvement covers all parts of the organization (and should be group-based);
- Improvement includes every person in the organization (and success is recognized);
- Including all costs of quality;
- Getting things 'right first time', i.e. designing-in quality rather than inspecting it in;
- Developing the systems and procedures which support improvement.

Even if TQM is not the label given to an improvement initiative, many of its elements will almost certainly have become routine. The fundamentals of TQM have entered the vernacular of operations improvement. Elements such as the internal customer concept, the idea of internal and external failure-related costs, and many aspects of individual staff empowerment, have all become widespread.

Lean as an improvement approach

The idea of lean (also known as just-in-time, lean synchronization, continuous flow operations, and so on) spread beyond its Japanese roots and became fashionable in the West at about the same time as TQM. And although its popularity has not declined to the same extent as TQM's, over 25 years of experience (at least in manufacturing) have diminished the excitement once associated with the approach. Unlike TQM, it was seen initially as an approach to be used exclusively in manufacturing. Now, lean has become newly fashionable as an approach that can be applied in service operations. As a reminder (see Chapter 11) the lean approach aims to meet demand instantaneously, with perfect quality and no waste. Put another way, it means that the flow of products and services always delivers exactly what customers want (perfect quality), in exact quantities (neither too much nor too little), exactly when needed (not too early or too late), exactly where required (not to the wrong location), and at the lowest possible cost. It results in items flowing rapidly and smoothly through processes, operations and supply networks. The key elements of lean when used as an improvement approach are as follows.

- Customer-centricity
- Internal customer–supplier relationships
- Perfection is the goal
- Synchronized flow
- Reduce variation
- Include all people
- Waste elimination.

Some organizations, especially now that lean is being applied more widely in service operations, view waste elimination as the most important of all the elements of the lean approach. In fact, they sometimes see the lean approach as consisting almost exclusively of waste elimination. What they fail to realize is that effective waste elimination is best achieved through changes in behaviour. It is the behavioural change brought about through synchronized flow and customer triggering that provides the window onto exposing and eliminating waste.

It is easy to forget just how radical, and more importantly, counter-intuitive lean once seemed. Although ideas of continuous improvement were starting to be accepted, the idea that inventories were generally a bad thing, and that throughput time was more important than capacity utilization seemed to border on the insane to the more traditionally minded. So, as lean ideas have been gradually accepted, we have likewise come to be far more tolerant of ideas that are radical and/or counter-intuitive. This is an important legacy because it opened up the debate on operations practice and broadened the scope of what are regarded as acceptable approaches.

Business process re-engineering (BPR)

Business process
re-engineering

The idea of **business process re-engineering** originated in the early 1990s when Michael Hammer proposed that rather than using technology to automate work, it would be better applied to doing away with the need for the work in the first place ('don't automate, obliterate'). In doing this he was warning against establishing non-value-added work within an information technology system where it would be even more difficult to identify and eliminate. All work, he said, should be examined for whether it adds value for the customer and if not processes should be redesigned to eliminate it. In doing this BPR was echoing similar objectives in both scientific management and more recently lean approaches. BPR, unlike those two earlier approaches, advocated radical changes rather than incremental changes to processes. Shortly after Hammer's article, other authors developed the ideas, again the majority of them stressing the importance of a radical approach to elimination of non-value-added work. This radicalism was summarized by Davenport who, when discussing the difference between BPR and continuous improvement, held that 'Today's firms must seek not fractional, but multiplicative levels of improvement – ten times rather than ten per cent'.

BPR has been defined[6] as

'the fundamental rethinking and radical redesign of business processes to achieve dramatic improvements in critical, contemporary measures of performance, such as cost, quality, service and speed'.

There is far more to it than that. In fact, BPR was a blend of a number of ideas which had been current in operations management for some time. Lean concepts, process flow charting, critical examination in method study, operations network management and customer-focused operations all contribute to the BPR concept. It was the potential of information technologies to enable the fundamental redesign of processes, however, which acted as the catalyst in bringing these ideas together. It was the information technology that allowed radical process redesign even if many of the methods used to achieve the redesign had been explored before. For example, *'Business Process Reengineering, although a close relative, seeks radical rather than merely continuous improvement. It escalates the effort of* . . . [lean] . . . *and TQM to make process orientation a strategic tool and a core competence of the organization. BPR concentrates on core business processes, and uses the specific techniques within the* . . . [lean] . . . *and TQM tool boxes as enablers, while broadening the process vision.'*[7]

The main principles of BPR can be summarized in the following points.

- Rethink business processes in a cross-functional manner which organizes work around the natural flow of information (or materials or customers).
- Strive for dramatic improvements in performance by radically rethinking and redesigning the process.
- Have those who use the output from a process, perform the process. Check to see if all internal customers can be their own supplier rather than depending on another function in the business to supply them (which takes longer and separates out the stages in the process).
- Put decision points where the work is performed. Do not separate those who do the work from those who control and manage the work.

Example[8]

We can illustrate this idea of reorganizing (or re-engineering) around business processes through the following simple example. Figure 13.5(a) shows the traditional organization of a trading company which purchases consumer goods from several suppliers, stores them, and sells them on to retail outlets. At the heart of the operation is the warehouse which receives the goods, stores them, and packs and dispatches them when they are required by customers. Orders for more stock are placed by Purchasing which also takes charge of materials planning and stock control. Purchasing buys the goods based on a forecast which is prepared by Marketing, which takes advice from the Sales department which is processing customers' orders. When a customer does place an order, it is the Sales department's job to

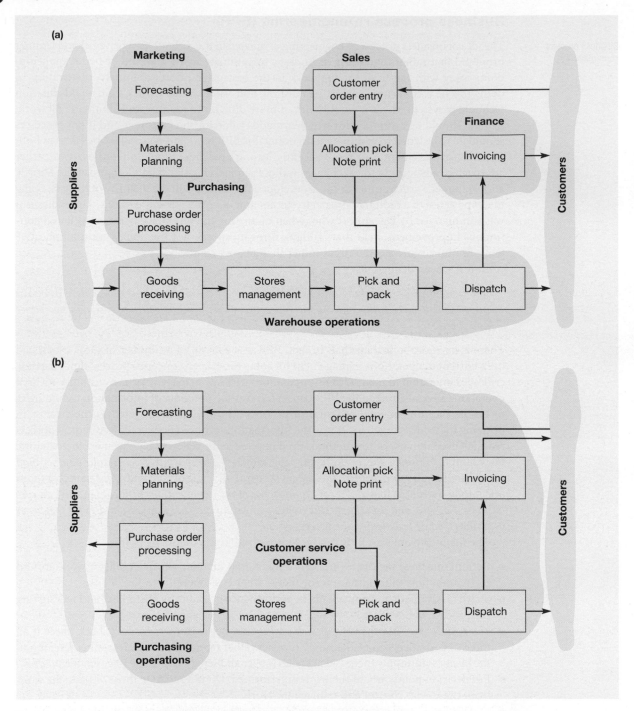

Figure 13.5 (a) Before and (b) after re-engineering a consumer goods trading company

instruct the warehouse to pack and dispatch the order and tell the Finance department to invoice the customer for the goods. So, traditionally, five departments (each a micro-operation) have between them organized the flow of materials and information within the total operation. At each interface between the departments there is the possibility of errors and miscommunication arising. Furthermore, *who is responsible for looking after the customer's needs?* Currently, three separate departments all have dealings with the customer. Similarly, *who is responsible for liaising with suppliers?* This time two departments have contact with suppliers.

Eventually the company reorganized around two essential business processes. The first process (called purchasing operations) dealt with everything concerning relationships with suppliers. It was this process's focused and unambiguous responsibility to develop good working relationships with suppliers. The other business process (called customer service operations) had total responsibility for satisfying customers' needs. This included speaking 'with one voice' to the customer.

Critical commentary

BPR has aroused considerable controversy, mainly because BPR sometimes looks only at work activities rather than at the people who perform the work. Many of these critics equate BPR with the much earlier principles of scientific management, pejoratively known as 'Taylorism'. Generally these critics mean that BPR is overly harsh in the way it views human resources. Certainly there is evidence that BPR is often accompanied by a significant reduction in staff. Studies at the time when BPR was at its peak often revealed that the majority of BPR projects could reduce staff levels by over 20 per cent.[9] Often BPR was viewed as merely an excuse for getting rid of staff. Companies that wished to 'downsize' were using BPR as the pretext, putting the short-term interests of the shareholders of the company above either their longer-term interests or the interests of the company's employees. Moreover, a combination of radical redesign together with downsizing could mean that the essential core of experience was lost from the operation. This would leave it vulnerable to any marked turbulence since it no longer possessed the knowledge and experience of how to cope with unexpected changes.

Six Sigma

Six Sigma

The **Six Sigma** approach was first popularized by Motorola, the electronics and communications systems company. When it set its quality objective as 'total customer satisfaction' in the 1980s, it started to explore what the slogan would mean to its operations processes. They decided that true customer satisfaction would only be achieved when its products were delivered when promised, with no defects, with no early-life failures and when the product did not fail excessively in service. To achieve this, Motorola initially focused on removing manufacturing defects. However, it soon came to realize that many problems were caused by latent defects, hidden within the design of its products. These may not show initially but eventually could cause failure in the field. The only way to eliminate these defects was to make sure that design specifications were tight (i.e. narrow tolerances) and its processes very capable.

Motorola's Six Sigma quality concept was so named because it required the natural variation of processes (± 3 standard deviations) should be half their specification range. In other words, the specification range of any part of a product or service should be $+6$ the standard deviation of the process. The Greek letter sigma (σ) is often used to indicate the standard deviation of a process, hence the Six Sigma label. Figure 13.6 illustrates the effect of progressively narrowing process variation on the number of defects produced by the process, in terms of **defects per million**. The defects per million measure is used within the Six Sigma approach to emphasize the drive towards a virtually **zero defect** objective. Now the definition of Six Sigma has widened to well beyond this rather narrow statistical perspective. General Electric (GE), who were probably the best known of the early adopters of Six Sigma, defined it as, 'A disciplined methodology of defining, measuring, analysing, improving, and controlling the quality in every one of the company's products, processes, and transactions – with the ultimate goal of virtually eliminating all defects'. So, now Six Sigma should be seen as a broad improvement concept rather than a simple examination of process variation, even though this is still an important part of process control, learning and improvement.

Defects per million
Zero defect

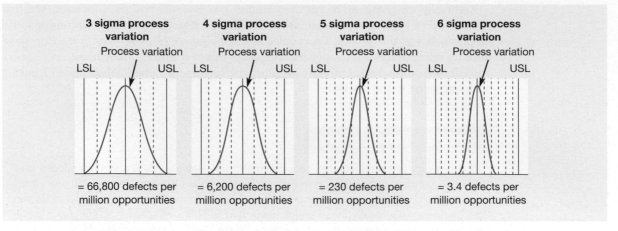

Figure 13.6 Process variation and its impact on process defects per million

Elements frequently associated with Six Sigma include the following:

- *Customer-driven objectives* – Six Sigma is sometimes defined as 'the process of comparing process outputs against customer requirements'. It uses a number of measures to assess the performance of operations processes. In particular it expresses performance in terms of defects per million opportunities (DPMO). This is exactly what it says, the number of defects which the process will produce if there were one million opportunities to do so. This is then related to the 'Sigma measurement' of a process and is the number of standard deviations of the process variability that will fit within the customer specification limits.

- *Use of evidence* – Although Six Sigma is not the first of the new approaches to operations to use statistical methods it has done a lot to emphasize the use of quantitative evidence. In fact much of the considerable training required by Six Sigma consultants is devoted to mastering quantitative analytical techniques.

- *Structured improvement cycle* – The structured improvement cycle used in Six Sigma is the DMAIC cycle.

- *Process capability and control* – Not surprisingly, given its origins, process capability and control is important within the Six Sigma approach.

- *Process design* – Latterly Six Sigma proponents also include process design into the collection of elements that define the Six Sigma approach.

- *Structured training and organization of improvement* – The Six Sigma approach holds that improvement initiatives can only be successful if significant resources and training are devoted to their management. It recommends a specially trained cadre of practitioners and internal consultants named after 'martial arts' grades, see below.

The 'martial arts' analogy

Master Black Belt
Black Belt
Green Belt

The terms that have become associated with Six Sigma experts (and denote their level of expertise) are, **Master Black Belt**, **Black Belt** and **Green Belt**. Master Black Belts are experts in the use of Six Sigma tools and techniques as well as how such techniques can be used and implemented. Primarily Master Black Belts are seen as teachers who can not only guide improvement projects, but also coach and mentor Black Belts and Green Belts who are closer to the day-to-day improvement activity. They are expected to have the quantitative analytical skills to help with Six Sigma techniques and also the organizational and interpersonal skills to teach and mentor. Given their responsibilities, it is expected that Master Black Belts are employed full-time on their improvement activities. Black Belts can take a direct hand in organizing improvement teams. Like Master Black Belts, Black Belts are expected to develop their quantitative analytical skills and also act as coaches for Green Belts.

Short case
Six Sigma at Xchanging[10]

'I think Six Sigma is powerful because of its definition; it is the process of comparing process outputs against customer requirements. Processes operating at less than 3.4 defects per million opportunities means that you must strive to get closer to perfection and it is the customer that defines the goal. Measuring defects per opportunity means that you can actually compare the process of, say, a human resources process with a billing and collection process.' Paul Ruggier head of Process at Xchanging is a powerful advocate of Six Sigma, and credits the success of the company, at least partly, to the approach.

Xchanging, created in 1998, is one of a new breed of companies, operating as an outsourcing business for 'back-office' functions for a range of companies, such as Lloyds of London, the insurance centre. Xchanging's business proposition is for the client company to transfer the running of the whole or part of their back office to Xchanging, either for a fixed price or one determined by cost savings achieved. The challenge Xchanging faces is to run that back office in a more effective and efficient manner than the client company had managed in the past. So, the more effective Xchanging is at running the processes, the greater its profit. To achieve these efficiencies Xchanging offers larger scale, a higher level of process expertise, focus and investment in technology. But above all, they offer a Six Sigma approach. *'Everything we do can be broken down into a process'*, says Paul Ruggier. *'It may be more straightforward in a manufacturing business, frankly they've been using a lot of Six Sigma tools and techniques for decades. But the concept of process improvement is relatively new in many service companies. Yet the concept is powerful. Through the implementation of this approach we have achieved 30% productivity improvements in 6 months.'*

The company also adopts the Six Sigma terminology for its improvement practitioners – Master Black Belts, Black Belts and Green Belts. Attaining the status of Black Belt is very much sought after as well as being fulfilling, says Rebecca Whittaker who is a Master Black Belt at Xchanging. *'At the end of a project it is about having a process which is redesigned to such an extent, that is simplified and consolidated and people come back and say, "It's so much better than it used to be". It makes their lives better and it makes the business results better and those are the things that make being a Black Belt worthwhile.'*

Rebecca was recruited by Xchanging along with a number of other Master Black Belts as part of a strategic

Source: Rex Features

decision to kick-start Six Sigma in the company. It is seen as a particularly responsible position by the company and Master Black Belts are expected to be well versed in the Six Sigma techniques and be able to provide the training and knowhow to develop other staff within the company. In Rebecca's case she has been working as a Six Sigma facilitator for five years, initially as a Green Belt, then as a Black Belt.

Typically a person identified as having the right analytical and interpersonal skills will be taken off their job for at least a year's training and immersed in the concepts of improvement and then sent to work with line staff as project manager/facilitator. Their role as Black Belt will be to guide the line staff to make improvements in the way they do the job. One of the new Black Belts at Xchanging, Sarah Frost, is keen to stress the responsibility she owes to the people who will have to work in the improvement process. *'Being a Black Belt is about being a project manager. It is about working with the staff and combining our skills in facilitation and our knowledge of the Six Sigma process with their knowledge of the business. You always have to remember that you will go onto another project but they [process staff] will have to live with the new process. It is about building solutions that they can believe in.'*

Critical commentary

One common criticism of Six Sigma is that it does not offer anything that was not available before. Its emphasis on improvement cycles comes from TQM, its emphasis on reducing variability comes from statistical process control, its use of experimentation and data analysis is simply good quantitative analysis. The only contribution that Six Sigma has made, argue its critics, is using the rather gimmicky martial arts analogy of Black Belt etc. to indicate a level of expertise in Six Sigma methods. All Six Sigma has done is package pre-existing elements together in order for consultants to be able to sell them to gullible chief executives. In fact it's difficult to deny some of these points. Maybe the real issue is whether it is really a criticism. If bringing these elements together really does form an effective problem-solving approach, why is this is a problem?

Differences and similarities

In this chapter we have chosen to very briefly explain four improvement approaches. It could have been more. Enterprise resource planning, total preventive maintenance (TPM), lean Sigma (a combination of lean and Six Sigma), and others could have been added. However, these four constitute a representative sample of the most commonly used approaches. Nor do we have the space to describe them fully. Each of the approaches is the subject of several books that describe them in great detail. And there are clearly some common elements between some of these approaches that we have described. Yet there are also differences between them in that each approach includes a different set of elements and therefore a different emphasis and these differences need to be understood. For example, one important difference relates to whether the approaches emphasize a gradual, continuous approach to change, or whether they recommend a more radical 'breakthrough' change. Another difference concerns the aim of the approach. What is the balance between whether the approach emphasizes *what* changes should be made or *how* changes should be made? Some approaches have a firm view of what is the best way to organize the operation's processes and resources. Other approaches hold no particular view on what an operation should do but rather concentrate on how the management of an operation should decide what to do. Indeed we can position each of the elements and the approaches that include them. This is illustrated in Figure 13.7. The approaches differ in the extent that they prescribe appropriate operations practice. BPR for example is very clear in what it is recommending. Namely, that all processes should be organized on an end-to-end basis. Its focus is *what* should happen rather than *how* it should happen. To a slightly lesser extent lean is the same. It has a definite list of things that processes should or should not be – waste should be eliminated, inventory should be reduced, technology should be flexible, and so on. Contrast this with both Six Sigma and TQM which focus to a far greater extent on *how* operations should be improved. Six Sigma in particular has relatively little to say about what is good or bad in the way operations resources are organized (with the possible exception of its emphasizing the negative effects of process variation). Its concern is largely the way improvements should be made: using evidence, using quantitative analysis, using the DMAIC cycle, and so on. They also differ in terms of whether they emphasize gradual or rapid change. BPR is explicit in its radical nature. By contrast TQM and lean both incorporate ideas of continuous improvement. Six Sigma is relatively neutral on this issue and can be used for small or very large changes.

Improvement techniques

All the techniques described in this book can be regarded as 'improvement' techniques. However, some techniques are particularly useful for improving operations and processes

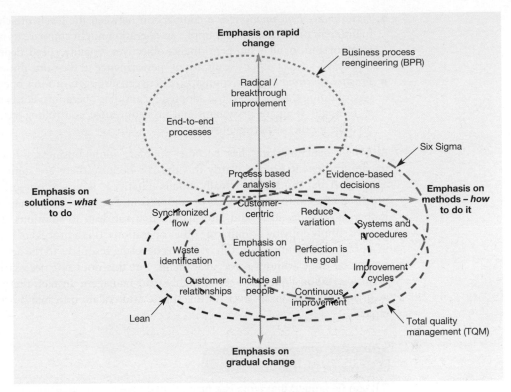

Figure 13.7 The four approaches on the two dimensions of improvement

generally. Here we select some techniques which either have not been described elsewhere or need to be reintroduced in their role of helping operations improvement particularly.

Benchmarking

Benchmarking is 'the process of learning from others' and involves comparing one's own performance or methods against other comparable operations. It is a broader issue than setting performance targets, and includes investigating other organizations' operations practice in order to derive ideas that could contribute to performance improvement. Its rationale is based on the idea that (a) problems in managing processes are almost certainly shared by processes elsewhere, and (b) that there is probably another operation somewhere that has developed a better way of doing things. For example, a bank might learn some things from a supermarket about how it could cope with demand fluctuations during the day. **Benchmarking** is essentially about stimulating creativity in improvement practice.

There are many different types of benchmarking (which are not necessarily mutually exclusive), some of which are listed below:

- *Internal benchmarking* is a comparison between operations or parts of operations which are within the same total organization. For example, a large motor vehicle manufacturer with several factories might choose to benchmark each factory against the others.
- *External benchmarking* is a comparison between an operation and other operations which are part of a different organization.
- *Non-competitive benchmarking* is benchmarking against external organizations which do not compete directly in the same markets.
- *Competitive benchmarking* is a comparison directly between competitors in the same, or similar, markets.

Benchmarking is the process of learning from others

- *Performance benchmarking* is a comparison between the levels of achieved performance in different operations. For example, an operation might compare its own performance in terms of some or all of our performance objectives – quality, speed, dependability, flexibility and cost – against other organizations' performance in the same dimensions.
- *Practice benchmarking* is a comparison between an organization's operations practices, or way of doing things, and those adopted by another operation. For example, a large retail store might compare its systems and procedures for controlling stock levels with those used by another department store.

Although benchmarking has become popular, some businesses have failed to derive maximum benefit from it. Partly this may be because there are some misunderstandings as to what benchmarking actually entails. Firstly, it is not a 'one-off' project. It is best practised as a continuous process of comparison. Secondly, it does not provide 'solutions'. Rather, it provides ideas and information that can lead to solutions. Thirdly, it does not involve simply copying or imitating other operations. It is a process of learning and adapting in a pragmatic manner. Fourthly, it means devoting resources to the activity. Benchmarking cannot be done without some investment, but this does not necessarily mean allocating exclusive responsibility to a set of highly paid managers. In fact, there can be advantages in organizing staff at all levels to investigate and collate information from benchmarking targets.

Critical commentary

It can be argued that there is a fundamental flaw in the whole concept of benchmarking. Operations that rely on others to stimulate their creativity, especially those that are in search of 'best practice', are always limiting themselves to currently accepted methods of operating or currently accepted limits to performance. In other words, benchmarking leads companies only as far as others have gone. 'Best practice' is not 'best' in the sense that it cannot be bettered, it is only 'best' in the sense that it is the best one can currently find. Indeed accepting what is currently defined as 'best' may prevent operations from ever making the radical breakthrough or improvement that takes the concept of 'best' to a new and fundamentally improved level.

The EFQM Excellence Model

In 1988, 14 leading Western European companies formed the European Foundation for Quality Management (EFQM). An important objective of the EFQM is to recognize quality achievement. Therefore, it launched the European Quality Award (EQA), awarded to the most successful exponent of total quality management in Europe each year. To receive a prize, companies must demonstrate that their approach to total quality management has contributed significantly to satisfying the expectations of customers, employees and others with an interest in the company for the past few years. In 1999, the model on which the European Quality Award was based was modified and renamed **The EFQM Excellence Model or Business Excellence Model**. The changes made were not fundamental but did attempt to reflect some new areas of management and quality thinking (for example, partnerships and innovation) and placed more emphasis on customer and market focus. It is based on the idea that the outcomes of quality management in terms of what it calls 'people results', 'customer results', 'society results' and 'key performance results' are achieved through a number of 'enablers'. These enablers are leadership and constancy of purpose, policy and strategy, how the organization develops its people, partnerships and resources, and the way it organizes its processes. These ideas are incorporated in the EFQM Excellence Model as shown in Figure 13.8. The five enablers are concerned with how results are being

The EFQM Excellence Model, or Business Excellence Model

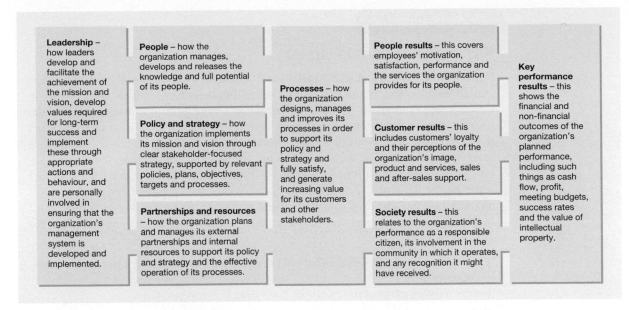

Figure 13.8 The EFQM Excellence Model

achieved, while the four 'results' are concerned with what the company has achieved and is achieving.

Self-assessment

Self-assessment

The European Foundation for Quality Management (EFQM) defines **self-assessment** as *'a comprehensive, systematic, and regular review of an organization's activities and results referenced against a model of business excellence'*, in its case the model shown in Figure 13.8. The main advantage of using such models for self-assessment seems to be that companies find it easier to understand some of the more philosophical concepts of TQM when they are translated into specific areas, questions and percentages. Self-assessment also allows organizations to measure their progress in changing their organization and in achieving the benefits of TQM. An important aspect of self-assessment is an organization's ability to judge the relative importance of the assessment categories to its own circumstances. The EFQM Excellence Model originally placed emphasis on a generic set of weighting for each of its nine categories. With the increasing importance of self-assessment, the EFQM moved to encourage organizations using its model to allocate their own weightings in a rational and systematic manner.

Scatter diagrams

Scatter diagrams

Scatter diagrams provide a quick and simple method of identifying whether there is evidence of a connection between two sets of data: for example, the time at which you set off for work every morning and how long the journey to work takes. Plotting each journey on a graph which has departure time on one axis and journey time on the other could give an indication of whether departure time and journey time are related, and if so, how. Scatter diagrams can be treated in a far more sophisticated manner by quantifying how strong is the relationship between the sets of data. However sophisticated the approach, this type of graph only identifies the existence of a relationship, not necessarily the existence of a cause–effect relationship. If the scatter diagram shows a very strong connection between the sets of data, it is important evidence of a cause–effect relationship.

Worked example

Kaston Pyral Services Ltd (A)

Kaston Pyral Services Ltd (KPS) installs and maintains environmental control, heating and air conditioning systems. It has set up an improvement team to suggest ways in which it might improve its levels of customer service. The improvement team has completed its first customer satisfaction survey. The survey asked customers to score the service they received from KPS in several ways. For example, it asked customers to score services on a scale of one to ten on promptness, friendliness, level of advice, etc. Scores were then summed up to give a 'total satisfaction score' for each customer – the higher the score, the greater the satisfaction. The spread of satisfaction scores puzzled the team and they considered what factors might be causing such differences in the way their customers viewed them. Two factors were put forward to explain the differences.

(a) the number of times in the past year the customer had received a preventive maintenance visit;

(b) the number of times the customer had called for emergency service.

All these data were collected and plotted on scatter diagrams as shown in Figure 13.9(a). It shows that there seems to be a clear relationship between a customer's satisfaction score and the number of times the customer was visited for regular servicing. The scatter diagram in Figure 13.9(b) is less clear. Although all customers who had very high satisfaction scores had made very few emergency calls, so had some customers with low satisfaction scores. As a result of this analysis, the team decided to survey customers' views on its emergency service.

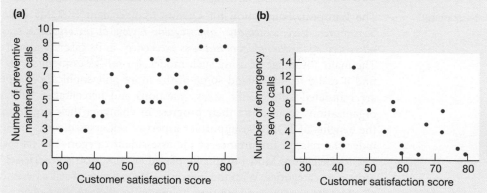

Figure 13.9 Scatter diagrams for customer satisfaction versus (a) number of preventive maintenance calls and (b) number of emergency service calls

Cause–effect diagrams

Cause–effect diagrams

Cause–effect diagrams are a particularly effective method of helping to search for the root causes of problems. They do this by asking what, when, where, how and why questions, but also add some possible 'answers' in an explicit way. They can also be used to identify areas where further data are needed. Cause–effect diagrams (which are also known as 'Ishikawa diagrams') have become extensively used in improvement programmes. This is because they provide a way of structuring group brainstorming sessions. Often the structure involves identifying possible causes under the (rather old-fashioned) headings of: machinery, manpower, materials, methods and money. Yet in practice, any categorization that comprehensively covers all relevant possible causes could be used.

Worked example

Kaston Pyral Services Ltd (B)

The improvement team at KPS was working on a particular area which was proving a problem. Whenever service engineers were called out to perform emergency servicing for a customer, they took with them the spares and equipment which they thought would be necessary to repair the system. Although engineers could never be sure exactly what materials and equipment they would need for a job, they could guess what was likely to be needed and take a range of spares and equipment which would cover most eventualities. Too often, however, the engineers would find that they needed a spare that they had not brought with them. The cause–effect diagram for this particular problem, as drawn by the team, is shown in Figure 13.10.

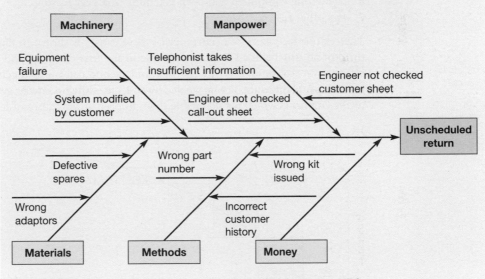

Figure 13.10 Cause–effect diagram of unscheduled returns at KPS

Pareto diagrams

In any improvement process, it is worthwhile distinguishing what is important and what is less so. The purpose of the Pareto diagram is to distinguish between the 'vital few' issues and the 'trivial many'. It is a relatively straightforward technique which involves arranging items of information on the types of problem or causes of problem into their order of importance (usually measured by 'frequency of occurrence'). This can be used to highlight areas where further decision-making will be useful. **Pareto analysis** is based on the phenomenon of relatively few causes explaining the majority of effects. For example, most revenue for any company is likely to come from relatively few of the company's customers. Similarly, relatively few of a doctor's patients will probably occupy most of his or her time.

Pareto analysis

Worked example

Kaston Pyral Services Ltd (C)

The KPS improvement team which was investigating unscheduled returns from emergency servicing (the issue which was described in the cause–effect diagram in Figure 13.11) examined all occasions over the previous 12 months on which an unscheduled return had been made. They categorized the reasons for unscheduled returns as follows:

1 The wrong part had been taken to a job because, although the information which the engineer received was sound, he or she had incorrectly predicted the nature of the fault.
2 The wrong part had been taken to the job because there was insufficient information given when the call was taken.
3 The wrong part had been taken to the job because the system had been modified in some way not recorded on KPS's records.
4 The wrong part had been taken to the job because the part had been incorrectly issued to the engineer by stores.
5 No part had been taken because the relevant part was out of stock.
6 The wrong equipment had been taken for whatever reason.
7 Any other reason.

The relative frequency of occurrence of these causes is shown in Figure 13.11. About a third of all unscheduled returns were due to the first category, and more than half the returns were accounted for by the first and second categories together. It was decided that the problem could best be tackled by concentrating on how to get more information to the engineers which would enable them to predict the causes of failure accurately.

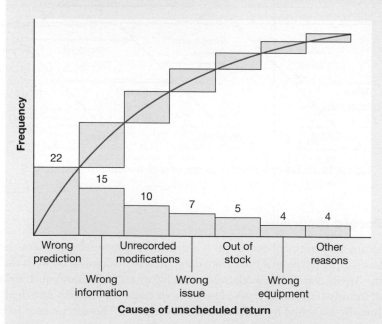

Figure 13.11 Pareto diagram for causes of unscheduled returns

Why–why analysis

Why–why analysis

Why–why analysis starts by stating the problem and asking *why* that problem has occurred. Once the reasons for the problem occurring have been identified, each of the reasons is taken in turn and again the question is asked *why* those reasons have occurred, and so on. This procedure is continued until either a cause seems sufficiently self-contained to be addressed by itself or no more answers to the question 'Why?' can be generated.

Worked example

Kaston Pyral Services Ltd (D)

The major cause of unscheduled returns at KPS was the incorrect prediction of reasons for the customer's system failure. This is stated as the 'problem' in the why–why analysis in Figure 13.12. The question is then asked, why was the failure wrongly predicted? Three answers are proposed: firstly, that the engineers were not trained correctly; secondly, that they had insufficient knowledge of the particular product installed in the customer's location; and thirdly, that they had insufficient knowledge of the customer's particular system with its modifications. Each of these three reasons is taken in turn, and the questions are asked, why is there a lack of training, why is there a lack of product knowledge, and why is there a lack of customer knowledge? And so on.

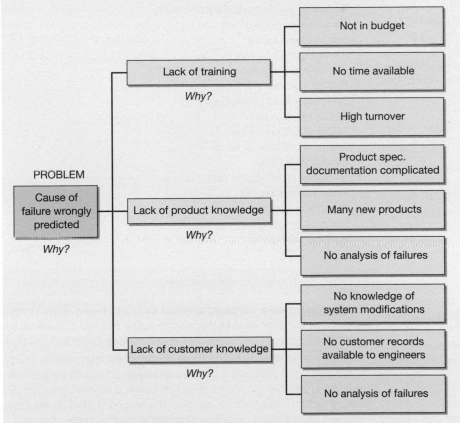

Figure 13.12 Why–why analysis for 'failure wrongly predicted'

Summary answers to key questions

 Check and improve your understanding of this chapter using self-assessment questions and a personalized study plan, audio and video downloads, and an eBook – all at **www.myomlab.com**.

➤ Why is improvement so important in operations management?

- Improvement (develop) is now seen as the prime responsibility of operations management. Of the four areas of operations management activity (define, design, deliver, and develop) the focus of most operations managers has shifted from planning and control to improvement. Furthermore all operations management activities are really concerned with improvement in the long term. And all four activities are really interrelated and interdependent.

- Companies in many industries are having to improve simply to retain their position relative to their competitors. This is sometimes called the 'Red Queen' effect.

➤ What are the key elements of operations improvement?

- There are many 'elements' that are the building blocks of improvement approaches. The ones described in this chapter are:
  - Radical or breakthrough improvement
  - Continuous improvement
  - Improvement cycles
  - A process perspective
  - End-to-end processes
  - Radical change
  - Evidence-based problem-solving
  - Customer-centricity
  - Systems and procedures
  - Reduced process variation
  - Synchronized flow
  - Emphasis on education and training
  - Perfection is the goal
  - Waste identification
  - Inclusion of everybody
  - Development of internal customer–supplier relationships.

➤ What are the broad approaches to managing improvement?

- What we have called 'the broad approaches to improvement' are relatively coherent collections of some of the 'elements' of improvement. The four most common are total quality management (TQM), lean, business process re-engineering (BPR) and Six Sigma.

- There are differences between these improvement approaches. Each includes a different set of elements and therefore a different emphasis. They can be positioned on two dimensions. The first is whether the approaches emphasize a gradual, continuous approach to change or a more radical 'breakthrough' change. The second is whether the approach emphasizes *what* changes should be made or *how* changes should be made.

➤ What techniques can be used for improvement?

- Many of the techniques described throughout this book could be considered improvement techniques, for example statistical process control (SPC).

■ Techniques often seen as 'improvement techniques' are:
  - benchmarking;
  - EFQM business excellence model;
  - scatter diagrams, which attempt to identify relationships and influences within processes;
  - cause–effect diagrams, which structure the brainstorming that can help to reveal the root causes of problems;
  - Pareto diagrams, which attempt to sort out the 'important few' causes from the 'trivial many' causes;
  - Why–why analysis that pursues a formal questioning to find root causes of problems.

Learning exercises

These problems and applications will help to improve your analysis of operations. You can find more practice problems as well as worked examples and guided solutions on MyOMLab at www.myomlab.com.

1 Sophie was sick of her daily commute. 'Why', she thought 'should I have to spend so much time in a morning stuck in traffic listening to some babbling half-wit on the radio? We can work flexi-time after all. Perhaps I should leave the apartment at some other time?' So resolved, Sophie deliberately varied her time of departure from her usual 8.30. Also, being an organized soul, she recorded her time of departure each day and her journey time. Her records are shown in Table 13.1.

(a) Draw a scatter diagram that will help Sophie decide on the best time to leave her apartment.

(b) How much time per (5-day) week should she expect to be saved from having to listen to a babbling half-wit?

Table 13.1 Sophie's journey times (in minutes)

Day	Leaving time	Journey time	Day	Leaving time	Journey time	Day	Leaving time	Journey time
1	7.15	19	6	8.45	40	11	8.35	46
2	8.15	40	7	8.55	32	12	8.40	45
3	7.30	25	8	7.55	31	13	8.20	47
4	7.20	19	9	7.40	22	14	8.00	34
5	8.40	46	10	8.30	49	15	7.45	27

2 The Printospeed Laser printer company was proud of its reputation for high-quality services and products. It was especially concerned with the problems that it was having with its customers returning defective toner cartridges. About 2,000 of these were being returned every month. Its European service team suspected that not all the returns were actually the result of a faulty product, which is why the team decided to investigate the problem. Three major problems were identified. Firstly, some users were not as familiar as they should have been with the correct method of loading the cartridge into the printer, or in being able to solve their own minor printing problems. Secondly, some of the dealers were also unaware of how to sort out minor problems. Thirdly, there was clearly some abuse of Hewlett-Packard's 'no-questions-asked' returns policy. Empty toner cartridges were being sent to unauthorized refilling companies who would sell the refilled cartridges at reduced prices. Some cartridges were being refilled up to five times and were understandably wearing out. Furthermore, the toner in the refilled cartridges was often not up to Printospeed's high quality standards.

(a) Draw a cause–effect diagram that includes both the possible causes mentioned, and any other possible causes that you think worth investigating.

(b) What is your opinion of the alleged abuse of the 'no-questions-asked' returns policy adopted by Printospeed?

3 Think back to the last product or service failure that caused you some degree of inconvenience. Draw a cause–effect diagram that identifies all the main causes of why the failure could have occurred. Try and identify the frequency with which such causes happen. This could be done by talking with the staff of the operation that provided the service. Draw a Pareto diagram that indicates the relatively frequency of each cause of failure. Suggest ways in which the operation could reduce the chances of failure.

Want to know more?

Goldratt, E.M. and Cox, J. (2004) *The Goal: A Process of Ongoing Improvement*, Gower, Aldershot. Updated version of a classic.

Hendry, L. and Nonthaleerak, P. (2004) Six sigma: Literature review and key future research areas, Lancaster University Management School, Working Paper, 2005/044 www.lums.lancs.ac.uk/publications/. Good overview of the literature on Six Sigma.

Pande, P.S., Neuman, R.P. and Cavanagh, R. (2002) *Six Sigma Way Team Field Book: An Implementation Guide for Project Improvement teams*, McGraw-Hill, New York. This is an unashamedly practical guide to the Six Sigma approach.

Xingxing Zu, Fredendall L.D. and Douglas, T.J. (2008) The evolving theory of quality management: the role of Six Sigma, *Journal of Operations Management*, vol. 26, 630–50. An interesting read, examining the evolution of TQM.

Useful websites

www.processimprovement.com/ Commercial site but some content that could be useful.

www.kaizen-institute.com/ Professional institute for kaizen. Gives some insight into practitioner views.

www.mxawards.org/home The Manufacturing Excellence Awards site. Dedicated to rewarding excellence and best practice in UK manufacturing. Obviously manufacturing biased, but some good examples.

www.ebenchmarking.com Benchmarking information.

www.quality.nist.gov/ National Institute of Standards and Technology. Well-established institution for all types of business quality assurance.

www.balancedscorecard.org/ Site of an American organization with plenty of useful links.

www.opsman.org Lots of useful stuff.

Now that you have finished reading this chapter, why not visit MyOMLab at www.myomlab.com where you'll find more learning resources to help you make the most of your studies and get a better grade.

Notes on chapters

Chapter 1

1 Sources include: company web site (2010), Baraldi, E. (2008) Strategy in industrial networks: experiences from IKEA, *California Management Review*, vol. 50, no. 4, IKEA plans to end stressful shopping, London *Evening Standard*, 24 April 2006, Walley, P. and Hart, K. (1993) *IKEA (UK) Ltd*, Loughborough University Business School.

2 We are grateful to Simon Topman of Acme Whistles for his assistance.

3 Source: Oxfam web site (2009).

4 Source: Discussion with company staff.

5 Quote from Chairman of the British Medical Association, speech from the Annual Conference, 2002.

Chapter 2

1 Sources include: press releases, Ryanair; Keenan, S., How Ryanair put its passengers in their place, *The Times*, 19 June 2002; Flextronics web site.

2 Hayes, R.H. and Wheelwright, S.C. (1984) *Restoring our Competitive Edge*, John Wiley.

3 For a more thorough explanation, see Slack, N. and Lewis, M. (2011) *Operations Strategy*, 3rd edn, Financial Times Prentice Hall, Harlow.

4 Mintzberg, H. and Waters, J.A. (1995) Of strategies: deliberate and emergent, *Strategic Management Journal*, July/Sept.

5 Also called 'critical success factors' by some authors.

6 Hill, T. (1993) *Manufacturing Strategy*, 2nd edn, Macmillan.

7 There is a vast literature which describes the resource-based view of the firm. For example, see Barney, J. (1991) The resource-based model of the firm: origins, implications and prospect, *Journal of Management*, vol. 17, no. 1; or Teece, D.J. and Pisano, G. (1994) The dynamic capabilities of firms: an introduction, *Industrial and Corporate Change*, vol. 3, no. 3.

8 Source: Lifting the bonnet, *Economist*, 7 October 2006.

9 Weick, K.E. (1990) Cartographic myths in organizations, in A. Huff (ed.) *Managing Strategic Thought*, Wiley, London.

Chapter 3

1 Sources include: BBC web site, BA managers leave after T5 fiasco, 15 April 2008; Browning, A., How do you clear a bags backlog? BBC web site, 19 April 2008; Fran Yeoman and Nico Hines, Heathrow T5 disruption to continue over weekend, Times Online, 28 March 2008; Kevin Done, BA to cancel hundreds more flights from T5, *Financial Times*, 30 March 2008; Kevin Done, Long haul to restore BA's reputation, *Financial Times*, 28 March 2008; David Robertson Why Heathrow's T5 disaster provide a lesson for Dubai's T3, *The Times*, 29 November 2008.

2 Source: Catherine Pyne and Nick Fuge, Lower Hurst Farm.

3 Sources include: Marlinson, C., The golden hour, *Sunday Times*, 21 Sept. 2006.

4 Sources include: Dabbawala web site (2009) www.mydabbawala.com; *The Economist*, The cult of the dabbawala, 10 Jul 2008; Ashling O'Connor, Big business learns a thing or two from the humble dabbawalas, *The Times* (of London), 21 April 2007.

5 Source: Fiona Rennie, Discussions with the News Team at the BBC.

6 Source: John Hendry-Pickup of Aldi.

7 Source: Miles, A. and Baldwin, T., Spidergram to check on police forces, *The Times*, 10 July 2002.

8 Skinner, W. (1985) *Manufacturing: The Formidable Competitive Weapon*, John Wiley.

Chapter 4

1 Sources include: *The Times*, Timeline – Airbus A380 super-jumbo, 26 October 2006; BBC news web site, Q&A: A380 delays, Monday, 30 October 2006; BBC news web site, Q&A: Airbus job cuts, 28 February 2007; Peggy Hollinger and Gerrit Wiesmann, Airbus is hampered by cultural differences, *Financial Times*, 15 July 2008; *The Economist*, Airbus Marathon man, 17 Jul 2008; *The Economist*, Boeing and Airbus – swings and roundabouts, 27 Nov 2008.

2 The Design Council website.

3 Sources include: Doran, J., Hoover heading for sell-off as Dyson cleans up in America, *The Times*, 4 February, 2006.

4 Sources: many thanks to Mark Taber and his site www.takelifeeasy.com; *The Economist*, Open, but not as usual, 16 Mar 2006; Ralph Kisiel, BMW wants joint effort to develop open-source in-vehicle platform, *Automotive News Europe*, 23 October 2008.

5 Sources include: Square fruit stuns Japanese shoppers, BBC web site, Friday, 15 June 2001; S. Poulter, Square melons on the way, *Daily Mail*, 3rd August 2006; we would also like to thank our colleague, Paul Walley, who first found this example for us.

6 With thanks to George Northwood, Manager of Daniel Hersheson's Mayfair salon.

7 Source: Think local, *The Economist*, 13 April 2002.

8 Bennis, W. and Biederman, P.W., *Organizing Genius: The Secrets of Creative Collaboration*, Addison-Wesley, 1997; new edn, Nicholas Brealey, 1998.

9 Hayes, R.H., Wheelwright, S.C. and Clarke, K.B. (1988) *Dynamic Manufacturing*, The Free Press.

Chapter 5

1 Source Horovitz, A., Fast food world says drive-through is the way to go, *USA Today*, 3 April, 2002.

2 Source: Genes, R. (2002) Smart ecology, *The Manufacturing Engineer*, April.

3 Hayes, R.H. and Wheelwright, S.C. (1984) *Restoring our Competitive Edge*, John Wiley.

4 Hayes, R.H. and Wheelwright, S.C. *op. cit.*

5 The Workflow Management Coalition (2009) www.wfmc.org

6 *The Economist*, A new departure for London's airports, 21 Aug 2008.

7 Based on work from the Advisory, Conciliation and Arbitration Service, ACAS.

8 Hoxie, R.F. (1915) *Scientific Management and Labour*, D. Appleton, Washington, DC.

9 Hackman, J.R. and Oldham, G. (1975) A new strategy for job enrichment, *California Management Review*, vol. 17, no. 3.

10 Bowen, D.E. and Lawler, E.E. (1992) The empowerment of service workers: what, why, how and when, *Sloan Management Review*, vol. 33, no. 3, 31–9.

Chapter 6

1 Sources: Paul Walley, our colleague in the Operations Management Group at Warwick Business School, Irisys web site (2009) www.irisys.co.uk, Martin, P., How supermarkets make a meal of you, *Sunday Times*, 4 November 2000.

2 Sources include: Devendra Damle; *Economist*, Nano wars, 28 August 2008; *Economist*, The one-lakh car, 10 January 2008; *Economist*, A new home for the Nano, 9 October 2008.

3 Source: 2003 Cedep Working paper, Paris.

4 Jonathon Carr-Brown, French factory surgeon cuts NHS queues, *Sunday Times*, 23 October 2005.

5 Sources: Interviews with company staff and Johnston, R., Chambers, S., Harland, C., Harrison, A. and Slack, N. (2003) *Cases in Operations Management*, 3rd edn, Financial Times Prentice Hall, Harlow.

Chapter 7

1 Source: For whom the Dell tolls, *Economist*, 13 May 2006; Rory Cellan-Jones, Dell aims to reclaim global lead, BBC Business, 14 April 2008.

2 Source: Grant, J., A cautionary tale of roof racks and widgets, *Financial Times*, 4 November 2002.

3 Brandenburger, A.M. and Nalebuff, B.J. (1996) *Co-opetition*, Doubleday, New York.

4 Hayes, R.H. and Wheelwright, S.C. (1994) *Restoring our Competitive Edge*, John Wiley.

5 Sources: Einhorn, B. and Zegels, T.M., The underdog nipping at Quanta's heels, *Business Week*, 21 October 2002; *Economist*, His hi-tech highness, 13 July 2002.

6 Fisher, M.L. (1997) What is the right supply chain for your product, *Harvard Business Review*, March–April.

7 This short case was written by Richard Small. Sources include: Helia Ebrahimi, Hedge funds put Gate Gourmet in the departure lounge, *Daily Telegraph*, 6 Dec. 2008; Maggie Urry, Northern Foods wins BA contract, *Financial Times*, 5 December 2008.

8 Parkhe, A. (1993) Strategic alliance structuring, *Academy of Management Journal*, vol. 36, 794–829.

9 Towill, D.R. (1996) Time compression and supply chain management – a guided tour, *Supply Chain Management*, vol. 1, no. 1.

10 Definition from the UK Government Purchasing Agency.

11 Source: Interview with David Garman, September 2006.

12 Source: Lee, H.L. and Whang, S. (2001) Demand chain excellent: a tale of two retailers, *Supply Chain Management Review*, 3 January.

Chapter 8

1 Sources: Ashworth, J., 'Met Office brings sunshine to the shops, *The Times*, 17 August 2002; *The Economist*, And now here is the health forecast, 3 August 2002; Jackson, H., Weather derivates are hot, *Wall Street Journal Europe*, 13 February 2002.

2 With special thanks to Philip Godfrey and Cormac Campbell of OEE Consulting Ltd. (www.oeeconsulting.com).

3 Sources: Lynch, P. (1991) Making time for productivity, *Personnel Management*, March; and Pickard, J. (1991) Annual hours: a year of living dangerously, *Personnel Management*, Aug.

4 Kimes, S. (1989) Yield management: a tool for capacity-constrained service firms, *Journal of Operations Management*, vol. 8, no. 4.

5 Sources include Robinette, S. (2001) Get emotional, *Harvard Business Review*, May.

6 Maister, D. (1983) The psychology of waiting lines, *Harvard Business Review*, Jan–Feb.

Chapter 9

1 Source: NBS web site and discussions with NBS staff.

2 With special thanks to John Mathews, Howard Smith Paper Group.

Chapter 10

1 Source: Interview with Joanne Cheung, Steve Deeley and other staff at Godfrey Hall, BMW Dealership, Coventry.

2 Sources: Jean Farman (1999) 'Les Coulisses du Vol', Air France. Talk presented by Richard E. Stone, Northwest Airlines at the IMA Industrial Problems Seminar, 1998.

3 The concept of $P:D$ ratios comes originally from Shingo, S. (1981) *Study of Toyota Production Systems*, Japan Management Association; and was extended by Mather, K. (1988) *Competitive Manufacturing*, Prentice-Hall.

4 Source: Walley, P. (2009) MBA Course Notes, Warwick University, UK.

5 We are grateful to our colleague Paul Walley for this section.

6 Source: Thanks to Lawrence Wilkins for this example.

7 Goldratt, E.Y. and Cox, J. (1984) *The Goal*, North River Press, Great Barrington, Mass.

8 Wight, O. (1984) *Manufacturing Resource Planning: MRP II*, Oliver Wight Ltd.

Chapter 11

1 Spear, S. and Bowen, H.K. (1999) Decoding the DNA of the Toyota production system, *Harvard Business Review*, Sept–Oct.

2 Kamata, S. (1983) *Japan in the Passing Lane: An Insider's Account of Life in a Japanese Auto Factory*, Allen and Unwin.

3 Based on an example in Womack, J.P. and Jones, D.T. (1996) *Lean Thinking*, Simon and Shuster, New York.

4 Source: Mathieson, S.A., NHS should embrace lean times, *The Guardian*, Thursday 8 June 2006.

5 Quoted in: Schonberger, R. (1982) *Japanese Manufacturing Techniques*, The Free Press.

6 Yamashina, H. Reducing set-up times makes your company flexible and more competitive, unpublished, quoted in Harrison A., *op. cit.*

7 This great metaphor seems to have originated from the consultancy '2think', www.2think.biz/index.htm.

8 Staats, B. and Upton, D. (2007) Lean principles and software production: evidence from Indian software services, Harvard Working Paper, Harvard Business School.

Chapter 12

1 Source: Interview with Michael Purtill, the General Manager of the Four Seasons Hotel Canary Wharf in London. We are grateful for Michael's cooperation (and for the great quality of service at his hotel!).

2 Parasuraman, A., Zeithaml, V.A. and Berry, L.L. (1985) A conceptual model of service quality and implications for future research, *Journal of Marketing*, vol. 49, Fall, 41–50; and Gummesson, E. (1987) Lip service: a neglected area in services marketing, *Journal of Services Marketing*, vol. 1, no. 1, 19–23.

3 Haywood-Farmer, J. and Nollet, J. (1991) *Services Plus: Effective Service Management*, Morin, Vancouver.

4 Berry, L.L. and Parasuraman, A. (1991) *Marketing Services: Competing through Quality*, The Free Press.

5 Mechling, L., Get ready for a storm in a tea shop, *The Independent*, 8 March 2002 and company web site.

6 Based on Parasuraman, A., *op. cit.*

7 Source: Scan avoids needless appendectomy, *The Sunday Times*, 23 Feb 1997.

8 Feigenbaum, A.V. (1986) *Total Quality Control*, McGraw-Hill, New York.

Chapter 13

1 Source: the EFQM web site, www.efqm.org.

2 Lewis Carroll (1871) *Alice through the Looking Glass*.

3 Imai, M. (1986) *Kaizen – The Key to Japan's Competitive Success*, McGraw-Hill.

4 International Standards Organization, *ISO 8402*, 1986.

5 Dale, B.G. (1994) Quality management systems, in Dale, B.G. (ed.) *Managing Quality*, Prentice Hall.

6 Davenport, T. (1995) Reengineering – the fad that forgot people, *Fast Company*, November.

7 Johansson, H.J. (1993) *Business Process Reengineering: Break Point Strategies for Market Dominance*, Wiley, New York.

8 Based on an example in Kruse, G. (1995) Fundamental innovation, *Manufacturing Engineer*, Feb.

9 For example, Davenport, T. (1995) op. cit.

10 Source: Discussion with staff at Xchanging.

Index